Spiritual Perspectives

Spiritual Perspectives

Maharaj Charan Singh
Answers Questions:
1960 – 1990

Volume II
Walking the Path

RADHA SOAMI SATSANG BEAS

Published by:
J. C. Sethi, Secretary
Radha Soami Satsang Beas
Dera Baba Jaimal Singh
Punjab 143 204, India

First edition 2010

17 16 15 14 13 12 11 10   8 7 6 5 4 3 2 1

ISBN 978-81-8256-932-4

Printed in India by: Thomson Press (India) Ltd.

CONTENTS

Volume II
Walking the Path

7 *A Personal Commitment*
Being pulled to the path   3
Initiation   12
Satisfying the intellect   31
The four vows   52
The vegetarian diet   56
Giving up drugs and alcohol   78
Ethics and morality   84

8 *Power of Meditation*
The circle of love   97
The power of meditation   104
Meditation and faith   122
Meditation as true prayer   129

9 *Practice of Meditation*
The practice of meditation   151
Come to the eye centre   158
Simran, dhyan and bhajan   171
Inner regions   211

The radiant form 230
Experiencing the shabd 239
Dying while living 243
Digest it within 250
Progress 258

10 *Effort and Grace*
Regularity and punctuality 277
Controlling the mind 292
Practical questions 303
Overcoming obstacles 322
Effort and grace 333
Responding to the inner pull 362

11 *Path of Action*
Living in the atmosphere of meditation 377
Doing simran all day 386
Living the principles 392
A constant struggle with the mind 396
Remaining in his discipline 410
Overcoming weaknesses 413
Falling and getting up 420
Being a friend 434
Making devotion our priority 438
Loving not calculating 447
Do it now! 452

APPENDIX 455
INDEX TO BIBLE QUOTES 459
SUBJECT INDEX 475
ADDRESSES FOR INFORMATION AND BOOKS 501
BOOKS ON THIS SCIENCE 507

Volume I
Understanding the Basics

1 *Mystery of Creation*
Mystery of creation
God as reality
Creation as a projection
    of the Lord
Continuation of the creation
Creation as the Lord's play
Kal
Good and evil

2 *Shaping Our Destiny*
Shaping our destiny
Clearing karmas
Duty and karma
Transcending karma
Sanskaras
Sowing seeds of karma
Destiny and free will
Reincarnation

3 *What Are We?*
Relationship of the soul
    to God
The human form
Self-realization
    and God-realization
Relationship of the soul
    to the mind and senses
The mind
Ego
Attachment and desires

4 *The Soul Has No Religion*
Give him any name
The soul has no religion
Arresting the teachings
One path, many religions
Scriptures and holy books
How the saints teach

5 *Lost and Found*
Lost in a maze
Suffering and loneliness
    as grace
Happiness
Improving the world
Peace
Marked souls
Grace to be pulled
Association with a master

6 *Role of the Master*
What is a master?
All masters are one
Need for a living master
Purpose of the master
The masters' miracles
Masters are above karma
One flame lighting another

Volume III
Living the Life

12 *Master and Disciple*
   Relationship of master
      and disciple
   Shabd is the real master
   Finding the master within
   Darshan
   Separation and longing
   Running after the master
   Parshad
   Awareness of his presence
   Passing of the master

13 *Satsang and Seva*
   Importance of satsang
   Atmosphere of satsang
   What is seva?
   Types of seva
   Charity and desireless action

14 *A Balanced Life*
   A balanced life
   Making decisions
   Worry
   Swim along with the waves
   Surrender

   Living in the Lord's will
   Becoming humble
   Criticism and anger
   Forgiveness
   A peaceful and relaxed life

15 *Facing Life and Death*
   Attachment and duty
   Marriage and family life
   Children
   Animals
   Physical and mental health
   Suicide
   Facing illness and death

16 *The Real Miracle*
   A positive approach
   A fresh perspective
   A loving and
      compassionate heart
   Love is a gift from the Lord
   A grateful heart
   A miracle at every step
   True and eternal happiness
EPILOGUE

Spiritual Perspectives

❧

Volume II
Walking the Path

❧ 7 ❧

A Personal Commitment

BEING PULLED TO THE PATH

1   *Master, how may a devotee realize the true value of the teachings taught by a true saint or a real holy person, so that he may act accordingly? How can we know we are in the company of a saint?*

Actually brother, it is very difficult to know whether we are in the hands of the right person or the wrong person. At our level it is impossible to know this. Whatever the signs may be, however intellectual we may become, still we can be deceived. We can only depend on the grace of the Lord to give us the understanding to be in the right hands. That is a straight, frank statement. Generally we try to convince ourselves intellectually and by so many other ways and means. But still we can be deceived. So the real understanding must come from within. And also it depends upon the grace of the Father.

2   *How can we judge the spiritual level of a mystic?*

We have to depend upon the grace of the Father, because there is no way to judge this at the level of the intellect. The conviction, the reality must come from within. There is something in you which automatically induces you to believe in a person. You will feel that you are where you want to be. If you try to judge somebody with the intellect, you can be deceived; so we can only know through the grace of the Father.

3   *In our country we meet ever so many saints and masters. How do we know which is the one to be followed? Whose name do we take? I'm really desperate at this moment and have to say so publicly.*

Well, sister, to be frank, it is extremely difficult for us to know about any master at all, about the spiritual height of any master. But first we should become convinced of the philosophy; and when we're convinced about the philosophy, then we should seek a master according to that philosophy which we want to follow.

The main thing is the teachings. When I know that a teaching is meant for me, when I want that teaching, that teaching appeals to me, then I must find a master who teaches according to that teaching.

What if the teachings sound alike? They sound the same from master to master.

Yes, sometimes teachings are definitely the same, because every real master will have the same spiritual truths to give you. They don't have different teachings at all. So it will come from within you, who is meant for you. You will automatically be drawn to him.

4   *Disciples of the master accept the master as the genuine deity, but actually in practice they do not know it at all. They know it only when he appears to them in his radiant form inside, for it is then that they see him as he is. However, I think it is all right to accept the master, who*

we think is very right by his grace, but what I mean is
that he is not the be-all and end-all. There are lots of
professors who can talk the same language in the most
beautiful way and express the divine order, but when it
comes to practice, some of these great men fall short. So
what is the criterion for recognizing a perfect master? I
mean, we should be honest with ourselves.

Brother, you are exactly right in what you are trying to analyze. In one of our meetings, I discussed it, that we must make a thorough research before we submit ourselves to any master. Even if our whole life is spent in making an investigation, making a research, it is not time lost, it is time gained. We are building on a very deep foundation, we are building on a rock. So we should not be deceived by the emotions, we should not be deceived by the masses or mass psychology, nor should we be deceived by the speeches. We have to make an inner research within ourselves to know who is the right or the wrong master. And once we are convinced, then we should forget about this research. We should give it a fair trial, but we first have to accept it. If we are happy within ourselves, we must give it a fair trial, then perhaps we may know, but perhaps we still may not know.

His grace is required to put us on the right path, to bring us in contact with the right master. We have a very limited intellect with which to find out. We can be deceived. We have to depend entirely upon his grace for guidance, real guidance. And, if we are sincere, I assure you, he puts us on the right path. He does guide us. It may take time; it is a question of some opportunity; but if we are sincere, he will definitely put us on the right path.

5   *I have been studying, reading every source that I find. But*
     now will you tell me how to contact the living master?

Well, sister, the main thing is to feel the necessity of the living master.

I do feel it.

Then the Lord will put you on the path. It is not you who are seeking. It is the Lord who is seeking you. The Lord is pulling you from within, and when the Lord makes you receptive, he will automatically put you on the path through someone. You just have to be receptive to the pull of the Lord. In Saint John, Christ said: Only those will come to me who are marked for me, who are allotted for me; they will automatically be drawn to me.[93]* They will automatically hear my voice and have faith in me.[109] So when we become receptive, when we are sincere seekers, then the Lord will pull us, will put us on the path.

6   *What if the Father doesn't want us to follow a spiritual path?*

We should never try to follow anybody, any path, unless there is a strong inner urge, a pull from within which we can't resist. We should never jump into any philosophy or rush to follow any teacher. We must always know where we stand and then be receptive to the urge which comes from within.

7   *Does a guiding hand pull people to you?*

You mean somebody guiding?

Yes, guides individuals to you? I mean, does the hand of God pull people to you during their lifetime?

---

*References to Bible quotes are numbered according to their order in the Bible and appear in a separate index. The Ten Commandments appear in their entirety at the end of the index.

You have read in the Bible – you are a preacher – you know that Christ said that he had been sent for the marked sheep, marked souls.[52] The hand of God is at the back. They will come to Christ, those who are marked for him. They are his sheep, and they will come to him. They will be brought back to him. You call it coincidence. There are no coincidences here. You do not know how one is being drawn to that side, what had led us to come to that side. So many factors have played a part; then suddenly we find that we are on the path. When we try to analyze it, we have no explanation for it. Suddenly, overnight, we feel that the teachings appeal to us. How simple they are! Why did we not think about it before? But it is not really very sudden, for we do not know how many things we had to rough through to come to this. We call it just coincidence, but there are no coincidences.

8   *I know that we've privately discussed this before. I consider you a friend of mine, and this may be impertinent. But why should I keep coming here? I've come here twice but I have no urge at all to ask you for initiation.*

You see, that pull has to come from within, and the Lord knows best how to create it and when to create it. Without him we would never even feel the necessity for the Lord. But when he wants it, he creates that urge within us. He creates the circumstances, the atmosphere which compels us to follow the path. Then we can't even resist that. Our own intellect fails, our own resistance fails when he wants it. The urge has to come from within, and when it will come and how it will come, he knows best. Nobody can predict that, nor should we even try to.

9   *Master, how can we ... I know I probably won't be able to make sense, but we know that we have to ask for help*

just to accomplish any sort of love for the master. How can we overcome being ashamed even to face the master with our being so worldly and empty of true love? How can we overcome feeling ashamed even to face the master and ask for initiation?

Well, actually, sister, it has to come from within. You can't prepare yourself for initiation. That urge comes from within and then you are automatically led by that urge to follow the path. The urge must come from within. There is someone within us who's always pulling us towards himself, and he creates that urge and love and devotion in the soul. You should try to seek and search and then the soul will automatically find the path. The urge has to come from within. The pull has to come from within.

10   *I remember on a tape about a year ago you saying we are all like children, playing with dolls, with pleasures. And we cannot drop the doll and seek the real one and the real pleasure until we find it or we see it. But how do we get past the point where we can't quite exert the effort to see the real one? And we don't quite have the discipline, or have the patience to give up the one we have been following?*

Well, sister, the Lord prepares us for that. All this comes from within and with an intensity so great that you are no longer interested in dolls. You will be able to leave all the dolls when you are attached to something better. Only attachment can create detachment within us. Unless we are attached to something better, it is impossible for us to detach ourselves from the world or from the worldly sense pleasures. When the urge comes from within, then we try to find something better than sense pleasures. And the Lord prepares us to accept that which is better, which is kept within every one of us. And when we know the reality, we don't run after shells. Then we are not interested in these dolls and in these toys.

11   *Besides reading, attending satsangs and talking to other people, how can one fight the doubts that come into one's mind?*

As long as you have doubts, you should go on asking questions. Satisfy those doubts. Never hesitate to ask any question; never hesitate to discuss with anybody whatever doubts you may have. One must dissolve all one's doubts about the philosophy. Most answers are in the books. But if you have any remaining questions, you should never hesitate to ask.

And then the pull must come from within. Our questions are never answered, but they're just dissolved. They become meaningless to us when the pull comes from within. Such a strong force comes from within that you can't resist it. Then automatically all your questions will be dissolved.

12   *Master, sometimes the master will give you the grace so that you have enough longing to come to the path without even the intellect interfering ...*

When your time comes, your intellect and your questions and your doubts automatically are dissolved. This intellect bothers us with so many questions, so many doubts. Everything bothers us. That is the habit of the mind. But when the pull comes from within and your proper time comes, then it isn't that questions will be solved, they'll automatically be dissolved and they'll become meaningless for you. You then think that these teachings are for you and you must practice them. But actually it is nothing but the grace of the Father.

13 *I would like to know whether a person who has had a mystical experience, some sort of revelation which has left a memory in him, would you say that person is on the way, or is he being tempted and is likely to fall by the wayside, possibly?*

Well, if he is getting spiritual experiences, it is due to the grace of the Father. Naturally, he is preparing him to follow that spiritual path. It is definitely the grace of the Father.

14 *Maharaj Ji, I haven't been initiated because I am still a scholar, but I believe and have faith in you as my master. I would like to know whether you guide and protect me like you guide and protect the already initiated souls?*

My dear child, the Lord is in every one of us and he protects all his devotees. If you are filled with his devotion, with his love, naturally it is his grace which is pulling you from within, and if he's creating that pull he will not forsake you, he will not ignore you at all. He will always be guiding you.

15 *When does a seeker come upon the path, Master?*

When the Lord wants you to follow him, to know him, to go back to him, he will give you the understanding and the urge. He will pull you from within and you will not be able to resist the pull. That is what Christ is trying to impress upon us: You cannot receive anything unless it is given to you. And by our own effort, we can never search for the Father.[93]

We are all blind; only he has eyes. No blind person can catch hold of a person with sight unless he is led to him or hears him. So it is for the Father to pull us. We cannot seek him; at the most we can be receptive to that pull. Without his grace we achieve nothing. When he wants us, he will automatically put us in such an atmosphere, in such conditions, that we can't help worshipping him in spirit. Till then, we have to wait for the pull.

16 *Do you think it is from dissatisfaction that we have gotten this longing?*

Whatever the reason may be, there are two ways of coming to the Lord. One is because we have longed to meet him; another is because we are tired of the world and we want an escape in his love. Some lucky people instinctively love him. They worship him only because they want to meet him. They have no other motive or desire. Other people are being driven to him because they are completely tired of this world. They want an escape into his love and devotion. Both are all right, but the degree of love in the first type cannot be compared with anything else, as that is the superior type of love.

17 *Master, could you explain something about meditation for those who have not been initiated?*

I told some of the students that it always helps to concentrate at the eye centre. When you close your eyes you see nothing but darkness in your forehead. You are not concerned with anything in the world at all. Keep your attention in the forehead, in the darkness here, and repeat any name of the Lord. This will help you in concentrating at the eye centre. This will prepare you also for initiation, and will be to your advantage in meditation after initiation.

But while you are trying to concentrate here in the darkness, you should try never to strain your eyes. And you should not try to focus at any particular point, otherwise you may damage your eyes or feel a strain in your forehead. You should absolutely forget your eyes. If, when you're concentrating in the darkness, you see some flashes of light or some colour, you shouldn't feel frightened at all. That is normal. That is bound to come with the help of your concentration. I can give only this advice, before initiation.

18 *Maharaj Ji, last week in Delhi, a seeker asked you about meditation, and if it was all right to repeat "Radha Soami" over and over again, and you said no. I was wondering if that's just personal advice for that person, or is that advice in general for all seekers?*

Well, brother, generally I never advise any seeker to repeat the words "Radha Soami" without understanding the teachings, without being convinced fully about the teachings, without their making up their mind that they want to follow these teachings. Sometimes they become so used to that repetition that it becomes difficult for them to come out of that practice and turn to the real simran. But seekers are anxious to do something, so they do it. Many times they are told, well, if you can't help it, then do it. But it is better to wait till they really understand the teachings, till they have made up their mind to follow the teachings, to live the teachings, to change their pattern of life. There's no harm in waiting.

INITIATION

19 *Is the master within you before initiation?*

The word [shabd] is always within us. Right from the creation, the word has always been within us. But it's no use to us if we are not attached to it. Fire is always in wood, but unless you take the fire out of the wood, you don't see it and you can't make use of it. Now this wood we are sitting on has fire in it. But unless we activate the fire within it, we will not be able to burn the wood. So master is always within us. The word is always within us. We have to find that word within us. Only when we find it can we make use of it.

20   *This might be a foolish question, Maharaj Ji, but now you say that you get placed here in our third eye. What was there before, before you placed yourself in our eyes when we became disciples?*

You see, nothing is put within us at the time of initiation which is not already there. Everything is there; we are just brought in touch with that sound. The soul is within, the sound is within. We learn the method and the technique of how to become one with that sound; with help and practice we become one with the sound. Nothing is added into us; everything is within us, even the Lord. He won't come from anywhere outside.

You see, even though this bulb gives such a strong light, if there are twenty or thirty black coverings around it, you won't see that light. The light is there; but you can't take advantage of that light, you can't see that light and you don't even know that under this covering there is a light. But if somebody explains it to you and you put your faith in him and go on removing these coverings and use this method, the light will start shining. And slowly and slowly you will see the whole light, you will be able to achieve that light – provided you put faith in that person, provided he is able to reach you and you are able to follow his instructions. The light hasn't come from outside at all; the light was there, but due to the coverings you are not aware of it.

Let us say there's a piece of hard substance, and it is covered with a lot of dirt. You think it is just another piece of stone and somebody tells you, "Wash it with soap." Slowly and slowly a diamond will reveal itself. The diamond was already there but due to the dirt around it, you did not know that the diamond was in this dirt. You just took it as a piece of dirt. So if you follow that person who told you to wash the dirty stone and have faith in that person and go on washing the stone, with patience you will be able to remove all the dirt and get the diamond out of it. It will shine, it will have the price of a diamond. That man has not added anything into that dirt. He has told you the method and you have been able to believe in him and you get that diamond. So everything is within us; nothing is coming from outside. The saints teach us and we put faith in them, and with that practice we are able to see that light over which there were so many coverings before, that light which was always there.

Christ explained in Saint John that light is the life of man and light is in everyone, but due to the darkness we comprehend it not.[72] Because this darkness of ego, of ignorance is there, we do not see that light within. Then he says: There was a man who has come from God, his name was John.[73] When the Father wants you to see that light and remove that veil of darkness from within you, he sends a man to our level. At that time it was John the Baptist. The Lord gave him the privilege of being at our level while also being at the level of the Father. He says, you have to meet somebody who has come from God to our level, and being at our level he has the privilege of still being one with the Father. God has given only him this privilege so that through him you will be able to experience that light.

This privilege is given to him so that we will be able to put our faith in him and practice accordingly, and then we also will experience the same light which the Lord has kept within every one of us. That light, that sound, doesn't come from outside at all. It is already within us. But unless the Father sends somebody to our level and we are able to place our faith in him, and then practice and do the needful, for our part we cannot eliminate that veil of ignorance or darkness and see that light within, which he has kept within every one of us. So the master doesn't put anything inside of us – it is already there.

Christ said: If thine eye be single, thy whole body shall be full of light.[23] You have only to open that eye to see that light. The light's already there. But now our whole consciousness attends to the whole world through the nine apertures. Because right from the eye centre, our tendency is downward and our consciousness has spread into the whole world through these nine apertures. When we are able to close these nine apertures and open that single eye, which is actually the central eye or third eye, then we see the light. Christ doesn't say the light will then come from somewhere outside – the light is already there. There is nothing but light, but unless we are within that realm from where we can see the light, we see only darkness. So everything is already here. We just have to come here to see that light.

A needle is always attracted by the magnet, but only when it comes within the realm of the magnet, within its reach. Then the magnet pulls the needle. If it is far away, the magnet will not be able to pull that needle. So we have to come within that circle, within that realm, to see that light. In order to come there we have to use the technique of simran and dhyan [repetition and contemplation] so that we can see the light. But the light is already there.

21 *Please, would the master discuss the subject of initia-*
    tion – not so much the formal ritual involved but the
    significance of initiation?

Actually, the significance of initiation is meditation. The purpose of initiation is meditation. And you know the purpose of meditation. We want to meditate because we want to go back to the Father, we want to escape from this birth and death.

That is the purpose of meditation. In order to do meditation you have to be initiated. You have to be baptized; you have to take a new birth.

It is all a matter of withdrawing your soul current to the eye centre and attaching it to the sound within, and being one with the light; that is the purpose of initiation. And we have to live meditation, just for the purpose of realization of the soul. There's no other purpose.

22   What is initiation and how can we prepare for it?

You see, brother, initiation means following the path, following the technique which withdraws your consciousness back to the eye centre and puts you in touch with the sound and light within. That is the initiation that Christ has referred to: new birth, baptism; they're the same thing. Christ says: Unless you take a new birth, you cannot get everlasting life.[77] That is initiation. But before initiation we must understand the teachings thoroughly. We must satisfy our intellect that this path is meant for me. Will I be able to follow this path? Am I convinced that this is for me? Will I be able to live the way of life that the teaching demands from me? That is very, very essential because that is the foundation on which we have to lay the structure, to build our meditation. And when that stage is covered, we are convinced; we feel quite a pull to the path and all our doubts are dissolved. Mental conviction is there, intellectual conviction is there.

Then what can we do before initiation? We can prepare ourselves to concentrate at the eye centre. We can practice withdrawing our thoughts to the eye centre. We can try to hold our attention at the eye centre. Our consciousness is spread into this world in two ways: by thinking and by contemplating. When we are here, we are thinking about our family, our children, our country, and all that. We are also contemplating on those objects, on those forms. So by thinking and contemplating, our consciousness is spread into the whole world. Whatever we are thinking about is all perishable.

So the saints advise us instead to think about the Lord, to repeat the name of the Lord and try to hold our attention here at the eye centre. So keeping your attention here, you repeat any name of the Lord which is familiar to you. To begin with, it is immaterial because the Lord has no particular name. All the names we give the Lord are out of our love, affection and devotion. So you can refer to the Lord by any name, as long as the love and devotion are there behind the name. So keeping your attention here at the eye centre, you can repeat any name of the Lord. You can practice that for twenty or thirty minutes every day. That will create a habit in you to sit for meditation, to sit still and to control the mind and withdraw the mind to the eye centre. This is a great help before initiation because after initiation we also have to follow the same process. The names are a little different, but the technique is the same. So that is the only advice I can give before initiation. We can sit still and try to hold our attention here at the eye centre, preferably by repeating any name of the Father.

23   *Can you experience the light and sound at initiation?*

At initiation you are told the technique and method. According to their own individual background, some people do experience light and sound. But it is not essential that everybody, at the time of initiation, must experience sound and light. But you are in the process of seeing that light and hearing that sound. Some people have had an association with the path in their previous births. They had made certain progress, so they now need only a matchstick to have light. Others need a wick and wax before they can become a candle, before they can become the light.

It is not essential that at the time of initiation everybody must hear the sound or see the light. But ultimately everybody must hear the sound and must see the light.

24   *Maharaj Ji, in the initiation I remember there were several things towards the end of the initiation that the master said – that if we follow those things we would be saved from returning to the world again. There were five or six prescriptive things the master said, like reading the books, keeping good company …*

At the time of initiation, we are told only about meditation, nothing else. We are told that this is not a religion. Now you know the art of simran and dhyan and hearing the sound. You should not feel that you have to cut yourself off from all your worldly activities, that you have become superior or better than everyone else or that you have to separate yourself from your worldly obligations. Then we are told to digest whatever we achieve within, not to divulge or to vomit outside but to digest all this within ourselves. We are told that we should try to attend the meetings to derive strength from each other. There are many problems which come in meditation which are generally solved in satsang. And if we have no opportunity for satsang, we should read the books. Then if you still don't find the answer, you can write to me. That is all in the initiation instructions. Only these things will help you and nothing else. The instructions are very simple.

25   *Can we have love for the master even if we are not initiated by him personally?*

Love will come by meditation. Love is not just in initiation or in who gives the initiation. That doesn't create any love. Love is created by meditation within us. Meditation creates it, strengthens it, helps it to grow. That is meditation. It is immaterial who gives us instruction. It's just a means. Ultimately our relationship is with the master, not with the representative, and we have to establish that contact by meditation.

26 *Master, I have a question that concerns many of us and we all know the answer but to hear it from you would soothe us greatly and this is the question: When I was initiated, I know that you initiated me from 11,000 miles away, and that Mr Replogle merely gave us the five holy names and some procedures. I would like to know, to feel that those whom you personally initiated are no higher than I am.*

Brother, I think I discussed that question yesterday in the evening. There is absolutely no difference whether the master physically, personally initiates you or initiates you through his agents. The master is responsible. But a disciple feels nearer if he comes in contact with the master in person. Otherwise, as far as the master is concerned, he is near to every disciple, whether he initiates personally or he has initiated by proxy – there is absolutely no difference.

27 *I read in one of the books that unless one has actually met the master personally, it is impossible to go inside and reach Sach Khand. Is it a fact that one must actually meet the master in person, first?*

Unless we have a living master – that is what it means.

I understood from the book that unless one had been initiated by the master in person – is that a fact?

That may not have been understood correctly, for when the master initiates us through somebody, he is responsible, for it is actually he who is initiating us. The one conducting the initiation is not responsible, as he is just an instrument on the way. So by this means the applicant has actually met the master. According to the philosophy of Sant Mat, we have got to contact or meet a living master. If we can come physically in his presence, that is very good; if we cannot do so, it is for him to connect us through some other channel. That is equally good.

How about the contemplation of the master's form, the dhyan part of it?

While doing simran [repeating the five holy names], we should contemplate on the form of the master, keeping his form here, at the eye centre. But if we have not seen the master in person, we can just keep our attention here and do the simran, and even then the master will appear inside. We are just to hold our attention here, at the eye centre, and do the simran. The same master will appear. If you have met him, have seen him, you can contemplate on his form; but you should never contemplate on any picture or photo. That is not advisable.

When the master initiates, whether he does it personally or by proxy, he is personally present to initiate the soul. Space and distance make no difference as far as the master is concerned, but definitely there are certain advantages that at least a disciple feels in the personal presence of the master, which otherwise, perhaps, he does not feel. But in spiritual practice, the advantages will be the same, whether you have met the master face to face or not; whether you are initiated by him personally or through someone designated by him to give the verbal instructions. It is the direct initiation as far as you are concerned. You will get the same result in your meditation that you would get otherwise. A disciple does always feel much better if he can come into the presence of the master or have his own contact with the master. However, from the meditation or spiritual achievement point of view, it makes no difference at all.

28 *Do sponsors take seekers' karma until the master takes over? I guess sponsors are relying on the letter in Divine Light that says that "the responsibility of a sponsor ends as soon as the applicant is accepted by the master."*

No, even before that, the sponsor has no spiritual responsibility at all, in the sense that he will not have to share the seeker's karma or anything like that.

Even if the sponsor knows that the seeker may not have met the prerequisites?

Then the sponsor is failing in his duty, but to say that he has some spiritual responsibility and will be punished – that is wrong. These are only matters of procedure, so to say.

29 *What is your responsibility when you sponsor a person for initiation?*

You mean, does the sponsor have any responsibility? I think even if you want to sponsor someone, one who has to come to the path will ultimately come to the path. You have only a responsibility to your conscience, that you've rightly sponsored a person, that you feel that he's sincere and willing to follow the path. You have no other responsibility. You don't have any spiritual gain or any spiritual responsibility.

30 *Even though we are initiates this time of a perfect master, Professor Bhatnagar said there's no guarantee that in our next life we will meet a master.*

Then you didn't understand him, I think. He said, don't think that if you have been brought on the path you have been initiated in the right sense. He said that the real initiation starts when you see the radiant form of the master. What is initiation? To be led on the path back to the Father. So actually, you start your spiritual journey from the point where you see the radiant form. It's a way of interpreting, a way of speaking. But to reach the radiant form of the master, you also have to know some technique and method, so that is also a form of initiation. But the real initiation is when we are led by the master within, back to the level of the Father. But he never said that if you are initiated, you won't get a human birth the next time. Definitely, once you have been initiated, you don't go down at all.

31 *Maharaj Ji, once I heard on a tape that you have said in a satsang here in India: I declare hereby with the rolling of the drums that a satsangi who is initiated is already in Sach Khand. Could you please comment on that?*

When I take a particular shabd in satsang,* I refer to Baba Jaimal Singh's letter to the Great Master in *Spiritual Letters*. He says, the day you are initiated you have reached Sach Khand. The rest is only your karmic account which you have to go through. It means your roots have been planted there, the seed has been planted. It will sprout one day. A child is born to become a man, but he has yet to become a man. So when the soul is initiated it has to become God, to go to that level. Every soul potentially is God, but it has to become God. When it is connected with that voice of God, you say it has become God, or it is in the process of becoming God. As Christ said: You have become whole,[85] meaning now you are in the process of becoming whole.

---

* *Ram gurpaaras pars kareejai.* Guru Nanak, Adi Granth, M1, p. 324.

That is what Baba Ji wrote to the Great Master. The moment a satsangi is initiated, you can take it that he has reached Sach Khand – that is, that he must reach Sach Khand sooner or later. The rest of his account of karmas has to be cleared, which he has to clear by meditation. It is assured that one day the seed will sprout, the soul will reach its destination. But it's a long way that you have to travel. You can't say you have reached there. When the water evaporates, it has to go back to the sea. It first becomes a cloud, then it becomes rain, then it falls and flows back into the sea. You see, a process has to go on.

32   *Maharaj Ji, was the foundation to be initiated laid in our past life?*

He knows best when he has sown the seed. We don't know when he has marked us, when he has sown the seed. He knows best. But now that seed is growing. Whether it has been sown this time, whether it was sown before, he knows best, but the seed has to grow. The meaning of Christ saying that unless you take a new birth, you will never be able to go back to the Father[77] is that after a birth, the baby starts growing. So after the initiation, after the baptism, after coming on the path, we have to spiritually grow and grow and grow to become one with the Father, just as a child grows and becomes a man.

So become like a babe, just as a child when he takes birth doesn't claim he knows anything at all. He knows nothing, he's an absolutely blank slate – you can write anything on his mind; his mind is absolutely blank. Then he grows according to what he is taught and to his environment. We mould that child, we teach that child because he's innocent. So similarly, disciples should become like a babe. We should have a simple mind, a clean mind, and then we have to grow according to the teachings, according to our meditation.

33 *Pardon me, Master, the other morning in your garden
you talked to a young lady on a point regarding rebirth
and initiation. I was wondering whether you could give
a little more detail about that, please?*

Rebirth and initiation? You see, Christ has said that you cannot
enter the kingdom of God unless you take another birth.[77] By
taking another birth he means meeting a master and getting
initiated by that master. It is said to be taking a new birth because
you start a new life completely – you become entitled to go back
to your Father from the day of your initiation. So it's absolutely a
new life, a new page in the book of your life. And it's also called
a birth because a child always gives himself to his parents, and
the parents become responsible for bringing up that child until
he can stand on his own legs. So when we follow the path, when
we get initiated, the master becomes responsible for us, for our
spiritual development, till we go back to the Father. Just as a child
is brought up, stage by stage, at every step, so similarly a new initiate is brought up. His spiritual development takes place under
the care of the master. That is what I was trying to explain to her
because she's writing a book. I was trying to tell her that she must
explain in detail to seekers what Christ means by a new birth.

34 *I want to know why I was not on the list to be initiated.
I don't know at what time I asked for initiation. Maybe
I'm on the next list coming up.*

Sister, I appreciate your anxiety to follow the path. But everything comes in time. When you read the Bible, Christ says to
one seeker: The time will come when you will worship the Father
in spirit.[83] So everybody has a time when he is to worship the
Father in spirit. You shouldn't be anxious. Whatever advice is
given to you, it is in your own interest.

Every seeker must have sufficient time to know himself, to know what he is going to do, because initiation is not a ceremony. It is a pattern of life. You have to change the pattern of your whole life. You have to live a certain way of life for the rest of your life. So you should never hurry for initiation. Give yourself as much time as you possibly can to understand the teachings and to know your own self: whether you can stay on the diet, whether you can attend to meditation, whether this pattern of life will suit you. When you are sure about it, you are always welcome.

35   *Would you clarify the reason for the age requirement for initiation?*

Well, many things we just learn by age. I always like every seeker to give himself sufficient time to understand the teaching which he is going to follow, because he's not going to follow it for six months or one year. It is going to be the way of his life; his whole life pattern will be changed. So he must have sufficient time to determine for himself whether he is able to follow the teachings and whether he is mature enough to understand.

When the mind is at a tender age, we are generally influenced by others – by our friends, by our relations, by our parents – and our decisions are generally influenced by them. That is why I always try to tell them that they must grow and become mature enough to make their own independent decision, not influenced by anybody at all. That is why age is a consideration, because at a certain age you get maturity, you get that wisdom to make your own right decisions. That is why everybody should give himself time. He must understand the teachings properly and thoroughly.

36   Why is there an age limit on initiation?

You see, you should be mature enough to understand what you are going to follow. Generally, children are influenced by their parents, by their elders, to follow the path. It is not their own decision. They make a quick decision under the influence of their parents; and when they grow and become mature they may think they have taken a wrong step. So I like children to grow to understand, and to make their own decision and not be influenced by anybody at all. They must satisfy their intellect.

First you must grow to build your intellect, and then, with that intellect, try to decide what is right for you. Generally we do not initiate a child. He has to become mature in order to understand that his decision is right. Otherwise, there's no age limit at all to follow the path.

37   If one is under the age limit and therefore waiting for initiation, is it possible to concentrate on dhyan in meditation until one is initiated?

My general advice is that you should never be in a hurry for initiation on this path or any path. Proper time must be given to deciding whether you really understand the teachings and if your decision is a mature one, uninfluenced by anybody else. Age teaches us many things. That is why I advise those young boys and girls who are very anxious to follow the teachings to try first to understand the teachings in the right perspective. They should not be influenced by their parents or associates. They must be mature in order to understand the necessity of this path and then decide if they will really be able to follow it. So they should never hurry to follow any teaching.

They are advised to adhere to the diet, to observe the principles of Sant Mat, to read the books, to attend the group meetings and if there is a question they are most welcome to write to me. They must give themselves time to understand the teachings properly, because it is not only a question of giving time to meditation. Sant Mat is actually a way of life to be lived. So they should not decide to follow the teachings simply under emotional excitement or because someone is influencing them. They must be mature enough to understand it themselves because it is a way of life. That is why I don't encourage youngsters to apply for initiation, not because they are not welcome.

But before they are initiated, I always advise them to give some time to concentration at the eye centre; to close their eyes and look into the darkness. They should try to still the mind in that darkness. This concentration will help them after initiation. This practice can easily be done for fifteen, twenty or thirty minutes, every day. And they should never strain their eyes or try to invert the eyes in an effort to see something within. Whatever we see within has nothing to do with these physical eyes. When we close our eyes, we are automatically where we should be. And being where we are, we should try to still our mind in that darkness, and slowly and slowly it helps the mind to stay there. This practice of concentration in the interim is helpful after initiation.

38 *Master, I guess you've heard this before but I suspect there are many people here besides me who would like to know. I'm destined to remain a seeker for some time still. And I'd like to know from you how I should live my life until I can be initiated.*

We should try to attend the meetings, read the books and try to understand the philosophy. We should try to lead a neat, clean, moral life. And we should try to remain on the diet. And we must give ourselves sufficient opportunity to understand the teachings we are going to follow; to decide whether or not we will be able to follow them, whether we will be able to live that way of life. Because you are not on this path for a year or two – your whole life will have to be spent on this path. So you must give yourself sufficient time to know whether or not you can live this pattern of life, this way of life. Your whole concept of life will be changed when you become initiated. That is why you should never hurry for initiation at all. And meanwhile, the only thing you can do is prepare yourself to understand the teachings in order to determine whether or not you'll be able to live the teachings.

39   *Master, you just said that two kinds of people are initiated: those who come to the master and those who live the Sant Mat way of life. Is it possible for the master to initiate someone inside who is dying, who has lived a Sant Mat way of life and who calls to the Father and calls to the Lord? Is it possible for him to be initiated?*

Sister, sometimes in very rare cases they do. Sometimes the master initiates some people inside, without coming physically in contact with them straightaway. Then the master must be physically living. You can't depend upon the past masters.

40   *I know some people that say they were initiated on the astral plane and never attended a regular initiation. Is that a possibility?*

Generally not. Very rarely will a soul be initiated inside. It is only those souls who have to die very soon after that, not for those who have to live. Even those who are initiated inside will have to come back in the body again for initiation. Only the sanskaras of initiation have been put in their mind. But they must take birth as a human to be initiated again.

41   *Master, if someone attains the first or the second region by his own efforts, without being initiated by a master, is it possible for him to get initiated on that plane by a master?*

First thing, it's very difficult for him to reach the second region. And then, he has to come to the flesh for initiation. If he has been initiated here in the flesh once, then he can be helped from the second region upward. But if he has not been initiated in the flesh, then he cannot be helped by the master in the second region. In the Bible Christ said: Who is my disciple? Who has seen me and who follows my teaching, he is my disciple indeed.[92] 'Seen me' means that he's in the flesh and the disciple is also in the flesh. Then we see each other. It means the disciple and the master have to be contemporary, in the flesh at the same time. The disciple becomes the master's disciple when he follows his teaching. Then it becomes the duty of the master to take that soul back to the Father. Whether he pushes that soul from the second region upward, from the third region upward or takes it from here, that is his job then. But the soul has to become a disciple first. Unless he becomes a disciple, the responsibility of the master doesn't come at all. You can only become a disciple, Christ says, when you take a second birth – when you have seen me, and when you follow my teaching. Those are the conditions for making a disciple. It is very clear in the Bible.

42   *Does a soul have to be initiated in this lifetime to reach Sach Khand? If somebody was initiated in another lifetime, do they have to be initiated again in this lifetime?*

They will have to be. The soul must be initiated in that lifetime. But that soul will pick up the thread from where it left off in the last birth. It will make better progress. It will start from that very point in its mental and spiritual progress, and then start to progress upward. But it has to be initiated.

43   *One could say that the physical eyes and the physical ears are the windows of the soul, and I would like to know how and if it is possible for a blind person who is also deaf to come to the Creator.*

Sister, the melody which we have to hear has nothing to do with our outside ears. The light which we have to experience and visualize and see within has nothing to do with our outside eyes. That is why Christ said: Having eyes ye see not; having ears ye hear not.[69] We don't hear with these ears; we don't see with these eyes. We use a different faculty to see within, a different faculty to hear within. So it doesn't make any difference at all if a person has become blind, because the soul has its own eyes and its own ears within – the faculty to see and the faculty to hear.

If a man is born deaf it doesn't make any difference at all. But a man born blind has very heavy karmas – having come to this creation, he cannot see anything. Then his problem is that if he has not been able to see the master outside, he will not be able to recognize the master within; he can be misled by any entity which can take the form of the master within. So he can be deceived. That is why mystics generally don't initiate people who are born blind.

44   *Maharaj Ji, is it possible for a person who is either blind, deaf, dumb, or crippled in any way to receive this nam?*

Well, brother, that divine melody is within every one of us. It has nothing to do with our outside ears, nothing to do with our eyes, nothing to do with any defect in the body. Anybody having no eyes or being deaf who is able to withdraw his consciousness to the eye centre will be attached to the melody within. It is a different ear within which hears the voice of God. It is a different eye within which sees the light of God. So these eyes and ears don't make any difference at all, if the soul is marked and is pulled within. The soul may finally pass within. The soul may come to the path, in spite of all these handicaps.

45 *Going back to the topic of controlling the mind, would a person blind or deaf have an advantage over the others in containing or controlling the mind?*

No. Their minds may always be running about, thinking that they would like to have all that people are explaining to them, or wondering what they are missing or desiring to have what others have.

Satisfying the Intellect

46 *I have been searching for a long time. How do I know that this is it, or should I continue to seek? My second question is: How do I remove the guilt of leaving a more traditional Christian approach?*

Well, sister, the first thing is that we should go on searching until we are intellectually satisfied. Unless we feel satisfied from within, unless the pull is from within, we should try to resist following any path at all. The conviction must come with a vengeance, with force from inside, and we should not be influenced by outside influences. We should feel our own individual intellectual satisfaction, and we must feel that pull from within. And even if our whole life is spent coming to that conclusion, it is not time lost, it is time gained. Then you are building on a rock, not on sand. Then nobody can shake you. So from that point of view, we should never worry. And we should give quite a fair trial to ourselves, to know ourselves, to know where we stand before following any path.

We should not carry any guilt at all for following our traditional paths; they are all steppingstones. Unless we understand those traditional faiths, we will not even be able to understand Sant Mat. Because these traditional faiths create our background, they create our foundation. At least they fill us with love and devotion, and they are the foundation on which we have to build. There is nothing wrong with our traditional faiths, but we have to understand those traditions, the basis of those traditional faiths, and then Sant Mat will just come right from those traditional faiths. Because it is not a new science, it is not a new teaching; it is the same old teaching which the old mystics have been giving to us, but now they have become traditional faiths because we have taken to rituals and ceremonies and dogmas rather than to the teachings. So we have given them shape and the names of traditional faiths. But actually, they were the right teachings originally.

For example, the teaching of Christ in the Bible was the right teaching. Moses' teaching was the right teaching, John the Baptist's teaching was the right teaching. But today these have become traditional faiths because the reality has been lost; today we have given them a more ritualistic, dogmatic approach. Rather we should try to give them a mystic approach, a spiritual approach. Faith will come right from those very teachings, from nowhere outside. So we should have no feeling of guilt at all for following those faiths as taught. They are our base, they help us to understand. It is difficult for a man to understand Sant Mat who has no background at all of any kind. It is easier for people who have some sort of faith. It becomes easier for them to find out about the path if they are a little open. So the question of feeling guilty should not arise at all.

47   *Master, would you please talk about how to talk about the master to people who are not on the path?*

We should always approach the seeker from his own background, in which his mind has been conditioned. If a person has a background of Christianity, we should try to explain the reality, the truth to him from the New Testament, from the Bible, and then the mind rises above these traditions and becomes open. Then he is prepared to accept anything and finds the same spiritual truth everywhere. So it depends upon the background of the seeker to whom we try to explain the teachings. Some people are absolutely closed, you can't reach them, and there is no need to waste your time. But if you find them to be real seekers, if you find a real hunger for spiritual truth in them, then you have to come to their level to explain to them.

48   *Maharaj Ji, along with a lot of other satsangis, I find that it is very easy to get enthusiastic about the path initially, but it is very difficult to sustain the enthusiasm.*

Well, brother, you are perfectly right. Sant Mat teachings are so simple, so convincing, that we find that they are for us. But they're very difficult to follow; it's very difficult to live the Sant Mat way of life, so we get confused.

I always advise seekers – and I'm never tired of saying it – that they should not be influenced by anyone to come to the path. They should not be influenced by their partners, by their friends, by their relations. It is an individual search, and they must feel their own pull from within. They must satisfy their intellect from every aspect. Unless the intellect is satisfied, it will come in our way and we will not be able to make any progress within. Intellect will never lead us back to the Father. But satisfaction of the intellect will give us faith, and faith will automatically force us towards practice. And that will bring us deliverance. That is the only way.

So we should not be influenced by anybody to run to the path. Even if our whole life is spent in investigating, in searching, it is not time lost, it is time gained. We are building on a rock, not on sand. Nobody can shake us then. If we are easily influenced by one another, then we find the path very hard to follow. We should never be hasty. We should read as many books as possible; we should ask as many questions as possible. Mostly, questions are answered in the books – there's hardly any question which is not mentioned in the books or on the tapes. But still, if anything bothers us, if anything stands in our way, we should never hesitate to discuss it; we should never hesitate to ask. And unless we feel an urgent pull with a great strength from within, we should not try to follow the path at all.

Before making a decision to join the army, a person should take his time. But once he has joined, the soldier has no option but to do his duty. Similarly, we should spend as much time as possible satisfying ourselves about the path, but once we have taken it upon ourselves to follow it, then we must give it a fair trial. Then we must live the teachings, follow the teachings and attend to our meditation. I always say that. I will remind you again – I don't mind.

49   *I see everyone asking a lot of questions. How do you get down to it? How do you get into the thing? I would like to know in baby words and not in intellectual words: How does one enter into paradise? Karmas exist in this world, illusions; what is true and what is not?*

Well, brother, everyone has his own approach. Some people are very intellectual, and unless their intellect is satisfied they will never be able to follow the path. Some people are simple, and they may accept the path in a very simple manner. But everyone who is a seeker and has been initiated has to follow the path. If one is fortunate or unfortunate to be intellectual, he must satisfy his intellect. As long as the intellect is a barrier in his way, he will not be able to follow the path. So intellectual people should be given all the opportunities and facilities to satisfy their intellect. Unless the intellect is satisfied, the intellect will not let you follow the path.

Intellect will not take you to the destination, but it can become a hindrance in your way to following the path. Ultimately, faith and practice – not intellect – will take you to your destination. But intellect can become our friend if we satisfy it. If we try to follow the path and set aside the intellect, it will again come in our way, it will again obstruct our progress. But by first satisfying the intellect, we are building on a rock because we are laying a deep foundation on which to build our meditation. Either we should be fortunate enough to be very simple, which we are not today – it is an age of reasoning – or, if we have developed our intellect, we must satisfy it, otherwise we will not be able to follow the path. So everybody has a different approach.

Can the intellect be satisfied as we go in?

To some extent. Naturally we have to pierce the veil of intellect with the intellect. You have to satisfy your intellect with your intellect.

But the intellect is illusion.

Of course it is illusion. It is an obstacle in the way. If you have intellect, you must satisfy the intellect. Once the intellect is satisfied, no one can shake you. Then faith and practice will take you to your destination.

50 *Master, you said before that we should convince ourselves first about a certain philosophy, but we know that on this physical plane, and with our intellect, no matter what conclusion we come to after studying various philosophies, there will always be some other great minds on the other side of the fence who will still not accept the conclusion we have come to. And this we see all throughout history. So even though I may feel very attracted to a certain philosophy, I also know that perhaps I'm in the dark, perhaps I'm still blind, and some other mind can see things differently.*

We must satisfy our intellect. Unless the intellect is satisfied, you will not be able to follow any philosophy; you will not be able to practice any philosophy; you will not be able to get results from following any teaching. The intellect must be satisfied. Even if your whole life is spent in satisfying your intellect, it is time gained, not time lost.

This intellect is a great barrier in your way. But you have to pierce the veil of that barrier valiantly. You have to satisfy your intellect. Unless your intellect is satisfied, faith cannot come; practice cannot come. And without faith and practice, you will get no results. We would be lucky if we were not at all intellectual, but we aren't that fortunate. We are very intellectual, so we must satisfy our intellect. And once the intellect is satisfied, that intellect will be our best friend, our best guide. Then nobody can shake us. We'll be building on rock, not sand. If a simple person who doesn't try to satisfy his intellect is influenced by other people and starts following a particular teaching, he can be led astray at any time. He can be put on some other path. But intellectual people will never be shaken once they have satisfied their intellect, even if the whole world turns against them.

I often give the following example: If one wants to drive from New York to Washington, a simple person will just ask anybody on the road for directions and as soon as a route is pointed out the simple man will start driving on that road. If someone meets him along the way and tells him that he's going in the wrong direction, the simple man immediately tries a new route. He believes anybody who comes along. Even if he were the first to start, he may be the last to arrive.

If intellectual people are told about a road leading to Washington, they will not believe only one man. They'll want two or three corroborations; and even after that they will check a map. Then they will drive a little and study the road signs. And once they have satisfied their intellect, nothing can convince them they're wrong. Any number of people can stop them now on their journey and tell them they're on the wrong road, but they won't listen. Their intellect is not taking them to Washington. Now the faith, which they have developed by satisfying their intellect, and their driving – their practice – that's what is taking them to Washington. They have never been to Washington before, but they have satisfied their intellect. And by the satisfaction of the intellect they have developed a certain faith in the fact that this particular road leads to Washington and so they're driving on that faith and they will be able to reach there. Now they cannot be shaken at all.

So if there is any doubt in our mind about the teachings or about the teacher, we shouldn't try to follow the teachings at all. We should, we must, make a very thorough research, a very critical research. And once we have satisfied our mind, then we should not let the mind interfere at all. Then we should set our mind aside and give the path a fair trial; we must practice.

51   *Will intellect allow you to do anything you want to do?*

Even if your whole life is spent in satisfying the intellect, you are not wasting time. You are utilizing your time, you are digging deep. Your foundation will be very deep. You are building on a rock. If you don't dig deep you are just building on sand.

52 *Master, before, I was listening to Professor Puri, and he said that on this level, on this plane, and with our intellect, everything is really subject to doubt. We can never really be sure 100 percent.*

I know you can never be sure 100 percent unless you reach Washington. But still, you have developed a certain faith and practice as you're driving to Washington. You can only be sure 100 percent when you reach the spot. So you have to build some sort of faith. I mean, if somebody is being taught that A comes before B, he can't ask "why A?" He has to start with a certain faith that A is the first letter. You have to build faith, but still you have to satisfy your intellect. There may still be some doubt until we actually reach the spot. But when you see the road signs, when the route is corroborated by the map, you won't be bothered by the length of the road.

53 *Should we strive for intellectual knowledge? Is it not inclined to interfere with spiritual progress?*

Intellect is very good to live by in this world. We know the ways and means for spending our life comfortably with the help of intellect. But intellect does not lead us to the Lord. We have to leave the intellect in order to follow that path. What we require is practice and faith. I do not say an intellectual man cannot follow the path. Intellect is a barrier in our way, no doubt, but we have to pierce this barrier with the help of the intellect. Unless the intellectual man is convinced that the path is right, he will never follow it. He can never have faith in the Lord as long as his intellect is not satisfied. But once his intellect is satisfied, he does not need intellect to follow that path. What he needs then is faith and practice.

I do not say that intellect is not required. For an intellectual man, intellect is required in the beginning to understand everything. But a simple man can also follow the path. He does not require the intellect to be convinced, but as he does not have much of a foundation, he can be led astray. The intellectual man is not led astray. Once I am convinced that this is a horse – it has all the signs of a horse – and I am intellectually convinced that this is a horse, even if the whole world tells me that it is a buffalo, I am not going to believe it. If to a simple man two people say that it is a horse, he will say, "Yes, it is a horse." Then if another ten people say to him that it is a buffalo, he will say, "Yes, it is a buffalo." The simple man is easily shaken. We do need intellect, but intellect does not lead us anywhere. Ultimately the faith and practice will lead us to that destination.

54   Is it possible to get hold of a wrong teacher?

That is possible too, why not?

Could one spend his whole lifetime working and holding on to the wrong teacher?

I generally advise the seekers that even if they spend their whole life in seeking, it is not time lost, it is time gained. We should never plunge blindly into anything. We must satisfy our intellect so that this intellect may not become a barrier in our way. We must satisfy it before we can progress on the path. If we spend our whole life satisfying our intellect about a teacher, about a path, I assure you it is not time lost, but time gained. We are just building a strong foundation. We are digging deep for a building. The deeper the foundation, the bigger the construction you can put up. We must build on a rock, make a thorough research into what we are going to do, and not just plunge blindly without investigating or satisfying ourselves that this is the right path for us. And once we have satisfied our intellect, then we should not let our intellect interfere with our progress. We should set aside the intellect. What we need then is practice and faith. Practice and faith, not intellect, will take you to your destination.

55   *Even in our daily life we have insights and ways of know-ing ordinary things; that is, better ways of knowing than trying to figure out the why and the cause and effect of certain circumstances. We use a faculty that takes us much nearer to the point. So why not try to understand the enormous things that way?*

No. As long as the intellect is there, it has to be satisfied. 'Why' and 'how' are kings of this age. We call it the scientific age. 'Why' is the first thing: Why should I do? How should I do? Because the intellect is there, we must try to satisfy the intellect, at least to some extent; otherwise, it will not let us try to meditate. Intellect is a great barrier in our way and we have to pierce this barrier with the intellect itself. Unless the intellect is satisfied, our mind does not go at all on the path of medita-tion. So we have to satisfy this intellect with the intellect. That is the purpose of all these discussions, all the satsangs, all this literature, all these group meetings. It is for no purpose other than to satisfy the intellect. Saints will just tell us, "Do it!" and we should start doing it; but we do not, unless first we satisfy the intellect. We must first be satisfied that it is the right path and it can lead us to the Lord. So we have got to satisfy our intel-lect, but intellect does not solve all our problems nor answer all our questions.

The reason we do not eat meat or take alcoholic drinks or that we accept you as master is largely an intuitive knowing?

That is right, but we still try to satisfy ourselves intellectually. These decisions are made on a much higher level. But in order to satisfy ourselves, we always say that our intellect has done it.

56   *There are many different ideas about God, what God consists of, what God is. Do we reach a point where we really understand God?*

Not by intellect in any way. When we go beyond it, then we will know what God is. To know him is to merge back into him. That is the only way to know him, not intellectually.

57   *I was wondering: You say that we must use our intellect to be sure we are not led astray by someone who claims to be a master, and be sure intellectually; then to leave our intellect aside. At the same time, do you not say that we have to accept the theory of reincarnation?*

No. I say that we have to accept all these theories now with our intellect. But to be able to understand them fully, we have to experience them. As long as the intellect is there, we have to satisfy ourselves intellectually about these theories.

But can we ever be sure of that intellectually?

We will be sure as far as intellect is concerned. Beyond that we cannot be sure unless we experience it. How are we sure about the Lord? Only intellectually. We are not yet sure through experience. So we have to accept these theories intellectually or reject them intellectually.

*58   In the early beginnings, at least, there are doubts that
arise in our contacts with those around us in our work
and regular living. Are those doubts of great hindrance to
progress?*

Brother, I said the other day that if we have doubts, they definitely stand in our way of progress. Our mind must be satisfied
before we can make progress. That is why I always insist that
applicants must satisfy their intellect before coming to the
path. After that, they should not let the intellect interfere in
their progress. Then all that is needed is devotion, meditation,
practice – nothing else. Doubts have no place on the path. Once
we have accepted it, then we know – then we need practice and
devotion – no doubts, no questions. They are automatically
resolved. As long as there are doubts, we should try to clear
them. We must clear our doubts, otherwise they gradually
become a stumbling block in our way.

*59   Well, we are trying to satisfy our intellect before we
start.*

That is right. And intellect ultimately will bring you to this conclusion, that you have to rise above it. The intellect will advise
you to cut the roots of attachments to this world. It can take you
no farther. It only helps us to understand what we should do;
but the release is gained only through spiritual practice.

*60   Master, sometimes when you're giving satsang in Pun-
jabi you use an English phrase: A rolling stone gathers no
moss.*

You see, it's very simple: A rolling stone gathers no moss. If you
are running everywhere – from one precept to another precept,

from one philosophy to another philosophy, from one path to another path – what moss can you collect? You have to build faith, and only then will the mind let you practice. Because without faith, there can be no practice. But if one is rolling about, then definitely one has no faith and one can never practice anything at all. So one has to be one-pointed towards the path. Shabd is the path, and through the master you can be in touch with the shabd. And if we try to go to the right or left – let me try this philosophy also, let me try that philosophy also – if the mind is wandering like that, it will collect nothing.

Before following the path we should try to satisfy our curiosity, our intellect. We must have intellectual conviction before we follow the path. Even if our whole life is spent in making a research, trying to find the right path, I think it's not time lost, it's time gained. Because then you are building on a rock, not on sand. The intellect is a great barrier in the way, and we have to pierce the veil of intellect through the intellect. Intellect doesn't help us on the path, but it definitely becomes an obstacle on the path. So we must satisfy our intellect before we can make any progress on the path. When the intellect is satisfied then faith will develop, and then you will be able to practice. Without satisfaction of the intellect you can never build faith, and without faith you can never practice, and without practice you can never achieve any result. So even if our whole life is spent trying to satisfy the intellect, it is time gained, not time lost.

I often give an example: If you want to drive from here to Delhi, and you have never been to Delhi before, naturally you will ask people about which road leads to Delhi. Somebody will tell you that this road leads to Delhi. But you are hesitant to drive on that road because you are not convinced by the statement of just one person. You need at least nine, ten corroborations to feel convinced that this road really leads to Delhi. And then also you would drive a little slowly and try to see milestones or road signs which would convince you about the direction of the road towards Delhi. You have never been to Delhi before and when you are convinced this road does lead to Delhi, then you have built faith that this road is leading to Delhi. Then you will drive on; you will keep going. Then even if a hundred people meet you on the way and tell you that you are wrong, that this road doesn't lead to Delhi at all, that somebody has misguided you, you won't bother about them because you have satisfied your intellect. By satisfying your intellect you have been able to build faith, and now that faith is forcing you to drive to Delhi, where you have never been before. And ultimately you reach Delhi. But intellect hasn't brought you to Delhi; faith and practice – driving – have brought you to Delhi. But satisfaction of the intellect was essential before you could build that faith that would enable you to drive.

With a simple person, if you tell him that this road leads to Delhi, he will at once start driving on the road. But if anybody meets him on the way and says: "Oh, you are on the wrong road – you have just missed the road on the right that was going to Delhi," the person will at once turn to the right. When he meets another person who says: "No, you are absolutely wrong, that other road leads to Delhi," he will go to that other road. So he's just moving about. Whatever anybody tells him, he just turns to the right or left, so he will never be able to reach Delhi. He may be the first to start, but he may never be able to reach there.

So he's the rolling stone that will not gather any moss at all. But if he's one-pointed, if he has been convinced, if he has satisfied his intellect, then he has been able to build faith, and now he can practice that faith. So faith is the rock on which we have to build our meditation.

That is Soami Ji's *shabd* [hymn] where I use this phrase. Soami Ji says that when you have come to the path you must be one-pointed towards the shabd. Don't think that by going to some holy tank you will be able to wash your sins; or let me read the holy books and this will help me on the path; or let me go and hide myself in the Himalayas – perhaps that will be essential in order to go back to the Father; and let me do this ritual or that ritual. Soami Ji says that these things will not lead you anywhere. You must be one-pointed towards the shabd. If your mind is wavering on every path which you come across; if everyone whom you meet you want as a guide, Soami Ji says, you will not get anything at all, you're just wasting your time, like a rolling stone which gathers no moss.

61   *Maharaj Ji, does a disciple sometimes ask a question, the answer to which is beyond his level of understanding?*

What can the disciple understand? Because if you ask a question which is beyond your mental understanding, what is the sense of giving that answer which is also beyond your mental understanding?

You see, a question actually means that which stands in the way of faith, that which becomes a hindrance in our meditation. We are bogged down with old orthodox religious traditions, and we want to rise above them. The mind has become very conditioned with those dogmas and with those preconceived ideas, and something within also pulls us to the path. So conflict comes, and then the intellect wants to be satisfied. Questions come which stand as obstacles in our way, but then they become clearer and clearer. The questions are not so much answered, but they dissolve – they become meaningless.

I find that many people are asking questions, but they're hardly interested in the answers which you have given. They're hardly even attentive to the answers, what to say of even interested. But they just ask. So naturally you can't be very serious about those answers. The real question is only that which becomes a block in the way of meditation and we are fighting to get rid of that. We definitely need help to rise above it; and we do get the answer and we do get the help to rise above it. Otherwise, with intellect, one can ask a hundred and one questions; there's no limit to them.

Should one wait and see whether the question resolves itself?

Don't worry. If there's any question, you can ask. That's why I say: If any question is bothering anybody and coming in conflict with his meditation, he must ask; he should ask. Why let it grow? You see, actually it is faith which forces us to practice. Faith. And faith only comes when the intellect is satisfied, so the questions are more or less to satisfy your intellect.

We have built so much intellect, especially in the modern age, and we also feel that we are real intellectuals, so we want to satisfy our intellect, otherwise it comes in the way at every step. So satisfaction of the intellect will give you faith, and faith will help you to practice. Intellect will not lead us anywhere; faith will lead us to the destination. Satisfaction of the intellect without faith can never lead you to practice. But satisfaction of the intellect does create faith in us.

We would be fortunate not to be intellectual at all, but in this modern, scientific age, everybody is very intellectual – that is, at least we all think we are. Unless we satisfy our intellect, our mind won't let us follow anything at all. But our intellect doesn't interfere with our traditional beliefs. I have seen many scientists – I have read their works – who can accept many unnatural things in the Bible, in the New Testament, and all those things don't bother them at all because, in spite of their deep knowledge of science, they don't let that knowledge interfere with their serious beliefs, howsoever contradictory those things may be. Because their minds have been conditioned right from birth, they accept all those things, or they never bothered to go too deep into them or use their knowledge of science even in this life.

62 *Is it important during our lifetime to study from the books about what is going to happen to us at the time of our death, or is it sufficient to leave it in the hands of the master, who will meet us at that time?*

I think these books are all more or less just for our intellectual satisfaction. The main thing is the experience. Even if you are not told anything about what is going to happen, when you are on the road you yourself will see what is coming in your way. Rather than preparing yourself and remembering the lesson of what you are going to see, you automatically see what comes before you. The experience is more essential than knowledge about these things, and knowing about these things is just for satisfying the intellect, so that intellect may not become a barrier in our way, hinder our progress and shake our faith. All these things are just to satisfy the intellect.

Either we are fortunate enough not to have any intellect at all, which is very difficult in this modern, scientific age, or if we have intellect to some extent, then we must satisfy it. Otherwise it will become a barrier in the way. It will never let real faith, real devotion come in. It will always make you shaky if you don't satisfy it. Intellect will not lead you anywhere. But satisfaction of the intellect will create love, faith, devotion and practice in you, and faith and practice will lead you towards your destination. Satisfaction of the intellect, not the intellect itself, will give you faith and lead to practice.

So if you try to set aside your intellect and try to build faith, it will become shaky in no time, and your mind will never be happy in practice because you are not sure what you are doing. But when you have satisfied your intellect, then nobody can shake you, and then automatically faith comes in, and when faith is there, automatically practice is there.

63   *If one has not got faith, how does one acquire it?*

Well, brother, faith just comes by his grace. We can't acquire it. We may think that we have acquired faith, but actually it is given by him, when he pulls us from within. Only then do we start worshipping him, thinking about him. When he wants to put us on a certain path, he helps us from within, to satisfy our intellect. Satisfaction of the intellect will give you faith and faith will give you practice. Without satisfaction of the intellect there can be no faith. You can't brush aside your intellect and say that I have built faith. Again intellect will jump in the way with more force, more vigour. So it's always better to satisfy your intellect.

64   *Master, what would your answer be to someone who accepts the path as a workable way of life, accepts the necessity of a master in this life, and yet it seems as if the only thing that apparently stops them accepting the path and the master completely is a complete disbelief in any afterlife at all. They simply do not believe in any existence, either spiritual, mental – or any existence whatsoever – after death.*

I don't think his disbelief will make any difference at all, as long as he's following the path, and he's attached to his meditation. You see, believing alone doesn't help. We have to follow the path. Mere belief doesn't take us anywhere at all unless we follow that belief, live that belief. This is only intellectual satisfaction. But then we have to live it in practice, we have to attend to meditation. That is more essential.

> *But it's just that it seems that they would like to follow the path. The person I'm speaking about is not initiated and yet …*

You see, a girl is intellectually convinced that a particular man is the right husband for her – he's a wonderful man; from absolutely every point of view he would make an ideal husband. But what is the use of this belief unless she marries him? The real marriage can start only after marriage. Even if we believe in the whole path and we don't follow it, practice it, that belief is of no use. It is only intellectual satisfaction, that's all. And that doesn't lead us anywhere. It creates our sanskaras and helps us in a way – someday next life it may help us – but otherwise, unless we follow it, we're not getting anywhere at all.

> *Then if this person came to you, Master, and said, "I would like to believe in the path, I would like to be initiated, but I do not believe in any existence after death," what would your reply be to that person?*

I'll tell you when I've replied to him, because he has not asked me this question yet. All the books are full of such replies, you see. Whatever letters come from seekers, these questions come in these letters, you see, and we try to satisfy them in every respect. It is the intellect which still stands in the way, which wants to be convinced about a certain philosophy, certain theories. But I personally feel that when the time comes for a person to follow the path, when the pull comes for him to be on the path, automatically the answers to all of these questions come. All these questions just get dissolved. You feel you're absolutely convinced. All these questions become meaningless to you, so you come on the path.

After all, not everybody comes on the path after satisfying his intellect about all the aspects of Sant Mat. They're on the path, but they don't know why they're on the path. It is a self-deception to think that I have thoroughly studied it and thoroughly weighed it from every angle and I'm fully convinced of all the aspects of the teachings. There is maybe justification for our doing certain things, but there is someone else who's pulling from within, who throws us on the path, and then we start justifying our being there. So when the time comes, these questions automatically get dissolved.

65 *Would it be reasonable to say that satsangis, initiates, who go off the path after being initiated by the master – would it be reasonable to say that the cause is the intellect?*

You see, generally people read books. They jump to conclusions, and they think they understand the path and they try to follow it. Actually, they have not made a thorough research. They have not satisfied their intellect. Their intellect and subconscious are not satisfied. So when it gets a chance, again that becomes a stumbling block in their way. So it's always better to satisfy the intellect and take as much time to understand as one really needs. But once we've really satisfied our intellect, then we shouldn't worry about the intellect at all. Then we don't need any book or any intellectual discussions at all. What we need is practice and faith.

66 *Yesterday we heard from Professor that a living master goes up daily through the regions and back. If I tell nonsatsangi friends that this is so and they do believe that, do you have any proof I could tell them about to*

*demonstrate the regions? I know there are certain sat-
sangis who have seen this.*

You see, we can only help other people by giving them the
literature to read. They have to satisfy their own minds. We
shouldn't try to influence them or impress our dogmas or our
thinking upon anybody. Let him make his own research and
his own investigation and acquire his own conviction. That
will be more solid for him, rather than to accept another person's decision and try to base his own thinking on it. All these
books, all these meetings, all these discussions are meant for our
individual conviction, individual research. We should never be
influenced by the decisions of others. We must feel convinced
ourselves that this is for me. It must come from within. And
the purpose of all these books which have been written is just
to satisfy our intellect. The books won't give you anything at
all. They will only satisfy your intellect so that you can develop
faith, so that then you can practice.

67   *Maharaj Ji, you once said that Sant Mat is so easy, you
just have to open yourself. Can you tell us a little more?*

It is so easy to understand, but very difficult to follow. It's
very simple. But sometimes it becomes very difficult for us to
understand simple things in a simple way. We are so intellectual,
especially in the modern age. Unless someone presents something to us in an intellectual way, we don't try to understand
that thing at all. So we never accept simple truths in a simple
way – unless they're put to us in a very intellectual way, then
we are very happy. Then we are satisfied because our intellect is
satisfied with that approach. Otherwise, Sant Mat is very simple
to understand. Our mind is in the habit of creating problems,
then trying to solve them, and then taking satisfaction in having

solved them – or feeling frustrated after not solving them. I don't understand the necessity of creating problems to begin with. We create problems and then we try to solve them or try to find answers to them. We don't accept simple things in a simple way.

THE FOUR VOWS

68 *Master, if my study of the teachings is correct, it seems that one of the primary aims for the initiate is to live in the will of the master. My mind has this idea about trying to live in the will of the masters. Could you speak on this subject?*

You see, to be firm on the principles on which we have to build our treasure in heaven, the first thing is to live in the will of the master. Then you need to attend to your meditation daily, as explained to you. If you keep to these four principles, the other things will automatically be shaped in your interest. If you don't compromise with these four principles of Sant Mat and you adjust your way of life accordingly, you are automatically living in the will of the master.

69 *You said that we should not sin any more. Well, what you consider a sin and what I consider a sin ... Well, I mean, how do you know if you're sinning or not?*

You see, sister, anything which keeps us away from the Father is a sin. And anything which takes us towards the Father is not a sin. You have to be steadfast in the teachings. At the time of baptism, at the time of initiation, a certain way of life is explained to the disciple. If you stick to that way of life, then you can say you are not sinning. You must stick to the teachings, to the way of life which I am trying to explain to you, in order to follow the spiritual path. If you do not stick to those principles and try to meditate, then your balance may remain the same.

We are told at the time of initiation that we have to lead a clean moral life. We have to abstain from meat, fish and eggs. And we have to abstain from drinking and anything that leads us into vices. We should be strict on these principles in order to build our meditation. Then we are in the process of becoming whole. If you do not stick to the principles, then you are not in the process of becoming whole.

70 *Maharaj Ji, would you tell us, besides being on the diet, not taking alcohol and so forth, and besides not killing and the regular abstinences, what some other karmic actions would be that we could avoid in this life?*

Nothing else. All other good qualities will come automatically with devotion to the Lord. If we make the Sant Mat principles a part of our life, then we abstain from meat, fish, fowl, and eggs or anything containing them; we do not take alcoholic drinks; we have a good moral character and we devote time regularly and punctually to the spiritual practice. When we do that, I personally feel and think that all other good qualities of a human being appear in us like cream on milk. You do not have to do anything else to get or develop those qualities, for they naturally will come in you. The nearer we are to the Lord, the more devotion we feel for the Lord, the more the good qualities automatically will come within us. We will become part and parcel of those qualities, without doing anything else.

71 *Master, most of us have in our religion the Ten Com-mandments, and the first commandment states that I*

*am your Lord. I am One and you shall not make any
images before me. I am trying to translate that from a
different language. You probably know it in different
wording. But I would like to know from you, are you in
favour of all Ten Commandments? Are you familiar with
the Ten Commandments?*

Brother, these are all set principles or set rules as to what we
should do and what we should not do.[138] We will automatically
know and practice all this when there is devotion and love for
the Lord within us. When the love and devotion of the Lord
comes in us, all these good qualities are manifested in us like
cream on milk. Then we need not tell our mind, "You are not
to kill, you are not to do this bad thing, you are not to tell a lie,"
for all that automatically will become a part of our life when we
live according to the teachings of the saints.

*But there are other human beings that are not so enlight-
ened, and for their start it is very important?*

It is good. All these things are just to guide us towards the
path. They are like cleaning the vessel, preparatory to putting
something into it, and it is necessary for the vessel to be clean
before putting anything into it. So by merely trying to follow
the Ten Commandments without being on the path, we shall
find the vessel still empty. We have to follow them and tread the
path, and by treading the path we are automatically following
the Ten Commandments too.

Yet, who gave them?

The saints tell us; the saints give us.

We understand that God gave them.

Well, God sent the saints. After all, God has never come into the world to write a book. The writings had to come through someone. Everything that we get through the saints we get from God. It is very clear in the Bible where Jesus indicated: If you have seen me, you have seen the Father; for I have seen the Father, so you have also seen the Father through me.[119] He also indicated: Whatever I tell you is what my Father wants me to tell you, for of myself I do nothing. The Father in me doeth all things. Christ makes it very clear in the Bible: All that I am trying to give you is not my own, but comes from my Father.[120] So the Lord tells us in this way. He gives us instructions through his saints, who have seen him, who have merged back into him and who therefore know his will. The Lord has given us these commandments. Whatever he gives, he gives us through the masters. He will always give his teachings through some human being, through his human incarnation.

I want to know why you doubt that he did not give them.

No, I do not doubt. I say that all the teachings of the saints are given by the Lord through his saints. The Ten Commandments are also teachings of the saints. So whatever the teachings of the saints are, they are given by the Lord through the masters.

It is in the Old Testament that the Ten Commandments were given to Moses in order to keep the people in line, these very primitive people.

So they have come through Moses. They were given to Moses for us, so we have received them through Moses. That is what I am trying to say. All the teachings of the Lord will come to us only through the saints.

THE VEGETARIAN DIET

72 *I would like to know why, if a person practices the Ten Commandments and does good to everyone regardless of whether they be good or bad, why is it that he has to abstain from meat?*

Sister, I will explain to you. All that you see in the world can be divided into five divisions or categories, based on the five elements – earth, water, fire, air and ether. The human body is made up of all five elements, but the soul, the essence of the Lord, gives it life. Because it is only the human body that contains all five elements, it is called the top of creation.

The first division is that of the plant kingdom, the main or active element of which is water. The second is that of insects, reptiles, and worms which live under the ground. They have most active in them the elements of earth and fire. [Fire and air predominate in insects that live above the ground.] Fowl, including all types of birds, belong to the third class, and the three elements most active in them are water, fire and air. Those belonging to the fourth category are the four-legged animals, such as cows, buffalo, horses, and the like. They lack only ether, the power of discretion. Human beings are in the fifth class, at the very top of creation, as all the five elements are active in them.

One's feeling is in proportion to the number of elements that are active and the degree to which they are active. For example, if you pluck a flower from the garden of your neighbour, there will be no punishment. She will only abuse you or frown at you, or you will just incur her displeasure. If you kill her chicken, she may file a suit and you may be fined; if you kill a horse, you may be imprisoned; and if you kill a human being you may be hanged or receive some other form of capital punishment. However, in this world, we can never live on the dead; the living can live only on the living. We cannot live by eating stones, nor can we live just by drinking water or by breathing air. Life has to live on life. So the saints advise us to collect the least amount of karma while living in this world, and for that reason they advise us to live on fruits and vegetables. They belong to the first division, and even they have souls; but the karma involved in eating them is not as great as that which we would incur by living on or in any way destroying the life contained in those belonging to the other categories.

Yet it is impossible to live in this world without some so-called innocent killing; for instance, when we walk, we kill insects; when we talk, we kill insects; when we breathe, we kill insects, though they are not visible to the naked eye. This whole room is filled with creatures; we are killing these creatures without even realizing it. We are killing by talking, by breathing and even when shaking hands. Whatever we are doing, we are killing. The room is full of souls.

If you are given 180 pounds of weight to carry, you will be crushed under it and will not be able to go even a step. So saints always advise us to collect the least amount of karma. That means that because we have to live and we can live only on the living, they advise us to collect the least possible load. That is why we depend upon plant life, which is a very insignificant amount of karma to collect and which can be cleared with even one or two days of meditation.

If on the one hand we are meditating, and on the other hand we are killing every day, we are only balancing what we are doing and we are back where we started. How to get rid of the load we are carrying? We are advised not to collect anything for the future, and whatever we have already collected, to clear it with meditation. Then only can we go back to the Lord. That is why we are vegetarian.

73   Master, do you advise a vegetarian diet?

There is no question of whether or not I advise it. We must follow it. There is no other way for spiritual progress. If you have only a shirt on your back, you can run; but if you are given a tremendous load, you cannot even take a step. As life must live on life in this world, the saints say that we should limit our intake to things containing one element, and that means vegetation, the plant kingdom. We should try to take the least burden from this world, just like wearing a light shirt, which does not bother you, as you do not feel that load. We should not accumulate so much bad karma, such as by killing, by eating meat, that we are just crushed under it and cannot make any spiritual progress.

If we kill, we will be killed. We should never forget that. Christ said, love thy neighbour.[67] All creatures are our neighbours. The surroundings in which we are living, that is, the whole universe is our neighbour. When you love anybody, you do not kill that individual; and when we love the whole creation, we cannot kill intentionally, nor could we find it in our heart to have it done for us by someone else.

74   Master, my children often come home from school having been told about the Ten Commandments –"Thou shalt not kill" – and they are told that these commandments apply to human beings, not animals, and that in the Bible, Moses said what type of meat you can eat. How can I explain it to them from a Sant Mat point of view?

Sister, the words are very simple: Thou shalt not kill.[138] Where is it written animals or humans?

You see, after some lapse of time, we forget the real teachings. We want to hold on to just the shell and lose the reality. We want to hold on to traditions, organizations; we want to belong to some sort of religion, and don't want to follow the teachings of those mystics at all. We think it is sufficient to say, Buddha is my master, Jesus is my master. That is all that we want to feel. We don't want to go deep into the reality of their teachings because that is very difficult to follow. It is very difficult to mould our way of life according to their teachings. So we start compromising and go far away from the teachings and from the reality.

No mystic advises killing. There should be no contradiction in their sayings, in their teachings. If on the one hand he says, thou shall not kill, and on other hand he says, you can eat meat, then that is a contradiction. How can these two things be reconciled? There is something wrong in our understanding.

75 *The doctrine of nonresistance, nonviolence – particularly not taking life – has been an important part of Indian history. What is the teaching of Sant Mat on this point?*

We practice nonviolence. We do not kill birds or animals for food, nor are we to kill anything for sport. That is nonviolence, and nonviolence is based on the karma theory.

76 *Maharaj Ji, why do you ask for a strict vegetarian diet with this meditation?*

The reason is: whatever you sow, so shall you reap.[133] If you kill, you expose yourself to being killed, and we want to avoid this killing.[14] That is why we have to be strict about our vegetarian food.

No doubt it is very difficult to stay in this world without killing anything at all. When we walk, we kill. When we breathe, we kill. When we talk, we kill. When we drink, we kill. Since the whole world is filled with souls, we can't exist in this world without killing.

Every killing involves punishment. But there is a difference in the degree of punishment. So saints tell us that whatever we eat in this world involves killing and a degree of punishment, and while being in this body we should try to collect the least amount of karma. If you have only a shirt on your body, you can run. You hardly feel the load. But if you are given a 100-pound weight, you can hardly walk. So that is why we are to collect the least amount of karma while in this human form.

And whatever we have collected, we can burn up through meditation. If we are attending to our meditation, then whatever little killing we do in the way of eating vegetables or fruits or our walking, talking and so forth is automatically taken care of by that meditation. But if the balance remains the same, then how can we escape from birth and death? On the one hand, we are trying to meditate, while on the other we are killing day and night. So the balance always remains the same. We remain tied down to this world.

We are always advised to remain strictly on the diet, because whatever has been done will be cleared by meditation. At least in the future we should not sow such seeds, so that we will not have to come back to this world to face the consequences. We must be vegetarians. We have to eat something to exist in this world. We cannot exist on dead things such as sand and stones. The living must live on the living. So that is why saints tell us that we should try to collect the least possible load and try to live on vegetables and fruits.

77 *Do you think a high master could be born in a meat-eating country?*

It does not make any difference. You may be eating meat, but when he wants you to drop it, you drop it as a glass from your hand. You do not have to be prepared for it. I know people who have been taking meat even till the time of initiation and then became very strict vegetarians. They leave meat-eating when they have to leave it, and they just leave it.

I meant, could a soul that is to be a master be born in such a civilization?

Yes, why not? He has to pay for his past karmas. He has to satisfy his unfulfilled desires, cravings which he had in his last birth. Probably he could do it best in this atmosphere, these surroundings, this environment, and after doing that, he is to make his own way on the path. So he will be led, too, according to his destiny.

78 *I am from India, and so many of my friends, American friends, always ask about the diet. Some of them want to eat meat. Now afterwards the question comes – they ask, if the law of karma applies to drinks and meats, then who is the bearer of the karma: the killer of the cow or the eater of the meat?*

Both. If the eater is not there, the killer won't be there. If the demand is there, the supply will be there. So the eater creates the demand and the killer supplies that demand. Therefore, both are responsible.

They try to follow the diet and suddenly within two days they're sick; they can't eat because of mental conditions.

You should advise them to leave off meat slowly, not suddenly, not all at once. We have many cases – many of them are sitting here – who were ferocious meat-eaters. Perhaps they are healthier now than before they came on to the diet. It's just a matter of habit. I don't think that meat-eaters are healthier, nor do you become sick if you stop eating meat.

79 *Say a patient is suffering from extreme malnutrition, at the point of collapse, and has been a lifelong vegetarian, and the medical doctors say she must have meat and cannot substitute, so she decides to have a homeopathic physician who will give her vegetarian food. But that won't be accepted by the medical physician. And the patient needs a medical certificate to satisfy the government that she is ill and so forth. And the medical physician won't take care of her under those circumstances, and a homeopathic physician won't be recognized by the government. What should she do?*

These are difficult situations. I understand it. As I have told you, we should try to remain firm on the principles of Sant Mat and do our best. Death will come one day, even when one is on a meat diet.

Never yield?

We should not. But there are slips here and there, I admit. However, you cannot compromise with a principle, whatever it is. A wrong is a wrong. Health of the soul is more important than that of the body.

80 *What can a satsangi do if she has to go to the hospital, she is very ill and the doctor doesn't agree with her being a vegetarian, because, he says, patients can't get well without eating meat or eggs? And if he says that she has to get it or he will get her to eat it, what can she do?*

Well, sister, I can understand your problem, especially in this country. But a principle is a principle. I find there are so many vegetarians in Europe now. Doctors should try to understand. If one doesn't want to eat these things, he shouldn't be forced.

You could go to another doctor who believes in all this. Being a vegetarian, there is more chance of your being healed than if you were not a vegetarian.

81   *Master, it's claimed that in this country there are no fertile eggs sold. Is it because of killing that we cannot have eggs or is there another reason?*

Well, sister, I agree with you. Those eggs have no life at all. I admit, you are not destroying any life if you eat those eggs. But if you start with that type of egg, you will end up with the other type of egg. You will not discriminate between fertile and infertile eggs. You will develop a taste for eggs and then you will start justifying every other type of egg. From that point of view, we are advised to abstain from taking eggs. I know these infertile eggs have no life at all. I made that point very clear in *Divine Light*. I wrote to some disciple a very long letter on fertile and infertile eggs, and I refer you to that letter in *Divine Light.**

82   *But why can we not eat an infertile egg? We are not killing?*

I know that infertile eggs have no life, and from that standpoint you can justify it. But when you start with that, you start with the other also. You get the taste of that and there will be no end to it. If you just start innocently with a kiss, you do not know where you will end; so then you start justifying things. It is better to be strict, and when we are strict about a certain thing, there is no question of compromising. We remain strict, but if we become just a little loose in this way or that way, we do not know where it will lead. Besides, the eating of even an infertile

---

* See Appendix for letter 439 in *Divine Light*.

egg hardens the mind by exciting animal instincts, which are antagonistic to spiritual progress.

83   *Master, if an initiate should stray from the vegetarian diet two or three years after initiation, what would be the effect on the initiate?*

I think you have given quite a lot of latitude – two or three years. You are perhaps referring to your wife, who was initiated today?

No, no! I am interested in all of us.

Then why worry at all? Why should an initiate stray at all from the vegetarian diet? Why worry about this question? If a child commits a mistake, even a little crime, the father does not hand him over to the police. But the father never hesitates to spank him, to beat him or to punish him in some way in order to set him right, to reform him; but he will never hand him over to the police or to the jail authorities. So if we fall, we do not go back but we have to pay for that. We are given punishment just for our reformation. A mother loves the child most, but still she has to keep him right. Sometimes she has to spank him – not because she hates him, but because she loves him and wants to keep him disciplined, to set him right. So in the same way, the master also admonishes us, and we have to face the consequences of what we do; but he does it with a loving hand and with loving care, just for our own advantage.

84   *What about a wife whose husband is not a satsangi and eats meat, but she wants to become a satsangi and doesn't want meat? What can she do?*

She should not eat it; but let her husband eat it.

*She can let her husband eat it without incurring karma
on herself?*

How can she force him to leave it? She herself should not eat it,
but let him eat it if he wants to.

She can buy it for him and cook it for him?

Yes, she can buy it and cook it for him. She has to do her duty.
But she herself should not take it. I would not like to create any
dissension between husband and wife. But the main thing is
that the disciple should not eat it at all. And if, under compul-
sion, the disciple has to entertain somebody who is a nonveg-
etarian, then there is no harm. But the disciple should not take
it. That is the main thing.

85   *Would you advise us as to an occupation involving cooking and serving meat to others?*

I understand the difficulty, especially in the case of some satsangis whose partners are not satsangis. But I never like Sant
Mat teachings to create any disharmony in the family. So I won't
mind if the wife or the husband has to cook meat for the other
spouse. But we ourselves should not partake at all. We must be
strong in our own principles. But if the partner insists on our
doing the cooking, I think we should do it.

86   *Is it wrong to be in a business selling meat and fish in a
restaurant, and to sell alcoholic drinks?*

As far as possible, it is better to avoid such things.

87   *There are situations in families which are difficult. There
may be parents, old people and other family members who*

come to visit their home. They try not to give meat, but sometimes they feel that the other would be displeased.

If you have to sometimes, you do it. We just should never take it ourselves.

88   *How about people who work for you and are used to eating meat?*

You pay them their wages and let them buy their own meat. Let them prepare their own meat.

If I give them money to buy their own meat, is that right?

You give them their pay and you don't know where they spend it and how they spend it. You are not responsible for that. You are only to pay their salary or wages.

89   *Master, what is the responsibility of a satsangi when he has a guest either in his home or in a public eating place to provide for that guest? Supposing that the guest wants meat?*

Brother, you do what is possible under the circumstances. You see, sometimes we are caught up in such situations, and we find it practically impossible to escape. We do it, but we are not happy that we are doing it. Then we try to avoid or escape from such situations where we are not happy about what we have to do. When we ourselves do not eat or drink what is harmful to spiritual progress, there is no reason why we should serve it to others. If we are doing it, perhaps we are not happy within ourselves. If you are not happy within yourself that you are doing it, a time will come when you will refuse to live against yourself; you will refuse to do it; you would like to avoid it.

It is better then that we should not want to do that?

If you feel guilty about doing it, then you should not do it. If you honestly feel that it is all right under the circumstances, I do not bother, I do not mind – go on doing it. You should not do anything that makes you carry a sense of guilt with you, for that will not let you sit in meditation, it will not let you live with yourself, and it will not let you be happy. We should always do the best we can under the circumstances. Sometimes we are caught in such a net that we find it difficult to escape. We just have to do what is practically possible in that situation. We do many things which we cannot justify, which we should not justify, but we have to do them. But all the same, the law of karma will take its own course.

> *Maharaj Ji, when a satsangi is having friends at home and his particular friend delights in eating meat and things other than fruit and vegetables, should a satsangi serve meat to his friends when he has to invite them to his home?*

Brother, it depends on the situation. If he has to do it, let him do it. But the main thing is that we are not to take it ourselves. And I tell you, when we do not take it ourselves, we are never happy to do all these things. What is the use of serving anybody meat or drink, if you carry that sense of guilt always with you of what you have done? Then you do not live with yourself. You are torturing yourself. You are unhappy with yourself, and gradually perhaps you yourself begin to take it. You will not be happy in such circumstances. You will not be happy in that atmosphere or company.

> *Then it is best that you let them know that in your home none of these things are served?*

I tell you, it is much better to be strong within yourself. There is no need to feel inferior in this society that we are vegetarian and do not drink, also that we do not serve such things. If people do not really love you, you have no concern with them. Do not bother about them. If they are interested in you, they will respect your principles. They will respect your feelings. And if you think they are not interested in you to that extent, I do not think they are even worth meeting.

90 *Master, in my business there are times when I have to take people out to lunch or dinner and they order meat, and I have to pay for the meals. Am I taking on karma by doing that?*

Well, if you want to know the exact answer, you are. We can't run away from it. We are creating a demand, and that supply comes and we become the means. We are getting involved. But it depends upon certain circumstances. If one can avoid it, it is always better.

91 *If somebody serves meat to his children or to other people or to friends, or liquor to other people, is this a demerit to him, or to the people who eat or who drink?*

It is a vicious circle. It is bad for both. When you yourself do not eat meat and do not drink, you yourself are never happy to serve these things. As a result you always carry a feeling of guilt in you, and that in itself becomes a block in your progress. You are not happy with yourself; you are never happy in such situations, and naturally, when your mind is always feeling like that, you will never concentrate, you will never make progress as long as you are carrying that feeling of guilt with you. So why not just throw it away by discontinuing those things that make you feel like that?

92   *Now, taking the reverse situation, when people invite you to their homes and they eat meat, and of course, the satsangi does not eat meat, what is the situation in regard to him when he gets the odour of meat right under his nose?*

We have to live in this world. We cannot convert the whole world to our own view, to our own way of thinking. You have to make the best use of the situation to the extent that you should not take it yourself. You do not bother about what they do. You are to be strict only with yourself. You are responsible for yourself, you are not responsible for the world. You cannot solve the problems of the world, but you can rise above those problems and not let them affect you. You are only concerned with your own food. Let them do whatever they want to do.

93   *How should one answer a friend who says that I know that eating meat is wrong; however, more bad karma is made by hurting the feelings of a host or hostess than by eating meat?*

You can just pity him, that is all. I assure you that when we stand on Sant Mat principles, we are not hurting others, not even a little bit, for our principles. Actually, when our beloveds and our friends know our principles, if they are interested in us, they respect our principles. If they are not interested in us, I do not think we should bother about them at all. We should not compromise with our principles. Our real friends will always appreciate and respect our principles, because they love us and they always like to do what pleases us. Otherwise, if they are selfish, you can easily be indifferent to them.

94   *Master, what is the simplest way to explain to one's children the reason for not eating meat?*

I think the simplest way is just to set ourselves up as an example to our children. They do not want any reasoning when they see that the parents do not eat meat. Generally, they try to do what the parents do, and we can explain to them from the humane point of view that it is not kind but it is cruel to kill anybody. I know of a particular example: When my sister was newly married, her husband used to take meat. Though, of course, she was an initiate and did not eat it, yet she did not like to interfere in his life, and when she got a child, her husband tried to rear the child according to his own views. My sister, of course, never liked that; so one day when her husband was out, the servants were going to kill a chicken, and she took her son right to the spot. Naturally, the chicken was crying out and resisting, and the child just could not stand it. After that he automatically became a vegetarian in spite of his father's persuasions, and ultimately the father also became an initiate.

Children do not know what they are eating, but if they know how these chickens and animals are being killed and slain and what they have to go through, probably the children would never eat meat. Their hearts are so sensitive and tender that they cannot stand it. So I think it is more or less for the parents to explain to them, or to be an example to them, but not to insist too much, especially to this modern generation. You see, they do not want any decisions made for them; they like to think that it is their own decision. But we have to prepare them for making good decisions.

95 *What can I do about my children, who prefer to have meat in their diet on occasions? I would rather not have it in my home.*

Well, sister, this is naturally a problem. You, and not your children, have taken a decision to follow a path. So as far as you are concerned, you should never compromise with your principles. You have to be strict with your principles. As for the duty of a mother to her children, if they want meat, I would advise you not to shirk your duty to serve them. But if you can explain to them, if you can advise them and you can put them on the vegetarian diet, perhaps you will be happy and they will be happy. If you cannot do it, you should not worry about it at all. But you should never compromise with your own principles.

96 *Master, I have two very small children, and it does not concern my husband or myself to give up meat. But when people hear that we are not giving meat to our young children, in our society, we are made to feel a little that we are depriving them of nutrition. A few words from you would put our minds at ease. For a young child, is a vegetarian diet sufficient?*

Well, sister, you can bring up your children in any way you like. Many people who have never tasted meat in their life are in better health than those who have taken it. It is the responsibility of the parents as to what they want to give to the child. The child himself has to make his own decisions when he becomes mature. Then you leave it to him what he wants to do. As far as Sant Mat is concerned, we are only concerned with the initiates. They are not to compromise with the diet; but with others we are not concerned at all.

But if I were thinking of initiation at some time, would it be better for me to keep my children vegetarian?

No, you have only to pledge for yourself. You have no right to pledge for anybody else. What you do not do for yourself you will always hate to do for others. It is for the parents to decide what is best for the children until they are mature. Then they can decide for themselves what they want and what they do not want. We are only concerned with the seekers, with the initiates. The initiate has to take a pledge to be vegetarian.

97   *Maharaj Ji, I think some of us are worrying about eating sugar, because we understand that bone products are used in processing the sugar?*

I think you are trying to analyze too much. If you try to do that, I wonder if you will even be drinking water! I wonder if you would even like to breathe if you knew what you were breathing in. It is the human habit to do too much hair-splitting, and when you go on analyzing too much you will find that it leads nowhere. We have to live in this world. We need food, we need shoes on our feet and we need clothes. If we try to analyze everything, perhaps we would not like to live. That is why saints always advise us that this world is not a place for us to call our home at all. Why not leave it and go back to the Father? That is the reason why all our efforts should be to go back to him. Personally, I am not against taking sugar. I do not take it, not because I have anything against sugar, but because I am a little diabetic. Otherwise, there is no harm in taking sugar at all, as far as Sant Mat is concerned.

98   *Has an apple from a tree got a soul just as much as the tree has?*

Yes, as long as it is a part of the tree, the soul is also there. The whole tree is one soul.

And the apples too?

Naturally, that is a part of the tree. But when the apple separates from the tree, then the soul is not there. You have deprived that apple from that life energy which was there, which the apple was enjoying when it was a part of the tree. It's the same as if you were to say: Then since I have killed the bird, the soul is not there, so I will eat it.

Would it be better to let the apple rot on the ground?

Justify anything, sister. You can't run away from the karmas in this world. Justify it in any way. How much spraying do you do on the trees? We kill so many insects. While going to the orchard to pick the apple, you have killed thousands and thousands, millions of insects. Just in order to go to pick that apple, you are walking, you are talking, you are breathing. At every step we are killing souls. You can't escape. So the best thing is to escape from this creation.

99   *Is it part of a moral life not to go to war when your country goes to war, and to avoid killing as much as possible?*

As much as possible, we should try to avoid killing. But even still, with our best intention and best motive, we are part of a chain in this vicious circle. We can't help killing sometimes. Even out here, when we are talking, you don't know how many germs you are killing. You are walking and you don't know how much you are killing. You eat fruit, you don't know how much killing has been done before the fruit has come to your plate. There is so much spraying of insecticides on these fruits. So many germs and insects have been killed before we are able to get that fruit which is nourishing you. You take milk: You don't know the fodder which is given to the cow, how many germs have been killed by these insecticides, these chemicals, before the cow can get its fodder and before we are able to get that milk.

So in that way, we are all killing because one can never live on the dead. We can only live on the living. But saints advise us that we should try to collect the least possible load in this life. As I said, we can't live in this world without killing, but we should try to collect the least possible load during the span of our life. And that least possible load can be easily taken care of if we are attending to our meditation. If, on the other hand, you are attending to meditation and you are killing birds and animals and humans, you are collecting much more karma than what you are trying to clear by meditation. What good will your meditation do?

You see, if you don't throw the rubbish from the house every day and you go on collecting rubbish, naturally it will accumulate. If every day we clean up what little dust is there, the house will always be clean. So we should not kill humans, and we should not kill birds and animals unnecessarily. If we can live on vegetables, then why kill birds and animals for our food?

100 *Master, many of us have animals, and we keep worrying about what we should feed them. Many satsangis say, "I feed my animal nothing but vegetables," which gets to be a hassle. Some dog food companies make products with a little meat in them along with cereal. What sort of karma are we creating?*

To be very frank, we shouldn't feed anybody meat when we ourselves don't take meat. But sometimes we have to entertain or feed people – that is different. Generally, you will not be happy within yourself if you feed somebody meat when you yourself don't eat it. We take on an unnecessary responsibility for an animal when we feed it meat. If you want to keep an animal, keep it on a vegetarian diet; otherwise why keep an animal at all? Where is the necessity of keeping that animal?

101 *I think it's impossible to feed an animal without using animal products.*

Well, sister, not only animals, even some humans also think it is very difficult to live without meat and fish, but we are all living. So similarly, animals can also live on the vegetarian diet. They can also live without meat.

102 *If you agree that a dog must eat meat and men must provide that meat by killing, how would that fit into your teaching?*

We must not kill birds for the sake of a dog. A dog can kill for himself. Our problem is that we have taken on the responsibility of feeding a dog, but nature has given him the freedom to feed himself. So he's responsible for his own karmas. We are trying to collect his karmas on our shoulders. Why should we kill for him and give him food? It is for him to find his own food. Since we have made him a pet, we are also sharing whatever we are giving him. We are responsible for whatever we are giving to the dog because through us he's collecting bad karmas, and we are also responsible for the fact that birds are being killed in order to be given to dogs.

103 *Concerning the food of the dog, is it the same case if you give the dog some prepared food containing meat from a shop?*

Meat is meat. Whether you buy it and prepare it or buy a preparation containing it.

104   *Sometimes the man I work with goes out of town and
      asks me to feed his dogs, and so I go to his house and I
      feed his dogs. But I have been really worried about feed-
      ing them meat, so I think I should feed them cottage
      cheese or something else.*

Well, sister, I can't say it is all right. If it's your duty to do it, try
to change your duty. When you are not feeling comfortable,
when you are not feeling happy doing it, then you are living
with a sense of guilt with yourself. Why live with any sense of
guilt at all? When there is a strain on your mind, that what you
are doing is not right, why not get rid of it?

      *Is it all right if we don't feel guilty? If, say, you are doing
      it for another person because that person is ill?*

You see, if you are compelled to do it, it is a different thing, but
if you have an option, then you shouldn't do it.

105   *I'm a little concerned because I have some suede skirts,
      leather purses and a suede jacket, and they're all made
      with animal skin. So I wondered how much karma I'm
      collecting.*

Well, your part is there. We can't avoid that because the supply
comes when there's a demand. Even for our shoes, animals are
killed. Even for our purses, animals are killed. We can't justify
it by saying that we don't kill them. That would be even worse
if we killed them. But still that supply comes because there's a
demand for it. So we become part and parcel of all that. But
since we live in this society, we cannot help it.

106   *If it's bad karma to eat meat, is it also bad karma to wear*
     furs and suede and such things?

Well, sister, to some extent we are definitely helping to add to
our karmas. When we create a need for these things and when
killing is done to satisfy our need, we definitely add to our karmas. I can't deny that if you wear leather or furs, you are adding
to your karma. But when you walk, you kill. When you talk,
you kill. There are so many insects living in this world which
strike against us and die. You can't escape from killing in this
world. Even vegetables have life. When we eat vegetables, we
are also adding to our karma. But this load is so light that it is
automatically taken care of by meditation.

Since we have to live in this world and are part of this creation, we have to draw a line somewhere in order to exist in this
world. So there's no harm in wearing shoes and all that.

107   *Master, while using leather from animals for shoes, we*
     are not consuming flesh, but we do voluntarily give con-
     sent to the death of these animals. Is that sanctioned?

Yes, sister, that is right. There are no restrictions on wearing
apparel. We have to take a practical, objective view in this life,
and to collect the least possible load, which should be cleared
by meditation and devotion to the Lord. Our main purpose of
living in this world should be God-realization. Then we can
justify wearing leather shoes, wearing clothes and eating fruits
and vegetables; but all the same, the karmas are there.

   But, could we not give up these things?

If you can do without, there is nothing like it. But if you even do
without shoes and clothing, it does not make much difference
as far as incurring karma is concerned; for, as I told you, even

when breathing, walking or drinking water, you are killing. So we have to take a practical view in life and try to collect the least possible load, which should be cleared by meditation and devotion to the Lord.

108 Maharaj Ji, if the soul is marked as it comes into the world, why are we allowed to eat meat and drink liquor and do all these wrong things before we find the path?

To go though your karmas – you have to go through your karmas. You have collected so much rubbish in the past, sown so many seeds in the past; you can't erase their effect – you have to go through all that.

Actually normal, natural food for a child is vegetarian. The natural food that a child starts with is milk. It is the parent's fault when they start giving children meat and eggs and this and that – it is the parent's fault, I must say.

Even smoking, you just start in a society, like a fashion, and it becomes a habit. Drinking starts in the same way – it becomes a habit. So similarly, people get in the habit of eating meat, but it's not natural.

GIVING UP DRUGS AND ALCOHOL

109 What do you think about drugs?

Probably it's a new thing I'm going to have to face in my trip to the United States. Six years ago when I came, nobody here knew even the names of drugs. And now I am told, and I find, that many people think that just by taking drugs they will get spiritual experiences. I wish it could be so easy. But it is not as easy as people think. They are trying to escape reality by taking these drugs.

Drugs are very harmful, not only to the body and the mind, but also to the soul. So many scientists have written about drugs. So many doctors have given advice in books. I have nothing to comment on that. But I can only make a plain statement: In following a spiritual path, drugs and alcoholic drinks are no good at all. They will not lead you anywhere, they will not take you anywhere at all. You'll just wreck your body, wreck your health, and you will not get anything in return. If you really want to follow the spiritual path, you should abstain from all types of intoxicants and drugs, especially LSD and marijuana and so many others I don't know the names of.

110 *There is a drug called* LSD, *which gives people inner experiences that seem to be rather along the lines of what we see, or hope to see as initiates of the master. What is the attitude of our master to the taking of this or any other drug?*

Actually, I was expecting this question, right from our very first meeting. Because we always like to have experience without working at anything, without doing anything. We want the results, but we don't want to work for the results. So it's very convenient and easy if we can have a pill or two and get all the internal experiences. But fortunately or unfortunately, that is not so. Our experiences differ. I have read a little of LSD – some article in *Life* magazine and here and there. Whatever little I could find out, the experiences of those people who take that drug differ from each other. But spiritual experiences do not differ from each other at all. They are bound to be the same, though our approach may be different.

For example, if you drive from here, London, to Edinburgh, your main experience, what you see on the way, is bound to be the same. But what is different is that sometimes you give more attention to one part of the country, sometimes you give more attention to another part of the country, sometimes you skip one scene, and you give more importance to another village. But all the same, the general experience is bound to be the same for whoever travels on that road. But whatever little I have read about this drug, experiences differ with different individuals. Actually, the experiences are just of their own mind, mental experiences. They have nothing to do with spiritual experiences.

This drug may give you a little physical concentration, it may put you in a little trance – you may be in a half-conscious state, or in a sleeping conscious state, and you may see something over which you have no control. But a true spiritual experience is within our own control. We can go up there when we want to, we can come back to the flesh when we want to. But the moment the effect of the drug is gone, nothing is in your control. You are again a victim of the senses, and you become again the same sort of human that you were before. But spiritual experiences differ from that. They make us much finer, better humans, and we are no longer slaves of the senses. We become able to control our mind and then our mind starts controlling our senses. But by taking these drugs, we remain a slave of the mind and a slave of the senses. So these are absolutely useless experiences.

I can only advise that we should not try to find short cuts in order to have those experiences. We have to practice, we have to concentrate, we have to open that door and find those experiences for ourselves which are permanent. Not only permanent but eternal – experiences which will take us back to the Father. Perhaps you may get some sort of experiences by overdrinking, by taking some other sort of drug which makes you a little semiconscious. Even chloroform – I have seen many people, when they take chloroform, they become senseless. They have many things to tell about what they have seen. But they have absolutely no control over what they saw in that state.

So this LSD is something very different from spirituality. I can only advise that we should not dabble in these things and should keep only to our own path, keep to our own practice.

111 *Maharaj Ji, in this country, many of us are living as animals, especially spiritual seekers who have been deluded with drugs. And in seeking, we become addicted to these drugs, or become somewhat helpless, even satsangis. And we need your help. Could you advise us?*

Well, sister, I must say I appreciate one point. Especially in your country, so many young people are being attracted to the path, attracted to spirituality. At least they are seeking. Sometimes their search leads them to drugs. It is not their fault. People exploit them; people misguide them. It's not that drugs are leading them to spirituality. Their search for spirituality sometimes leads them to drugs.

These drugs are very harmful to the body, to the mind, and to the soul. But the one good thing is that they are sincere. They are seeking something. They are trying to revolt against the old hypocritical conventions of society. They are trying not to live in the old beliefs. They are trying to find something, and this that they are seeking may help them someday to find the path; may help them someday to find that spirituality.

Personally, I think it is a good sign. I have found very beautiful souls, very beautiful people in the young boys, in the young girls. But it is really unfortunate that they have been led by or exploited by people to go towards drugs, because drugs just kill their mind and body and smother the soul. These are positively harmful to their body, mind and soul. If they can just leave drugs and try to understand what the real spiritual teachings are, they will find that which is in them, which I find and appreciate in them. If they will put in the effort, the grace of the Lord will be with them.

112 Do you think drugs are a fair tool to use?

Well, brother, plainly speaking, I am absolutely against the use of drugs. They are very harmful. Never use them in an attempt to attain any spiritual experience. The result of taking drugs may be hallucination, it may be anything, but it definitely is not spiritual experience. These drugs are harmful to the mind, the body and the soul.

113 What do you mean about not taking drugs? Does that include medicine?

We should not use drugs in order to obtain spiritual experiences. But from a medical point of view, if a doctor gives you some chloroform, or something for an operation, that is not harmful. You are not getting used to that drug, you see. You are not taking it for spiritual experience or to go back to the Father. But narcotics, LSD and other hallucinogenic drugs are not good for the soul or for the mind or for the body, at all. They do not lead to spirituality and are extremely harmful in every way.

114 Do you believe that certain chemicals they are using now in modern psychiatry for transcending the ego can give us a certain amount of spiritual experiences?

They will not give you spiritual experiences. They put you to sleep, or you may feel that you are in a trance, or you may not know where you are, or you may have some sort of hallucinations. You would not have any power to go up or to come back. Just as intoxicating drinks put you out and you have no control over yourself, similarly those tablets or capsules or that drug may have the same effect as that of alcohol or other drugs, as far as the mind is concerned.

*115 I have met many people who claim that by using these
      chemicals they have gone into a region of ecstasy which
      they believe is the Supreme. Some claim they have gone
      into another world and have drawn pictures of creatures
      they have seen ...*

I think these must be the advertisements of the commercial
firms for selling these chemicals.

> *I do not think so. These things are on the black market.
> I have heard that Hindus use these things for various
> spiritual purposes.*

We have in India what is called *bhang*, which is another name
for hemp. Some people drink it and they become inebriated.
It is another way to get intoxicated. One may say that he is not
drunk, but it is all the same; there is absolutely no difference. The
use of any narcotic for sensual pleasure is a definite hindrance
to spiritual progress.

*116 Master, could you explain what the harm or the side
      effects are of alcohol and hallucinogenic or mind-
      affecting drugs?*

They are very damaging from the spiritual point of view. From
the physical point of view, doctors can advise you much better.
They make you absolutely a physical wreck. You have become
so dependent on these drugs that you can't live without them.
This leads to so many types of crimes, so many other things.
It deranges your mind. You're not normal human beings. You
see a sober person, and then see when he is drunk. What is the
difference in his attitude? That too is a drug. So much has been
written, you see, even by scientists, even by doctors.

117   *If you are under the influence of alcohol and drugs, will that stop spiritual progress altogether?*

We should abstain from alcohol and other drugs forever. Unless you uproot a weed from the roots, it will grow again. You have to use very strong language against alcohol and drugs. You have to uproot the weeds right from the roots. There is absolutely no question of any compromise with it. You can interpret that in any way, whatever you like.

118   *Why is taking marijuana forbidden on the path?*

Tomorrow you will ask me why eggs are forbidden, why drinks are forbidden, why meat is forbidden. You would like me to start from the ABC now? Hmm? Have you started taking that? And you are trying to justify it? Forbidden is forbidden. There's no why. Even if we know the why, it will not convince us unless we are strict with ourselves, unless we keep ourselves disciplined. Anything forbidden is forbidden. There's no question of why. There's no reason for it. Reasons are only to satisfy the intellect, just to get support for abstaining from those things. Otherwise, a soldier, once he joins the army, he has no reason to refuse. He has no right to refuse. He never asks why. We have taken a certain discipline on ourselves, and we have to abide by it.

ETHICS AND MORAITY

119   *I understand that you enjoin us to be ever honest and truthful. Could you kindly elaborate on how we can best live up to this principle and what exactly the words mean?*

Actually, we have to be truthful and honest with ourselves, not with others. When we are truthful with ourselves, then we can live with ourselves; otherwise we are always at war within ourselves. We are always miserable within ourselves if we are not honest and truthful with ourselves. So we shouldn't try to deceive ourselves. We must face facts, and we must understand the reality, and we must be honest with our own feelings, with our own self. And if you are honest with yourself, you'll be honest with others also. If you are deceitful to yourself, you'll be deceitful to others also. One always knows whether one is being honest with oneself or not. You don't require anybody to tell you about that; you know within yourself whether you are truthful to yourself, honest with yourself or not.

120 *Maharaj Ji, would you give us a little amplification on the third requirement for a satsangi: the moral values, the moral principles that we should live by? Not especially the sex angle – we understand that, perhaps – but the broad concept of living with our fellow man in the business world and still being a good satsangi.*

You see, it is very difficult to explain every little thing in detail. But the main things are explained to us and if we are able to stand on these main principles, then we will also be able to get other qualities. If with the help of meditation we are filled with love and devotion for the Father, all other qualities will just come like cream on milk in us. Automatically we'll be filled with those qualities also – we'll be very soft-hearted; we will not injure anybody; we will not deceive anybody; we will not cheat anybody; we will not like to hurt anybody. All these qualities automatically will come in us, if we are attending to our meditation. So it's very difficult to lay down "don't do this" and "do that" – we ourselves know what to do. Our whole attitude towards life changes – by meditation.

121 You've already mentioned that religion today has been redefined as morality, and this is being expressed by doing good works – social reform and relieving the injustices of our fellow man. To what degree should we, as satsangis, involve ourselves in this expression of morality?

You see, Professor Puri didn't say that morality is bad. He said morality alone is not sufficient to take your soul back to the Father. You have to be moral to go back to the Father – morality is essential. It is a base on which you have to lay the foundation; you have to build your meditation on morality. But morality itself is not sufficient to take you back to the Father. Morality comes automatically when you're filled with love and devotion for the Father. That is the outcome, just as cream comes on the top of milk. Similarly, all these moral qualities will come in a satsangi when he's following the path, living the life of Sant Mat. You will be helpful to other people, other humans; you will want to help them, you will want to be kind to them, you will want to be good to them, you will not deceive them, you will not cheat them, you will be humble, you will have patience. Automatically you'll be filled with these qualities.

What Professor Puri was trying to point out is that these qualities alone are not sufficient to take you back to the Father. They are the effects of meditation; they are the effects of following the path. They are essential prerequisites on which you have to build your meditation, but they alone are not sufficient to bring you back to the Father. Cleaning a vessel is not sufficient, unless you also fill the cup with milk. To lead a moral life is just cleaning a vessel, but cleaning a vessel for what? To fill it with love and devotion for the Father, with spirituality. So cleaning is essential before filling – without cleaning a cup, you will not be able to put milk in it. To be moral is essential for building your meditation, but cleaning alone is not sufficient unless you fill your cup.

122 *Maharaj Ji, could you say that politics is neither moral nor immoral, but amoral?*

Politics means you and I together. Politics is not something confined to any individual. I mean, we are all politicians, because we are part of a country's politics. We make the politics of a country.

123 *Supposing you want to do something very good, but there's an obstacle; let's say, for example, we want to keep land for the poor, but unless you bribe one thousand rupees, you won't get the land. Is that right?*

Well, if our means are corrupt, our end automatically becomes corrupt. If our means are noble, then the end is noble. Howsoever noble our cause may be, if we adopt corrupt means, we cannot justify the end at all. The means should be as noble as the end.

You see, if I want to become the ruler of a country and I don't care how, and I kill thousands of people to get at the helm of affairs, you would not be able to justify those means. The means must justify the end. If the means are corrupt, the end automatically becomes corrupt. I don't want to comment on a particular example, but that's the general policy, the general principle.

124 *Is it right that satsangis go into the army?*

There's no harm. Baba Ji [Baba Jaimal Singh] was in the army. Great Master was in the army. It is just a profession.

But isn't the army a school for killing other people?

You mean to say those people who are not in the army, they don't kill each other? How many people die from overdrinking and driving; have you ever noticed in the paper? People die twenty times more in car accidents or by overdrinking than in the wars. How many people die of starvation due to our own negligence, our own poor system of distribution of wealth and food? Aren't we responsible for that? This is just a profession, sister, and if you don't want to kill, well, his grace is there; the Lord won't give you an opportunity to kill.

Maharaj Ji [Maharaj Sawan Singh] used to tell us about Baba Ji Maharaj. There were always disturbances on the frontier with the Pathans, you see. Baba Ji was in the British army. So they were always in conflict with each other. Both sides were always firing, here and there. So sometimes Baba Ji would just keep his gun and sit in meditation. Anyone who would come and pass by him would say, he's some fakir, he's some sadhu. Nobody would say anything to him, and they would pass.

125 *What about the situation when countries are at war and you are in the service and you are forced to kill? Should one become a conscientious objector then?*

Brother, if you are really sincere and you do not want to kill, the situation will be such that you will never kill. You are always helped not to kill. There is a guiding force behind you which saves you from such situations. The Great Master was in military service; his guru was in military service; and they both served until the age of retirement, but they never killed anybody. The Lord is always there to help us in such situations.

What is a satsangi's position in the case of a nation going to war?

He has no option but to be a part of that war; yet there is some other force to protect him and to help him under such circumstances, if he does not want to kill.

126 Master, why is marriage a sacred bond?

Well, sister, it is a sacred bond, and it should be taken in that light. Otherwise your mind becomes so restless and runs about so much that it can never concentrate. There are certain human needs, bodily needs, which we have to satisfy to some extent. If we let them run wild, you will never be able to concentrate. To some extent they have to be satisfied. And marriage is the only institution in which you can do that.

127 If such a karmic debt to a mate is predestined, and you've returned here to work it out, I don't understand what's so important in the ceremony of marriage. I've been living with an initiate of Kirpal Singh for three months, and I feel that we're married, but ...

Well, brother, there's nothing in the ceremony of a marriage, provided you are honest with a woman and you take the responsibility of that lady as a wife for the whole of your life – then there's nothing in the actual ceremony. Ceremonies are only binding us to certain conventions, certain responsibilities.

Then if you acknowledge these responsibilities and maintain your search for the Father within ...

And when you want to acknowledge a responsibility, where is the harm in falling in line with society? Where is the harm in going through the ceremony and satisfying the legal requirements? Where is the harm? When we are fulfilling so many other legal obligations as a citizen, where is the harm in fulfilling this obligation also?

I don't understand – someone from the Kirpal ashram told us this morning that the relationship that we were living under was improper, and I haven't felt that within. And I don't understand how – if a master such as you or Kirpal Singh were to perform something that they called a marriage, perhaps I could understand that, but the way it was put to me was, if we went to City Hall and we got a piece of paper, and we went to a justice of the peace and he said some words and we performed a ceremony, that would make it proper. And I truly don't understand that. I don't see how such a ceremony could possibly consecrate or ...

You see, the ceremony brings with it certain responsibilities. It creates certain restrictions on your mind.

Aren't those the exact type of restrictions that are karmic debts? Isn't that the exact kind of thing that you would want – at least I would want – to liberate myself from? Like, I saw a Zen master a few weeks ago, and he said that if a married couple were truly, truly honest with each other, every time they saw one another, they'd say, I've never seen you before. We're new people every moment. I don't want to restrict the freedom of our relationship by making a vow that I don't understand. All I can say to Lauren is that I know you now, and I'm with you, and I feel your spirit, and I feel we're together. I can't understand a vow that I have to take ...

Actually, that vow is the ceremony.

Pardon me?

That vow which we take as a man and a woman to live together in the presence of the Lord, that is a ceremony. Whether you take it in a church or take it anywhere, you take a vow, before the Lord, that you will live together as man and wife, and each discharge your responsibilities. That is a vow that should be binding on both, husband and wife.

> *I vowed long ago, with Lauren, to keep our hearts as pure as possible, and to keep our eye on the master, whenever we could, whenever his grace would allow. I felt that was enough.*

The mind always plays tricks with us. Sometimes it deceives us, and it tries to run away from the situation. But when there are certain restrictions on the mind, then it is very difficult for the mind to run out of such situations.

> *I understand exactly what you just said, but I don't understand whether the end of that statement is that therefore you should make the vow or therefore you shouldn't? What did you just say?*

We should take a vow.

> *OK, is the vow that I made with Lauren in the woods months ago, is that vow sufficient to keep us pure in the eye of the master?*

You know best what vow you have taken – I don't know.

> *Does a certificate mean that if a man doesn't love a woman anymore, I mean, can't seem to work it out because they just seem to have other things …*

I would advise you to read Saint Matthew in the Bible. He talks very clearly about marriage.

> *Well, what if they have other karmas to go through and they just, you know …*

These are all justifications of the mind to run away from each other. I don't analyze every situation, but generally we try to justify what we do.

> *But in different lives we've had different karmas with people ...*

Yes, that's right.

> *Sir, if two people have agreed on a pure relationship, why should they go to a corrupt priest or a corrupt City Hall in order to secure a license?*

Well, you can go to a court, if you don't want to go to City Hall. You see, a marriage is performed to legalize things because there are so many other responsibilities resulting from it – children, property, so many other things. I would suggest that since we have so many books written in English, you should try to read these books. It's very difficult to know the teachings in one or two sittings, or by asking a few questions. Most of our problems are the same, most of our questions are the same, and practically all these questions that I've been trying to answer have been discussed in the books. So I advise you to read those books very thoroughly, and if anything still is not clear you are most welcome to write to me at my place.

128 *My boyfriend wants to know why I have to be celibate before initiation.*

Well, sister, it is not that alone that determines the whole thing. The point is, when we are initiated, when we follow the path, we are supposed to live a moral, clean life, and we must be sure that we will be able to live that way of life. That is why I was a little discreet in my statement that we must know whether this way of life will suit us or not. We have to lead a good moral life. And if we think we can't lead a moral life, according to the principles of Sant Mat, I don't think we should apply for initiation. Perhaps that is why the representative wanted to be sure that, since you are not married, you will be able to live that way of life. You have to be sure of yourself.

129 *In the teachings one requisite on this path of love is the moral life. Could you explain to this young seeker the place of love, of sex and of the man-woman relationship?*

Love is something very different from lust. Lust is the instinct of the body. But love is something very different. In love, we have to lose our individuality. We have to merge back into the Being. So I don't think any explanation is required. You all know the difference between lust and love.

130 *Master, I'm troubled by the mutual exclusiveness between nam or shabd and kam or lust. Specifically, can there be sexual relations between husband and wife in the pure light of nam, without an element of kam? Or if not, can there be nam in the morning and kam in the evening?*

This is why married life is preferred on the path rather than being single. It's difficult to fight with this instinct of lust. When you build suppression, you fight the instinct, and your mind becomes very wild and runs here and there. It can never concentrate. A controlled married life is advised for a satsangi. And it is up to a husband and a wife to mutually adjust – how much they can help each other. They must help each other. They should not have differences on this point. There should be the right type of understanding between them. It is very difficult to draw a line, you see, between these things in their relationship. But a married man is only concerned with his wife for the satisfaction of this instinct, while the unmarried person runs to many places – his mind runs in many directions. So that is more difficult, it is more of a problem to bring the mind back to the eye centre.

131 *Maharaj Ji, I have a question regarding attachments. We spoke the other day about marriage. And your answer was very clear. We are to get married if we want a relation- ship. However, some of us, especially in the West, have had relationships. And we have children, and maybe the relationship broke up, but we still have the attachments. We have attachments not only to a wife, but also to a mother-in-law and father-in-law. And we just feel that with going into another marriage, we will just gain that many more attachments. Now my question is, if I'm quite content with the amount of attachment that I have in this world at this stage, is the only choice getting mar- ried again or to live a life of celibacy?*

Well, brother, it is better to be attached to one than to many. Marriage means attachment to one person. And if you don't marry, God knows how many people you are attached to, how many women you are attached to. And the attachment with a wife, after some time, the infatuation goes away. It becomes a matter of duty for the sake of children. And you just stay together as a matter of responsibility and obligation. And you run through your span of life very happily. Attach- ments just fade out, after some time. That infatuation, that attachment which we have at the time of marriage, doesn't stay forever in a marriage. But the unmarried man is always running after women and he's always attached to another one, another one, another one. Unnecessarily he's collecting karmas and sins.

132 *Master, a few minutes ago you were speaking of divorce and parents' responsibilities to their children. You said that a parent has a very strong responsibility to the children for having brought them into the world. And my question is: If it's that parent's karma to leave the children, and if there are no outside influences – like they are being forced to leave because of war or something like that – if it's just their karma to leave the children, then what can you say of that responsibility?*

We shift from partner to partner and start justifying our destiny, our karmas, and refuse to accept that it is our mental weakness, our weakness of the mind. How do you know that you are not sowing new seeds rather than going through your destiny? Who is the judge? How do you know whether you have sown a new seed or whether you have gone through your destiny?

133 *This question stems out of a conversation I had with a seeker. We were discussing the moral principles of Sant Mat, and I was explaining to him that any sexual familiarity outside the bonds of marriage was strictly forbidden because it takes the attention down and out and so one can never make spiritual progress. Okay, he was able to grasp that point. But as it turns out, in the United States, in a number of states, it's legal for a man and woman to live together without having gone through any kind of formal marital ceremony. So the question he posed to me, which I was unable to answer properly, is why then is it bad karma for people to have sexual activity outside of marriage, and the same activity within the bonds of marriage would not be considered bad karma?*

You see, there are always certain rules to a game, and we have to build meditation on certain principles. There must be a foundation on which you have to build your meditation, and this is one of the foundations, one of the very strict rules. You can't find any answer to it or justification one way or another way. We have to live absolutely within the four walls of the Sant Mat principles. Whether they mean anything to anybody or not is immaterial. If you really want to make spiritual progress, you have to live within these walls. There's no other way. It was never illegal to live together. In no country was it ever illegal to live together. People kept so many friends and all that, always. It was never illegal, but it was always immoral. So even if it becomes legal, still you can't make it moral. So we must be very strict with our morals, if we want to really make any progress within. You can't justify it, that married and unmarried is the same thing. It is absolutely wrong.

134 How does one trade kam for nam? That is, sex for shabd?

Kam means the desires of the world, and nam means that holy spirit within. When you are attached to the holy spirit, when you are attached to that shabd, that nam within, naturally no desire for the world is left in you. When you get diamonds, you do not run after shells.

135 I have read in one of Mahatma Gandhi's books that self-realization is possible without celibacy, but for God-realization celibacy is a must. Is that true, Maharaj Ji?

No. You see, when your mind goes beyond the first stage, you automatically become celibate. Without that, you wouldn't be able to achieve self-realization. Automatically your mind won't run to those things. It's not that you have to fight with your mind. You don't have to fight for that at all; automatically your mind won't run to those things.

⚘ 8 ⚘

Power of Meditation

THE CIRCLE OF LOVE

136 *If a person is full of love but has not the power to medi-*
     tate, is the path still open or is it shut? Is there another
     possibility?

Without love there can be no meditation at all. By meditation
we travel on the path which leads us back to the Father. And
without love for the Father we will never try to travel on the
path at all. Love is the first essential quality. Rather, it forces us
to travel on the path. So love automatically leads us back to the
Father. And what is love? As you have often heard: Love is God
and God is love.[136] Love has the characteristic of making you
lose your own individuality. So we have to lose our own individuality, eliminate our ego and become one with the Father.
That is love. So love is an essential characteristic of meditation.
Love for God is in itself meditation. Love forces us to follow the
path which leads us back to the Father.

137 *Master, when we know that this is the right path and we*
     have the faith and yet there is no love in our heart, how
     shall we go about it?

Sister, if you are attending to your meditation, love will come automatically. You do not have to work for love. It comes when it comes. Even in worldly love, you know, if you analyze yourself – you do not work for it. God gives this gift, and it just comes.

By the grace of the master?

When God wants you to love him, he will give you that love; but it comes by meditation, as instructed by the living master.

138 *Maharaj Ji, I have often heard and listened to tapes about doing our meditation with love and devotion, feeling that love and devotion. It appears in the beginning that so much of that love and devotion is emotional and physical. Will that gradually become more of a real sense of love and devotion? The emotion and the physical sense that we have in the early stages, will that grow into a deeper feeling of love and devotion?*

Sister, meditation creates that love. Meditation strengthens that love. Meditation helps the love to grow, to grow to the extent that we become one with the Lord. It is all meditation. Meditation is nothing but love. What is love? What are the characteristics of love? To merge into another one, to become another being, to lose your own identity, to lose your own individuality and to become another being is love. And what is the purpose of meditation? To merge your soul back into the Father, to remove all the dross from the soul and to make it shine and to make it one with him. That is meditation. So that is why meditation itself is love. That is why we say that love is God and God is love, because God has the characteristics of love. Love of God is a characteristic of love. We become one with him. We lose our own identity.

*139 How may we always keep our love for you in the first
position, as our highest desire? How can we keep it there
if we do not display it so much?*

Brother, display is on the outside. The real love is expressed
within. Meditation automatically creates devotion and love for
the Lord. When we love the Lord, we also love the travellers on
the same path, and we all become nearer to each other. Supposing
you are away from your wife, and somebody comes from your
wife. You like to talk to him about your wife, and he also becomes
dear to you because he is talking about your wife to you, and you
always like to hear about your wife. So he also becomes dearer
to you. Similarly, saints or masters always come and talk about
the Lord and thus create his devotion in us. So they also become
dear to us. We also love them. The meditation, as advised by the
saints, creates this affection, this love and devotion in us.

140 How can we increase our love for God and the master?

You see, only meditation creates love. Meditation increases love.
Meditation helps the love to grow to the extent that we can
become one with the Father. We can only do meditation, the
rest we leave to the Father. Meditation will help us be receptive to his grace. He gives the love – we have only to become
receptive to this love. He is the one who gives his own love. He
pulls us from within. We want to be receptive to his grace, and
meditation makes us receptive. Then his love is reflected from
within us automatically. So meditation strengthens our love, it
creates our love, it helps to grow our love. Meditation is the only
means to achieve all these things.

*141 I have read in books that love may be generated to any
degree, but it doesn't tell one just how to do that. When*

you get to a certain age and take stock of yourself, you realize that most of us are stupid, egoistic and selfish, and that all that hard shell of the ego might be cracked if we had more love. How can we generate that love?

You can be receptive to the Lord's grace. When it is raining, if you keep your cup upside down, it will collect no water. And if you keep the cup right-side up, it will collect water. So you can be receptive to his grace. The Lord has given us this environment, this facility, this company in which we can strengthen each other's love and be helpful to each other. These are all means for generating love, so we can be receptive to all these things. But still, everything is in the hands of the Lord. He creates his own love in us. We then feel that we love him or that we are separated from him and we want to become one with him. He's the one who is pulling us from within. That is entirely in his hands. Unless he gives us the means, we can never generate that love ourselves. Meditation generates love. Meditation creates that pang in you, that desire in you to become one with the Father. Meditation makes you realize that life is worthless without him. Meditation makes us realize our false pursuits in this world. That is all his grace. That is all the effect of meditation.

142 *When we're sitting in your presence and looking upon your face and into your eyes, is there any way that we can become more receptive to what you are showering upon us?*

You see, brother, meditation makes us receptive, enables us to receive the Lord's grace. Meditation is nothing but to make us receptive. He is always giving, always giving. He's more anxious to give to us than we are prepared to take, and meditation makes us receptive to receive his grace. There's no other way which can make you receptive to receive his grace, only meditation. If there's heavy rain and your cup is upside down, it won't catch even a single drop of water. If you put it in the upright position, it will be filled. So we have to become receptive, and it is always raining. His grace is always there.

143 *Master, I wish that I could love the guru more. May I pray for it, or is it better that I wait quietly?*

Don't wait quietly, just attend to meditation quietly. And that will help you in every way. Meditation creates love, strengthens love, helps the love to grow to the extent that you become one with the Father. It helps you to lose your own identity, your individuality and become one with the Father. That is the height of love.

144 *Master, I have one question. Will you please speak to us about how we can create love and devotion in meditation and how to relax.*

Well, sister, the seed of love is within every one of us. We are only to help that seed to grow and grow and grow to become one with the Father. As I said, the soul is a drop of the divine ocean and is always soaring towards its own origin. Soul is always anxious to go back to its own source. Love and devotion are in the soul. It is the mind which is keeping us attached to this creation, while the soul is becoming very unhappy in this creation. It's very unhappy. That is why we have the feeling of loneliness, no matter what we have in this creation. We always feel lonely. We feel that nothing belongs to us and that we do not belong to anybody. We are just trying to deceive others, and they are trying to deceive us. This is the soul, because it really belongs to the Lord and he belongs to us. That divine spark of love is within every one of us, so we have to help that divine seed to grow by meditation.

If there's a lot of rust on a knife and you go on rubbing it on the sandstone, slowly and slowly the rust goes and the knife shines. So similarly, we are rubbing our mind with shabd and nam within, so that all the rust of the mind vanishes, it all fades away and the soul shines from within. That is real love; that is real devotion. That is why we say God is love and love is God, because the real form of the Lord is love and only through love can we go back to him.[137] Love means to become another being, to merge into another one, to lose your own identity, to become another one. That is love. You do not exist any more at all, only the object of your love exists. That is love. Then only the Lord exists and we are no more. That is love.

The purpose of meditation is to create that love and devotion for the Father within, because the relationship of the soul and the Father is that of love. It is not of any religion, not of any caste, any creed. That is why Christ said: Love thy Lord with all thy heart, with all thy body, with all thy soul.[67] That is love. He also said: Blessed are those who mourn, for they shall get comfort.[8] Those who miss him, who are restless to become one with him, who have the longing to become one with him, they are the fortunate ones.

145 Why do pain, grief, and loneliness turn one to God, while pleasures, mink coats and wealth turn one away from God?

Sister, as you have heard in my discourse, we should not look to God as an escape from these worries, or from these miseries, nor should we forget him in times of pleasure and affluence. We should look to him with devotion and love; we must base our meditation on love, not on fear. The basis of spirituality is love, not fear. We should not try to worship the Lord thinking that in return he will relieve us of our miseries or with the idea to fulfil any of our desires. This is a very inferior type of meditation, inferior type of worship of the Lord. We should worship him because we love him, because we want to go back and merge into him. With that devotion and love we should try to worship him. But naturally when we are in agony, when we are in trouble, we want somebody to lean on. And there cannot be anyone better to lean on than the Lord. So, in times of worry and turmoil we naturally look to him, we try to lean on him. Well, even that is all right. It is a blessing in disguise. But that should not be our reason for worshipping him. It must come out of love, and not as an escape from reality, from the world.

146 *Maharaj Ji, how does a satsangi's love grow from an intermittent thing, to one of God-absorption?*

There is one very special process. And that is *the* very special process. That is meditation. You see, meditation creates love. It strengthens love. It deepens love. It grows love. Ultimately, it illuminates you and it makes you God. That's all meditation. I can't suggest to you any bypass. There is no short cut or bypass. That is the only way.

So by doing our meditation we're loving God?

That is the height of love. That is why Christ said, sin against the holy ghost can never be forgiven.[46] That's the basic teaching of Christ. If you turn your back to your meditation, to shabd and nam, you can never be forgiven. Forgiven for what? For what stands between you and the Father – our karmas, our sinchit karmas. We can never be forgiven for those karmas if we turn our back to meditation. Only meditation invokes the forgiveness of the Father. Only by meditation are we able to repent for what we have done in the past or to seek his forgiveness. And then we become the Father, ultimately. He says other things can be forgiven because meditation will help you to get forgiveness from the Father for anything you do in this life. But if you don't attend to meditation, then how can you ever be forgiven? So meditation is the main thing.

THE POWER OF MEDITATION

147   What is repentance? How can a man repent?

Repentance is to be sorry for what you have already done and not to repeat that mistake again. But once we take this birth we have absolutely forgotten what we have done in past lives, and we cannot feel sorry for what we don't know. We can't be sure we will not repeat that mistake again. The past is absolutely blank to us. We know nothing of what we have done in the past life, so this repentance cannot be taken literally.

We generally take repentance to mean to be sorry for what we have done and try not to commit that sin again. But in the spiritual sense, repentance is meditation. Meditation makes you really repent for what you have done in the past and helps you not to repeat those mistakes again. That, in turn, helps you to obtain forgiveness from the Father. Meditation helps us to get his grace and his forgiveness. His grace helps us not to repeat those mistakes again which might pull us back to this world.

148   Master, is there any way to avoid the effect of desires that the mind has created before coming on to the path? Is there any way to avoid their effect?

You see, unless you have a ladder, you can't rise above the ground. It's very difficult to get out of these desires without meditation. Because unless the mind has something substantial within, it doesn't leave the sensual pleasures. Desires always pull you to the senses, towards the senses. Unless you are able to concentrate at the eye centre and are attached to the shabd and nam within, you can't get rid of all these desires. They are bound to be there. Only the shabd can pull you up from these desires. And then they just fade out.

149 *Master, will meditation over time cleanse the mind, or is it essential for the disciple to actually renounce his desires, particularly those desires that lead to action?*

You see, meditation helps you to detach from those desires. By fighting with those desires without meditation, you can never succeed. The mind will again rebound back to those desires with greater force. Suppression will not lead you anywhere. Only attachment can create detachment in you; detachment can never create attachment in you. The mind is the same, whether its tendency is downward or upward. When its tendency is upward, it doesn't run to the senses at all. But when its tendency is downward, then naturally it's a slave of the senses. Mind is the same. Christ says, either you can worship mammon or God.[24] When the mind is pulled upward – after coming back to the eye centre, it is attached to the light and sound within – we're worshipping God. When it is being pulled down by the senses, we are worshipping mammon.

So you can't fight with your desires without meditation. Meditation is a sword by which we are armed to fight all our worldly desires, which are pulling us back to this creation. Guru Nanak gives a beautiful example: It is just like catching a snake and putting it into a basket. By putting a snake into a basket you can't feel secure; it may come out of the basket at any time, and then you may have to face its sting. But if you take its sting out – the poison out of the snake – then you can leave it, you don't have to put it in the basket at all. Meditation is just taking the sting out of the snake. Otherwise, without meditation, fighting with your desires – by discipline, by strong willpower – it's just suppression, putting a snake into a basket. You never know when the mind may deceive you and make you dance to its tune. We have to fight our desires to some extent by bringing the mind back to the eye centre and attaching it to the sound and light within. Then automatically that sound and light pull the mind away from the senses.

I often give an example: A river is flowing and you can build a dam to control the water – you can hold the water for some time by building a dam. But when there is too much water in the catchment area, it will not only break the dam but also flow over the banks and create devastation. But if, after building a dam and holding the water, you make another channel for the water to flow, then the dam remains permanent and there's no danger to the banks of the river at all. So similarly, with simran and dhyan we are building a dam to help us withdraw our attention to the eye centre. But that is not the end-all and be-all of our meditation – we have to give another outlet or channel to the mind, so that the dam remains permanent. And that channel is to attach it to the light and sound within. When the mind gets that taste, when it starts flowing in that direction, then the dam is permanent; then the mind doesn't come down below the eye centre.

150 *Is it possible to rise to some level where you can negotiate with the mind and these attachments and balance them without actually having to live through the karma? As an example, if a man in his normal span had to live three lives, could he reach a certain level and negotiate with the mind and balance these karmas without actually*

*having to live the three lives? Does one physically have
to go through the karma, or can one balance the karma
mentally at some higher region?*

We can always burn our karmas. They can always be destroyed.
That is the purpose of meditation; otherwise, we would have
taken hundreds of lives to fulfil those karmas. But by meditation
it can be done in one, or two, or three lives – four at the most.
The object of meditation is to destroy those karmas, to clear those
karmas. Kabir says that if you have a big stack of hay, it takes only
one match to burn the whole lot. Similarly, one little portion of
nam or shabd, an atom of it, burns thousands and millions of
our karmas. We actually burn or destroy and rise above them,
and do not make new ones in the process. These old karmas have
relations with our mind. When, with the help of nam or shabd,
our mind goes back to its origin, these karmas just drop down.
However rusty a knife may be, if you hold it against a revolving
grindstone, all the rust is removed. The knife again shines like
new. It becomes pure. That is the condition of the soul when it
leaves the mind after coming in touch with the nam or shabd.

151 *Is there any short cut through our fate karmas that pays
     them off?*

Well, brother, there is a short cut; meditation is a short cut to
get rid of the karma, otherwise you have to come back to this
creation to go through all that. And while going through all
that, you may collect much more than what you had to go
through in the first place. So meditation is a short cut for going
through the karma.

152 *Master, in* Quest for Light, *one letter says that if we don't
     have any anxieties or worries and we sit for meditation,*

we will get some pleasure in our meditation. So is it our karmas that get in the way? Is that what keeps us from really getting into the meditation, really enjoying it?

You see, while sitting in meditation, you should never think about how much karma you have cleared. We don't sit in meditation to clear our karmas. We sit in meditation to enjoy that bliss and peace and happiness and to become one with the Father, and these karmas are automatically taken care of. We shouldn't always be conscious of sitting in meditation to clear our karmas. We don't have to be calculating in that way. If we are, then we accomplish nothing. These are the effects of meditation, not the purpose of our meditation. Our purpose is to go back to the Father, to become one with him.

153   Is it possible to change your destiny through meditation?

You can't change the main course of your destiny, but you can eliminate some of the effects of the destiny by meditation. At least you'll get the strength to face your destiny without losing your balance. You will face all those karmas smilingly and cheerfully. But you have got to go through your destiny. The pain may be eliminated to some extent.

154   Master, is it possible to break strong attachments without pain?

Well, you can only break strong attachments by experiencing joy, joy from becoming one with the sound and light within. That bliss and peace which you get by attending to your meditation, that will break your strong attachments and strong bondages, so then the question of pain doesn't arise at all. Then you are happy to get rid of those attachments, because you have got something much better.

If somebody gives a beggar a 100-rupee note, he will automatically drop the paisa from his hand — he doesn't feel the pain at all. He's so attached to the collecting of paisas and shells, but if you give him a 100-rupee note he won't feel the pain of dropping those shells — he'll be happy to get 100 rupees. So you don't experience pain in getting rid of those attachments, you experience joy and happiness to get rid of those attachments because only attachment will create detachment, and that attachment within will give you peace and bliss and happiness.

155 *Does the sound current actually change one's personality? By that I mean: Is one able to analyze a person's reaction to something that happened a long time ago in the past, in a previous life, subconscious though it is?*

It is not a question of reaction. By spiritual practice we rise so high that we can meet anything, we can know anything. We advance spiritually. Our mind becomes refined, matured, and we can know anything. That is how spirituality should help us, in developing within ourselves. It must make us a better person. If it does not, then it is not spirituality. When spirituality — that is, devotion to shabd, nam or the word — grows within us, all the other good qualities of a human being come in us like cream on milk. We do not have to fight in order to learn or to develop those qualities. They come automatically within us. When we have the devotion of the Lord within us, that devotion, that love brings all the qualities within us. It just transforms us; our whole outlook is changed. The more we go near to him, the more we find ourselves close to each other and the more we love one another. The more we find peace within, the more we find peace outside. It makes us true humans. We then try to understand each other on a human level, and not merely on political, social or economic levels; not on religious, national, caste or creed levels – just on the human, real human level. But only the devotion of the Lord and nothing else brings these qualities within us.

156 Master, outside of master's grace and meditation, is there any hope of conquering the five passions?

It is just by meditation. We can only fight with these enemies with the help of a sharp sword in our hand. Guru Nanak gave a very beautiful example of the sandalwood tree. It has a good fragrance, and its effect is very cooling. Snakes have a lot of poison in them, and the effect is very hot. So they always coil around the sandalwood because they like the coolness and the fragrance of the tree. Now if you want to take a branch of the tree, how can you go near it, because the snake is there? So Guru Nanak says that if you take a sword in your hand and cut the snake into pieces, then the whole tree is yours.

So this human body is like a sandalwood tree. The fragrance of the Lord is there within us, always, and this life is the most precious opportunity given to us, but the snake-mind has coiled around it. So unless the mind is captured and subdued, you cannot get what the Lord has kept within everyone of us. So Guru Nanak says: Go to a mystic; he will give you the sword of nam. Cut that snake of your mind with your sword of nam, and then whatever treasure the Lord has kept within you is all yours. There's no other way to capture the mind, to subdue the mind, to fight with these passions without the help of meditation, because it is the mind which runs to the senses. Right from the eye centre, the senses are pulling you to their own level. So unless the mind gets a better pleasure than the sensual pleasures, the mind refuses to leave the sensual pleasures. The Lord has kept that better pleasure within every one of us at the eye centre. When we withdraw the mind and attach the mind to

THE POWER OF MEDITATION

that better pleasure, the divine melody within, then it doesn't come down to the senses.

As Christ said, either you can worship God or mammon.[24] Above the eye centre you are worshipping God; below the eye centre you are worshipping mammon. When the mind is attached to the shabd and nam within, it finds a taste which is better than the sensual pleasures, so naturally how can it be a slave of the senses? That is the only way to control your mind – not by austerities, rituals, ceremonies, or running away from the events or situations of life. That doesn't help you much.

157   Can you say something about divine light and divine love and sound?

As long as the tendency of the mind is downward we are involved in worldly love. When the tendency of the mind comes upward with the help of that sound and light, then we are involved with divine love, as you call it. Divine love is that which makes us divine, which makes us merge back into the Father. That divine love will only come with the help of that sound, with the help of that light. When the mind is absorbed in that light, when the mind is absorbed in that sound, then worldly detachment will come and the godly attachment will come. When we become attached to that light and sound within, automatically we'll be detached from the senses, automatically we'll be detached from the world. So then we will be filled with a divine love.

As Christ said, either your mind can be the master or God can be the master. Either the devil can be your master or God can be your master.[24] When mind is below the eye centre, then we are under the sway of the mind. When we come back to the eye centre and the mind is attached to the shabd and nam, then we are on the divine path, then we are attached to that spirit or holy ghost. And that light comes from that sound, and sound is in that light. Ultimately they become one and the same. So we have to see that divine light and hear that divine sound too.

158 *Master, the mind knows that this is good and that is bad, and you say to the mind that we're going to do this because this is good, and mind says, "Yes, but I want to do that." And so after some time the mind eventually gets almost ready to explode with anger or frustration or whatever, and then you lose control altogether, worse than ever.*

That is why we attend to meditation. It is not only by the intellect that we can rise above those weaknesses. It is not only by strong willpower that we can rise above those weaknesses. When we attach the mind to something higher than the worldly pleasures, then it leaves the weaknesses. That is the purpose of meditation. Because mind is fond of pleasures, it will only cease running to the sensual pleasures when it is attached to better pleasures. That is the purpose of meditation, to give the mind a taste of that nectar within so that it will not run down to the senses.

I have given examples so many times. If there is a lot of water in the catchment area, you can build a dam to hold the water, and you will be able to hold the water for some time. But if there is too much water in the catchment area, it will not only break the dam, but also overflow the banks of the river. But if after building the dam you make another channel for the water to flow, then the dam is permanent. By simran and dhyan we are building a dam to keep the mind from running down to the senses again. But you cannot hold it permanently at the eye centre; when there is too much suppression, then the mind breaks all the rules and regulations, and breaks all the chains. But if after holding it here you attach it to the shabd and nam within and it starts tasting that nectar within, then the dam remains in place and the mind doesn't come down from the eye centre, because it has something better to hold on to than the senses now. So both are essential – building the dam and creating another channel where the water can flow.

That channel is daily meditation and tasting that nectar within, that divine bliss and divine light within. That holds the mind at the eye centre. Otherwise, with your strong willpower, with austerity, with your intellect, you're only building a dam, but when the suppression becomes too much, then you will break all the chains. That is the difference between Sant Mat and other practices that only believe in denying the mind all the pleasures of the world but don't believe in giving anything to the mind to do. Then the suppression is horrible. They run away from the situation in the world, to the forest; they don't wear clothes, they don't do anything, you see, they run from every situation and hide themselves in the forest. But for how long? They go on building, building, building; suppressing, suppressing, suppressing; and then the result is horrible sometimes. Either they become mad or they become worse than normal human beings. But when we are able to attach our mind to the shabd and nam within, then it automatically gets detached from all these things. That is the difference between holding the mind with austerities and holding it with shabd and nam.

First, go on building a dam. At least that you can do. Then the channel will also open. If you refuse to build the dam, then how can you hold the water at all? So start with simran and dhyan and then generally the Lord's grace is always there to create the channel for the mind to flow in a different direction.

We are trying to withdraw our mind slowly and slowly, so that there's not much suppression. We are leading a householder's life; we are having all the activities of life, all the innocent pleasures of life. What are we building? We are slowly and slowly withdrawing the mind, so the dam remains permanent. And we are also opening a channel, you see. We're not running away from situations so that we build up too much suppression. We are living with the situations every day.

159 *Master, could you speak to us about equanimity?*

Peace of mind? You see, the purpose of meditation is nothing but to obtain that peace of mind. Actually, all this tension and depression that we feel is due to the scattering of our mind. When our attention is scattered, we become very restless, unhappy and lose that peace. The more we concentrate at the eye centre and our attention is upward, the more peaceful we become, and only then can we enjoy that bliss and happiness within. The more our mind is scattered from the eye centre through these nine apertures in the outside world – whatever the reason may be – we become depressed, unhappy and miserable. The only way to obtain peace is to withdraw our consciousness back to the eye centre and to have our attention upward rather than downward. We get peace only beyond this eye centre. As long as we are below the eye centre, we are miserable.

The Lord may give all the gifts – everything – to us, but we can never obtain peace. Peace we can only obtain when all coverings from the soul are removed. When the soul shines, when the soul becomes whole and it becomes worthy of merging into the Being, into the Lord, only then can we get peace. As long as the soul is separated from its source, we can never get peace. And the soul can only become worthy of becoming one with the Lord when it leaves the association of the mind, when all coverings of karma or of sensual pleasures are removed from the soul. Only then does it shine, only then can we obtain peace, and only then can we radiate that peace.

In order to get tranquillity and peace, the only method is meditation – to take our mind back to its own source, to get release from the mind, to remove all the coverings from the soul, and to let the soul shine and become whole. Only then can we get peace, not otherwise. We can never find permanent peace in worldly objects or sensual pleasures. These are short-lived, these so-called pleasures, and their reaction makes us more miserable, makes us more unhappy sometimes. So the only way to obtain peace is to go back to the Father and become one with him.

You see, everything is at rest when it goes back to its own source. As long as we are separated from our source, we can never get peace. So even bodily pains – the body is made of five elements – when these five elements [that together constitute the human body] merge into the five elements [that constitute the creation], then we get comfort of the body. We get peace of the body, we get rid of all the diseases. So as long as these five elements are separated from the other five elements, the body is not at peace. When the soul is separated from its own source – from the Lord – the soul is not at peace. And when the mind is separated from its own source – Trikuti – the mind is not at peace. So we get bodily peace, mental peace, and peace of that soul – bliss of that soul – only when they all merge into their own source. That's the only way to obtain peace.

160 *Is it all right to be relaxed on the path? Is this a good path to be relaxed on?*

When are we tense? When our mind is scattered. And we are relaxed when our mind is concentrated at the eye centre – we are most relaxed at that time. If you see your blood pressure before you sit in meditation and then after you get up from meditation, you will know how relaxed it makes you. Why should we remain tense? We should always feel relaxed. But you can't have calculated relaxation, it has to come from within. If you're happy within, you will radiate happiness wherever you go. If you are miserable within, you will radiate misery wherever you go. You go to a miserable person, he will make you miserable. You go to a happy person, he will make you happy in two minutes. You always give what you have. So the purpose of meditation is to relax our mind, to create that bliss and peace within ourselves. Now we are not living within ourselves at all. We try to live only with others, we are always tense. When we learn to live with ourselves, we are always relaxed. And that self is within every one of us. So meditation should make us relax – rather it does make us relax. It doesn't create any tension in us.

161 *Master, can we expect to receive some peace of mind in our meditation before we actually have inner experiences? And what kind of peace would that be?*

You see, when you sit in meditation, whether you make any progress or not, you definitely feel bliss and peace and happiness within. Concentration gives you peace and bliss. The more your mind is scattered, the more unhappy and miserable you will be. The more your mind is one-pointed and concentrated, the more happy and relaxed you'll be, and there'll be no tension at all. So you feel the effect of meditation before you actually see any progress within. You'll be mentally at rest, at peace, you'll feel the bliss, you will feel that atmosphere within yourself, and there is some sort of contentment. Your attitude towards the events of the world is also changing. You are developing a detached outlook on everything by meditation, though you may not have experienced any progress within at all.

162 *It just seems to me that, at least for me, I have to almost psych myself into meditating. I have to say, "Well, listen, if you meditate two and a half hours this morning, you're going to be able to deal with your life and your worries*

better today." So it just seems like it's so good to be enthu-
siastic each day, to go on.

Daily attendance to meditation definitely gives you some bliss
and peace and happiness within yourself. You can go through
your routine of the whole day without losing your balance much
if you are attending to your meditation every day. You always
feel that bliss and happiness and peace within yourself. Even
if a blind man cannot admire the beauty of flowers, definitely
he can enjoy their smell, and when he'll get eyesight, he will
enjoy the beauty also. So we enjoy this smell, the fragrance of
meditation to begin with.

163 How can we better accept the conditions of our lives?

Well, that is what the meditation is training us to do: to accept
everything which comes in our destiny. Meditation is nothing
but training our mind to accept or to live in the Lord's will. That
is the object of meditation: to surrender to him, to keep us in
any way he likes. We accept both joy and misery with the same
balance, the same attitude.

164 Maybe we should accept pain with pleasure?

Accept pain as a pleasure. Accept pleasure, but don't get lost
in it. But you can only accept what he gives you when you are
above the eye centre, when you are one with that holy spirit
within. Then, whatever happens below the eye centre, you are
not worried about it all, whether it is pleasure or pain.

165 Can you give me a reason why there is absolutely nothing
to worry about as a satsangi?

Well, if one is a satsangi, then there's nothing to worry about. You see, we worry about things which we don't expect to happen but which we think will happen. But when we say our destiny is set, the events of life are already chalked out and we just have to go through that, good or bad, then what is there to worry about? It's not going to change the events of life. If we have that attitude, then why worry?

We worry because we want certain things to happen in the way we want them to. We have certain desires, certain wishes to fulfil, certain ambitions to fulfil. And we are always worried about whether we'll be able to achieve them or not, whether we'll be able to satisfy those desires or not. That keeps us worrying. If we leave it to the Father, if we live in his will, he knows best what to give us. We just prepare ourselves to accept what he gives. Then what is there to worry about?

The purpose of meditation is just for that. The purpose of meditation is to train ourselves to adopt that attitude. It's not easy; it's a lifelong struggle, no doubt. But that is the purpose of meditation – to develop that attitude of accepting things as they come.

166 *Last night, Master, you talked about Jesus Christ and his story about the seeds, the sowing of the seeds, some in fertile ground and some in unfertile ground where they would bear no fruit. I feel like I have been cast like a seed that's on a rock where there is no fertility at all. What can you do consciously, what could I do consciously to change that?*

You sit in meditation consciously to change your consciousness. Meditation, brother, is the only answer. Anything else is just an excuse. Meditation solves all problems. There are many questions, many problems in life for which there is no solution, but we can always rise above them with the help of meditation.

167 *Would you consider the practice of meditation as a form of unfolding or as a form of being – as a form of becoming, or developing?*

To become one with the Other, to lose your own individuality and to become the Other, that is a real spiritual experience. To become the Father, to lose your own individuality. You can give any philosophical term you wish for that.

168 *Master, does the soul retain its individuality as it progresses?*

The soul maintains its individuality until it merges back into the Creator. We want to lose that individuality and become one with the Creator. The whole purpose of meditation is to lose our identity, lose our individuality, and to become one with the Creator. That is the whole purpose.

169 *Maharaj Ji, can you give us some criterion or some sort of sign that lets us know that we are too self-important? The great disease is the disease of individuality or self-importance.*

Ego, you mean?

Yes, how can a satsangi be made to realize when that disease is too strong in him or her?

That disease is very common and strong in every one of us. But for that disease, we would not be in this world. The fact that we are here is a clear indication that we are victims of the disease of ego, and the disease of ego will go from us only when we are attached to the word, to shabd or nam. That drives ego from us and creates humility within us. This shabd or nam drives out the I-ness from us, what we call I, I, I. Then we just become Thou.

For example, when we are in love with someone, we never like to do what we want; but we always like to do what he wants or she wants. We are always in readiness to please the other party, crushing our own views, fighting our own views, adjusting them to the other one. The same principle is in meditation. When we merge into the shabd, when we fall in love with our meditation, with devotion to the Lord, to the master, slowly and slowly and automatically this I-ness is being driven out of us. We take pleasure in merging, in blending into him, rather than making him bend to our dictates. This ego is automatically driven out.

Without attachment to him you can never be detached from anything in the world. Attachment to worldly possessions, attachment to worldly faces is ego. First we always look at things and a distinct impression comes in. Then we want to possess them. In order to possess them we work hard. Then we find that we are a slave to them. For example, a spider has woven its own web happily, and when it has woven it so beautifully, it finds that it has become a prisoner of it and cannot escape out of it. And that is what I think we are doing. We are making so many scientific investigations for modern worldly achievements, working hard day and night; we are weaving our own net and ultimately when we get all that, we find how much a prisoner we are of these things. They have possessed us. They have taken us and we have no more freedom. Then we find it difficult to get out of that net. That is ego. We can break that net only by shabd, meditation or nam.

170 *Could it be, Master, that the emotional joy the mind eventually experiences from achieving spiritual union begins to take the consciousness up?*

That joy is a state of consciousness, but mind is mingled with it; mind is mixed with it. We can only get rid of the mind when we go beyond the realm of mind and maya. Till that stage, that emotional joy is just a state of consciousness – it is a higher mind, a noble mind, but the mind is still there. You see, actually this meditation, this love that we're trying to develop is for the mind. The soul by nature, by instinct, is in love with the source, in love with the divine ocean, since it is a drop of that divine ocean. So the characteristic of love is actually there in the soul.

And it is the same love which is in the Father. Potentially every soul is God. Potentially it is in love, but due to the over-powering of the mind, it is helpless. Because mind is dominating, soul is helpless. So we should try to develop love within us for the Father. Actually we are developing love in our mind for the Father. We are making this mind more noble, purer, higher, more sublime, and in this way trying to get rid of the mind. When the mind goes to its own source, automatically the soul goes to the Father, because it is already filled with love for the Father.

The soul is potentially in love with the Father, as it is part and parcel of the Father. So all our efforts in meditation are for creating our love, devotion, faith – it is all for the mind. You see, we have to win the friendship of the mind and get rid of its animal instincts. You cannot get a better friend than the mind, and you cannot get a worse enemy than the mind. So we have only to convert the enmity into friendship in order to achieve our object.

That is why we often talk of this meditation as being 99.9 percent for the mind – in a sense, for the karmas and sins which have been collecting in past lives, because all that is dross on the soul now, a weight on the soul. Slowly and slowly we want to remove that weight from the soul.

171 *It seems like our life is just a school – just a school where we have to learn devotion?*

The purpose of this human birth is nothing but to fill ourselves with love and devotion for the Father, nothing else. Because what is the purpose of meditation? To detach ourselves from the creation and to attach ourselves to the Creator. To turn our back to the creation and to face the Creator – that is the whole purpose of meditation.

MEDITATION AND FAITH

172 *Could you please comment about faith?*

It's not in your hands at all. It comes from within. A girl falls in love with a man. She has no reasoning. She cannot say, "To what extent should I have faith, to what extent should I have this and that?" She is absolutely blind. No matter how much you explain to her, she can't get out of it. She may be deceived, but she has faith. So love creates faith. The more love you have, the more faith you will have in the person concerned. And faith enables you to practice. Then you will follow another person's advice. If you love somebody, that builds faith in you. When you have a problem, you consult another person, and whatever he has told you, you always like to follow it. You think what he has said must be for your good.

So these factors are very essential for following the path. Love will create faith, and faith will create practice. Without faith, mind doesn't go straight on practice. It finds one excuse or another – a hundred obstacles come in the way. You brush them away; again they come. They come and they go. But faith makes you absolutely straight. You do what pleases another person. You never do what annoys another person, what might displease another person – you have built so much faith in that person. And the base of all that is love.

173 *I would like to have true faith. Is that the meaning of meditation?*

You see, faith actually is built by meditation, faith comes by meditation, faith comes by experience. Otherwise the mind always remains shaky. Meditation will be able to create that faith. It generates faith, it creates faith, it strengthens faith. Faith grows by meditation.

174 *Maybe, Maharaj Ji, it would be a good time to talk about having faith in the teachings and faith in the master, about the importance of faith.*

Well, sister, the importance of faith is there, nobody can deny it. Without faith we don't make any progress at all. But first we have to build intellectual faith in the philosophy. And in the light of the philosophy, we have to weigh the master. And then real faith will come only when you practice. Actual faith comes by experience, and faith comes from within, it doesn't come from outside at all. The faith which we build by seeing other people doesn't have much depth at all; it's very shaky. The faith that comes from within by meditation – which strengthens our faith, rather it creates faith – that is unshakable faith. Faith is very essential before we can put forth an earnest effort to practice.

175 *What's the best attitude for the disciple?*

You have to have preliminary faith in order to practice. In order to do research in the laboratory, preliminary faith is required. Otherwise you will refuse to do research. But actual faith comes only when you are able to get satisfaction from that research. Then your faith comes, not before that. On the outside, we feel that we have a lot of faith. This is just a self-deception, I would say. We have no faith at all. Christ said that if you have even as much faith as a grain of mustard seed, you can move mountains.[55] That faith we develop only from within, by practice, by testing within. Not outside.

176 *Master, when Christ said that if we had faith we could move mountains, what did he mean by that? He didn't mean physical mountains, did he?*

Well, brother, with your faith you can move the Creator of the mountains, what to say of mountains. Who created the universe? Who created the mountains? The Lord. By your faith in him, you can move him. You can become him. If you become him, you can move anything.

177 *Professor just mentioned that all doubts must be left behind when we embark on the path and, of course, that is what we have read over and over again, and hear over and over again. It's easier said than done. The thing that bothers me is when I first read about Sant Mat, Dr Johnson made the analogy that we choose our ship or our airplane carefully, but once we have boarded the vessel that is going to transport us, we entrust ourselves completely to the captain. That's the kind of faith that Dr Johnson felt should bring us to the path. That I understand. It seems to me that the analogy is somewhat faulty, however, in that, when we embark on an earthly voyage we have some idea of the time it takes, to start off with. Then I can trust myself to the captain for a week or for a month, however long the voyage is going to be,*

as far as I know. But this voyage might take my lifetime or several more lifetimes, and that is where the problem comes in: How long can one remain without wondering whether one is getting anywhere?

Real faith you will be able to build up only by experience, and you get that real faith not with the whole experience, but with glimpses of experiences, I would say. For example, if you drive from Beas to Delhi, you want an intellectual faith that this road will lead ultimately to Delhi. And for that you see the road map, you see the road signs, you ask another nine, ten passers-by, and when you are intellectually convinced this road does lead to Delhi, only then do you start driving. But real faith will come only when you are able to reach Delhi. Before that, according to your map, according to the information given to you, if you see those signs on the way – road signs, certain scenery is explained to you, certain monuments coming on the way – then, actually, you get faith that you will reach Delhi. But actual faith you will get only when you reach Delhi. But still those signs which have been told to you for your information before you started – after you have been able to build up intellectual faith – give you the faith to reach Delhi.

If you meditate, you do start seeing the signs. It may be glimpses, it may be visions, it may be some other sorts of things. You start seeing the signs and that deepens your faith; that strengthens your faith. Actual faith you will get only when you have the right experience, not before that. So we have so many types of faith, I would say. Before you start, you must have intellectual faith, because without intellectual faith, you will not start. And then you must have some faith from some signs along the way, here and there. Actual faith will come only when you reach the destination.

178 Master, is faith a quality of the soul or the mind?

Faith has to start with the mind. Without faith in the mind you cannot experience the faith of the soul. This emotion, this faith, it has to start with the mind. Soul always has faith in the Father. Soul is always yearning to become one with the Father. Soul is full with love and devotion for the Father. It is the mind which is holding it back. So faith, to begin with, has to start with the mind. Even our emotion – so-called love, devotion – it has to start with the mind. Guru Nanak gave a very beautiful example. He said this mind is iron, and the divine melody or word is a philosopher's stone. As soon as iron is brought in touch with the philosopher's stone it becomes gold. He says the iron is within you, and the philosopher's stone is also within you. The mind is in your body, the nam is within your body. With the grace of the master, they are brought in touch with each other. And then your mind becomes gold, it becomes pure. It becomes your best friend. So it has to be brought in touch with the philosopher's stone. Only then does the soul get released from the bondages of the mind.

179 Master, what part does the disciple's understanding of Sant Mat play in the progress towards reaching the eye centre?

Intellectual understanding doesn't bring you back to the eye centre. You get learning. You become a learned man about the teachings, about the philosophy. But unless you practically withdraw your consciousness to the eye centre, how can you succeed within? Intellect won't lead you there at all, learning won't lead you there at all, wisdom won't take you there at all. Your effort and then your experience – that will bring you there.

I have often said that either we should not be intellectual at all, but if, fortunately or unfortunately, we are, we must satisfy our intellect. Otherwise intellect will become a barrier in our way. Unless intellect is satisfied, effort will not come. Faith will not come. Experience will not come. Satisfaction of the intellect will give you faith. And faith will lead you to practice. And then you will be able to experience within. But intellect will not take you there. Satisfaction of the intellect will take you there.

180 Is it permissible to express a disagreement with Professor Bhatnagar when we ask questions?

I think you have all misunderstood Professor. What he means to say is that if you are able to develop faith, then automatically all your questions are dissolved, no question is left, then you have no question to ask, if you are able to develop that much faith. But all these meetings are just to help develop that faith. We meditate to develop that faith. We are becoming a source of strength to each other just to develop that faith. Once we come to that level, then naturally there will be no questions. Christ himself says in the Bible: Now you ask me so many things and I put you off. And then you will have no question to ask me. And if you have any, I'll have to answer you straight.[127] All endeavour is to develop that level of faith. First we start with our intellectual faith, I would say even intellectual love, to start building our meditation. But with that experience, with that progress within, we are able to develop that deep faith, that deep love and devotion. Then automatically all questions vanish, all questions dissolve, all questions become meaningless. That doesn't mean that right from the beginning you will be able to develop that faith and that you will have no questions. We are trying to reach to that level.

*181 Can the intellect ever really be satisfied except by the
touch of the master's love?*

Whatever the reason may be, how it is satisfied, that is a different thing, but intellect definitely gets satisfied. And definitely
its satisfaction gives you a certain faith, and definitely that faith
leads you to practice. All your questions become meaningless to
you. When the time comes, all the questions which have looked
to you like the Himalayas, they will become meaningless to you.
You won't bother or care about them.

182 How can we deepen our faith?

By meditation. Meditation will strengthen your love, strengthen
your faith, strengthen your devotion. Your roots will go very
deep, and then nobody will be able to shake you from the path.
There is no other way – only by meditation.

   We are carried away with certain atmospheres: of satsang,
of group meetings, of good satsangis to some extent, but all that
becomes shaky very soon if we don't try to supplement it with
meditation. Then it becomes a permanent intoxication, and it
creates a very deep faith which nobody can shake.

   If you have experienced personal knowledge that this is a
horse, let the whole world say it is a cow – you will never believe
it. If you have never seen a horse before, you can be fooled even if
somebody tells you a cow is a horse. Personal experience creates
depth in our faith, and that we can get only with meditation.

*183 Maharaj Ji, I don't have faith and I don't understand
faith in the master. There seem to be so many facets
to the understanding of faith in the master. Could you
please discuss faith in the master?*

I don't think love can be discussed or faith can be discussed. Love you feel within, faith you experience within. And you can only know from within how much faith you have. What will you discuss about faith?

There is nothing about love and faith to discuss. It's just what you feel, what you go through, what you experience, something within you that tells you where you stand. Nobody can analyze your faith except your own self. We always know where we stand.

MEDITATION AS TRUE PRAYER

184 *Maharaj Ji, when we come before you and we just feel so relaxed and excited to have an interview with you, so often we're so enthusiastic and nervous that we aren't able to say all the things that we are feeling, or sometimes we don't even say what we are feeling. Do you pay more attention to what our words are saying or to what our heart is feeling, or do you listen to both?*

The Lord knows even what we don't say. The Lord is not deaf, yet you are shouting to reach him. He hears even the noise of the ant moving about. So we should not worry about what we have been able to say, what we could not say, or what has been left to say. Whatever is said is sufficient.

Instead, we should give more attention to meditation. Meditation is nothing but knocking at his door for mercy, to seek forgiveness from him. Meditation is nothing else – it is just our expression of gratitude towards the Father, just to tell him how anxious we are to become one with you, how restless we are to be with you, reach you. That is what meditation is, so what we say is absolutely immaterial – it is more or less for our own mental consolation, nothing else.

We feel light after saying things, but he knows even before that and he hears even unsaid things. But still, if we feel right by writing or by saying, there's no harm in it, but the real saying is meditation – nothing else.

185 *Maharaj Ji, about the Lord's Prayer, does it help a person to say the Lord's Prayer?*

Sister, what is a prayer? Prayer is real love and devotion within us – the desire to go and merge back into the Father. That is a prayer – yearning of the heart to go back to its own source, yearning of the soul to merge back into its own source. For that we don't need any mechanical words. No words are required. It is a prayer of the heart to the source. That is your prayer. What we think of as prayer is asking the Lord to fulfil our worldly desires. But that is not prayer. That is creating desires and asking the Lord to fulfil those desires, and then we have to come back to fulfil those desires.

I am not against prayer. Prayer gives you strength to face a situation, to go through that situation. It may not be able to change your destiny, but definitely you get strength to face that destiny. But real prayer is whatever time we give in his love, in his devotion, in his meditation. That's our prayer. We are knocking at his door so that it may be opened – that is, praying day and night to go back to him.

But we generally take prayer as asking the Lord to give us this and give us this and give us that and give us that. And if he does not, we become frustrated that our prayer has not been heard. You see, if a child is ill and he asks his mother to give him sweets, which are not good for his illness, the mother will not give that child something that will irritate his fever. Not because the mother doesn't love the child, but because she loves him so much that she cannot stand to see him suffer more. So she will give only a little so that the fever may leave him.

The mind creates desires, and then we want the Lord to fulfil them. We are the slave of the mind. We are not trying to explain to our mind to remain in the will of the Lord; we are trying to explain to the Lord to remain in the will of the mind. We are not devotees of the Lord; we are becoming devotees of the mind. And then if he doesn't come up to our expectations, we become frustrated with him. It is good to pray for worldly things if we know just what is best for us, but actually we don't know what is best for us. Sometimes we pray to him for four, five years to get something out of him, and then we may have to pray another twenty years to get rid of those things. Because we don't know what is best for us.

So the real prayer is submission to him. He knows what is best for us. That is what Christ has tried to explain in the chapter on prayer in Saint Matthew. He says: When he looks after even the fowl, even the birds who don't work, he gives them what they need – you think he is unmindful of your desires, your demands?[25] He will give you what you require only if you have faith, if you can submit to him.

I'll give you a little example. Our maid in our house, if she does her duty dutifully, lovingly, smilingly, we always want excuses to give her more and more. We are so happy with her devotion, her work and duty. If on the other hand she doesn't work at all and she is always grumbling for more pay, we always find excuses to get rid of her.

Our real prayer is to do our duty, dutifully, lovingly to the Lord, whatever he expects us to do. That is our daily prayer. The teaching in which we live, the time which we give to meditation, the life we are trying to live – that is all prayer. And this prayer will lead us – not the prayer by the mind of creating desires and asking him to fulfil them day and night, then feeling frustrated if he doesn't do it and then forgetting about him. That is no prayer at all. The real prayer is submission to his will, facing our destiny cheerfully, and that we can only do if we live in meditation.

186   Is it permissible, or advisable, to alternate simran with other prayers addressed to the Lord?

You see, actually whatever time you are devoting towards meditation is praying to the Lord. What is prayer? Prayer is not to ask him for worldly goods or to fulfil worldly ambitions or to get material wealth. That is not prayer at all. The real prayer is to take us back to him, that he should merge us back into him. That is real prayer.

There's no harm in praying to the Father. It gives you strength, and you'll be able to face situations without losing your balance. That is the effect of prayer. But the time we are devoting to meditation we're doing nothing but prayer. Every minute, every second is a prayer. Whenever we are living in his love, living in his devotion, living in his memory, trying to devote our time to meditation, that is all a constant prayer to the Lord.

We're all knocking at his door to give us admission. That is prayer. Prayer is not asking him for anything in the world. There's no harm in asking the Lord for that – after all, that is the only door we have on which to knock – but it does not mean that he will give us what we want. He will only give us what is best for us. Prayer will give us strength, strong willpower to face situations. Either the desire will leave us or the desire will be fulfilled by him. If something is not in our interest, he will not give it to us. You see, when a child is sick, has a fever, if he insists that his mother give him sweets, she will never give them to him. It's not that the mother doesn't love the child – she probably doesn't love anything better than her child. But she knows that this sweet is not good for the child. Perhaps bitter quinine would be better for the child. So whether the child cries or weeps, she puts the bitter quinine in his mouth. The child doesn't know what is best for him. His mother knows what is best for him.

So sometimes we pray for worldly things – we knock and knock and knock, and day and night we ask for those things. And if the Lord gives them to us, perhaps for another ten, twelve years we may have to pray to get rid of those things. We don't know what is best for us. So when we are so blind that we don't know what is best for us, why not leave it to the Father to give us whatever he thinks best for us? You follow my point?

Moreover, you see, it is the heart which desires, which creates the desires, the longing for worldly things. We are praying to the Father to fulfil the desires of the heart, the mind. We are not trying to explain to the mind the need to remain in the will of the Lord; we're trying to explain to the Father the need to remain in the will of the mind. But we're not devotees of the mind, we're devotees of the Lord. We have to do what pleases him, not what pleases the mind. We have to explain to the mind that it must remain in the will of the Lord. Whatever he gives us, we should be happy. We should accept it cheerfully. That is prayer – not asking him and pressing him to fulfil the desires of the mind.

The mind is always there to deceive us. The mind is not our friend, it may put us astray. Christ speaks very beautifully about prayer: These birds in the air, they don't sow anything, yet the Lord takes care of them.[25] He knows they need to eat, and he gives them food. They never need to do anything at all. Without their even asking, he supplies them with what they need. So if we want to pray, we should give our time to meditation. That is prayer. And meditation will help us to remain in his will, to eliminate our mind, to eliminate the ego, eliminate the will of the mind, and will help us to remain in the will of the Lord. That is the real prayer.

But sometimes the mind wants to say prayers that are not connected with desires.

These set prayers are of no use at all. Prayer must come from the heart. A set repetition of a certain prayer is no prayer at all. That is just like putting a tape recorder on. The soul must speak, the heart must speak, and that does not need any language, any set prayer at all. It should be the language of the heart. The heart should pray to the Father. And no words are required there. No set prayers are required there. If we just remember a prayer like a parrot and say it five, six times a day, our mind is not even in what we are saying. If our mind is there, then words are not required at all. Our mind should be in tune with the Lord when we are praying to him. Then where is the need to remember all those words? Mind is not there anymore – it is tuned in to his love. So for real prayer, no set prayer is required at all.

187 *Is prayer and faith enough, no matter what age a person may be?*

I have discussed prayer from the Bible. Christ says, prayer does not mean submitting a demand list before the Father.[20] The Father knows what you need.

Prayer is just submitting yourself to the Father and accepting what he gives you and having faith that whatever he gives you is best for you. That is real prayer.

Whatever time you devote to meditation or living in the teachings, or living in his love and devotion, is time devoted to prayer. Meditation is prayer. He said, prayer is living in the will of the Lord.[20] We only live in the will of the Lord when we are able to eliminate our own will. Then we go beyond the realm of mind. Then only can we live in the will of the Father. At present we're living in the will of the mind. But real prayer is to go beyond the realm of the mind. And that you can only achieve by attaching yourself to the spirit within. So when you give time to your meditation, you are praying.

188 Does that mean, Master, that prayer is something where we become aware of the presence of the Father within?

You see, in prayer there should be nothing between you and the Father. No set words are required for prayer, no set phrases are required for prayer, no language is required for prayer; the heart is required and the Father is required. There should be nothing between your heart and the Father. No worldly desire should exist between you and the Father. It is just your heart which should speak to the Father. No words are required, no language is required at all. You should be just one with the Father, that is a prayer to him. You exist and he exists. The whole world doesn't exist for you when you pray to him. That is a real prayer. When we ask for worldly things and to fulfil worldly ambitions, then the whole world exists between you and the Father. All those worldly things and worldly desires exist between me and the Father, so it means that I am not in touch with the Father, I am not in tune with the Father. There are so many barriers between me and the Father. There should be no barriers at all between me and the Father. That is real prayer.

189 Is it okay to talk to the master within when we pray? Should we try to stop doing that, or should we start doing simran?

Do meditation. Meditation is nothing but a prayer. Meditation is nothing but knocking at the door of the Giver. Meditation is begging the Father for his grace, for his forgiveness for what stands between us and the Father.

You see, meditation alone can never clear all our karmic accounts. The attitude of the mind which we develop by meditation, that helps us a lot. That fills us with devotion and with love and makes us feel the separation from the Father, and we become restless without him. Our whole attitude towards the world is then changed. If you think that by mere meditation we can ever account for all the karmas we have been committing in previous lives, it is impossible. Nobody can do it. What to say of doing it in four lives, even in twenty lives we could not do it – that's how much dross we have collected. But when the Father sees our attitude, when he sees the devotion and love within us – which we can only develop by meditation, by living the Sant Mat way of life – that invokes his grace to forgive all that stands between us and the Father.

190   *Maharaj Ji, can you tell us about the function of prayer on the path?*

The real prayer is knocking at the Lord's door for forgiveness for the actions which we have been collecting from birth to birth, from body to body, from house to house. That is real prayer, to ask for forgiveness. And that forgiveness we get – or rather, we are able to repent for all those karmas – only by meditation. So meditation is the best prayer. It gives us moral strength and also strong willpower to face our present karmas. It gives us strength to go through our destiny without losing our balance. It gives us strength not to sow any new seeds that would force us to come back to the creation. And it invokes his forgiveness for what we have been collecting in the past. So meditation is the best prayer.

191   *When we leave, when I go back home, I was thinking that there might be situations when I'll want to beg for your forgiveness, or call out to you, and I was wondering if I should try to develop some kind of relationship with*

the inner master, or could I call out to what I experienced
of you here? Now there'll be you, the way I experienced
you here, in my memory. I don't know whether to call out
to that or to the inner master?

You see, your master's always within you, and whatever time you
are devoting to your meditation, you are calling your master.
Instead of just addressing your own mind within, it's better to
attend to your meditation. We waste our time, we try to pray,
we try to call and talk to our own master within. Actually you
are talking to your own mind. You are just talking to your own
mind, nothing else, so it's better to put it in simran, put it in
meditation, since meditation automatically helps us in every
way. Because the Lord knows what we need, what we want, we
don't have to tell him, we don't have to express ourselves to him.
He knows our language of the heart. Our tongue doesn't have
to move there at all. So just attend to your meditation.

192 *Your Holiness, would the devotional approach that we*
have in the West, a simple prayer, be sufficient for us to
attain the goal, rather than the more complicated sahaj
yoga *rules, which I personally find rather difficult?*

No doubt this is a very difficult subject to understand. The main
thing is, what is prayer? Actually, our whole meditation is nothing but a prayer before the Lord, nothing but a prayer from the
heart, the soul, to merge back into the Lord. Real prayer is only
to pray to the Lord to have mercy on us, to give us his grace and
guidance to live in his will, to give us such circumstances that
we can meditate on his name. That is real prayer. Prayer does not
mean that we should pray for worldly things, or that we should
pray for the fulfilment of a desire. That is not the process for
getting back to the Lord at all but is, in fact, just sowing seeds

which make us come back into the world again to reap the results of those prayers. The real prayer is from the heart; it's submission to the Lord. He is not unmindful of what we need. If we are dutiful in our meditation, he who knows what is best for us will definitely give us what we need, whether we ask him or not.

193 *Yes, I know that the lowest type of prayer is a prayer of petition; but can we say, "God, thy will be done" or "God, give me guidance, I have a difficult decision to make," to help in making that decision?*

We should always pray to him for his mercy and guidance. And for that, whether or not you say the spoken word, it is immaterial. Real prayer comes from the heart. Generally, we have set prayers. We remember them and repeat them every day, several times a day. That is mechanical prayer, whereas it is the heart that should speak. No words are required, and no particular time is required for that; in fact, a true lover is in constant communion with the Lord. When the heart speaks, he hears, he gives. So we should pray to him to guide us, to be merciful to us, to redeem us from birth and death, to take us into his own lap; in fact, to merge us into himself. That is real prayer.

However, any other prayer is not bad. It makes your willpower strong. Whether he gives you anything or not, when you pray to him, even your mechanical prayer makes your willpower strong, and you can face life a little more boldly. You can adjust yourself to situations and circumstances even by means of these mechanical prayers or prayers of petition. But actually, you are not praying to the Lord, you are explaining to yourself what you want. You are developing your mind, and that helps you to adjust to these circumstances and to face them boldly. Any type of prayer helps, provided it is sincere. But the best prayer is just to submit to him and ask only for his guidance and grace.

194 *When a person prays for something and the prayer is answered, is it God that necessarily answers it? It happens quite frequently that a person will pray for something material; for example, a person prays for a new car, and he gets it, or a million dollars, and he gets it. Now, who gives it to him?*

What you mean to say is that when we pray, whether it is due to our prayers that we get those things, or even otherwise we would have gotten them? I think that even otherwise you would have received them. The Lord does not want us to be asking and begging him to fulfil our wishes, nor does he want us to think that our wishes have been fulfilled because we have asked him. He is so merciful he gives us even without our asking.

Our karmas bring us all these things that we are wanting. But by prayer we develop ourselves to that extent that we make our willpower strong. That is all. We have never prayed to the Lord: "O Lord, whatever we have, take it from us and give it to other people!" We have never prayed to him like that – we are always asking and asking. But it is good to pray. Prayer is not bad.

195 *Do you just ask, or just talk to the Lord?*

Mechanical words are not necessary. Prayer should come from the heart, and the heart speaks without language, without words. No set prayers move him, but the prayer from the heart moves him. We should be in tune with the Lord, with our heart; that is the right prayer – to be always in constant communion with him. So real prayer is always from the heart, from within. Set prayers are all right. I am not against them. They also give us certain strength. Our willpower becomes so strong that we face our karmas quite boldly and gracefully. But that type of prayer does not take us back to him. The real prayer is meditation, the spiritual practice, which alone enables us to contact the shabd, the sound current, and that will take us back to him.

Meditation is nothing but prayer for his guidance, for his grace. That is the only purpose of meditation. We hardly devote any of our time in meditation, but devote all our time in asking for fulfilment of our desires. If we are dutifully loyal in our meditation, we are actually praying to him. He is not unmindful of what we need, but he will not give us anything that is not good for us. Perhaps when we are not getting what we want, he has some greater blessing for us in that he may want us to detach ourselves from the world. He wants to take us back to him. We think that he is not hearing our prayers, when actually he is hearing our prayers. But he will not give us a burning hot coal that would burn our hands, just because we ask for it. He is hearing our prayer, but we do not know whether what we are asking for is right or wrong. He alone knows it. Sometimes we think we are not being heard and that the Lord does not help us. That is a wrong notion. We do not know what is best for us. Just leave it to him. That is the right prayer.

196 *We should not place our desires or our wishes before God, but should cheerfully accept whatever comes, with confidence that whatever he does, he is doing for our own good. Is that correct? Will you please elaborate?*

Yes, that is right. We have to adjust ourselves. We should not try to adjust the Lord to our wishes. Mind creates the desires and we are knocking at the Lord's door, asking him to fulfil them. We are actually slaves of the mind, not slaves of the Lord. We have to become the devotees of the Lord and not of the mind. We have to tell our mind to remain in the will of the Lord, and not ask the Lord to remain in the will of the mind. So our real prayer is the longing and desire to merge back into him; and to accomplish that we ask for his grace, his love and devotion; and when we get that, nothing else is left to be desired.

If you bring a millionaire to your house, the money automatically comes with him. But we are only desiring the possessions of the Lord and not the Lord at all. We generally attach ourselves to what he gives and not to the Giver at all. We forget the Giver and enjoy only his gifts; but if we realize the Giver within us, we automatically get everything. He is the owner of everything, he knows what we need, and he will definitely give us what we need. But we are only to ask for him. That is the real prayer.

197 What about praying for other people?

If we do not know what is good for us, how can we know what is good for others? Whether you alter anything or not by praying, it is difficult to say. But you do get inner strength by praying to the Lord. We pray for others when we are concerned about them because they are ill or poor, or we want their wishes fulfilled. This is due to our attachment to those people, and it is the mind which creates all these desires to be fulfilled, and when we pray for others, we may even be asking for something which is not good for them. For example, if a child is ill and wants some sweets, though he weeps and begs, his mother will not give them to him. She loves the child and knows that sweets are not good for him when he has a fever, and she may have to give him a bitter pill instead. But the child cries for the sweets because he does not know what is good for him. He wants sweets, but the mother does not give them to him, because she loves him and knows that they are not good for him. On the other hand, if she concedes to his request and gives him sweets, I think she really does not love him at all. His fever may go higher and his illness may even become worse because of the sweets which he begged for and received.

Similarly, the Lord or the master will give us only what is best for us and for those for whom we are praying. He does not want us to be attached to the world. He wants to detach us from the world. He will not give us those things which will make us forget the Lord and take us back to the senses and again make us slaves of karmas. He will give us only those things which detach us from the world and take us nearer to the Lord. We do not know what is good for us or for others; but he knows what is good for everyone. So why not leave everything to him and just do our duty? Real prayer is not by the lips, not by set words. It comes from the heart, and the heart does not need any language, any words, in order to pray. The real prayer is just submission, surrender to him.

198 When a body is dead, if we say some prayers so that the soul may hear it, and to help the soul, does the soul hear us?

No, the soul does not hear our prayer. These prayers are said for the benefit of the bereaved ones. All that we do is to console those people whose relatives or friends have left them. Practically, we can do nothing for the departed soul. It has to answer for its own karma. All the ceremonies, prayers and things that we do after anybody dies are, in fact, to console the survivors and ourselves, and not that departed soul. We do not help the dead at all. His or her karma will take care of that. Generally when we pray for the dead, I think we are really praying for ourselves to be able to bear our loss and separation. We do not help the departed at all.

199 Master, I go to school with many active Christian pupils, and I would like to know if a Christian or Muslim who leads a very good life and prays to the Lord for guidance and forgiveness – will their souls go back to the Father, or will they have to come back and follow the path of Sant Mat?

Well, sister, there's no harm in praying. Every child knocks at the door of his father. The Father is the giver, and we are always the beggar. So we have no other door at which to beg but our Father's. Prayer doesn't mean that the events of life will change. We have to go through whatever our destiny is, whether we pray or don't pray. Prayer doesn't change our destiny; prayer doesn't change the events of our life. It just gives us strength, strong willpower to face those karmas, those events of life, but they will remain as they are.

And happiness lies in our adjusting to the events of life. Happiness doesn't lie in changing the events of life, because they will never change at all. Events of life have already been set, so we can only be happy not by praying to the Father, but by adjusting ourselves to the events of life. For example, the weather changes; summer comes, and the cold weather comes. If we adjust according to the cold weather, naturally the time passes, and if we adjust according to the summer, time passes – we don't feel miserable at all. But if we refuse to adjust to the weather, we are the ones to suffer. Weather will change. We cannot stop the change of weather, but we can adjust ourselves according to the weather. So similarly, according to our destiny, we have to adjust to those karmas.

Prayer doesn't mean that events of life will change. Prayer only gives us a sense of strength, strong willpower to face those situations.

And then there's another aspect. If the Father is in a position to give, he's also in a position to know. He doesn't have

143

to demand that the child must ask. A loving father is always anxious to give to his child without demanding anything of the child. So we have to become the loving children of the Father. He automatically will take care of us. As Christ said in the Bible: O ye of little faith, you are praying to the Father for worldly achievements, worldly needs, worldly desires. You have no faith in the Father, that he knows all that, and he will do all that. He says, if you ask anybody for any help, they are always anxious to help. Won't your Father help you when you are the top of the creation? Then he gives beautiful examples. He says: Who feeds the insects? Who feeds this grass, which just today is, and tomorrow will not be? When he looks after even these things, won't he also look after you, who's at the top of the creation?[25]

So the Father is always looking after us, whether we pray to him or not. Prayer only helps us to face situations. It doesn't change the course of the events of our life.

Then, we do not even know what is in our best interest to pray for. We are blind. The Father knows what is best for us, and we do not know what is best for us. There are many things that we spent many, many years praying to the Father to get. And when we get them, perhaps we may have to pray for an even longer time to get rid of those things, because we are blind, we don't know what is best for us. So when we are so blind and we do not know what is best for us, why show our lack of faith in the Father? Why not leave it to him? He will give us what we deserve, he will give us what is in our best interest. That is real prayer.

Meditation itself is a prayer. Meditation is just knocking at the door of the Father for his grace and to forgive us for what stands between us and the Father. Meditation is nothing but asking for forgiveness. Meditation alone will never be able to make the soul pure or make the soul whole, because we have such a huge layer of karmas. If you go on scratching the ground, you will never be able to reach the bottom. It is the same with us and our karmas. By meditation we can never burn them at all.

Meditation is just an excuse to ask for the grace of the Father to forgive us, whatever we have done in the past. So we are repenting by attending to meditation, and that repentance is nothing but a prayer to the Father to forgive us and then make us one with him. Just to become one with the Father, that is real prayer, but there's no harm in other prayers for worldly things, whether he gives them to us or not. At least it gives us strong willpower and makes our minds strong to face the situation so that we don't lose our balance so easily. But prayer doesn't change the course of the events of our life. Yet there's no harm in praying to him.

200 Jesus taught his disciples a prayer. Could you shed some light on that prayer?

He made it very clear. He said we should never pray to the Father for worldly desires or to fulfil worldly achievements. We should only pray to the Father to give us strength to go through our destiny. Because our Father knows what is best for us. So there should be no repetition of any set prayer. And no words are required to pray to the Father. Only our heart is needed. Our heart needs no language. Nothing should be between you and the Father when you pray. Prayer to the Father does not mean putting a list of demands before the Father.

These desires are created by the mind. And we are asking the Father to fulfil these desires. We are not explaining to our mind to remain in the will of the Father. We are, on the other hand, explaining to the Father to remain in the will of our mind. When we pray for things, we become the devotee of the mind, not of the Father. So prayer to the Father involves unconditional surrender to him. Give yourself to the Father, and face happily what he gives you. Live in his love, in his devotion, and attach yourself to the spirit within. That is a real prayer. Whatever time you devote to your meditation, whatever time you devote to the spirit within, you are devoting to the prayer of the Father. This has nothing to do with the reading of certain prayers five or ten times a day.

201 *A lot of people, when they receive initiation and get their instructions and begin focusing, start looking for something, but a very advanced disciple said to me years ago, "Think of the Giver and not the gift," which I take to mean: Think of master, don't think of everything else.*

The idea is that in our prayers we should all ask for the Giver himself from the Lord, the Giver rather than his gifts. We are always worried about his gifts, about the favours he should do for us, but we never try to seek the Giver. We are always running after the gifts, but not after the Giver. If you get the Giver, the gifts automatically will all come to you, because gifts belong to the Giver – everything belongs to the Giver and if the Giver is with you, there's no dearth of gifts. But we generally just ask for gifts from him and never bother about the Giver. So that is what generally is impressed upon us, that we should try to ask only for the Lord from the Lord. Because all the gifts come from him, and if he is with us, then all his gifts are automatically with us.

202 *As a child, I was taught that we had a direct line to God, that we could ask God for help. As an example: "Please help this person. Please heal this person. God, please help this husband." And my prayers have always been answered. Now in Sant Mat I am told that this is wrong, that I should just do my simran and leave the rest to God. I really feel very lonely about it. Would you comment on that?*

You see, sister, in prayer there is no question of allowing or not allowing us to do anything at all. Prayer is between the disciple and the Lord. There are no set words in prayer. No language is required in prayer. Only you exist and the Lord exists, and that is your prayer to the Father. Nobody and nothing should come in the way – not even words, not even your thoughts. Just surrender yourself to the Father and be one with him. Attune yourself to him. That's prayer. Meditation is nothing but a prayer. What is meditation? If we think we can clear all our debts to Kal by dint of our meditation, it is impossible. Meditation is only a prayer to the Lord to forgive us for all that we have been doing, for all that stands between us and him. Meditation only helps us to seek forgiveness of the Father. Meditation is nothing else. We are knocking at his door just to seek forgiveness. So that itself is a prayer. There can be no better prayer than meditation. In prayer, no set words are required, no language is required. Between you and the Father, nothing should exist. The whole world should cease to exist when you are praying to the Father. That is a real prayer.

203 *Many people believe in so-called faith healing, and that by prayer people can be healed. There are so many examples in religion …*

It's okay if anybody prays for you – let him pray. You sit at home. Let him go on praying for you. We are happy if we are able to pray for ourselves.

But what about prayer and karma?

There is no question of karmas involved in it. Prayer doesn't change the course of the events of your life. It only gives you strength to go through those events. Prayer doesn't change your destiny. Prayer doesn't change your karma, the course of your karmas. It only gives you strength to face those karmas, face that destiny, without losing your balance very much. That is the only advantage of prayer. You can just take charge of the situation at that time by praying to the Father. Otherwise you become emotionally too upset. But prayer is not going to change your destiny at all, because your destiny is interlinked with so many people. How can one man be picked out from destiny? What about the karmic connections with other people? What will happen to them? In prayer, we speak to God. We expect something from him to fulfil our desires. In meditation we hear God, we submit to his will. In meditation, you hear the voice of God, and you submit your will to him. You live in his will. In prayer you are asking the Lord to fulfil the desires of your mind. You are dominated by your mind, and you are using the Lord to fulfil those desires. In meditation you just resign yourself to the will of the Father. You give yourself to him. Whatever he gives you, you are happy, contented. That is the difference between prayer and meditation.

204   What is the place of prayer in Sant Mat?

The real prayer to the Lord is submitting ourselves to the Lord. What is prayer, as it is ordinarily understood? Our mind creates desires, and we are praying to the Lord to fulfil those desires. We are not explaining to our mind to adjust to the will of the Lord, but we are trying to explain to the Lord to adjust to the wishes of our mind. Actually, we are a slave of the mind and not of the Lord. We have to become a slave of the Lord, and then there is really nothing to pray for. We are just to submit to what he wants us to do. We should pray to him to give us strength to face gracefully and boldly whatever he wants us to go through.

When we are devoted to the Lord, naturally he is not unmindful of what we need. For example, if a maid works in your house and she does beautiful work, is always willing and pleasant about it and never asks you for anything, then you always feel like giving her something, without her asking. You are so appreciative of what she does and of her attitude that you want to give her something, more than if she had asked for it. If another maid does not work well or even if she works well but is always grumbling and asking for something, you do not feel like giving her anything, and you would even like to dismiss her.

Generally, we pray to the Lord for worldly possessions – health, wealth, and prosperity for ourselves and our loved ones. In the first place, we do not know what is best for us, much less for anyone else. Many things are received from the Lord after praying for four or five years, and perhaps we have to kneel in prayer for another ten years to petition him to relieve us of the very things that we had been praying for. When we ask, we do not know what is good for us. When we do not know what is good for us, why not submit to him? He will give us what is best for us.

~ 9 ~

Practice of Meditation

THE PRACTICE OF MEDITATION

205 Can you explain to us what meditation is, and why we need to meditate?

Meditation is very simple. We all know there is one God, and that he is within every one of us. And God has made us all alike. If he is within every one of us, and if there is only one God who can only be found within ourselves, there cannot be more than one path leading back to the Father. It has got to be the same path in a Muslim, a Christian, a Hindu, a Sikh or any other person because the Lord has made us all alike. For those who try to seek him within, there is only one path. Those who try to seek him outside are just lost in illusion, and that will lead them nowhere at all.

The Lord is within every one of us. The path leading back to the Lord is also within every one of us. Our spiritual journey starts from the soles of our feet and ends at the top of our head. In the body, the soul and the mind are knotted together here, at the eye centre. From here our mind spreads into the whole creation through the nine apertures: the two eyes, two ears, two holes of the nose, the mouth and the two lower apertures. Through these nine apertures our thoughts are spread into the whole creation.

151

How are our thoughts spread? We are always thinking about one thing or another. The mind is never still. No matter how much you close yourself off in the darkest room, you will not be there – your mind will be scattered into the whole creation. And whomever we are thinking about, their form appears before us. If I am thinking about my child, my child's form will appear before me. If I am thinking about my wife, my friends, I will start visualizing their forms. Automatically we start visualizing the faces of whomever we are thinking about, and slowly and slowly we get attached to them, so much so that we start dreaming about them. And at the time of death, all their forms appear before us as on a cinema screen.

Those attachments and that love pull us back to the level of creation after our death. Mystics tell us that unless we are in love with the Father, unless we are attached to the Father, we will not be able to go back to the level of the Father. They tell us that with the same method by which you are attached to the creation, you should try to attach yourself to the Creator. The mind is in the habit of doing simran – thinking day and night about what we see is known as simran. And whatever we try to visualize is known as doing dhyan. So the mind is in the habit of doing simran and dhyan, but simran and dhyan about whom? Those faces, those objects, all that we see in this creation, are perishable. So mystics tell us to think about the Lord. Visualize the form of the Father. By the same process we use all the time, you try to withdraw your consciousness back to the eye centre.

The mind is fond of pleasures, and it has become a slave of the senses because it is very fond of the pleasures of the senses. Unless the mind gets a better pleasure than the sensual pleasures, it refuses to leave the sensual pleasures.

The Lord has kept within every one of us at the eye centre that better pleasure, which is known by different names. Christ refers to it as the holy ghost, word, spirit, name; Indian mystics generally call it shabd or nam. Some call it *akash bani,* some call it *kalma* or *baang-e-asmani,* but we are not concerned with the words at all.

That divine melody is within every one of us here at the eye centre. When, with the help of simran and dhyan as taught to us by the mystics or saints, we withdraw our consciousness back to the eye centre, then we are in touch with that divine melody within, which has its own sound and its own light. With the help of the sound, we know the direction of our house within. With the help of the light, we know the path which we have to travel. So slowly and slowly, stage by stage, we start making progress within ourselves.

In order to go back to the Father, we have to withdraw our consciousness back to the eye centre. This is known as meditation – withdrawing our consciousness from the nine apertures and holding our attention here at the eye centre and attaching our attention, our consciousness, to that divine melody or divine light within. The more we concentrate at the eye centre, the more we will be in touch with that divine melody and divine light within. The more we enjoy that divine light and divine melody within, the more we start withdrawing from the attachments of the creation. Attachment to the divine melody automatically creates the feeling of detachment from the senses, detachment from the creation. Only attachment can create detachment in us. Detachment can never create attachment in anyone.

When we are attached to that divine melody within, it starts pulling us away from sensual pleasures, from worldly love, from worldly pleasures. That is why it is known as *amrit* – because from it we get immortal life. Christ calls it the living water, Muslims call it *aabe-hayaat.* Once we taste it, we become free from birth and death. So that is shabd and nam, which the Lord has placed within every one of us here at the eye centre.

But unless we withdraw and hold our attention at the eye centre, we cannot taste that nectar within, we cannot enjoy that silent music which the Lord has placed within every one of us, and we cannot be one with that divine light within. Once we are one with that divine light and one with that divine music or divine melody within, then automatically detachment from this creation starts in our mind. That attachment to the divine melody starts detaching us from the creation and slowly and slowly attaching us to the Creator. This is meditation; this is the process which we have to follow.

206 What is meant by the journey of the soul?

We have to withdraw the consciousness from our feet to the top of our head. Our journey consists of two stages. The first stage is to the eye centre, and the second stage is upwards, above the eye centre. With the help of simran and dhyan we have to withdraw our consciousness back to the eye centre. And once we are here, we have a door at which we can knock. Whenever we go to our house, unless the door is open, we can never get entry into the house. So the door of our house, where our Lord resides, is here at the eye centre and we have to knock here. With the help of simran and dhyan we have to open our third eye, open our faculty to see within. Seeing within means to be in touch with that sound there, to be in touch with that light there. With the help of our concentration at the eye centre, we will hear that sound, which will become clearer and clearer, and we will start seeing that light, which will become brighter and brighter. With the help of sound, we know the direction of our house. With the help of light we travel on that path, and stage by stage we go back to our destination.

You can call it shabd, you can call it nam, you can call it light and sound; you can give it any name, it is immaterial.

This is the only process by which we can travel through those stages and go beyond the realm of mind and maya. Because our soul and mind are knotted together, unless the soul gets release from the mind, it doesn't become pure, it doesn't become whole. And unless it becomes whole, unless it becomes pure, it doesn't become worthy to become one with the Father.

Only the pure soul becomes worthy to become one with the Father, and the soul becomes absolutely pure when it gets released from the clutches of the mind. The mind is fond of the senses, so at this stage the mind is a slave of the senses. When the mind gets the better and more absorbing nectar within, the mind automatically leaves the senses. The more we taste that nectar within, the more we are detached from the creation and from the senses.

With the help of sound and light, the mind goes back to its own source, Trikuti. The moment the mind goes there, the soul gets released from the clutches of the mind. All our karmas – our kriyaman karma, our sinchit karma – become ineffective; they cannot pull our soul back to the level of the creation because now the soul rules the mind and the mind rules the senses, rather than the senses ruling our mind and the mind ruling the soul. We have to reverse the whole process by meditation. As Christ said: You have become whole, so sin no more, lest a worse thing come unto thee. So when he put that man on the path, he said: If you go on practicing this meditation you will become whole, provided you don't add more to your sins.[85] Whatever sins are there, you will be able to clear them, and if you don't add more to your sins, automatically you'll become whole. When we become whole, automatically we have merged back into the Father.

207 Master, can you speak on the importance of meditation?

Our soul is a spark of the divine ocean, but having taken the association of the mind, it has become a slave of the mind. Nor is the mind itself independent. It has become a slave of the senses, so the soul also has become a slave of the senses.

Whatever karmas we commit now under the influence of the mind, the soul has to pay for them. And to account for those karmas, we have to shift from one flesh to another flesh, from one body to another body, from one house to another house. Wherever we take birth, we are unhappy and miserable. Even if you come as a king or a ruler, you can never be happy in this creation because the instinct of the soul is always towards its origin. The soul can be happy only when it goes back to its own source. So we are all miserable in separation from the Father.

Unless the soul seeks its own origin, it can never get peace, it can never get happiness. The only way the soul can achieve that level is when it escapes from the clutches of the mind. And the mind also will only come to its own source when it abstains from the senses. But since the mind is fond of pleasure, unless the mind gets a better pleasure than the sensual pleasures, it refuses to leave the worldly pleasures.

The Lord has kept the better pleasure within every one of us, irrespective of caste, creed or colour, here at the eye centre. That better pleasure has been referred to by so many mystics in so many ways. When we are able to withdraw our mind from these senses, with the help of simran and dhyan, and come back to the eye centre and attach the mind to that better pleasure, which is far superior to the pleasures of the senses, then the mind refuses to go back to the senses. But unless you give the mind a better pleasure than the sensual pleasures, it refuses to leave the sensual pleasures. And the Lord has kept that better pleasure within every one of us. When we are in touch with that word or logos or name, that spirit, that holy ghost – Christ has referred to it using these four or five terms – then we experience its light. We experience that inner silent music, and the mind gets absorbed in that light, in that music, which is much more absorbing than the sensual pleasures. With the help of that, the mind comes to its own source, Trikuti, and the soul gets released from the mind. At that point all coverings are removed from the soul, and then the soul shines; it becomes whole, it becomes worthy to become one with the Father.

So only with the help of meditation can we achieve or reach to that level of consciousness where the soul gets released from the clutches of the mind, where the soul becomes whole, where the soul shines and there are no longer any wrappings on the soul. Then these karmas which we have been collecting for ages from previous births all become ineffective because they are attached only to the mind – but the soul is no longer a slave of the mind. Now the soul controls the mind and the mind controls the senses.

With the help of bhajan or meditation, we have to reverse the whole process. Now the senses control the mind and the mind controls the soul. But with the help of bhajan or meditation, the soul controls the mind and the mind controls the senses. Only then can the soul go back to its own source. That is the advantage of bhajan.

208 *What qualifies as meditation? Does spiritual reading, and then thinking on the truths represented by the writings, qualify as part of meditation?*

No. Meditation is giving proper time to the practice as taught by the masters. But all the other things help us prepare for meditation. Reading Sant Mat literature helps to remove our doubts; it creates devotion and faith in us and builds an atmosphere of meditation around us. It helps in that way. It is a means, not the end in itself. The real meditation is the time that we devote to our usual daily practice. That is real meditation.

All of these things definitely help us. They lead towards this thing, as does seva, as I explained earlier in the morning.

But the main thing is that we should have no doubts in us. We should sit for meditation with an absolutely relaxed mind, and not with any excitement or doubts. All these group meetings, the reading of the literature and getting our doubts cleared, all help us to build that atmosphere of meditation around us.

COME TO THE EYE CENTRE

209 How can we start to meditate? How can we learn it if we have never done it before? We have to start at one point, but how?

As I have just explained, the soul and mind are knotted together here, at the eye centre. All our thoughts are spread into the whole world, coming from here and running out through the nine apertures of the body. Sometimes we think about our friends, about our country, about our children and so forth.

Your mind is not concentrated at its headquarters even when you shut yourself in a room. It is always running out. You are constantly thinking about something or another. And whatever you are thinking about, you are also contemplating on its form. If you think about your friend, your friend appears before you. The objects and faces about which we are always thinking, we are also visualizing their forms at the same time.

Consciously or unconsciously, we are getting attached to those objects and those faces, so much so that even at night we start dreaming about them. At the time of our death all these forms appear before us like on a cinema screen. And then these attachments pull us down to their own level. What created this attachment in us? Our constant thinking about and contemplating on those forms.

Saints therefore advise us that since we are already in the habit of thinking and contemplating, instead of on these forms, try to think of and contemplate on the name of the Lord. Thinking about the Lord means repeating the name of the Lord with the attention here, at the eye centre. The Lord has no particular name at all. All these names have been given by us out of our own love and devotion. The relationship of the mother with her child is that of love, not words. Words only express her love for the child. She can call her child by any name. Her relationship is that of love, not of words. Similarly, the devotees of the Lord have referred to him by so many names. Actually, the Lord has no name at all. So you can refer to him by any name, out of your love and devotion, keeping your attention here, at the eye centre. In fact, it is the attention that is to do the repeating. Thus you will be able to withdraw your consciousness back again to the eye centre. That is the first step in meditation.

As I have told you, the eye centre is the door which you have to knock on and open before you can get in. As Christ said, knock and it shall be opened unto you.[29] So we have to withdraw our consciousness by constantly repeating the name of the Lord, by keeping our mind still here at the eye centre, the third eye. That is how we knock at the door, and when we knock, the door opens. And then we find the real path on which we have to travel to go back to the Father. That path is shabd and nam. But you cannot follow that path unless you open this door.

So the first step in meditation which you eventually have to learn is to still your mind here at the eye centre and to withdraw your consciousness to the eye centre. Beyond that, there is only one path that leads to the Father: You have to hear that sound and see that light. The soul has two faculties, the power to see and the power to hear. The soul will hear that sound and see the light of that sound. Call it sound, call it word, call it truth, call it spirit. It all comes to the same thing. You can only achieve all that when you are able to concentrate at the eye centre with love and devotion. This is the first step which you have to learn in meditation.

210 Why do the older forms of yoga require the cultivation of the lower bodily centres?

Brother, yoga, as we take it to be today, is something different from the teachings of the saints. I should say the teachings of the saints are the real yoga. Yoga means something which unites your soul to the Lord. It really means 'union'. But some yogis, as I call them, rather than do the real yoga, try to make progress from the lower centres upwards to the eye centre, and then think of going higher up. If you are in the middle of a hill and you would like to reach the top, you would not like to come back to the bottom and start from there to reach the top; you would like to make a start from the middle upward. We are all sitting here, in the eye centre. This is the seat of the soul and mind knotted together. If you forget anything and you want to think about it, recall it, your hands automatically touch your forehead. This is the headquarters which has to do with our thoughts – this is the thinking centre. The saints say that from here we should try to go up rather than first draw our attention down to the lower centres and then again slowly take it from there to the eye centre, which is already our headquarters. Why not just concentrate here and go up with the help of the sound?

Sant Mat, the teaching of the saints, is quite different from those of the so-called yogis, who try to come back to the lower centres instead of taking the attention up from its present headquarters. Some saints have described those centres so that the yogis may not think that the saints do not know about these centres. Soami Ji, Kabir Sahib, Guru Nanak and many others have described them; but all the same they advise us not to get entangled in these centres. We have to rise above them eventually, so why waste time in going down to them and perhaps even getting stuck there and forgetting our goal? Nothing is gained thereby. Besides, even if we do not get deceived and detained at the lower centres, which is unlikely, why take that chance and waste precious time? In this modern world, when our life span is so short and we are so absorbed in this world, in our struggle for existence, we would never be able to achieve our goal if we started from the lower centres.

211 *Is there a centre in the solar plexus as well? Through reading various philosophies I find that some of them seem to say that a centre of subconscious feeling is there in the solar plexus, and the yogis talk about the solar plexus chakra?*

They start from the lowest chakra in the physical body and try to go up slowly and slowly by passing through the various chakras below the eye centre. However, the saints have modified the process so that we need not go through all the lower chakras of the physical body. Our thinking centre in the body is the eye centre, and this is the seat of the mind and the soul in our conscious state. From here we have to go up. Supposing you are in the middle of a hill and wish to reach the top. Would you like to go to the foot of the hill first and then climb upward or go straight up from where you are? You are already at the eye centre. Why not go up from here rather than go down to the solar plexus and then cover the arduous journey upward?

We have just to concentrate here, at the eye centre. When our thoughts are running out from this place, we have to bring them back and try to hold our thoughts here, keep our consciousness here, and from here our spiritual journey begins. We need not bother to go down and then again come up to the starting point.

212 *If a person meditates according to the raja yoga method, it seems that forces could be aroused, as I have heard, by the kundalini rising within an individual, and he could find himself in certain difficulties. Is that why the raja yoga approach is not so safe?*

Brother, I would not like to comment on any other method of meditation. But let me tell you that in modern times it is very difficult to follow these yogas, or to try to awaken the kundalini. You cannot control it. We have neither that health nor that energy nor that time to do these yogas in this modern age, nor are there practical guides who can help us on that path. They are more or less a thing of the past, I would say. By raising the kundalini within you, what you will get is power or control of the mind to perform some supernatural things – that is all; nothing else. For example, you will be able to make your body so light that you can fly, but to what purpose? You have planes to fly over thousands of miles. There is absolutely no use in dabbling in these things at all. We have to do spiritual practice for spiritual advancement, for having the real bliss and real love of the Lord. That is the purpose.

With these other methods, sometimes the ego sprouts in us: "I can do this; I can do that." But with spiritual practices, we learn to digest the Lord's grace and humility comes to us. The more humble we become, the more he gives us. The more we get from him, the more we digest and the more humble we become. But in these other practices we generally become egoistic, and this takes us far away from our destination. We have to develop our mind. We have to develop our spiritual consciousness. We have to come to that stage nearer to the Lord so that we can merge into that divine will, that divine light, that divine music and get real peace and happiness within.

> I was referring to the type of yoga by which a person concentrates here, and my thinking has always been that if a person concentrates between the eyebrows, the kundalini will automatically arise.

No, with this practice we do not arouse the kundalini at all. We are unconscious of the body. We are not conscious of any organ of the body at all when we start spiritual practice. We do not even feel that we are in a body, what to say of arousing the kundalini. We have a split consciousness, so we feel that our body is somebody else's body moving about or sitting – we are the onlookers. This spiritual practice that I am trying to explain, this surat shabd yoga as we call it, or Sant Mat, or attaching ourselves to that divine power or shabd or nam, has absolutely nothing to do with the kundalini, which is aroused at one of the lowest centres in the body. Our concentration starts above this; in fact, we start at the highest centre in the body, which is the eye centre.

213 *You spoke of concentrating between the two eyes. The Zen masters say to concentrate the consciousness at the lower abdomen. And for them it seems to work.*

I understand what you mean. When you are at the middle of a hill and you want to go to the top of the hill, you don't come down first and then try to go up. You start from where you are and try to get to the top. In this body we are here, at the eye centre. If you forget anything, if you want to recollect anything, automatically your hand comes to this point in the forehead. This place has something to do with our thinking. This is our thinking centre. From here our attention goes out into the world. So why start at the lower chakras, bringing the attention down to all those chakras and then going up? This would all be wasted effort. Right from here we should go up.

We should be able to withdraw the consciousness back to the eye centre, where we are, and right from here we should try to go up. Vedanta does not say you should go to the lower chakras at all. There are some schools of thought that tell us to start from the bottom. There are many schools of thought, but the saints tell us to start right here, from the eye centre upwards, rather than first coming down and then trying to go up.

214 *In the case of meditation, if a person concentrates between the eyebrows, let us say a person had one of these mantras, he repeats the mantra and suddenly drops it and holds the mind in blank – I am not thinking of satsangi territory – does one hold the mind in blank after repeating the mantra, or does one keep it in a circle going continuously?*

Brother, the first thing is that you should always ask your own master what you are supposed to do. But since you are asking me, I would like to comment, but I would not like to put you off from what you are already doing. You see, we should try to repeat the mantra while keeping or holding our attention here, between the eyes, in the darkness, and we have also to visualize our master's form, because our mind will not stick here unless there is something to hold on to. So we contemplate on the form of the master and repeat that mantra, and then only, slowly and slowly, do we withdraw to the eye centre. It is a constant struggle with the mind. You do it, and your mind will forget it; again you do it and your mind forgets it again. When you make a habit of concentration, then automatically your mind will come back to this point.

Concentration and meditation?

Meditation is a general word or term. It covers everything which concerns what we do for our spiritual progress. It has three parts: simran, dhyan and dhun. Simran means the repetition of the holy words. The purpose of it is to withdraw the attention currents up to the eye centre. Dhyan is contemplating on the form of the master in order to hold our thoughts at the eye centre. And dhun is shabd or word or logos, with the help of which we have to go up. So everything is included in meditation. All this, combined, is known as bhajan in Hindi, or 'meditation' in English, which actually means devotion to the Lord. Whatever practice we do to develop this devotion, that is meditation.

215 *What is the difference between stilling the mind and blanking the mind?*

There is a great difference. If you try to blank your mind, it will never stay there; it will run out again. That is why I use the phrase, "when we are attached, we are automatically detached." When we are attached, the question of blanking does not arise. We have something to hold us there, and that is the shabd. Blanking can only be if we have nothing to hold us there. That is detaching by austerities, by discipline, and there is nothing to hold our attention there, but we are trying to withdraw from the world. That is a very temporary phase, after which the mind will react and rebound with even greater force.

What is blanking?

Blanking means negative thinking: "I do not want this; I do not think about this; I do not think about anything; now I am blank; there is nothing in me."

What if this happens automatically? Where is one's mind?

You will be conscious only of what you are thinking, so your mind can never be blank. It never sticks here, at the eye centre, but runs out with one excuse or another. We only change the direction, the subject of thinking. The mind is never blank. If a river is flowing and you put in a dam, how long will you hold it back? When the water accumulates to such an extent that the dam can no longer hold it, the dam breaks, the water flows beyond the banks and even causes destruction. But if you put in a dam and divert the channel of the river, the dam is complete and permanent, and the water flows in a different direction. When we are blanking, we are actually putting up a dam without giving our mind another outlet. We think we can control the mind by putting up a dam, by withdrawing from the world, by withdrawing all thinking, by not letting our mind go to the senses. But this is just another way of suppression, a negative way of trying to hold the mind there, and a temporary measure at that.

Only attachment creates detachment. Detachment does not create any attachment. When we try to hold the mind blank and do not give it another direction in which to flow, we think we have conquered it. But when it is suppressed too much, it reacts with even more vigour. The method of Sant Mat or the philosophy of the saints differs in that we have to attach our mind to a better object than the sensual pleasures. And that better object, the word, the logos, the sound current or whatever name you give it, is here, at the eye centre. We have to withdraw our attention up to this point, concentrate it here and attach it to that sound. That attachment will automatically detach us.

216 *This gentleman says that he's absolutely sure that all beings in this world are totally impregnated with the divine presence. He has made a very thorough investigation,*

and he believes also that only a master can help us, and if he is between God and us we are able to withdraw our consciousness inside. This gentleman says that he's making a sort of pilgrimage to come here. But he would like to know, when you speak about the third eye, what you think about concentration on other centres below the level of the eyes, because many other people speak about that kind of concentration, particularly on the region of the heart. He thinks that through the region of the heart, there could be an interesting path to follow. So, he asks, is it possible to attain God and to withdraw the conscious-ness either through the heart or through the third eye?

I have followed your question, brother. I'll try to explain. In our body, the seat of the soul and mind is here at the eye cen-tre. If you forget anything and you want to remember it, you automatically come to this point, you strike this point on your forehead. You do not strike the heart or any other part of the body. Saints advise us that because we are already at the mid-dle of a hill and we want to go to the top of the hill, it would not be advisable first to come down, then to go up. Right from here, we should see that our mind doesn't come down at all. And whatever consciousness has already spread, we should try to withdraw it to the eye centre and hold it there, and not let it come down to the senses at all. And then from there upward, we can go very easily.

There are many schools of thought which people follow to come back to the eye centre. Some people want to come to the heart centre first and then go upward. Some people concentrate on the lower chakras, lower centres. They also want to come to the eye centre and then go upwards. So for coming to this third eye, there are many schools of thought, many ways of doing things, I would say. But from here onward there is only one way and that way is through the divine sound and divine light. There's no other way at all. Saints advise us that it is easiest for us to concentrate at the eye centre because we are already here at the eye centre. Whenever we forget anything and want to remember, automatically our hand comes to this point. So it is easier to concentrate here at the eye centre rather than concentrate first at the heart centre and then try to come back to the eye centre. Because ultimately, from the eye centre we have to go upward. That is why saints advise us not to concentrate on the lower centres, such as the heart. We should try to concentrate here at the eye centre because we are already at the middle of the hill and we want to go to the top. We would not like to come to the bottom first, and then try to go to the top.

217 Is the pineal gland the third eye?

Yes, that is right. But the third eye itself is not a physical part of the body. If you dissect the body, you will not find it.

218 Am I right in my perception that just as the soul and the mind have no actual location in the human body, the third eye also has no particular location?

Yes. Just as we see everything in this world through the physical eyes, so we call whatever faculty with which we see within the third eye. There is no particular location. It is explained at the time of initiation that you do not have to find any particular spot at which to concentrate. You just have to keep your mind here in the darkness, and being here, you have to do simran; then you automatically will be there. There is no particular spot. It is just that faculty which sees that light – in India we call it *nirat*. Because it is a function of an eye to see, we call it a third eye.

Maharaj Ji, what I meant to ask was: Suppose a surgeon performed a post-mortem examination on the human body ...

He won't find any gland there; you certainly won't find any third eye there. Otherwise it would be very simple to operate on it and open it.

219 *Maharaj Ji, what does it mean when without any effort we are behind the eyes? What does it mean to be behind the eyes?*

When you close your eyes, you are automatically within. Our thinking centre, the third eye, or the single eye as it is referred to in the Bible, is just in the centre behind the eyes. But it is not physical. There is nothing physical about it. You just close the eyes and you automatically will be behind the eyes, when you have fully concentrated at the eye centre. That is what I mean.

Since you point to this spot, is that here, about the middle of the eyebrows?

I would like to make it clear: You should not try to find any particular point within yourself. You should not physically try to invert, pull or stretch your eyes or focus them on any particular point. In this way you are liable to harm your eyes. There is no particular point on which you have to focus. When you close your eyes, you see darkness. You feel you are in this darkness. Mentally, keep your attention in this darkness and do the simran with the attention of the mind. Do not try to find that you are at the centre of the forehead or that you are to the right or to the left of the forehead. You cannot physically find that point inside. It has nothing to do with these physical eyes. You are just to close your eyes, and when you close your eyes you will automatically be behind your eyes in this darkness. It is natural. Just keep your attention there and do the simran. Mentally keep concentrating in the darkness and do not try to follow anything. Do not try to pursue anything. You are only to keep your attention mentally in the darkness and do simran.

220 *Maharaj Ji, in meditation, we are enjoined to use the power of the soul to both hear the sound and see the light. Are these the same?*

We have to withdraw back our consciousness at this eye centre. Then we have a single eye. Now, in this world, we are seeing with two eyes. So we are a victim of duality. When we withdraw back behind these two eyes, we open that single eye – the third eye, as you call it – only then does our soul see that light. Actually, there is nothing but light here, but we don't concentrate to that point where we can see that light. When we withdraw our soul, our consciousness, back to that eye centre, then we see that light, then we hear that sound. So ultimately it is the same thing. The soul hears the sound, the soul sees the light, but they are just different aspects of the soul. You are one; the soul is one. The soul sees, the soul hears, inside.

221 *Maharaj Ji, does meeting the Lord in every sense other than Sant Mat infer a spiritual insight?*

Why 'other than Sant Mat'? That too requires spiritual insight. Why not? How else can we see the Lord except through spiritual insight, through that inner eye, the single or third eye? That is spiritual insight, when we have opened that inner eye. It is only with the inner eye that we can see the Lord. He cannot be seen with the physical eyes.

222 *Could you say what concentration is? Some have called*
it letting go, while it is also regarded as a kind of intensi-
fication of effort.

Concentration is stilling your mind at the eye centre. The real
concentration is to be here at the eye centre because this is the
seat of the soul and mind knotted together. From here our
consciousness spreads into the whole world through the nine
apertures. To withdraw the attention to the eye centre, to still
the mind, that is concentration. Real concentration can only
be when you are here at the third eye. Be still, still your mind
and be with God. Only then can we be with the Father, can
we be on the path which leads back to the Father. So we have
to still that mind. We have to withdraw our attention back to
this eye centre.

SIMRAN, DHYAN AND BHAJAN

223 *Could you explain to me about doing simran with love*
and devotion? To me these are just words, and I don't
understand what they mean.

Put your whole mind in these words; you will automatically
feel the love and devotion. Let no other thought come in your
mind. Let the whole of yourself, the whole of your mind, be
in the simran. Love comes automatically. The idea is that love
creates faith, and faith helps us to practice. If we love someone,
we naturally develop faith in him, and if we have faith in him,
naturally we always like to follow his advice. So if we have love
for the master, love for the teachings, faith will come in us. And
if we have faith that what we are doing is right, then practice
will come automatically.

224 *I'm a little afraid to ask this question because I read recently in Bulleh Shah where he said, "My mind posed a question to the Beloved and the Beloved ran away and hid himself." But I do have this question. There seems to be an inconsistency in my mind. When we do our simran to reach the Lord, to reach the eye centre, our mind is active and busy in that simran, but the masters in the books talk about a state of inner silence and inactivity of the mind. I wonder if you would discuss the transition between the simran and that state of silence.*

I'll tell you, sister. We do simran to eliminate thoughts from our mind because the mind is in the habit of always thinking about something or another. The purpose of simran is to eliminate all those thoughts so that we may not think of those worldly things at all — to achieve that silence where the mind can be absolutely still. If, without doing simran, we can still our mind, it's most welcome. If no thoughts of the world of any type come into your mind, if the mind doesn't think anything at all, if it is absolutely blank at the eye centre, if it is 100 percent there, that is the purpose of real simran; that is real concentration.

With that kind of simran, would the mind be repeating the names or would the mind be still?

The purpose of simran is only to eliminate thoughts. The moment that you are there, that you have been able to eliminate worldly thoughts, light and shabd will absolutely pull you, will catch you there. It will not let you remain in a vacuum.

225 *I have a question about simran. The other night I believe you said that paying attention to the pronunciation or to the speed will not help you to gain concentration. I also read that Great Master said that the devotee should*

repeat the names as if one is calling out for the Beloved. I'm just confused because sometimes simran seems to course through the mind very quickly, and all trace of clear pronunciation is gone.

Your mind should merge in those words. Your mind should become part and parcel of that simran. It is not that the words you repeat are different than your mind. Your mind should become part and parcel of that simran. It should merge in those words – only then does concentration come. If you are repeating those words in your mind and thinking about all the activities and problems of the world, concentration will not be there. The mind must merge into the words. You should be in those words, not somewhere away from them.

226 *Can you talk about simran and dhyan and their relation-ship to each other? What are they exactly?*

The mind is never still. It's always thinking about something or another – either about the children, country, work, or whatever. No matter whether you are in the darkest tomb, the mind is never there, it's always running out, it's always thinking. This thinking is known as doing simran. And whomever we are thinking about, their form also appears before us. If you think about the children, the children come before you. If you think about the house, the house will come before you. That is known as dhyan. Everybody is in the habit of doing simran and dhyan. But of what? Those things which are perishable, which belong to this creation. So saints say, try to make use of this habit of the mind. You are already in the habit of doing simran, already in the habit of doing dhyan, but do simran on the name of the Lord and contemplate on the form of the master, just to eliminate worldly thinking and worldly contemplation. It is a positive step. When you are doing simran on the name of the

Lord, naturally you won't think about anything of the world. When you are contemplating on the form of the master, all other forms automatically will disappear from your mind, and that will help you to concentrate your mind at the eye centre and hold your mind there. With the help of simran we have to withdraw the consciousness to the eye centre. With the help of dhyan we have to hold our mind there because it is difficult to hold the mind in a vacuum.

The mind has two faculties. Both faculties have to be occupied: the faculty to think and the faculty to contemplate – that is, to visualize. When they are both occupied with simran and dhyan, then naturally our concentration becomes complete at the eye centre, and that is essential before we can be in touch with that melody within, before that sound or shabd can pull us upward. Dhyan is not a must, but simran is a must. Dhyan is a great help. Even otherwise, if you can't contemplate on the form of the master, you can feel you are doing simran in the presence of the master. Even that will help you to hold your attention at the eye centre. But if you can contemplate on the form, then there is nothing like it. Otherwise you should think you are sitting in the presence of the master and you are doing simran there. Someone is there, in whose presence you are doing simran. That also helps you to hold your attention in that vacuum, in that darkness. Only then can we be pulled by the sound within, and if you see the light, then the light automatically catches your attention and you can go on doing simran. But the real dhyan is when we see the radiant form of the master. That automatically catches our attention, doesn't let it go anywhere, and that holds us there.

227 *If somebody that is very close to you in your family has an ailment, is it incorrect to do simran in the company*

of this person, in order to try to alleviate the pain, or is it the right thing to do?

You shouldn't try to use your simran to alleviate the pain of anybody, but there's no harm in your doing simran at his bedside. It will give you strength with which to face the ailment of your dear and near one. It will not involve you with the other person's ailment and will help you not to unnecessarily lose your balance. So it's better for you to keep yourself in simran. Help that person as much as you can, but you can't use your meditation to eliminate the ailment of anybody. That may not be good for you to do.

228 *Master, I've heard it said to keep your mind 100 percent in simran and feel that you are doing your simran in the presence of the master. Does this mean that we are to feel that our master is sitting across from us in a chair in our room, as he is now?*

Well, brother, what I mean to say is: Be 100 percent in simran, because the mind is in the habit of projecting many things at one time. We do simran and we also start thinking about other things, so that means the mind is not 100 percent in simran. By 100 percent I mean that we should do only simran and nothing else. Nothing in the whole world exists except for the simran.

About the presence of the master, what I mean to say is that first we should try to visualize the form of the master, but if we can't succeed, then we should mentally feel that we are in his presence doing simran. But we shouldn't try to visualize the master in a chair or in his room or anything like that. When you are in the presence of your beloved or a lover, you don't look around to see where you are. You only know your pivot, your object. Other things don't exist for you at all. If you are still conscious of other things, it means there is some deficiency in your love. When we are confronted with the beloved we just lose ourselves in the beloved – we are not conscious of anything else at all. So in that way, we should be in the presence of the master.

229 *We must be attached to the guru, the instrument with which to hold the mind, to direct the mind?*

That is what we are discussing. That can be done by simran. It is a very long process to explain. Now our thoughts are scattered in the world by thinking about things, and whomever we think about, those faces also appear before us. We are sitting here, and as you are thinking about your son, his face appears before you. So it is always the habit of the mind to think about something, always to contemplate on the forms of people, places or things. That is the nature of the mind. In the same way, we have to withdraw from all this by thinking about the Lord, by contemplating on the Lord. We withdraw ourselves to the thinking centre and attach ourselves to the audible life stream inside. We have to withdraw up to this eye centre, hold the attention here, and attach ourselves to the shabd. In this way we are to detach ourselves from the senses.

230 *If one gets greater pleasure from a devotional approach, should one not stick to it?*

Brother, it is wonderful if one can get a devotional approach. The object of repetition or simran is only to concentrate or to withdraw to the eye centre, and this is just a means. The end is to attach ourselves to that sound, or that shabd, that nam inside. If by any other practice you can concentrate and bring your consciousness back to the eye centre, you are most welcome to do it; there is absolutely no harm in doing that.

231 *Master, we are told to apply the test of simran when we*
go inside to test whether or not the mind is playing tricks.
Is there any test we can use outside, when we are making
decisions, to stop the mind from leading us astray?

I'll tell you why we have to do simran: in order to know that
no entity is deceiving us. Mostly it is our mind which deceives
us within, because our mind projects in many forms, in many
ways, and if 100 percent of your mind is in simran, then who
is going to project before you? The mind only projects when it
is 10 percent or 15 percent or 20 percent in simran. Then that
remaining 70 or 80 percent starts projecting in different forms,
different entities, this and that, you see, so we get deceived. If
your mind is 100 percent in simran, then it has no chance to
project in any other form, so you're never deceived.

Does that work on this plane also, when we are using our
mind to make decisions?

On this plane, there is a certain destiny we have to go through.
By attending to meditation, our willpower becomes strong,
which helps us go through our destiny. But naturally the decision has already been taken – you are not making any decision
at all. Whatever has to happen has already happened. You have
to go through that, but now you are better equipped to face the
situation, to face the events of life. You don't lose your balance
in going through those events – but you can't change them. So
meditation definitely helps us. We should do our best and leave
the result to the Father.

232 *Maharaj Ji, I once understood from a satsangi that during*
the simran part of meditation, if an image of a person or a
group or something comes into your mind – say my child
comes into my mind while I'm trying to concentrate – I

can just imagine the child doing simran, or if my mother comes into my mind, I can imagine her doing simran, so that I have every image in my mind doing simran. Is this all right to do?

Even if you don't do simran, those faces are always before you. These are our attachments, which always project themselves before us. We want to get rid of those forms, those attachments, with the help of simran and dhyan. If we go on contemplating on their faces while doing simran, we are creating more of a bond with them rather than detaching from them.

There once was a school of thinking which taught this type of practice – that is why you find statues being worshipped, idols in temples and other places. There was a school of thinking that taught that one should contemplate on their forms and do simran. But then you get so attached to a particular idol or statue that you find it difficult to detach yourself and then to attach to the shabd and nam within. You become part and parcel of those idols. You may be able to hold your attention by contemplating on them, but then that doesn't take you up because then you can't detach your thoughts and attach to the shabd.

But when we contemplate on the form of the master, the master automatically takes the form of the shabd. We don't have to detach our mind from the master's form because the master is going to merge into the shabd. The master *is* shabd. So our attachment actually helps us. But attachment to statues or idols pulls us down – it doesn't let us go ahead at all. That school of thinking taught that to hold our attention we should contemplate on the statue, then we should detach from the statue and try to attach to something else. But that is very difficult to do, and even if you succeed with that method, it does not take you beyond the realm of the mind.

233 *Should simran be perfectly automatic or should it be visual? I mean, one is concentrating at the third eye. Wouldn't doing that and at the same time concentrating on each name be difficult?*

We should never try to find a particular focus or a point within. Neither should we physically try to invert or strain the eyes to bring them to a particular point or focus. That would damage the eyes. We should absolutely forget about the eyes during meditation. We should just keep our attention here, in the forehead, and close the eyes without straining them at all. We are not to concentrate on the words. It is our attention that is to repeat the words and concentrate here in the darkness.

We should not try to see the words?

No. There is nothing to see in the words. They have no form. They are just there to hold our attention in the darkness. If we have seen the master, we can contemplate on his form to hold our attention there. Otherwise, just keep the attention in the darkness and just do the simran. You are not to contemplate on or see the words or try to think about them.

234 *Are the Father's holy names the same as the Father himself?*

Yes. Mystics have given these names because we can understand only with words; things can be explained only with words. But there's no language as far as the Father is concerned. Every language has its limitations, its origin, its time. These languages can't tell us for how long the Father has existed. These are just names given by mystics referring to his characteristics.

We should do as the mystic tells us to do. But these words don't take us to the Father. They help us to concentrate at the eye centre, but the real thing which will pull us back to the Father is the shabd, which has its own voice and its own light. Shabd consists of music and light, and that is what pulls us upwards. There's a door of the house – the beginning of the journey. From there the journey begins, just with that music and light. The words – repetition, simran – help us to keep our attention there. It is that music and light which pull us upward. Mystics can give any names. Maharaj Ji [Maharaj Sawan Singh] used to give different names to Arabs and Persians than to Indians.

Then in a way the names are the Father, aren't they? He's giving them to us.

That's right – for us these are the holy names because we have to do this. We have to repeat them. Their sanctity is because they have come from our master, not otherwise. Words by themselves have nothing in them, but since they have come from the master, they have their own significance and power within them.

Within those names, then, we can begin to live in him?

Definitely they will lead us back to the Father because they will unite us with the shabd and light within.

235 *Maharaj Ji, I have a threefold question, and I wrote it down so I wouldn't ramble too much. How do you bring the attention to the eye centre to do simran there when it has apparently been coming from lower down, probably from the throat? And how do you stop the simran flowing from lower down, where it has been going on automatically for a very long time?*

Sister, I'll tell you. If you are at the middle of a hill and you want to go to the top, you don't have to come down to the bottom and start going upward again. You start right from where you are and go upward. We are all at the eye centre. If you forget anything and you want to remember it, automatically your hand comes here [Maharaj Ji pointed to his forehead]. Sometimes you forget, and automatically your hand comes here to remember what you have forgotten. This is our thinking centre. This is the place where the soul and mind are knotted together. So instead of going down to the lower chakras and pulling upward by simran to the eye centre, and then trying to go up from here, why not go up right from the eye centre? We should not be conscious of the lower chakras at all. Forget about them.

Master, I don't know if it's at a lower chakra, or where it is. It seems that the attention gathers in the mask of the face. I find it very, very difficult – almost impossible – to bring it to the eye centre, with the exception of times when I feel that master himself is pulling my attention up and focusing it there. I don't understand the place of effort, because I'm not able to make it go up where it should be. You said the other day that some of us don't know how to knock or where to knock. Well, intellectually I know that we knock at the eye centre and we knock by simran, but I don't know where and how to do it, and I'm not able to do it myself. It seems like the only time it happens is when it's master's special grace.

Sister, you should try to contemplate on the form of the master while doing simran. If you cannot succeed in visualizing that form, then think that you're sitting in the presence of the master and doing simran. You have to feel that you are sitting in his presence and doing simran. That will help you to be there, and to concentrate there.

Should that be done, Master, whenever we're doing simran, or just during our meditation time?

When you're doing simran. And when you're able to reach to the light, then you need not worry about visualizing the form of the master. Then you can keep your attention in the light. The light will serve as dhyan. Then keep your attention in the light and do simran. That will help you to concentrate there.

> *And then in meditation, Master, should I begin the names at whatever level I can reach, and hope and beg for the master to pull the attention up?*

Just do simran. Automatically that prayer is there. Meditation itself is a prayer.

236 *Master, we're told that if the master's form appears inside, we should test it with simran, and it will disappear if it's false. Why is it that when one tries to do simran and to create the form of the master inside, simran doesn't destroy that image that you've created whilst you do dhyan?*

Because we are trying to visualize the form of the master — simran helps us to visualize the form of the master. It isn't a question of destroying it; it builds it.

> *So it's not negative?*

No. Simran builds the image of the master, you see; it doesn't destroy the image of the master. We only visualize other forms, or think about other forms, when we are not attentive to the form of the master within. Simran helps us to be attentive to the form of the master, and then other images automatically disappear. Simran doesn't let you waver from dhyan, from that particular spot, because simran helps you to concentrate there, where you want to be with your master. When you are so concentrated with the help of simran, automatically other beings will disappear. Because they don't exist for you then at all.

Even in this world, when you are in love with some-body – when you're looking at somebody that you love – any-body may come and go and you hardly notice. You're not even conscious of who has come and who has gone, because you are so absorbed in your own self and your beloved. Similarly, in that intensity of being one with the master, when it's complete, the mind doesn't waver or go to anything else at all. All those forms that we see within are nothing but projections of our own mind – our mind is projecting all that within. But the mind has no time now to project anything because it is so concentrated on the form of the master; it is one with the master.

The mind can project many things. Now we are talking here to each other, and the mind runs to so many places, think-ing about so many other things. But with the help of simran, the intensity of focus on the master becomes so great that the mind doesn't run out at all from the master. Those other forms automatically disappear. All of the mind is there, not part of the mind.

237 *Would you advise us to repeat the names slower so that the mind would be forced to concentrate?*

No, speed of repetition does not make any difference. Whether we do it fast or slow does not make any difference. We should just do it at normal speed. It is concentration which matters here. That is the main thing. You should do your simran with the attention and while keeping it here, at the eye centre.

238 *Maharaj Ji, there are many words with which to try to describe and understand the Lord and the creation, and there are also many mantras. My question is, are some words actually more holy or more powerful?*

The most holy and powerful is your level of consciousness which you achieve by doing that simran. It is the level you achieve with the help of simran that is powerful. No matter how powerful the words may be, if the concentration is not there, you're not able to achieve that level of consciousness and there's no use. So the power lies in your level of consciousness, not in the words.

239 *In some teachings, they refer one to the mantras, the "om" sound, before meditation. We understand that our body has to be tuned first to the sound, which enters the heart, and the vibrations come in closer and we are readier and the mind is easier to discount?*

Sister, that is not a physical sound. When we create sound by saying "*om, om*", we are trying to copy that sound. That sound seems like that, but by repeating that sound, we are not in touch with the real sound.

240 *With our simran, are we really calling to the master all the time?*

Yes. In meditation, there's nothing else. In meditation we're calling the master at every stage, all the time, even to the last moment. For a disciple, meditation is nothing but the master, at every level.

241 *You've spoken of closing the nine doors of the body, but what happens when the consciousness withdraws from the body and goes through the tenth door? What happens to the breathing?*

Never synchronize your simran with breathing. Now you are talking to me and I'm talking to you, and neither of us is conscious of our breathing. Breathing is a natural function of the body, so let it function. You're only to be here at the eye centre mentally, not physically. Mentally you have to withdraw your mind to this eye centre, but the breathing will just continue. You see, the problem is that some people who are in the habit of doing pranayam, breathing exercises, try to synchronize simran with breathing, and they develop a lot of breathing troubles. Then they find it difficult to stop synchronizing their breathing with simran. Or sometimes, due to our associations of past births, we get involved with breathing while doing simran. But simran has nothing to do with our breathing at all.

242 *Master, it is my understanding that simran is what takes us to your radiant form and that the real shabd is not given until we have reached your radiant form. So our primary concentration should be on simran until we reach your form inside?*

Yes, simran helps, and shabd also helps. Shabd starts pulling us, and simran helps us to concentrate. They are both essential. One is not at the cost of the other. The object of simran is to withdraw the consciousness to the eye centre and the object of shabd is to pull us upwards. Just with the help of mere simran we can't go upwards too much. Shabd ultimately has to pull us upwards.

So the simran is the knocking at the door?

Yes, simran is knocking, but then the door has to be opened. Shabd breaks down that door and pulls you upwards – it admits you in.

243 *I would like to know the difference between simran and bhajan.*

You see, brother, the only purpose of simran is to withdraw our consciousness to the eye centre, to hold it there so that we may hear the sound within. Once we are in touch with the sound, it starts pulling us upward. At a certain stage we leave the simran, for its purpose is achieved. Only then do we hear the sound, and only with the help of this sound are we able to go up.

But simran goes a long way to help us to still our mind, to hold our mind there and to bring us in touch with the spirit, the sound. That is the purpose of simran. But simran doesn't go with us all the way. Shabd, the sound, goes with us all the way until the end.

244 Master, could you explain dhyan?

The purpose of simran is to withdraw your consciousness to the eye centre, and the purpose of dhyan is to hold your attention at the eye centre. It becomes very difficult to hold your attention in a vacuum because we are in the habit of contemplating on some form or another. The form of whomever we are thinking about automatically appears before us. That is the natural habit of the mind.

So since we do simran on the name of the Lord, we also have to contemplate on him to hold our attention in the vacuum, because we get attached to whomever we contemplate, unconsciously or consciously. We fall in love with them, so to say. We get so attached to them that we even start dreaming about them, and at the time of death their forms appear before us like on a cinema screen. And those attachments often pull us down to the level of this creation. So we have to analyze on whom we should contemplate, since we do not know the form of the Father.

Saints advise us to contemplate on the form of the master because his real form is shabd. As you have read in the Bible, masters are the word made flesh, shabd incarnate. There is nobody else in this creation worth our contemplation. You can't contemplate on the vegetable kingdom, you can't contemplate on insects, you can't contemplate on birds, you can't contemplate on mammals or humans. So we contemplate on the form of the master, because his real form is shabd. The masters come from the shabd. After attaching us to the shabd, they merge back into the shabd. If we contemplate on their form, we unconsciously get attached to their form, and since they ultimately merge into the shabd, our attachment to them ultimately leads us to the shabd also. So the purpose of dhyan is just to hold our attention there at the eye centre, and then our soul is attached to the shabd within.

So with the help of simran we have to withdraw to the eye centre, and with the help of dhyan we have to contemplate on the form of the master. But if you have not seen the master, naturally then you can't contemplate on his form. It's not right to contemplate on pictures or on sculptures, because they can't pull you, they can't hold your attention at the eye centre. If you haven't seen the master, you should just keep your attention in the vacuum, in the darkness, thinking that your master is there. You can visualize that your master is there, that you're sitting in the presence of the master and doing simran. You can also adopt that attitude if you have seen the master but can't contemplate on his form: that your master is within you at the eye centre and you are sitting in his presence doing simran. That also will help you to concentrate your consciousness here at the eye centre.

The main purpose of all this dhyan and simran is just to hold our attention, to still our mind here at the eye centre. And then automatically, like a magnet, the soul becomes attached to the shabd within. With the help of that shabd, slowly and slowly, stage by stage, we progress upward. That is the purpose of dhyan.

*245 Master, could you just discuss very briefly the role of
dhyan during meditation and at what stage it is most
advantageous?*

Well, as you all know, the seat of the soul and mind is at the
eye centre. From here our consciousness is spread into the
whole world. And how does it scatter? By simran of worldly
faces, worldly objects; by contemplating on worldly faces and
worldly objects. By the same process we have to withdraw our
consciousness back to the eye centre.

So with the help of simran we are able to withdraw back
to the eye centre. But then it becomes difficult to hold the mind
there in the vacuum, in the void. We need to contemplate on
some form or another, so we contemplate on the form of the
master to hold our attention there, because on whomever's form
you contemplate, you'll fall in love with that form. You will get
attached to that form, and that attachment will always pull you
to its own level. There's nothing else worth our contemplation in
this world because the master's real form is shabd. That is why
we contemplate on his form, and with that help we are able to
hold our attention at the eye centre.

If we can't contemplate on his form, we should feel that
the master is there and we are doing simran in his presence.
That also helps to keep our attention here. Otherwise, just in
the vacuum, just in the darkness, it becomes difficult to hold
the attention. So with that feeling we are able to still our mind
at the eye centre, and then we can be in touch with that sound
and that light within. Actually, real dhyan comes when we see
the radiant form of the master within, because when we see the
light, then something is there to hold our attention.

Even if you just see flashes of light, or colours or anything
within, there is something for you to hold on to. Without that,
there's nothing for you to hold on to. So you contemplate on

the form of the master – just to hold your attention there, to still your mind there. Once you start seeing the light and other visions, you don't have to try to contemplate on the form of the master if it becomes a problem or an effort for you. Then, when you see the radiant form of the master, automatically dhyan will be there. That is real dhyan, when we see the master within and contemplate on his form or are absorbed in his radiance there. That real dhyan doesn't let our attention fall down.

So dhyan is not a must in meditation, but it is a great help. Even otherwise, by keeping our attention at the eye centre or in the darkness, we are able to hold our attention there, but we have to put in a little effort. With dhyan it becomes very easy to hold the attention there. And once you see the radiant form of the master, then automatically that form absorbs your attention and will not let your attention drop down.

And during the period that we listen to the sound, would the dhyan still continue at that stage?

When you reach to that level where you see the radiant form of the master, then you are in the master – in the form and also hearing the sound. Both faculties are occupied – the faculty to hear and the faculty to see. We have to occupy both those faculties. The faculty to see can be occupied either by contemplating on the form of the master or by seeing those visions and light within, or seeing the radiant form of the master within. And the faculty to hear can be occupied by being in touch with or being one with the sound within. Unless both the faculties are occupied, our attention drops down.

246 Could you please give us the exact method of dhyan?

Dhyan is just contemplating on the form of the master.

189

Do you do it at the time you are doing simran, and then drop it when you do bhajan?

Yes. When doing simran we should try to concentrate on the form of the master. I have often discussed the purpose of doing simran. It is to eliminate the worldly thoughts, and the dhyan or concentrating on the form of the master is to eliminate the worldly faces and impressions, because it is the habit of the mind that about whomsoever we are thinking, we are also contemplating or visualizing those forms and objects. In meditation we want to occupy both faculties of the mind, thinking and contemplating. So while doing simran we should also try to contemplate on the form of the master, because it is difficult to hold the attention in a vacuum. At least you feel there is something which is holding your attention at the eye centre. Then it becomes a little easier to concentrate. But even without dhyan you can concentrate.

Simran is very essential, and dhyan helps in concentration. But at the time of listening to the sound you are not to contemplate on anything, otherwise your attention will miss the sound. So at the time of listening to the sound, you should give attention to the sound only; but if you are fortunate enough to see the light, then you have something to see also. Then the light holds your attention. But if you are not seeing the light and only hearing the sound, then whatever type of sound you are hearing, slowly and automatically it will become clearer and more distinct.

247 *After having seen the master, how do we practice dhyan?*

Well, sister, it is explained to us at the time of initiation. While doing simran, we should also visualize the form of the master because the mind has two faculties: the faculty to see and the faculty to think. So the thinking faculty is to be occupied by simran, while the faculty of seeing has to be occupied by visualizing the form of the master. It helps in concentration. Even if one cannot visualize the form of master, he can just do simran, keeping his attention here at the eye centre.

Visualizing or contemplating on the form of the master helps us in concentration, but it is not a must. You can achieve that result just by doing simran. Actually, dhyan of the master comes when you are able to see the radiant form of the master within. That is real dhyan. But in order to reach there, we need concentration. In order to concentrate and still our mind, we need simran and we need dhyan, both. But if you can't contemplate on the form of the master, you shouldn't worry about it much. Keep your attention there and try to do your simran.

248 *Maharaj Ji, should we contemplate on the master when we are listening to the sound?*

No, it is better to give your whole attention to the sound. And the stage will come when you'll be in touch with the sound at a certain level, and you'll be seeing your master automatically. Your master will project himself out of that sound, and then you will hear that sound and you will also see that light and you will also be seeing the radiant form of the master. They'll all be one.

249 *Maharaj Ji, I have a question about darshan. In the 1981 session at the Dera, while you were giving darshan, Mr Babani said, "Without the physical darshan, the inner darshan is impossible." Can you comment on that?*

It *is* impossible. You see, unless you have seen the master outside, how can you visualize his face inside? We only do dhyan and visualize the form of the master when we have seen him outside. Unless we have seen him outside, it is impossible to visualize him within at all. Then we just have to keep our attention in the darkness and do simran. That's what he meant. And moreover, you see, seeing the physical form of the master increases our devotion, the intensity of our longing, and that helps us in dhyan. You always try to visualize the faces of those whom you love. You don't have to put in any effort at all to visualize them. The lover always just tries to find a chance to see the beloved. He automatically gets pulled, wherever the beloved is.

250 *The books say one should contemplate on the form of the master but not on a photograph. What, then, should those satsangis and seekers do who have never seen the master?*

You see, we never advise them to meditate on the form of the master at all. We only advise people to meditate on the form of the master if they have seen him. Otherwise, we advise keeping your attention here at the eye centre and doing the simran. Those who have seen the master, they can contemplate on the form of the master. It's not right to contemplate on a photo. That's a lifeless thing that will pull you back if you're attached to that particular photo.

I'll explain to you the purpose of dhyan. The purpose of simran is to withdraw your consciousness to the eye centre. The purpose of dhyan is to hold your attention there. It is difficult to hold the attention in a vacuum. It becomes a little easier to hold your attention there if you contemplate on someone's form. So that is why we advise you to contemplate on the form of the master, because his ultimate form is the shabd, with which we want to merge. But if we contemplate on something else that is subject to birth and death, then we get so attached to that form that we also become a victim of birth and death. That is why it is safest to contemplate on the form of the master. That helps you to still your mind at the eye centre. Even without contemplating on the form of the master you'll be able to hold your attention here. Dhyan is only an additional help – it's not a must. Simran is a must; shabd is a must. Dhyan is a help to hold the attention here at the eye centre. Naturally only those people who have seen the master can do dhyan. How can those who have never seen the master contemplate on his form? They just have to hold the attention here in the vacuum and do simran.

251 *In dhyan, should we try to visualize one set expression or change and see you walking, talking and the like?*

We should never think about any expression at all. Just think about the face of the master and don't try to associate him with outside activities, because then your mind will run out and the purpose of dhyan is defeated.

252 *Can dhyan be used simultaneously with simran? Or should it be separate?*

If we contemplate on the form of the master while doing simran, we will have much better results, for then our mind will have something to hold it there while we are doing the mental repetition of the five holy names. They both go together.

253 *Master, for how long should we do dhyan? Should we do dhyan until we see the radiant form? Is that part of the concentration all the way until we see the radiant form?*

Sister, the real dhyan goes a very long way. First, we do dhyan along with the simran. This is more or less our imagination bringing the face of the master before us. But when you see the radiant form of the master, that is the real dhyan. We become so absorbed in that radiant form that we forget the whole world. We become blind to the world. Then our real eye is open – we see the Beloved. Our outside eyes are closed as far as the world is concerned, and our inside eyes are open as far as the Lord is concerned. That is real dhyan.

Then, ultimately, we lose our identity. We become so much in love with that form that we lose our identity, our individuality, and merge into that form and become one with that form. Christ says: You have become me and I have become the Father, so you have become the Father. My Father has come unto me, and I have come unto you. So we both have come unto the Father.[122] This is the purpose of dhyan. We lose our identity into the master, our individuality into the master, who has lost his individuality and identity into the Father. Then with his help, we lose our identity into the Father. That is the real purpose of dhyan – to lose our identity, to merge and to become one with that being.

254 *If we see the light, then you don't have to try to see the form of the master?*

You may not have to try much because that light and sound itself will take you to the radiant form within, where you will have the real dhyan of the master. We must have something that holds our attention here at the eye centre. But we become so used to contemplating on the form of the master that even when we see the light, we'll automatically be visualizing the form of the master. Because we fall so much in love with that form, visualizing it becomes a habit of the mind. That helps. You can see the light and also visualize the form of the master, but the real dhyan will be when you see the radiant form of the master there. Both of these faculties are to be occupied, and when you are able to hold your attention there, that sound becomes more distinct and then it starts pulling you upward. With the help of the sound, we have to know the direction of the house. With the help of the light, we have to travel on the path. And slowly and slowly we have to pass through those mansions.

255 *Maharaj Ji, a question has arisen several times, and I think your recent illness has perhaps brought it into focus. In terms of dhyan of the master, if you are initiated by a master and he then leaves the world, am I correct that the teaching is that one continues to do the dhyan of the master who initiated him, even if there is a successor whose satsang he attends?*

That is right. That is the teaching. Whoever has been initiated should contemplate on the form of that same master. Our relationship is only with the master who initiated us, not with anybody else. We can get strength and inspiration from the successor, and he can help dissolve our doubts, but we have to look to our own master, not to anyone else.

And, Maharaj Ji, those who say they have never seen their master physically, and then they see the new master, sometimes they say it's very difficult for them, having seen a perfect master ...

You see, dhyan is not the essential part of meditation. They can do simran keeping their attention at the eye centre. Dhyan supplements, helps concentration. Even without dhyan you can concentrate and any form may appear. But we have to look to our own master.

256 Master, could you talk to us about dhyan? This is the first time I've seen you.

In order to hold our attention at the eye centre, we try to visualize the form of the master because we have not seen the Lord – we do not know his face, neither his colour nor his creed. We have no concept of him, and there's nothing else worth our visualizing, worth our dhyan, in this whole creation. Everything is perishable. So we try to visualize the form of the master, just to hold our attention there at the eye centre. And when you hold your attention there, then naturally light appears. The light is there to hold your attention. That is the purpose of dhyan. Even if you have not seen the master, you can concentrate at the eye centre. Just be in the darkness and do simran. Don't let your thoughts go out. But visualizing the form of the master is a great help, no doubt.

257 Is there something we can do to cultivate dhyan?

Well, brother, actually the basis of dhyan is love. We'll automatically visualize the face of the person we love. We can't get rid of that face. And so it's all his grace, so to say. But the purpose of our dhyan, which we try to synchronize with simran, is just to hold our attention at the eye centre, because in the vacuum it becomes difficult to hold our attention there. So we try to visualize the form of the master, to contemplate on the form of the master. Because if we contemplate on somebody else, we may fall in love with that person and his love may drag us to his level. Since master ultimately has to merge into the Father, this love and devotion will lead us towards the Father. That is why we contemplate on the form of the master.

I find that when I try to concentrate, his form goes away, and when I'm not trying ...

You shouldn't try to run after it too much. You should just keep your attention here at the eye centre, and you can think you are sitting in the presence of the master and doing simran. Slowly and slowly we do get into the habit of visualizing his form. And then when we get light, when light is there to hold our attention, our attention stays there due to that light.

258 *I think there is one sect that uses eye meditation, and they stare at each other for a certain length of time.*

They try to focus their attention on one another? I don't know, I have never heard about it. You see, there is an Indian school of thought where they try to stare at a statue, say Rama, Krishna or anybody. The purpose was to withdraw your attention from everybody else and focus it at one point, that is to say, the statue. Then they used to take their attention out of the statue and try to bring it within and then try to go ahead. But the method is misunderstood now; they just try to stare at a statue – they think that is the be-all and end-all of their practice. But that practice was just to eliminate other thoughts from the mind by synchronizing their attention with the statue of any holy being – Krishna, Rama, or whomever. Then they used to withdraw their attention from that focal point and try to bring it within.

That is the same thing we do when we have darshan of the master. We try to gaze at him outside and then try to withdraw all that attention here at the eye centre; try to focus it within us. The mind is always thinking about something, and it is very difficult for the mind to be still in the darkness unless it has some object on which to focus in the darkness. So we try to visualize the form of the master in that darkness to keep the mind still. We eliminate our thinking by simran, and we eliminate visualizing other faces by contemplating on the form of the master. That is the object of dhyan and simran. But ultimately it is to withdraw our attention to the eye centre, where we attach it to shabd and nam. So dhyan is just a means of becoming one with the shabd and nam. Then from that shabd and nam the radiant form of the master manifests, and that is actual dhyan, the real dhyan, real darshan.

You see, there are different schools of thought about how to withdraw the consciousness back to the eye centre. Saints have tried to adopt the simplest way of simran and dhyan. In the earlier times people found it very difficult to detach themselves from those statues. They became one with the statues. They thought they were in love with a particular statue. If you would give them another statue, they became confused. They were more in love with the stone than with any being that the stone represented. So it became difficult for them later on to withdraw from that statue. But if you contemplate on the form of the master, ultimately, because he merges back into the Lord, our devotion to the master will enable us to merge back into the same divine bliss, the same divine shabd and nam. The radiant form of the master also emerges from that very shabd and nam. So that is why saints advise us to contemplate on the form of the master.

259 *Regarding the different incarnations that we may have to go through before we can get back to the Father, the infinite ocean of love, I believe that those who are really seeking shall never have to come back again. Is that true?*

It is the attachment which brings us back, and as long as we are attached to worldly objects and worldly possessions and things, we have to come back here. We have to detach ourselves from them and attach ourselves to the Lord. Then only will we go back to him. It is through the mind that we are attached to the senses and the worldly pleasures. So we have to detach our mind from the senses and the worldly pleasures and attach it to the devotion of the Lord. The audible life stream or sound current, whatever you may call it, reverberates within every one of us here, at the eye centre. We have to concentrate our attention back up to the eye centre, the thinking centre, which is the seat of the mind and the soul knotted together. From here our mind is pulled down through the nine apertures of the body by the five senses. So unless we withdraw our attention back up to this point, the eye centre, we are not capable of treading this path. Our real spiritual journey begins from here onwards, so we must have something that holds our attention here, and we must have something to pull us back on that path. With the help of simran and dhyan we withdraw up to this point and concentrate, to contact the sound that is reverberating there. And when we are attached to that sound, we are automatically detached from the senses and worldly objects.

This is the whole principle of Sant Mat. If we try to fight with the mind in order to detach ourselves from worldly things, we can never succeed. In order to overcome our mind, to sub-due it and to take it back to its own origin, we have to give it a pleasure which is greater than the sensual pleasures. And that superior pleasure, the shabd, the sound current, is right here at the eye centre in every one of us. It is here that we have to attach ourselves to that sound.

260 *Does the inner master control the ten – or eight – sounds below the eye centre? Does he pull one and change the sounds we hear at each level?*

No, that's not the point. The point is that we hear a mixture of sounds, and with the help of concentration the sound becomes distinct. The sound is always distinct and clear. It is our mind that is not clear. Our mind is not still, so we don't hear the sound properly. If a concert is going on here, on this stage, and you hear it from a distance, you can't recognize what instruments are being played. But when you come within hearing and seeing range, you know at once the instruments being played. The instruments are the same. The sound is the same. You are the same. But now you are within a zone where you can hear them properly. So the sound is always distinct and clear and pulling, but we are not within the zone. Our mind is scattered outside, so we hear only its echo – a mixed type of sound. When, with the help of simran, we come within that zone of concentration, the same sound becomes distinct and clear. It is not that the master is sending first one sound, then another sound, then another sound. And you don't have to discriminate one from the other. Don't try to choose the right type of sound. You hear them all. Otherwise you'll be lost, wondering which one is the right one and which one you're not supposed to hear. You just go on listening to it. With the help of concentration, automatically other sounds will fade out and only that sound will become distinct and clear and pulling.

261 *Soami Ji talks about five melodies. Are they the sound current?*

Soami Ji was explaining about the five melodies within. They are actually one melody, one sound, but since it is coming through five stages, many mystics have referred to it as five melodies, five holy sounds.

A river leaves its source and merges into the sea, but it has a different sound at different places, such as when it becomes a waterfall, when it passes over big boulders, when it spreads out and when it merges into the sea. In every place it has a different sound, but the river is the same river. Similarly, the shabd is one – it just comes through different stages. But mystics have tried to describe it in more detail and have generally referred to it as five melodies, five sounds.

262 Can all the disciples of a perfect master hear the sound?

Even other persons sometimes hear the sound within, but they don't know what it is. Many people who have come on the path say that they had been hearing the sound and seeing the light for a long time, perhaps fifteen or twenty years before they were initiated, but did not realize its value. Sometimes they were even frightened and consulted doctors. They would not like to sit in the darkness or close their eyes out of fear of that light. This ability to see and hear within was due to their past association with this path.

So it is not that other people who are not initiated will not hear that sound, but the sound they hear will not be able to pull them up to that level, as they have not been put in touch with it by a living master in this lifetime. Anybody who attends satsang and hears about the sound and light can try to hear the sound, but it will not pull that soul to the level of consciousness where we ultimately have to go.

263 Master, in addition to giving the larger part of our meditation time to simran, did I understand correctly that it must always be done first, before bhajan – or could one listen to the sound current first if it happened to be very loud at the beginning?

Sister, the procedure, especially for beginners, is to devote at least three-fourths of the time to simran and dhyan, then one-fourth of the time to hearing the sound. But if one is successful in concentration, if one is successful in withdrawing his consciousness up to the eye centre, and without any effort he is behind the eyes and hears the sound, then he can give less time to simran and more time to shabd. When the shabd is pulling, the shabd is attracting or the shabd is strongly audible within, then you can switch from simran to the shabd. There is no hard and fast rule that at the time of simran, we must avoid shabd. If at the time of doing simran the shabd is very strong, pulling and catching, we are not to resist it; rather, we have to submit to that sound.

The object of simran is just concentration, to be in touch with the shabd. Simran and dhyan are just a means to an end. We have to attach ourselves to that sound. So if one is lucky to hear it and it is pulling, he should not ignore it, nor should one insist on doing simran at that time. He can switch to the sound. Ultimately, the stage comes when you cease to do simran. You listen only to shabd and you merge into shabd, and shabd takes you back. Then you do not need simran at all, for the moment you close your eyes you are in shabd.

264 *Master, when we meditate with our simran and dhyan, we're bringing our attention to the eye centre. But with bhajan, especially at the beginning, often the sound is weak, and it's hard to hold our attention there. I know for myself, and I've heard this from other satsangis, too – perhaps we don't give as much time as we've been told to at the time of initiation. Could you talk to me about the importance of bhajan and the proportion of time that we should give to bhajan?*

You see, naturally in the initial stages, the sound is not very distinct and clear. The more successful we are in concentration, the more distinct, clear and pulling the sound becomes. So we have to give more time to simran and dhyan and less time to listening to the sound. But since we also have to develop the habit of listening to the sound even if we don't hear anything, we must practice every day. We give less time to listening to the sound and more time to simran. So normally, if we sit for two hours and thirty minutes, then we should give one and a half hours to simran and the rest of the time we should devote to hearing the sound. Whatever sound we may hear, even if we don't hear anything, keeping our attention here, we should be attentive to what may come. And in every sitting, even if we are sitting only for an hour, we should try to give three-fourths of our time to simran and one-fourth to the sound. When the concentration becomes better, and we are successful at holding our attention for a very, very long time, then we can decrease our time in simran and increase our time of hearing the sound. When the sound becomes very pulling, very sharp, very distinct and starts pulling us upwards, then we can decrease our time in simran and increase our time of hearing the sound. There are no hard and fast, rigid rules.

265 *Master, if we don't have time to do all our meditation in one sitting, how should we divide our bhajan and simran?*

I'll explain to you. The purpose of simran is to withdraw your consciousness to the eye centre. The purpose of dhyan is to hold your attention there, at the eye centre. The purpose of shabd is to pull your soul upward. So first we have to give our time to simran and dhyan, and then we have to give our time to hearing the sound. But both things should be done in every sitting. If you are sitting for two hours and thirty minutes, at least one hour and thirty minutes should be devoted to simran and one hour should be devoted to hearing the sound, even if we are hearing the sound during simran.

If you divide your meditation into two or three sittings, in every sitting you must first give time to simran, then to hearing the sound. At least three-fourths of the time should be given to simran and one-fourth of the time should be given to hearing the sound. Then eventually, with the help of simran, your concentration will become better and more complete. The shabd will become very distinct and sharp and will start pulling you upward. At that time you can give more time to listening to the sound and you can decrease the time for simran. This you'll know for yourself. But both have to be done.

266 *One thing I've wondered about quite a lot is the sound. It sometimes seems like I have contacted it, and at other times I am not quite sure. The sound I hear in my ears is ringing, and it is more or less continuous, and I wondered if it is a back echo, or what?*

In the beginning, you will hear that type of sound. You should give your attention to it. It is not a back echo. With the help of simran, when your mind is concentrated fully here at the eye centre, that very sound will become distinct and clear, and you will feel its pull upward.

267 *When sound is heard equally loud from both the left and right ears, should you listen to the right side or focus in the eye centre and listen to both at once?*

In the beginning, it is very difficult to know whether the sound is coming from the right or the left. Sometimes we feel the sound is coming from the right, and sometimes we feel the sound has shifted to the left. It is always better to keep our attention at the eye centre and try to hear that sound. When the sound becomes absolutely distinct and clear, then you will be able to distinguish sound from the right and sound from the left. Then you have only to give attention to the sound which is coming from the right, not coming from the left. But before that, you can just keep your attention at the eye centre. From whichever direction the sound may be coming, you should try to hear that sound.

268 *Master, again, about the technique of meditation. Is it not true that the plugging of the right ear is only until one reaches the stage where the sound is so clear that outside distractions are so nonexistent that one can dispense with it?*

That is right, sister. Plugging the right ear is necessary only in the beginning. When you are able to concentrate at the eye centre and you are in touch with the shabd, you do not need any plugging of the ear, for then you are automatically in touch with that and you are unconscious of your hand, your ear and your whole body. When you hear that shabd and it is pulling you, you are just to give yourself to it, and you will be in that shabd. But the plugging of the ear is the right procedure of practice for a beginner.

269 *Maharaj Ji, if some sound persists louder on the left, and it stays like that, what should we do?*

Give more time to simran. Keep your attention at the eye centre and try to hear that sound. With simran or with concentration, that sound will become very distinct and clear, and only then can you know whether it is coming from the right or left — not before that. Generally we get the feeling that it is coming from the left. Actually, the sound is never coming from the left. So keep your attention at the eye centre and just hear that sound. It will automatically become distinct and clear with simran. And when it starts pulling you upwards, you will know whether it is coming from the right or left. Then try to concentrate on or be in touch with the sound from the right, when it starts pulling you upwards.

270 *This lady has suffered a hearing loss recently and she is very much concerned about whether this will impede her spiritual progress.*

Our hearing with these physical ears has nothing to do with our spiritual hearing. Whether we hear anything with the physical ears or not, we have internal ears which we have to open to hear that sound. As you have read in the Bible, Christ so beautifully said: Ye have ears and hear not; ye have eyes and see not.[69] So it is not these physical eyes which see within; it is not these physical ears which hear within. There is an internal ear, which is not physical, which hears the sound. So whether you are able to hear with the physical ears or not is immaterial.

[Here the deaf lady said:] I would love to hear what you are saying.

That is all right, but I want to tell you that you are not missing anything if you do not hear from the outside, through the physical ears. The thing worth hearing is inside. Give your attention to that hearing. That sound inside will automatically pull you up and you will hear much better things than you were used to hearing outside.

271 *This question about the inner hearing having nothing to do with the ears, is that to say that a deaf person can be initiated as well as all of us?*

A deaf person can hear the sound as well as another person. It hardly makes any difference at all because the ears have nothing to do with that sound. Rather, the deaf are sometimes more fortunate to be in touch with the sound earlier, because their faculty of hearing the outside worldly sounds has been cut off. So their attention is not much scattered through the ears.

272 *This sound, Master, isn't exactly heard by your physical ears then?*

You see, to begin with, you feel that the sound is coming through the ears. But actually, when you're able to concentrate at the eye centre, you will realize that the ears have nothing to do with the sound at all. This hearing is just at the eye centre. But since we are in the habit of hearing with the ears, to begin with we feel that it is coming through the ears. But then you won't even need the help of ears at all. The moment you close your eyes, you'll be in touch with the sound. Sometimes when you're sitting alone – you're not even closing off the ears – you will find yourself hearing the sound very audibly, and it is pulling you up. So ears are not required at all. Even deaf people hear it.

And you are hearing the sound even if you are hearing other sounds at the same time?

Yes. It becomes more clear, distinct and absorbing, and then other sounds automatically fade. You see, sometimes you may be talking to a friend, and outside there may be drums playing, people coming and going. You're not conscious of them at all, because you're so absorbed in your talk with your friend. You don't know who has come to your room, who has gone out and whether the radio is on – you just forget all that. You're so absorbed in your friend's talk that those other sounds just fade out for you. Similarly, when you are absorbed in the sound, all other sounds automatically fade.

Master, when you hear the sound from a long distance, in the very beginning, can you still be thinking thoughts while you're hearing it? Can thoughts be coming through your mind while you're hearing it?

The mind will keep hearing the sound and then start thinking about something else again, because the mind is not still; it's still running about. When you are there, at the eye centre, you hear the sound. And when you are thinking about something else, the mind has gone away from that.

273 *Maharaj Ji, if while going to bed the sound comes, should one listen to the sound, but if the process keeps on going and we want to do simran, when?*

What do you mean by when?

I mean, when it is time for bed, instead of starting the five holy names, you start hearing the sound?

It is the same thing. If you want to hear the sound, you hear the sound; or if you want to do the simran, it is the same thing. As long as you are in tune to that side, whatever you do in his name is all right.

274 *Maharaj Ji, before listening to the sound current, one is supposed to do simran, but if the sound is so compelling, then what should be done?*

The object of simran is to concentrate, to bring our consciousness back up to the eye centre and to be in touch with the sound, the shabd. But if sometimes during simran that shabd is pulling us, we can easily switch over from simran to the shabd. There is no hard and fast timing, that this time must be given to simran and this time must be given to shabd. Sometimes, if during listening we do not hear anything and our mind is not at all in the shabd, we can switch over to simran. If sometimes during the simran the sound is so audible and so catching and pulling, we can switch to the sound. There are no hard and fast rules.

We are told these timings at the beginning when we have to start from 'A' and work towards the end, when we have to learn the ABCs, that this much time we should give to simran, and this much time to shabd. The more we are able to concentrate, we can decrease our time for simran and increase our time for the shabd.

275 *During bhajan, should all our attention go to the sound?*

While listening to the sound, we should not do any simran or contemplate on the form of the master. We should just be at the eye centre, trying to be one with that sound, trying to give our whole attention to the sound. If we see the light, then we can be in the light and try to hear the sound.

276 *When we do bhajan, how can we keep our attention where it should be without doing simran?*

We have to concentrate here at the eye centre with the help of simran and dhyan. Then you have to keep your attention here while listening to or trying to hear the sound. While listening to the sound we should just keep our attention at the eye centre, and whatever sound we are hearing, we should try to be fully attentive to it. Gradually the mind will be absorbed in that sound, and the sound becomes clearer and clearer. Then it starts pulling upward. But when you see the light while listening to the sound, then the two will go together, because their source is the same.

277 *Sir, several speakers have said that if you listen to the sound, that doesn't do anything, that the simran is what gets you up to the eye centre. And they also say that you should spend about one-quarter of your time listening*

*to the sound. If you just spent all the time doing sim-
ran, wouldn't you go up quicker than if you listened to
the sound?*

I don't know why you are confused in your question. There's no
question of going quicker or going slower. Simran is a means
to an end. Unless you come to the eye centre, you cannot be
in touch with that shabd within, and unless you are in touch
with the shabd within, it will not pull you upward. If you want
a magnet to pull a needle, you have to bring the needle into the
range of that magnet, from where it can then pull. Simran is
a means of withdrawing your consciousness to the eye centre,
and then shabd pulls the consciousness upward. So you can't say
that if you devote more time to simran you will make quicker
progress, or if you devote more time to shabd you will make
quicker progress. They both have to go together.

278 *Maharaj Ji? You told us that by meditation the willpower
becomes very strong and also that attachment to the body
can be very strong. Can you develop willpower so much,
by meditation, that you can leave the attachment for
the body?*

You see, attachment to the body will go automatically when you
are attached to the sound within. When you are attached to the
holy ghost within, your attachment to the body will go away.
Guru Nanak gives a very beautiful example. He says: This body
is a cage and the soul is a parrot. A parrot falls in love with the
cage and so lives in it forever. Unless he leaves the love of the
cage, he can never fly from that cage. Similarly, as long as the
soul is in love with this body, it remains imprisoned in this body.
But when the soul leaves the love of this body, then the soul will
fly. And how can it leave the love of this body? Guru Nanak

tells us: You attach yourself to the sound within and drink that nectar within. When you taste that nectar, that living water within, then you automatically will become detached from this body. Then you will not be in love with this body anymore, and the soul will fly back.

INNER REGIONS

279 *Maharaj Ji, does a satsangi have to explore all the inner regions before reaching Sach Khand? Or can a soul bypass them?*

The radiant form will take the soul through all the regions, but the soul of course will merge into the radiant form of the master. The master doesn't let the soul go away from him at all. Otherwise the soul would never be able to go through all those stages. There are so many temptations, so many snares, it would just get lost in the beauty of those regions sometimes. It would never be able to get through them at all. So the master merges the soul in himself and then takes the soul through those regions. We don't leave the radiant form of the master, but neither is there any bypass or short cut.

But does one have a chance to see the regions?

Yes, definitely. Maharaj Ji [Maharaj Sawan Singh] often used to give us an example. Say there are five stories in a house, and on the first story there are only shells, on the second story there are only coins, on the third story there are only pounds, on the fourth story there are diamonds, and on the fifth story is the king himself. If you just go to the first story, you feel so happy. Oh, God, so many shells! You just start collecting the shells and come back, and you are very happy that you have achieved something.

Another seeker may want to go up a little higher, and he becomes enchanted by the coins. He says: "Oh, I was a fool to stay back in the first story – I'm glad I've come here." So he just collects the coins and comes back. And a third is still more anxious. He tries to go still higher, and he sees that he was just wasting his time on the first and second stories. There are so many pounds here – all gold. So he tries to collect the gold and comes back. A fourth curious one goes still higher up, and naturally he is enchanted by the jewels. And then the fifth one, who would be free, goes to the fifth stage and finds the king, who puts a crown on his head and makes him the king of the whole universe.

So if we have a guide right from the beginning, he will always tell us not to waste time on the shells. There's much better than the coins further up. There's nothing in this gold. Try to seek the diamonds. And when you go to the diamonds, he says, why don't you become the king of the whole universe? Why don't you become God? What is in these diamonds? So ultimately he takes him from stage to stage, back to the court of the king, which is the purpose of that guide.

A man who reaches the third stage and sees the gold will never be happy to come back just to collect the coins in the second stage. He will always want to go to that stage where he has seen the gold. But when he was in the second stage, it was difficult for him to try to go up. He was happy because he had found something much better than the shells. If the master takes us to the third region and then leaves us alone, we would never be tempted to stay back in the first or second region because we have seen the glory of the third one. But if he had not guided us from the second to the third, we would have been lost in the second and contented with whatever we got there.

So we are not allowed to go astray at all to see the regions. When we go to the higher ones, we are allowed to see the lower ones. Then we are never tempted to stay there.

280   I have a question about some things I have read about the
higher regions. Sometimes it seems that Sat Nam is three
levels lower than Radha Soami, sometimes it seems there
are …

I'll just explain to you. I follow your point. Actually there are
only five regions. Generally saints mention five regions. But
some saints have subdivided the last region, Anami. Actually
it is only one region. Some have subdivided it, some have left it
as one region. It makes no difference at all. And some mystics
have referred to only two regions: below Brahm and above
Brahm – below the realm of mind and above the realm of mind.
They do not even deal with five regions. But their path is the
same; their destination is the same.

For example, when you go from San Francisco to Los
Angeles, you pass many cities on the way, so you count four or
five cities. Sometimes in the last, the fifth city, Los Angeles, you
start counting the suburbs also. But your destination is still Los
Angeles, whether you count it as eight stages, five stages or only
two stages from San Francisco. It hardly makes a difference as
long as the destination is the same, as long as the goal is the same.
So people are unnecessarily confused. Some say that there are
eight regions, some say there are five regions. Actually, Satnam,
Alakh and Agam are the subdivisions of the Anami region.

281   Why is there a region of darkness before the fourth region?

This is a divine law, and there is a certain purpose for it. After
Trikuti, when you go to the third region, there are no karmas to
hold you back to this creation. All coverings are removed from
the soul. The soul shines; it becomes naked. What is it that keeps
the soul away from the Father? It is the load of karma – the
covering on the soul. So when all those coverings are removed,

when the karmas are cleared, and the soul shines – then what is left to keep the soul away from the Father? That veil of darkness. In spite of everything, the soul can't pierce through by itself and go back to the Lord. That is a divine law. So, you see, the Lord, through the master, takes souls to that region. The soul has no problem there. But that is absolutely the grace of the Father. He brings that soul to his own level whenever he wants it after that. Because there is nothing left for the soul to be tied down to. All the coverings have been removed, the soul shines – there are no karmas to bind the soul to the creation or to the mind. The soul is absolutely light. It is only that veil of darkness which still keeps the soul away from the Father.

282 *Would it be possible to explain the location of the astral plane? Is it something beyond, or is it a consciousness?*

It is a stage of consciousness, a level of consciousness. There's nothing physical which can be explained at this level.

And we only attain that by ...

We can only experience it within; realize it within.

283 *When in meditation you come to the astral world, is there a danger that you will stay there, that you will not come back from the astral world?*

If you have the proper guidelines, there is no danger in meditation. You come back to this world again – you do not cut the silver cord at all; you are still connected with the body. When you get up from meditation you will be the same again. There is absolutely no danger at all.

I thought that when you come into the astral world...

That is what I say. You will leave this body and go there, and again you will be back in the body. As Christ said: I can ascend when I want to and I can descend when I want to.[108] Which means that with your will you can leave the body and be in the higher regions, and with your will you can come back into the same body.

284   Do we carry the five passions with us to the astral plane?

As long as the mind is with you, to a certain extent, the five passions stay with you. You will get rid of them completely only when you go beyond the realm of mind and maya.

285   In Sar Bachan *and* The Path of The Masters *one reads about the various deities that one must meet on the way up to Sat Purush. Are these deities also attempting to return to the source whence they have come?*

No. Certain deities have certain functions, to stop you on the way. They are the agents of Kal, tricks of the mind. You have read in the Bible that Christ also had the same experience inside when he said to Satan: Get thee hence, Satan.[6] Certain obstacles do come in our way – we have to cross them, and we need the help of a master to cross those barriers.

Are these deities souls which have originated from the same source?

Yes. Everything is soul, so to say. The whole creation is the Lord's creation. They are there for a certain object or purpose. He knows best.

286   Were Kal and other rulers of regions ever human beings?

They are just powers which rule these regions. Yes, the Lord is also a power. He is not a person or a man – he is a power. There

215

are certain powers which govern those regions and rule those regions, those mansions. But the disciple is not interested in those powers at all.

Neither the disciple nor the initiate ever comes across those rulers, because their master is the power of that region, the ruler of that region. That is what Christ meant when he said, I will come again and you will come unto me.[117] The master merges the soul into himself and then takes the soul through all those regions back to the Father. So the soul is not concerned with anybody there, with anyone else at all. The soul has come unto the master; and for the soul, the master is the ruler of that region at that time.

287 *Do I understand correctly that at a certain point in the unfoldment we are able to review all the past karma? If so, is it necessary, and/or is it of any advantage?*

Sister, we do know about our whole past when we go beyond Trikuti, the second stage. When the soul gets released from the mind, your past will be crystal clear to you, as if you are looking in a glass. This is possible only when you go beyond the second stage, and then perhaps you will not be interested in knowing your past. You are rather looking ahead, not back. You do not feel inclined to see what sins you have been committing, or what you have had to go through. You are not concerned. You do not bother, for you are looking ahead.

288 *Trikuti is the home or the source of the mind? But I under-stand that the soul has to wait quite a long time before it can see to the third stage. Would you comment on why?*

You see, the soul has to wait in Trikuti a long time because all these karmas have to be shed, have to be cleared. Even their impression has to be erased before the soul can leave the association of the mind. That is in Trikuti, not after Trikuti. Generally the soul stays in Trikuti for a very long time.

Would you tell us something about the region of darkness and karmic impressions on the soul?

Actually this is part of a divine design. Without the help of a guru or a mystic, the soul can never pass through that dark region and go back to the Father. So that dark region must have been kept just for that very purpose – that even if the soul shines to its best, even if it is totally pure, still it may not be able to go back to the Father without the master. That is the Lord's design. Nobody can question that. When the soul has no covering, no karma, when it has become pure, it shines – it has become whole. There is nothing to keep her back from the Father then, because only karmas keep her tied down to this creation and to the first two regions. After that, there are no karmas at all. Then what keeps the soul back from its own source is that dark region. It must be the Lord's design that he calls the souls at his own convenience, with the grace of the master – whatever he wants. But the souls don't come back to the creation once they go beyond the realm of mind and maya.

Impressions are what remain when you get rid of the karmas; but still some impressions on the soul are left – you can call them the soul's memories of the past. But the karmas have become ineffective. They cannot pull the soul back. But still the soul remembers those karmas, those impressions. Even the impressions are lost after some time in the third stage.

289 *Do we ever reach the height where we will not be attracted by mind again, to come down again?*

Sister, if you mean by height the higher stage, where the soul merges back into the Lord, then you cannot come back, because the mind is not there. You leave the mind far behind in order to reach that higher stage or place. The mind belongs to Trikuti, the second stage; but you go to the fifth stage to reach the Lord.

In the beginning, I mean?

In the beginning there is always danger of our coming back. Even from the third stage, sometimes we come back. But after that there is no chance of our coming back at all. We continue to go slowly and slowly upwards.

290 *Being separate in time and space and therefore separate from God, how can the soul have individuality beyond time and space when it rises above the physical, astral and mental planes?*

The soul is still attached to this body. That link is not broken during meditation. You may go to any spiritual height within, but you are still connected to this body as long as you are living.

291 *I was wondering about the sound and light within. Some people hear sound or some people see the light or have an inner experience. At what point do these two meet, where they become just experience?*

Sister, sometimes there is thunder in the sky, and then lightning comes. Isn't the source one? Thunder and lightning come from one source, and similarly that sound and light come from one source. Some people make a start with the help of light; some people make a start with the help of sound in the initial stages. Ultimately both have to go together.

Okay, but say you might catch the sound, and you keep just hearing echoes, like you said earlier, of the real sound.

And when you turn inside and see the light, you might just see echoes of the light. So they just seem like echoes, but I guess they will come more and more together?

You don't need to worry about bringing them together. They'll automatically take you to the same source. You just be in the light, because your faculty to visualize has to be occupied by seeing the light. Your faculty to hear has to be occupied by hearing the sound. So both faculties will pin your attention to a particular point.

292 *When somebody happens to go inside, I ask myself what he knows, having arrived in the first region. I know that it is a change of consciousness, a matter of consciousness. But to those who are already in the first region, does he just appear there?*

It's a level of consciousness. The spiritual development of the soul in the regions is just your level of consciousness, to what level of consciousness you have been able to reach.

But when you arrive there, are other souls already there?

Sometimes we do meet other souls, but generally we don't. It is not in our interest to meet other souls there, because we only meet those souls with whom we have some sort of association; there's always the danger of reviving old associations, old attachments, and your consciousness may fall back down again to the lower level. So it is not in our interest to meet anybody unless we go beyond Trikuti, and then you're not interested in anybody at all. Our curiosity in knowing anybody or meeting anybody there is only here, when you are in the flesh, but there you are not interested in meeting anybody.

You see, when a moth goes to the light, it is so in love with that light that it is not interested at all in how many other moths are there. They're not conscious of each other at all; they're only conscious of one light, the object of their love before them. So if they're conscious of each other, then they're not moths at all. They have one object there before them for which they have devotion and love; they're not conscious of or interested in anybody else at all. You can know if you want to, but nobody tries to know at all.

293 How many times is an inner experience just our imagination? How can we tell the difference?

You can imagine things once or twice, but if you experience the same thing every day, then it can't be your imagination. When your experience tallies with the experience of other mystics, then it can't be imagination. Mystics who have had no means of contacting each other, who have come in different ages, different countries, different nationalities, have all been trying to explain the same experience on the path. When you are also having that same experience every day, then it can't be imagination.

294 When we have a feeling, or an experience, how do we know if it is spiritual – if it comes from God – or if it is a figment of our own mind, our imagination?

Brother, we have all sorts of experiences. We have experiences of our imagination and we have spiritual experiences, too. But you can always differentiate whether you are having spiritual experiences or not. For example, when we are told that we are going to have such and such an experience through our meditation, we cannot call it a hallucination. We cannot call it imagination, because the same experience has been described by so many saints, in so many different countries and at so many different times. Consequently, when our experience is corroborated by the experiences of those people whom we have never even had the chance to meet, whose language we do not know, or whose countries we have not visited, we cannot say that that experience is just our imagination. When it is corroborated by so many saints, by so many other people, naturally our experience is genuine and has to be the same.

For instance, when you read in a guide book how to go from New York to London by sea, and what things you are going to see on your way – when you are on the ship, you see those things. You cannot say it is mere imagination because you have been informed beforehand about what you are going to see on the way. You have read in so many guide books from the travel agent what you are going to see on the way. When your own experiences are being corroborated by the experiences of all those people who have travelled on that path, who had the same things to see, the same things to do or to face, naturally you will feel convinced that your own experience and what you see is reality. You are not dreaming, you are not imagining. You are seeing what you are supposed to see, what you are told will be there. The same is the case with a spiritual experience.

295 *But how is one to know he is experiencing reality? He might be experiencing a figment of his imagination, and it might be a false power that he thinks he has.*

Imagination will last for a day, for two days, for three days. If the same thing happens to one, two or three people, one could say that it is imagination; but not when it happens to thousands. It can be imagination only if it happens just with you or another two or three persons; however, when the same thing happens with everybody, it cannot be just imagination. Anyway, at the time of initiation, you are told how to differentiate between the false and the real.

But how do we know that the same thing is happening with everybody until we compare notes?

We can read of these experiences in the writings of the saints. They have recorded their experiences, and you can find them in our literature. Then you can compare to see whether or not your individual experiences are the same. When the experiences of an Arabic saint, of one born in Persia, of one born in India, or of those born in other countries all happen to be the same, that could not be just imagination. When those saints never got a chance to meet each other, to exchange notes which were written at different times and in different languages, how could their experiences be the same if they were not genuine? When we compare our notes with them, we know that our experiences are not just hallucinations or imagination.

You say the saints have written these things down. In my small amount of reading I have not been able to come across ...?

That is found in all the Sant Mat literature which we are placing before the public. You have read just one article, but by making a research you will find corroborations from at least sixty people on the same point.

Well, let us say I see a house that is purple and it has sixteen windows in it. Will the writings tell me that what I am experiencing is not a figment of my imagination, that that house is at Trikuti level, or Sahansdal Kamal level, and what you find by going to your left after you reach this point?

Once you are on the path, if you will use the test given to you at the time of initiation, you will always know whether it is your imagination or whether it is real. These misgivings arise because we neither face the reality nor even realize the imagination. When we are there, we know whether it is a reality or imagination. Definite signs are given to us. Definite tests are given to us for our use to determine all this. Here and there we may exchange notes with our fellow travellers too.

296 *Maharaj Ji, imagination seems to be linked to belief to me. How does belief about experience interfere with actual experience? For example, we tend to imagine the experience of certain inner regions, or we often interpret the meaning of certain events the way we would like to, and these interpretations seem to be a function of our imagination and lead to expectation, which in turn may contribute to disappointment and confusion. How can we be sure that we are not letting our imagination interfere with our actual experience of growth and understanding?*

But why should we imagine the experience of the inner regions at all? We are never told that in meditation we have to imagine inner experiences. They're only explained to us so that when we are confronted with them, we know what they are and where we are. But we shouldn't try to imagine them or try to visualize them at the time of meditation. Otherwise the mind would be running to those things and would not concentrate at all. We need to eliminate every type of thinking. What has to come will automatically come before you – you don't have to think at all. Even when we try to do dhyan, we shouldn't try to connect the master with outside events. Even that causes the mind to run out. We just visualize him here at the eye centre, or think that he's there – that's all. We don't even associate him with outside activities; otherwise the mind always finds excuses to run out. So one should never imagine those experiences, you see.

297 *If I understand you correctly, there are many things we cannot possibly understand here, because there are so many things on the higher planes that do not resemble anything that we have here?*

That is right, but mostly there are many things that saints just do not like to explain because then we would have to take those things on faith and nothing else. Even if they told us, we would not be able to grasp them and it would only confuse us. These things have to be experienced inside.

298 *Maharaj Ji, can the master sometimes grant the disciple a 'going within' for a moment, for a moment of encouragement, before the disciple has reached the stage of seeing him inside?*

Yes, sister, it happens. Sometimes even before initiation it happens. We have some visions just to give us faith, or to keep us straight on the path. And even sometimes after initiation, before we have reached the stage of going in at will, we have visions, we have glimpses here and there, just to keep us on the path. But through spiritual practice we have to work our way up and then realize all those things. It does happen.

299 *Would you say that dreams are really spiritual experiences?*

Sometimes, definitely, some dreams are real spiritual experiences. You see, in a sense when the mind is tied to the body, it cannot have these experiences. But in a dream state, sometimes the soul just flies, leaves the body and has spiritual experiences within. But you don't have control over such spiritual experiences.

Sometimes you dream you are flying over the hills, flying over the oceans, you are trying to reach somewhere that you find very hard to reach. Many dreams have spiritual value, are spiritual experiences; but since they are not under our control, we can't depend upon these experiences.

300 Master, can we be deceived inside?

Yes, we can be more easily deceived inside than outside. But a satsangi knows how to distinguish the true from the false. A disciple of a true master can never be deceived.

301 Why is maya so incredibly dark?

You see, it's a great mystical thing – it's very difficult to explain. When we go beyond the realm of mind and maya, then we have no karmas at all. So what holds us back from the Father, then? Why should we not go back to the Father at once? At that point only the darkness of Maha Sunn keeps us from going back to the Father.

> The reason I mention that, Sir, is that at that time the soul has the divine light of twelve suns ...

That's what I'm saying. Without that darkness, the soul would shoot back to the Father at once. In spite of its radiance, in spite of its light, it cannot find its way in that darkness back to the Father. So it has to become one with the master there. As Christ said: When I have come unto you, you will become me and I'll become you.[122] We become one with the master. And then, through his grace, we go back to the Father. It is just a divine design, to keep souls separated from the Father. Unless the Father pulls them through the darkness and calls them back to him, those souls cannot merge back into him. But they will not come back down at all; they will not come down to the creation.

302 *When the soul does go back to where it belongs, the person finds that only then does the body have peace and strength that it has never had before.*

What gives life to this body? The soul in the body. As long as the soul is in the body you feel both happiness and misery. When your soul leaves the body, the body by itself feels nothing. When you are able to withdraw the soul current to the eye centre, and it is one with the spirit, you are not in the body at all and the body is automatically at peace. That is why it is known as dying while living, a living death. That's what Saint Paul means when he says: I die daily.[131]

I'm not speaking of dying ...

I'm saying that the body will be at peace when the soul is able to withdraw from it and be one with the spirit – then the body will be at peace. It may be suffering still from a worldly point of view, but it will be at peace.

303 *Master, does each region have its own particular sound?*

Sister, the sound is one, coming from the top of the head to the eye centre. Since it passes through five regions, as generally five regions have been explained by the saints, we feel that the sound is different at every region. Actually, the sound is just one. For example, a river leaves the source and merges into the sea. At the source, it has a particular sound. When it passes through rocks it has a different sound. When it spreads out on the plains, it has a different sound. All the same, the river is one. So that audible life stream, that shabd, nam, nad, word, logos or whatever name you may give it, is just one, coming from the top to the eye centre. Since it is coming through the many mansions in the Father's house, the saints have tried to explain to us, as well as it can be done in mortal language, the different sounds at the different regions or mansions of the Lord. Actually, the sound is one and the same.

304 The sound current purifies? Do we connect with the sound current before Trikuti, or only after reaching Trikuti?

Sister, the purpose of the sound current, the shabd, is to untie the knot of the soul and the mind and to take the soul back to its home. Our soul has taken the association of the mind, and the mind has become a slave of the senses. With simran and dhyan, we withdraw back up to the eye centre. When we are in touch with the sound, the attachment to that sound detaches the mind from the senses and takes it back to its own original home, which is Trikuti. Without attachment to the sound, the mind can never come back to its own origin, because the mind is fond of pleasures and every moment the mind runs to the senses. Unless we give the mind a better and superior pleasure to that of the senses, it will not leave the senses. In order to imprison our mind, subdue our mind, catch our mind or purify it, we have to attach it to the sound. When it is attached to the sound, all the dirt starts falling off and it gets purer and purer.

As long as our mind is being pulled down to the senses, nobody can be more inimical to us than our own mind, for it is our worst enemy. But when it is attached to the sound, the shabd or nam inside, and it is on its way back to its own home, it becomes our friend, a real friend and real guide, till Trikuti. Then the soul gets released from the mind and merges back into the Lord.

When the soul leaves the mind at its own source, then the soul has pure love and devotion for the Lord, and its longing to merge back into him increases. That pure love, devotion and longing takes the soul back to the Lord. The mind remains far behind in its own home, and all these karmas – actions and reactions, good and bad deeds to which we are a slave in this world – they all remain with the mind. That is how the soul becomes pure and merges back into the Lord.

305 When we start having inner experiences, will we see things outside as well?

It's not physical at all. We say the Lord is within in the sense that unless we reach to a certain level of consciousness within ourselves, we do not see him. We have to advance to that level of consciousness within ourselves, not somewhere outside. When you advance within yourself to that particular level of conscious-ness, then you see God. Mystics also say that when you see God within, then you see him everywhere. He is not confined to the body only – he's everywhere, but you have to reach to that particular level of consciousness to see him. Similarly, you have to reach to a certain level of consciousness within yourself to have all these spiritual experiences. The experiences are within yourself, not somewhere outside. That spiritual development is within yourself, so whatever you see is also within yourself.

306 You make greatest progress in the Pind region?

Yes, that is right. You always make better progress in the physi-cal body than in other regions. That's because there is so much misery around you that you always want to escape. And there's more grace and help because you always have guidance. There is somebody on your physical level to guide you, and that same guidance is also always within. So you always make better progress in the body than in the inner regions. But still, in spite of making progress here, we have to stay for a certain time in those regions and pass through them slowly and slowly. It takes a little time to go through them, stage by stage.

307 *Master, when we get to Par Brahm, are we alone with*
     you or are there lots of other souls around?

You have no association with anybody there. If you are conscious
of karmas with others, you will not be there – you will not be
able to go to that level of consciousness at all. You're concerned
only with your master, not with any other soul. And you are not
attached to anybody. Concern is just here; attachment is just
here. That is why we are not there. When we are there, we are
not here. These attachments do not exist when we are there.

308 *Master, when you speak of going within and up through*
     the different regions, does the soul actually leave the
     body, as in the final death state, or does all this happen
     within the body? Is the body itself a vehicle needed for
     this inner journey?

The soul is never disconnected from the body. The soul always
remains connected with the body. When Christ was baptized by
John the Baptist, he said: I can take this body when I want to, I
can leave this body when I want to.[108] I can be in the body and be
at your level, and I can be out of the body and be at the level of the
Father, or in those inner regions. But you still are connected with
the body – you don't disconnect yourself from the body at all.
Being in the body, you have to reach to that level of consciousness.
Human birth is given to us for that very practical purpose.

309 *Well, say I passed on from this body tonight, and I am not*
     very far along on the path. Would I continue to meditate
     wherever I go?

When you leave the body at the time of death, you have nothing
to worry about. Death simply means separation of the mind and
soul from the body.

THE RADIANT FORM

310   Master, do the lights that one first sees – flashes of light –
do they come from the radiant form?

You see, you probably do not have a very clear concept of the
radiant form. Master projects himself from the shabd and
appears as we see him outside. That projection is what we call
the radiant form of the master. He takes that form, the spiritual
form, from the shabd within. Otherwise we wouldn't recognize
him, and any entity could mislead us within. But since we know
our master, we cannot be misled, and unless he appears before
us we can be misled. So he appears before us just like he does
outside. He projects himself from that shabd within, and this
light is always here, but darkness comprehends it not, as Christ
says.[72] Because of the veil of ego and our attachment to the
creation, there's the darkness, so we do not see that light. The
moment we start concentrating, we start seeing that light, but
since we don't stay there permanently – we are there and then
come down – it looks like lots of flashes. The light is not coming
and going – we are coming and going. So the light appears to us
as flashes. Actually there is nothing but light and light. But we
are not permanently there. We just concentrate for a second and
again our mind runs out. So again we are in darkness. When
we are there we see the light; when the mind runs out we see
the darkness. Christ said, darkness comprehends it not. This
darkness doesn't allow us to see that light.

> *When the sun and the moon are talked about, are they*
> *like the physical sun and the moon?*

They are like that type of light. They are not exactly the sun and not
exactly the moon. Those are just examples to explain the type of
light. These things have to be explained with outside examples.

Master, when we see the radiant form of the master, is that the first rung on the ladder?

No. The radiant form is not the first rung on the ladder. You see, it depends on grace, on our karmas to some extent, on our efforts, on our sincerity, on our love and devotion. Even without going much within we sometimes see the radiant form – we find it there at once. And sometimes we have a lot of spiritual progress within and yet we don't see the radiant form. It depends on many factors. Sometime even people who are going astray will be surprised to see the radiant form of the master within, even when they are not sitting in meditation, because master wants to bring them back to the path, is pushing them back to the path. He just gives them the conviction and the courage to follow the path because ultimately he must lead those souls back to the Father. He knows best how to lead the soul.

We call that a vision.

Whenever you see master within, whether you call it a vision or you call it the radiant form, it is the same thing. As Christ said, then I will come unto you.[122] A physical body can't come into another physical body, so he will come to us in his spiritual form.

311 *Master, it's said that at the time of initiation, the master places the radiant form within each of his disciples. Let's say there are 500,000 disciples – does that mean that there are 500,000 radiant forms of the master inside? Also, when one goes within, is this radiant form that's put in each soul the form that takes one all the way up?*

Each soul has its own master within. You see, why do we have to see the radiant form of the master? It's a very simple thing – so that we are not deceived by any other power within. Outside, we have seen the master, so if he projects from the shabd in the same form, we know that we are meeting the right entity. If there is some other projection or some other face within, naturally we can be misled anywhere, and there are thousands of entities or powers trying to mislead us within. We have to see our own master; otherwise we won't get the right guidance and conviction within regarding where we stand. So he has to project from that shabd to us in the same form as we see him outside. That is why contact with the outside master is essential for guiding us within to the level of the radiant form of the master.

Have you heard the BBC news sometimes? How many transistors are in the world, with everybody, everywhere hearing the news? Is the speaker in every radio? How many televisions are watched every day? Are all those actors actually in every television? If this can be possible in this material world, why can't it be possible within – that master can be in thousands of disciples within? It's very simple logic.

> *Now, when we go inside – let's just say, for instance, that all of us in this room are on the astral plane – would we perceive one master and 500 disciples, or would there be a projection of one master – a one-to-one relationship between the master and each disciple, all the way to the highest region?*

It is the individual relationship of the soul with the shabd. It is not a collective or a mass relationship. Every soul has an individual relationship with its own master within.

> *I understand that. But as on the physical plane we have one body master, one physical master and many disciples, is this similar to the relationship as we move within in the inner planes?*

I've just told you, it's an individual relationship. You're not conscious of other people at all. If you become conscious of them, you're so much attached to them. But you're just conscious of your own master. There are thousands of moths on the light. Ask the moths, do they know that there are any other moths near about? No moth knows that there are any other moths near about. They only know one thing – that light exists and they exist. They're not conscious of anything else. Their love doesn't allow them to be conscious of anything else. And if they're conscious of each other, they're not the right lover of the light.

Each soul has its own master within. Why do we have to see the radiant form of the master? It's very simple – so that we are not deceived by any other power within. We have seen the outside master, so if he projects from the shabd in the same form, we know that we are meeting the right entity. If there is some other projection or some other face within, naturally we can be misled anywhere, and there are thousands of entities or powers trying to mislead us within. We have to see our own master; otherwise we won't get the right guidance and connection with him. So he has to project from that shabd to us in the same form as we see him outside. That is why contact with the outside master is essential for guiding us within to the level of the radiant form of the master.

312   *In meditation, if we imagine we are looking at your form,*
     are we looking at you or aren't we?

In the beginning you have to imagine, naturally. You don't see the master within. You have to try to visualize his face. You have to imagine, of course, that he is there and you are looking at him, and that will help you concentrate at the eye centre. And once you are concentrated there, then you will see that light. That veil of ignorance or darkness is eliminated from your way and you start seeing light. And when that develops into the radiant form of the master within, at that higher stage, then of course you will be looking at the master. Then you are not imagining or trying to visualize his form because you are seeing his form.

We are in the habit of thinking and also visualizing whatever we are thinking about, and those forms automatically appear in our mind. You think about your wife, your child or a friend, and immediately their forms appear in your mind. So in order to hold your attention at the eye centre, you have to occupy both faculties there – that of thinking and that of visualizing.

The faculty of thinking you are occupying by doing simran, and the faculty of visualizing you have to use by visualizing the form of the master, because it is a little difficult to hold the attention in a vacuum. So when you feel the master is there, at the eye centre, or you visualize his form there, it becomes a little easier for you to concentrate. But even otherwise, you can concentrate without visualizing the form of the master, just by doing simran with the attention at the eye centre. But dhyan, or visualizing the form of the master, definitely helps us to a great extent. However, people who have never seen the master and are initiated can, with the help of simran, concentrate at the eye centre; but having seen the master and being able to visualize him makes it a little easier. The real dhyan we can have only when we see the radiant form of the master.

Christ said, even so must the son of man be lifted up.[79] That is, when you will be able to lift up your consciousness to that level where you see the son of man, the master within – that is, the radiant form of the master – then you are able to pull yourself from the sensual pleasures. Then the mind does not come downward, but rises to go upward.

313 *Master, when we meditate upon the radiant form of the master and if we make that contact, is that a particular individual, or is it sort of a universal consciousness that we come in contact with?*

That particular individual comes in the form from the universal consciousness – the real form of the master is shabd. The master takes that form from the shabd, but we see him as we see him outside. Actually, that is the shabd. Christ very beautifully tried to explain in the Bible: Now I am with you, and you have no faith in me. After a little while I shall not be with you. And then again I shall be with you after a little while. Then you will have no doubts. All your doubts will be resolved.[127] In fact, he is pointing out that he is within the disciples and they will behold him in his radiant form within themselves after he leaves the body, because the disciples are feeling quite frustrated that he is going to leave them. He is assuring them that while he is in the body they have so many types of doubts, but when they will behold him within, after a little while, they will have absolutely no doubt.

So the radiant form of the master is inside, and actually that is shabd. Our real master actually is the sound, the shabd. Because in the physical world only a human being can be the teacher of a human being, so masters have to come from that shabd in the form of human beings to put us on the path and merge us back again into the same ocean. Therefore, we see the master as a human being outside; inside he takes his form from that shabd, from that universal consciousness.

Then we can be said to be in contact with all masters that ever were, once we make this contact with the radiant form?

When you contact the master's radiant form, he does not leave you – he guides you to the ultimate. He does not leave you there, where he meets you, but guides you to your home.

314 *I understand that we are always to follow the master who initiated us. But if we have desires to meet past masters, as we make progress along the path, can that be arranged?*

235

When you go within and see the radiant form of your own master, you are hardly interested in anybody else. But if you are still interested, your master will bring them along with him. But if they come by themselves, you are not to give them any recognition at all. Just as Christ has said, all that ever came before me are thieves and robbers[105] – we are never interested in the other masters when we go within. We are always so absorbed in our own master, in our own bliss and devotion, that we don't think about anybody else. But if you really want it, it is always arranged within.

315 If one can see only the shape of the master inside, can one ask him for help with our problems, or is this a trick of the mind until one has seen the radiant form of the master?

Sister, we are only thinking about these things as long as we don't see the radiant form of the master. When you come to that level of consciousness, you will forget all your worldly problems. You will never ask at all – you will forget what to ask; you are so absorbed that you will have no questions. Who will ask; who exists there? You don't exist there at all, so who is going to ask? These questions arise only as long as we are away from the radiant form of the master. A lover goes to meet his beloved with so many questions, with so many grievances against her, but once he meets her, he forgets everything. He's so happy to see her that he forgets all his regrets and grievances. He has no more questions left. If our worldly problems are still bothering us, even when we are confronted with the radiant form of the master, then what is the point of seeing the radiant form of the master? The point is just to rise above all those problems – we are not conscious of those problems at all. Master knows our problems. He himself may guide us, but we are so lost in him that we are no longer conscious of our problems.

316 *Maharaj Ji, we may have to come back in the human form three times more, right? So then altogether we will have four different masters. If we reach Sach Khand, do we see four different masters there, or do they all look the same in Sach Khand?*

All masters are the same. They are all waves of the same ocean. You cannot differentiate one wave from another. They all rise from the sea and merge back into the sea. Christ says that ultimately there'll be one shepherd and one fold.[107] That one shepherd is the Lord, and the one fold is all the marked sheep who go back to the Father.

> *But it is said that in the astral region, we meet the master in the same image that we see him here.*

Otherwise you would not recognize whether you are meeting a master or somebody else. You see, our master is the shabd. He's not the body. Through the body, we try to reach to that level where we see the radiant form of the master. But would we recognize him unless we have seen him before? How would we know whether it is the negative power who's trying to deceive us or whether it is the master? How would you differentiate? The only way is if you have seen the master outside. So he has to project himself just like that, inside. Only then can you be sure that you are with the master.

But ultimately you forget everything. You merge back into that shabd. You have no body there. The master leaves his body here; the disciple leaves his body here. The body doesn't go back to the Father at all. The soul is the real disciple, and the shabd is the real master. The shabd has to pull the soul back to the level of the Father. But we can only be in touch with the shabd when we are in the body and the master is in the body. It is he who brings us in touch with that shabd. So when we see him within, we have to see him as he is outside, otherwise we would not be sure whether we are in the right hands or the wrong hands. That is why we see the radiant form of our own master. Master projects his form from the shabd. He manifests himself from the shabd, from the nam within. That is why I said that all masters are the same, because they're waves of the same ocean. It's not the body. It is that creative power which is within every one of us – that is our master.

317 *Master, could you please explain the relationship between the radiant form and physical form and how can we transfer our love for the physical form inside when we don't have any darshan?*

You see, love for the physical form of the master will help us to contemplate on his form and then get attached to him slowly and slowly. And since his real form is the word, the shabd, we also will see him within as we see him outside. Because we are so attached to him outside, unless we see him in the same form inside, we will not be satisfied. Master projects himself from that shabd as we see him outside, so there's no question of severing our attachment outside and not being attached to him inside when we see the same thing. Actually, the radiant form is nothing but shabd – it is not the physical form of the master. To satisfy our love, so to say, satisfy our attachment, he has to project himself from that shabd within. Also, we can be deceived if we see some other form. But with the master's form, we will not be deceived, because we are so attached to him. And if we see any other form, we won't be mentally happy because we are so attached to him through dhyan. So we get that mental and spiritual satisfaction when we see his radiant form within, and ultimately that is nothing but shabd. It is not the physical form.

EXPERIENCING THE SHABD

318 So when we are initiated, what happens?

Then you know the process of being in touch with the shabd.
You are internally in touch with the shabd.

We are made conscious of it then?

That is right. You are made conscious of it and you are put in
touch with it also. A drop of water is on the ground. In the
sun there is always warmth – heat. But only when the light is
concentrated does the drop of water evaporate. So shabd is in
everyone of us irrespective of whether we are initiated or not, but
saints concentrate us, so to say – they put us in touch with shabd
and then with the practice of that, with the help of shabd, the
mind withdraws from the senses and then the soul withdraws
from the mind. Otherwise, shabd is in every one of us.

319 Maharaj Ji, in one of the letters in the book Spiritual
Letters, *Baba Ji writes to the Great Master, "The satguru
is always in the shabd form and is always with you and
protecting you every moment." Would you mind explaining, Maharaj Ji, whether this protection is automatic,
even if a satsangi is not thinking of the master every
moment of the day?*

You see, this letter is by Baba Ji Maharaj [Baba Jaimal Singh] to
the Great Master. If you reach to that level of consciousness to
which Baba Ji is referring, then protection is always there because
you are receptive to that protection. Now we are not receptive to
it. Shabd is always there to help us. What is the protection shabd
gives? The protection of the shabd is to pull you out of all these
attachments of the world and take you back to the Father. That

is the protection the shabd has to give to every disciple, every soul – to keep us straight on the path back to the Father. Shabd has to protect us so that we may not go astray or get lost in the illusion of the world, and it has to pull us back to our destination. That is the protection shabd has to give to every soul.

And we also have to play our part in seeking that protection. It is the duty of the shabd to pull the soul to the source. But if soul refuses to be pulled, if it always likes to remain in the domain of the mind and under the weight of the senses, then how can we get protection from that shabd? So we also have to be receptive to that protection. The letter is written by one great soul to another great soul, knowing what level of consciousness he is referring to. Protection is always there. When the soul travels through the regions inside, it has to be protected so that it may not get lost or go astray in those regions. It has to be kept straight all the way to its destination, so protection is there at every step inside.

This protection of the shabd always refers to inside protection. It doesn't mean that if it is in our destiny to meet with an accident, we won't meet with an accident, and if it is in our destiny to miss a train, we are not going to miss that train. We try to seek that protection for these things, which is just bringing that protection to a very low level. The real protection is within, pulling the soul back to its destination. The soul can never go back there without that protection.

320 *Does the soul first see a glimpse of light, and then the light becomes stronger and stronger, or is the sound and light a sudden, intense experience?*

When you read the life of Buddha, it's made very clear that first he saw flashes of light, and slowly and slowly the light grew stronger and stronger, and ultimately he merged back into that light. Actually, there is a very strong light within every one of us. It is our own consciousness, our concentration which is poor. We come to the eye centre and we see the light. Then our attention drops back again. We again come to the eye centre and see that light; then our attention again drops back. So it appears that there are flashes of light.

Actually, there is nothing but light there. It is our mind which doesn't stay there permanently. It goes there and drops back. The more it stays there, the more light we see, more and more, more and more of it. Actually, the light is the same – it doesn't become less or more. It is our consciousness, our mind which doesn't stick to that point. So the more concentration, the more light; the less concentration, the less light.

Buddha had the same experience. First he just saw a glimpse of light and he fainted. He couldn't bear it. But slowly and slowly he saw more and more of that light. Ultimately he merged into that light and he got nirvana.

321 *Yesterday you said that the way to detach the mind from the sense pleasures was to give it a better pleasure, to withdraw the attention to the eye centre and to attach it to the shabd within. It's also been said that the shabd is the purest of the pure and will not touch anything that is even slightly soiled – such as any attachment to the sense pleasures. Could you explain the seeming paradox of those two points?*

The shabd is absolutely pure, and when you attach yourself to the shabd, you automatically become pure. You have seen so many small streams falling into the sea, and when they fall into the sea they become sea water, absolutely pure sea water, no matter how dirty those streams may be. Once they go to the sea, they become part of the sea, and they become pure. What impurity is left then?

Shabd is just like a sandstone: When you rub a rusted knife on the sandstone, it shines. Similarly, when we rub against that shabd within, when our mind is rubbed against that shabd within, it becomes pure, it shines. All impurities are taken away by shabd.

What does it mean that the shabd will not touch anything that is at all impure?

Shabd itself is very pure. Even impure things, when the pure thing touches it, will become pure. Shabd is absolutely pure. Water in the sea is absolutely pure. No matter how impure the water is that you throw into the sea, it will become pure.

322 *Sometimes when you're speaking about the light, do you mean actual light to be seen with the inner eye, or do you mean a level of consciousness?*

It is the same thing, sister. You can't see that light until you reach that level of consciousness. The soul has two faculties – the faculty to see and the faculty to hear. The faculty to see will see that light and the faculty to hear will hear that sound. But you can only hear that sound and see that light when you reach to that level of consciousness. That is why we describe a different type of light at every stage and a different type of sound at every stage.

323 *I can accept that the human body is suffused with the shabd, but I can't comprehend it. And what I would like to endeavour to understand is: When I am concentrating at the focal point, even though I obviously am not reaching the master within, does the shabd, as it were, come down to meet me and make communion, or is there no*

communion until I actually reach that point within when I am with the master?

Shabd is always there. It doesn't have to come down at all. We have to come to that level to be in touch with it. Shabd is always there.

But until one gets to that level, one isn't really in touch.

We are in touch with the shabd even now. But since we are not at that level of consciousness, the shabd doesn't pull us. It's not very audible. It's not very pulling. But shabd is there even now.

324 *What does it mean in the Bible when John the Baptist says he saw the spirit descending from heaven like a dove, and it took abode in him?*

You see, a dove descends very gracefully, without any fluttering, without making any noise – it looks very beautiful and smart, you see. Similarly that spirit, that shabd and nam, comes just like a dove in us. This is just a myth, an image, just a way of explaining in a very loving way, a very soft way, that shabd and nam takes abode in us.

A dove is generally referred to as a bird of peace, a bird which brings peace. Similarly the shabd, the spirit, brings peace within us. So it's generally referred to as a dove.

DYING WHILE LIVING

325 *Why are physical death and meditation death painful?*

You see, at the time of death we have to pass through the same process as we do at the time of meditation. Whenever the soul leaves the body, it has been withdrawn to the eye centre – only then does the soul leave the body. And at the time of meditation also, we try to withdraw our consciousness back to the eye centre. That is why meditation is known as a living death. It is the same process which we have to follow at the time of death. That is why death is not painful for a satsangi – because he is passing through the same process every day. Actually, meditation is nothing but a preparation for death. We are trying to withdraw our consciousness back to the eye centre every day, and that is the same process we have to follow at the time of death. That is why Saint Paul said, I die daily.[131] Every day I withdraw my consciousness to the eye centre. That is why it is known as living death, dying while living.

Withdrawing your consciousness to the eye centre is dying, while you are living. So both are painful. But if you practice it, you overcome this pain, and then there is no pain at all. That is why the process of simran is very slow. Through simran, slowly and slowly we are trying to withdraw our consciousness from the body. At the time of death, if you are not in the habit of withdrawing your consciousness from the body, the soul suddenly comes to the eye centre and leaves the body, so naturally it is painful. If you put a cloth on a bush full of thorns and then pull the cloth off, the whole cloth will be torn to pieces. But if you remove the cloth from first one thorn and then another thorn, slowly and slowly, one by one, there is no pain at all to the cloth and it is not torn. Doing the practice of simran and dhyan, meditation, is removing the cloth from the thorns slowly and slowly, one by one. Our whole consciousness is spread throughout the whole body, and slowly and slowly we are trying to withdraw it. With gradual withdrawal there is not much pain, but if you have to withdraw suddenly, then the pain becomes unbearable. As I said, if you pull the cloth from the bush, it will be torn. That is why some people faint at the time of meditation, you see;

they concentrate with intense emotion or devotion. In satsang or otherwise, they become so full of emotion and devotion that they concentrate, and they are not in the habit of concentrating. The moment they see a little light, they just faint – they can't stand it. It becomes unbearable for them, so they faint.

If a thousand-candle bulb is suddenly shone into your eyes, you can't stand that light – you'll faint. But if we show you one candle, then two candles, then three candles, every day, slowly and slowly, you'll get into the habit of seeing that light, and eventually you'll be able to see a thousand candles without hurting your eyes. That happens slowly, with practice. Similarly, with the method of simran that has been adopted by saints, we have to withdraw our consciousness – which has been spreading into the whole world for ages and ages – very slowly, so that we do not faint or hurt ourselves or get so frightened that we stop sitting in meditation. If suddenly you see a light or you hear a very pulling sound and you can't stand it, you might become so frightened that you stop sitting in meditation. But if slowly and slowly you see a little ray of light and hear a little sound, gradually you become used to it, and then you are able to bear all that. You start enjoying all that. That is why this method is slow, but sure, and there is no injury to anybody.

326 Master, what is meant by dying while living?

Dying while living is often referred to by mystics. Saint Paul says, I die daily.[131] Guru Nanak also says that unless you die while living, you will not be able to achieve your destination.

You know that when death comes, our soul withdraws upwards from the bottom of our feet and comes to the eye centre. Only then does it leave the body. First the feet become cold, then the legs become cold, then the body becomes cold, but the soul is still in the body and sometimes we are still conscious of it. When the soul is able to withdraw up to the eye centre, only then is the body without the soul and we die.

By the same method, the same process, we have to withdraw our consciousness back to the eye centre. While living, we have to die; while living, we have to withdraw our consciousness up to the eye centre. That is dying while living. So unless we are able to withdraw our consciousness back to the eye centre and attach it to the spirit within, we do not die while living. And unless we die while living, we do not get everlasting life.

327 Can one reach perfection in this life, or does one have to die to go back to the Lord?

Sister, we have to die daily to go back to him.

I do not understand – what do you mean?

When death takes place, what do we feel? First our feet become numb, then our legs become numb, then our thighs and the lower portion of the body become numb. Still the soul is in us, still we are conscious, we are still living, life is still within us. When we withdraw the current up to the eye centre, the soul leaves the body and we say the person is dead. In our spiritual practice we do the same while living, the only difference being that the connection is not severed and we come back into the body after meditation. It is a method of dying daily. Some Christian saint said, I die daily.[131] That means that he daily practices the withdrawal of the consciousness right from his feet up to the eye centre, in order to follow the spiritual path within.

We are not to die physically to meet the Lord, but we have to die daily in our spiritual practice to meet him. We have to withdraw our consciousness up to the eye centre. This is dying while living. Then only will we be on the real path. We are not to leave the physical body permanently in order to go back to him.

If we are not able to achieve our destination in this life but are on the path, it is possible that we may achieve it in the next life or in still another life; but we need not wait until after death to meet him. We have to be on the path while living in a human body, and the aim is to meet him during our lifetime.

328 *In many of the Sant Mat books, we hear of the pain of death. Is the pain of death a physical pain, or is it a mental anguish?*

You see, what is this meditation? It's nothing but a rehearsal to die every day. When you have rehearsed yourself so much on that path, then you won't bother about death at all. When people are putting on a play, they rehearse so much that on the actual day, it's very easy for them to go through that whole play; but without rehearsal, we forget at every step. So meditation is nothing but a lifelong rehearsal to die, a rehearsal to learn to withdraw our consciousness to the eye centre and then leave the body. But it depends on so many other factors also. Sometimes many types of karmas have to be gone through in the body. So that a little leftover karma may not bring you back to the creation again, sometimes it is better to go through those karmas and get rid of them while in the body. Master knows best – we can't make any hard and fast rule about it. The Lord knows best about this.

329 *When we start withdrawing from the feet upwards, do we not have to bypass the lower centres?*

When you try to hold your consciousness at the eye centre, automatically you will withdraw the attention upward, without paying any attention whatsoever to any of the centres below the eyes. Somewhere in the Bible it is mentioned, *I die daily.*[131] This

247

is what Saint Paul mystically tried to explain to us. Every saint in the East explains to us that we have to die while living. We have to withdraw our attention from the body and bring our consciousness back to the eye centre.

To follow those yogic exercises is very difficult. We cannot do it in this modern age. Today we hardly have any time to sit for meditation even for an hour or two. The yogis who performed those difficult exercises in the olden times had to go through extremely rigid disciplines to achieve all that. And after all that, they still had to start from the eye centre if they wanted to go up. It is impossible for you and me to do those exercises in these days, so saints always advise us just to forget about all that and to keep our attention here, at the eye centre, and go ahead. The living master saves us from all that danger, hardship, confusion and delay.

330 *Maharaj Ji, most of the books tell us, or indicate at least, that prior to going in, the whole body becomes numb. Is that always the case, or are there cases occasionally where the person might go in and not have the feeling or sensation of numbness throughout the body?*

We may not be conscious of our body having become numb, and still we have withdrawn. We say we start withdrawing from our feet upwards, and we call that numbness. It does not mean exactly physical numbness. It is withdrawal of the attention, not being aware of the body – that kind of numbness. When our soul current is not spread through this body outward, but is being withdrawn inward, that is numbness. Sometimes we do feel a little numbness in the body, but even without feeling any numbness in the body, we can be 'in' – we can see many visions inside. But that is not within our control. However, when we have actually withdrawn, when our body has become absolutely numb, then it is in our control as to what we are seeing inside. Otherwise, too, it may happen that even before our actual withdrawal, we have a glimpse or experience of spiritual vision.

What do we mean by 'inside'? When you close your eyes, you are automatically inside. Holding your attention within – here, between the eyebrows – that is inside. There is no particular 'inside' that we have to see or search for. When you do not think about anything in the world, then you are here, in the centre behind the eyes. When your mind is not scattered and your attention is concentrated here, you are 'in' – you are within yourself, you are inside. Then naturally you start withdrawing upward and start seeing something inside. That is what we mean by numbness.

In other words, it may be a complete forgetting of the body itself, or any feeling in it at all, rather than a distinct feeling of numbness?

That is right. We are to become absolutely unconscious of our body, even as to whether it exists or not. Sometimes we feel that somebody else is sitting in meditation – we are just separate from the body and we are watching who is sitting in the body, and we watch who is moving about in this world, not feeling that it is our own body. We feel that we are the audience and we are watching ourselves. That is withdrawal from the body. By practice we get into this habit.

When we start withdrawing from the body, we feel the duality – that this body does not belong to us; we are in it and yet we are out of it. Sometimes you feel that there is somebody else sleeping or lying down and that you are away from yourself, away from the body. You are watching who is sleeping. We have that type of feeling sometimes. There is nothing to fear. One American lady wrote to me that she had to consult some doctors or mental specialists because she always felt that she was something away from the body. That feeling is bound to come within you. There is nothing to fear and there is nothing to worry about, as that is what we are trying hard to accomplish.

DIGEST IT WITHIN

331 Maharaj Ji, would you please explain to us the importance of never divulging any inner experience? Because there are so many stories going around – so and so said he went up, he saw light, and so forth.

Sister, it is not in one's own interest to share one's inner experience with anyone, because unconsciously there is always ego in it, when we discuss or share with another person our own spiritual experiences. We definitely become a victim of our ego, and the moment you become a victim of the ego, your progress stops and you lose what you have. That is the main purpose of not sharing our spiritual experience with anybody.

Also, it is an individual relationship of the soul with the Father – it's nobody's business, nobody else comes in our way, no relationship comes between the soul and the Father. No worldly relationship has any right to share that experience – that is just the relationship of the soul with its own origin, its own Father. Why would we want to share? A wife doesn't share all the secrets of her husband with anybody else; how can you expect the soul to share all the spiritual experiences and secrets within with anybody else? It should be digested, and the more you digest, the more grace you will find within and the more receptive you become to his grace.

There is also always a danger, if we start sharing our experience, of becoming a victim of performing miracles. Because ego inflates us – we think, I can do this and I can do that – and things do happen. Because you do have a certain level of consciousness within – in your progress within – and you are not even conscious of your spiritual powers, but you say things and miracles do happen. It's not that you want to perform them, but you have the power to perform them. Unconsciously you do those things, and you always do so at your own cost. So it's always better to remain obscure and just digest within yourself all that you have. One can say, "I'm happy in my meditation" – that's all.

Moreover, you see, when other people know that you are spiritually advanced, that you see the light or are very happy spiritually within, they start humouring you and praising you, and there's always the danger of your ego being inflated by that. They start showing you undue regard and respect, and they take you as a great man and spiritual leader and this and that, you see. You become conscious of all that honour, and the result is you lose all that progress – that danger is always there. And people are always selfish. They will be around you for their own selfish purposes, not because they're happy with your spiritual progress. They want to take advantage of your spiritual progress. Some want a child, some want worldly fame, some want their sick relatives to be healed; that is why they're hovering around you – for their own selfish purposes. They think that they can use you because you have some spiritual experiences, spiritual powers within. One becomes tempted by all this ego and then you lose everything. Unnecessarily people start giving you importance, and the moment any importance is given to anybody, there's always the danger of his falling. So it's always better to remain obscure.

332 If satsangis develop supernatural powers, they are not advised to use them, are they?

If we use the supernatural powers that we have gained through meditation, we do it always at our own expense. We lose what we have gained. The Lord does not bestow that power on us to become his rival. He just gives it to us for our own benefit, to clear our own karmas, to clear our own path to go back to him. If we start using these supernatural powers for other purposes, we inflate our ego and we lose what we have. So I personally advise satsangis never to dabble in these things at all.

333 *Master, why is Sant Mat and the experiences of the initiate so esoteric, so secretive? Why cannot the initiate compare notes with another initiate? It is my understanding of Sant Mat that it is a science of the soul; and any scientist, to test the validity of his findings, would like to compare notes with somebody else.*

Brother, there is always danger of ego coming in. When you share your internal experiences with anybody, you are inclined to give yourself airs, and you lose what you have. Also, when people know that you are spiritually advanced, they may try to take advantage of you, of your powers. Then you may be tempted and thus lose what you had gained.

334 *Master, I know we are not allowed to talk about our inner experiences, but if you know somebody quite well, and one day they suddenly leave the mind behind, would they be completely different then, would you know it if it suddenly happened to them?*

What is the advantage to you if you know that somebody has gone to a higher region? It's just your curiosity.

It would make me happy to know it.

You should be happy with your own progress, not with the progress of another person. You see, we generally build our ego by sharing our experiences with others, knowing that I have been able to achieve it, but you couldn't do it. We start putting on airs about it, and that becomes a stumbling block in our way. And then people can exploit your spiritual experiences also. They can use you. They will ask you for some boons, for some worldly favours, since you have the spiritual power to do some things, and you will be led astray. Sharing our spiritual experiences is forbidden. It has so many costs. You will collect so many sycophants around you, who will unnecessarily go on humouring you and praising you, and you will lose all that you have. You yourself will become self-important – it will build your ego. You have seen that if a crop is good, the fence around it is strong. If something is very precious, there will even be a guard with guns to protect it from thieves and trespassers. So something by which you become the king of kings, one with the Father – imagine how much protection is required, how much you have to guard.

Let us say you give your child some money to do some business. If he's doing it diligently, putting in hard work and increasing his wealth and then reinvesting it in the business, you become so happy that you give all you have to him. But if he starts squandering and wasting the money, you withdraw your hand – you don't give anything to that child. When we are so careful in our worldly affairs, you can imagine how careful the Lord will be that we do not misuse our spiritual treasure. A jeweller, if he gets hold of a diamond, always keeps it in a safe and never parts with the key. He is so secretive about it that he doesn't tell even his best friends that he has got such a precious, priceless diamond in his safe. But if a donkey man gets hold of the diamond, he will just put it round the neck of his donkey. He doesn't know its value. It is the same diamond.

So we have to appreciate the value of that spiritual treasure. Kabir says that after getting this wealth, we should keep it so close that even little fragments should not escape from you. He said people are not interested in this wealth at all; they're interested in worldly favours. They would like to have a child, they would like to have money, they would like to have status and position in this world, they would like to get rid of their diseases, they would like their children to be good; they only want to use your spiritual wealth for these things – they're not interested in nam at all. Christ also said, why throw pearls before swine?[28] Every mystic has been warning us about this.

335 Could you speak to us a little bit about the role of emotions on the path of Sant Mat – what we feel in our hearts?

If you channelize your emotions, then they are very helpful. If you let them loose, then they are just a waste. Channelizing your emotions means diverting them towards meditation. You see, when a river flows in a normal way, it is so useful to the public for navigation purposes, for irrigation purposes, for so many other advantages. But if the river floods and overflows its banks, then it creates nothing but devastation. So emotions are very good, very helpful, provided you keep them channelled in discipline, channel them towards meditation and you don't let them loose. Without emotion you can never succeed in meditation at all, but we have to discipline our emotion and direct it to meditation.

336 Master, if we feel an emotion towards you, should we try and channel that to simran?

Sister, try to digest your emotions and divert them to meditation, to your master within. He loves such emotions, within. There's no need to demonstrate them outside. Love demonstrated loses its depth. It has to be digested, to make a deep groove on your mind.

337 *You've talked about digesting experiences versus express-ing them, and I wondered how we can best digest that feeling of happiness that we sometimes get?*

We don't go to the top of the house to shout that we are happy. We are happy within ourselves. It will radiate from our face. Why lose the depth of that happiness by sharing it with anybody else? Those experiences will definitely make you happy, but you will lose their depth when you try to broadcast them, blow a trumpet about them.

So digest them within yourself. When you learn to digest, the Lord, with his grace, will give you more and more of that. I often give an example: If a father gives a little money to his son to start some business, and if the son is very attentive and is doing his best to expand the business, the father is very happy with him and gives him more and more money to expand. But if the son wastes his time and money and gambles with it, then the father withdraws his hand. So the son has to show the father that he is very attentive to his business. Then the father becomes so happy that he starts giving him more and more, and ultimately the father gives the son everything.

Similarly, we have to show the Father that we are capable of digesting his grace, that we are receptive to his grace. We don't want to put on any airs about it or try to show off to others that we are superior to them. So we digest within ourselves. And then he gives more and more to us.

338 *Maharaj Ji, many of us have experienced worldly love for another person. If something like that can't adequately*

be described in words, then how do we even begin to compare that with the true spiritual love that the disciple has for the master?

Well, brother, when we can't adequately describe our worldly love, how can we describe our devotional love for the Father? Words are inadequate to describe that love. No matter how beautifully we try to describe it, love can never be described. You can't even describe the taste of a toffee; a person has to taste it. The taste of a toffee is different from its description in a book. So love is to be experienced rather than read about or described. And then the more you experience it, the more you digest it within. You don't dramatize your love at all. You try to digest that love within, and the more you digest, the more it grows. So there's no necessity even to describe that love; it has to be experienced. Love, when described, loses its depth – it can only be experienced and felt.

And that is only experienced through your meditation?

Naturally. What is love? Love is losing your own identity and becoming another being. To lose your individuality and merge into another being – that is love. And only shabd can help you to achieve that, to eliminate your ego, to eliminate yourself from within yourself, to become one with the Father. Only meditation helps. Meditation creates love. That is why we say that God is love and love is God, because it is God's nature to become one with the disciple. When he pulls us to his own level, then we lose our individuality, we become another being. That becoming another being is love. If you exist, then he doesn't exist. If he exists, then you don't exist at all. And how can you describe that in words? You can only experience it, and those who did try to describe it were crucified; they were put on hot pans; they were killed. People couldn't tolerate their description.

Mansur [an Indian mystic] said: I am God. He reached to that level of consciousness, but he couldn't keep it within himself. He said, I have become God – and they crucified him. What happened with Christ? What happened with other mystics? So if we want to save our skin, we have to digest that experience within.

339 *Master, you give us so much love while we're here at the Dera, and every day it accumulates more and more, until we're filled to the brim. When we leave the Dera, is there a way we can put a cap on that love and not lose it?*

Sister, have a bigger container to hold the love so that it may not overflow. Have a very big container to keep it, to preserve it. Don't let it overflow.

But is it all that easy?

Well, that is what we have to do; we have to digest all that within. The more you digest, the more you get. The more you feel, the more it grows. Keep it to yourself. You see, love is only shared with the beloved, not with the masses. You don't blow the trumpet of your love for the beloved – it only concerns you and the beloved, no one else. It should remain between the two of you. It has to grow in secret.

340 *Master, you were saying that we should keep our spiritual experiences to ourselves. In the event one encounters obstacles in meditation, should one not speak of that also? Should one keep that a secret?*

Sister, the only one who can help you remove those obstacles is your master. There is no use speaking to others about these things, for nobody else will be able to help you. If you speak to your master, you will get guidance and help.

PROGRESS

341 *Between the totally illiterate person and the highly intellectual one, which of these two will reach Sach Khand more quickly, Maharaj Ji?*

You see, neither intellect will take you to Sach Khand nor illiteracy will take you to Sach Khand. Your meditation will take you to Sach Khand. His grace will take you back to Sach Khand. It's immaterial whether you're a literate person or an illiterate person. The intellect is not a barrier to going back to the Father, nor is illiteracy in any way a help. It's all his grace and according to one's individual karmas.

> *Will people who are illiterate have to take a rebirth before they become literate enough to understand Sant Mat and then make progress on this path?*

Illiteracy is not a barrier to going back to the Father. It's immaterial whether you're literate or illiterate.

342 *We find people throughout history with different grades of intellect and intuition. I would like to hear your comments on that.*

Yes, people can be of different calibres of intellect. Fellow travellers on the path can be of different grades of intellect, or of different stages of advancement spiritually also. But as long as the road is the same, it does not make any difference whether you have covered ten miles or fifty miles or a hundred miles, because if in this life you have covered ten miles, naturally you start again from the end of that ten miles in the next birth, and then cover perhaps another fifty or sixty miles or more, until ultimately you reach the goal. As long as the road is the same, the teachings are the same for us. So, basically, we can try to understand and follow the teachings under the guidance of a living master.

343 *The master has repeatedly said that there's no way that we can ever measure our spiritual progress and that maybe we shouldn't even be concerned with that, that that's in his hands and every moment of meditation is being accounted for. But in the last few years, measuring my progress as a human being, sometimes I get very discouraged, because even though I can see that certain modes of behaviour or reactions to certain things have been tempered, still, when I fall back into a habit that I think is unbecoming or react to someone or am sarcastic, which used to be a very big problem, it's ...*

Sister, we can only measure when we know how much we have yet to cover and how much we have already covered – only then can we know. If you know your destination is 100 miles away, and you have been able to cover one mile, only then can you measure. When you don't know how far your destination is, how can you measure your spiritual progress? How can you know how much of a dent you have been able to make in that big heap of karma? We can never know. But by meditation we definitely know how much our attitude has changed towards the whole creation, our environment, our relations. Through meditation our own attitude changes towards everybody, and we feel that bliss and happiness within ourselves. That is the measurement we can make, by which we feel that we are progressing in meditation. But how much we have covered and how much we have yet to clear, it's impossible to say. But definitely meditation helps us to get that peace, bliss and contentment from within. We don't get so easily upset. We take life easier and accept God's will as life comes. So our life changes in that way – that advantage you can feel, but you can't say how much you have already covered and how much is left. That is impossible to know.

344 Will we gain credit even when we're not hearing the sound?

Any minute you spend in love and devotion for the Father is to your credit. It's a steppingstone. You are making some progress — maybe at an ant's speed, but you are making progress. Any little bit of love and devotion for the Father is to your credit.

345 Is it master's will that helps our progress or mainly our own efforts?

When master initiates us, puts us on the path, naturally he wants us to make progress. If he didn't want us to make progress, he would not have put us on the path at all. When the disciple is able to withdraw his consciousness to the eye centre and become attached to that spirit within, the disciple is happy and the master becomes happy, because it is the duty of the master to take that allotted soul back to the Father. So when the soul is progressing within on its way to the Father, naturally the master is happy. The master always wants that disciple to try to follow the path. When the disciple is putting in effort, the master will not withhold his grace. The Lord is always there to help us.

346 You've said that our spiritual breakthrough is predes-tined. The time when we are going to go in and our effort up to that time is preparing for that?

Well, brother, when the Lord wants you to put in effort, you will automatically put in effort. You won't have any excuses to give at all. He will give you the environment, facilities, opportunity, the pull, the yearning within. You can't help but put in effort then. It's not that you are getting up at three o'clock in the morning – there's someone else who is awakening you. You will not get rest the whole day unless you attend to your meditation in the morning – there is someone who is creating that unrest in you, who is pulling you towards him. We are pursued, actually. But we should try to do our best. We shouldn't try to find any excuses. But when he pulls the soul, he will just pull it.

347 *Maharaj Ji, the other night we were talking about the soul and body and that some people have experiences from various causes, and they may not necessarily be spiritual experiences, in which they feel that they are looking down on their body. From what viewpoint is that, when the soul only goes to the eye centre and then remains in the body – how can they view their body then?*

You see, when your consciousness develops, it rises up and comes to the eye centre, and then you feel that you are separate from the body. Below the eye centre, you are one with the body and absolutely under the control of the mind, so you don't feel separate from the body. But when the consciousness is brought back to the eye centre, and sometimes the soul gets released from the mind, then you feel that this body belongs to somebody else and that you are just a spectator watching this body moving about in the world, doing all sorts of things, and you are something different. The soul is just gaining its identity, its individuality. The individuality of the soul is being developed by spiritual practice.

And then the soul starts watching your own self moving about in this world. You are watching yourself – you are not part and parcel of yourself. You are separating your soul from yourself, from the mind, the activities of the mind, and the soul starts watching your own body. You are talking to somebody, and you are just watching yourself talking to that person. You are moving about, watching yourself as if that body were moving about on a stage. This is the soul separating slowly and slowly from the mind and starting to observe all the activities of the mind. This only comes by spiritual practice, spiritual development.

Maharaj Ji, can it happen to someone who hasn't done any spiritual practices?

It can, sometimes. You see, spiritual practice means that on occasion everybody can rise to that level of consciousness, because we have had associations with spirituality in our past lives in one way or another. So at moments everybody can rise to that level of consciousness and have such experiences.

348 *Maharaj Ji, I've read that as long as the disciple thinks that he is the doer, he has no chance of meeting the radiant form inside; but that it's not until we see the radiant form inside that we fully comprehend who the master is. Will you explain that?*

You see, seeing the master as the doer means that you are so absorbed with your love and devotion that you merge into the master and forget your own identity. When you merge back into the master, you lose your own identity and you think that your master is moving about, that he's doing everything and you are just a spectator watching yourself. Sometimes you must have felt as if you were watching yourself moving about in this world. You withdraw from the body and watch yourself sitting in meditation, talking to people, doing all the worldly things, and you feel as if you are somebody different from the body which is walking about. You separate yourself from the body. This is withdrawing from the body, to some extent. So similarly, if we withdraw ourselves and merge back into the master, then he is the doer and we don't feel that we are doing anything – we feel that he is doing everything.

349 *After one has started practicing according to the master's instructions, what is the maximum time before one should start having contact with the master inside? How much maximum time would it take to realize the astral form of the master?*

The time it takes to make spiritual progress within depends upon the individual. It depends upon our individual karmas, our background, our past associations with the path of the masters; in fact, so many things count in achieving that experience.

350 *What would be a fair test to see if one has attained God-realization?*

A test is always of the intellect and mind, while this is something which you have to experience within, beyond the intellect and mind. Compare your experience with the recorded experiences of other mystics. Then you can know if you are following the right road. And when you see the milestones within, you will be convinced that you are on the right road. You yourself will feel it and will know it.

351 *Sometimes it seems that even with a lot of effort and determination, still it is impossible to keep from thinking and speaking and acting in ways that are wrong. At such times it seems like there is no progress being made, even sliding back. What I wonder is, if we are doing our meditation and doing our best to follow the vows, can we at any time really fail to make progress?*

Well, brother, the first step is to become conscious of our weaknesses. That is also a step towards progress.

352 *Can the five perversions be overcome all at once, overnight?*

No, sister. By and by, the more we are attached to shabd, the more we are being detached from the senses. It is always a slow process.

> *Master, do the five enemies leave all at the same time, or is it possible for one to leave and the other four to remain?*

They go slowly and slowly, one by one.

353 *Maharaj Ji, sometimes we feel that we are not progressing at all, we are just going backwards. You know, we read that the master says that we progress from the moment we are initiated …*

When we come to the path we start analyzing ourselves too much, because those things which we were taking credit for, we now feel ashamed of doing. So we start feeling guilty. Actually, we definitely make progress whenever we make effort. For example, if this room was absolutely dark, you would not see anything in this room at all. If a little ray of light were to come into the room, you would see so many things flying around in this same room. The light has not brought those particles which are in the room. They were already there, but the light is making them visible to you.

So we were full of weaknesses, but we were never conscious of those weaknesses before. When we come to the path, when we are filled with love and devotion, that ray of light comes into us and we start analyzing or seeing the weaknesses in ourselves. At first we were proud of those same weaknesses and now we are ashamed of them. So it is not that we have become worse.

When we come on to the path we are becoming better, we are becoming conscious of our weaknesses. Before that, we were not conscious of our weaknesses at all.

354 Wouldn't an individual in India make better progress because there are fewer temptations there?

No, I do not think so. As far as progress is concerned, the place does not make any difference. I sometimes find that the Westerners are more sincere than the Indians. Whatever they do, they do sincerely, after they have satisfied their intellect. It does not make any difference whether you are born in India or America, in the West or the East or anywhere else. You have to pick up the thread where you left it. It hardly makes any difference.

355 Maharaj Ji, is it possible to have unconscious attachments without really realizing it?

Sometimes we are not aware of our attachments. We feel that we are detached, but when the situation arises, we realize how attached we are. Our present attachments, as well as our previous attachments, can bring us back to this earth, because unless all our karmas, all our attachments are loosened, we cannot go up. We are now thinking about these present attachments. We may have some previous attachments of past births which may still be strong and for which we may still have to give an account. They may even pull us back to this world.

Even if we do make progress?

Even if we do make progress. But we will, of course, go ahead, not backwards. We will be born in much better circumstances where we can clear our karmic accounts in a much better way. Once we make a start, we will always go ahead, not backward at all. There are no failures in Sant Mat. We just go ahead. But unless our attachments are loosened, we cannot go back home. And meditation takes care of our previous attachments also. When we think that we are not making progress – we do not actually know what progress we are making. We do not know until that last little remaining veil is pierced through, even as to what is left to be pierced from the other side of the wall. We all have a store of karmas from previous births, and unless we clear those karmas, as well as our fate karma, and do not sow for the future, how can we go back?

Meditation takes care of all those stores of karmas. By meditating we are loosening those attachments, and when they are being cleared, sometimes in meditation we see many types of faces coming before us of gents and ladies, moving about. We do not know who they are. Those are our previous relations, our previous attachments. We are not to pay any attention to them. We are just to keep ourselves in meditation. Automatically they will cease to come before us. Their accounts with us are being cleared in this way. We are getting detached from them, and then we can go ahead. Meditation takes care of all these things. Only if we still have very strong attachments left at the time of death are we brought back into this world to clear them. Other- wise, even though we may not have made much progress, we can continue making progress and go up from some intermediate stage, and can thus be saved from birth and death. Yet it may be a long way to reach back to him.

356 *Master, once you get to the first stage, in other words, you get up there and cross over and meet the master in his radiant form, after that stage, even though he may appear before you there – suppose you get there in a life- time – is there a chance you may fall back down?*

Yes.

You mean there is no guarantee that once you get up there with him …?

Well, there are certain forceful karmas that pull us down again, sometimes even from the second stage. As long as the mind is there, you can never be sure. But when you get release from the mind, nothing can pull you back down.

357 *Master, we seem to have high periods and low periods of spirituality. Is this a trick of the mind or is it part of our development?*

Sister, ups and downs in meditation do come. You call them high activity or low activity. Our meditation, our spiritual practice, is never smooth. Sometimes we feel that we have gone up, we have made progress. Sometimes we feel that we have fallen down. Ups and downs always come in meditation. That is also due sometimes to our past karmas and so many other things pulling us, which we do not consciously realize. Unconsciously they are affecting us. But we should not worry about the ups and downs. Gradually we have to steer upward.

I seem to have such a time – I wondered if I was missing the right approach. But sometimes it seemed to me that I was there – I seemed to have a direct contact with the power – and at other times I seem so disturbed that it is hard to live with myself.

That is right. One gets such feelings, but one should not feel worried about it. We should just do our duty and give our time to meditation. Then we do overcome such feelings.

The main thing was that I just wanted to hear you say that I was doing right?

Oh, yes. You are definitely doing right. The sound is within every one of us, irrespective of anyone, so we need only concentrate at the eye centre, the thinking centre, to be in touch with that sound.

One just knows that eventually everything will be all right and one will understand?

Yes, that is right. We should never sit in meditation with any excitement or with longing to see something at once, for then the mind gets frustrated and runs out. We should attend to meditation with an absolutely relaxed mind and just do our duty. When it comes, it just comes. Our excitement or our anxiety does not bring anything. It is the concentration that brings it; concentration with love and longing and his grace bring it. So when it has to come, it comes automatically.

358 *The satsang Sunday morning was based on Soami Ji, but you used several English words: attachment, detachment, and "a rolling stone gathers no moss." Would you tell us what you were saying?*

With the help of simran and dhyan, we are creating a dam for a certain time to prevent the mind from running back to the senses. But this is not a permanent cure; it has only a temporary effect on the mind. But when you attach your mind to the shabd and nam, then its whole tendency is towards a different direction. Then it goes upward instead of coming downward. Then the dam remains permanent and the river flows in a different channel. So I used the words 'attachment' and 'detachment' in that connection. When your mind, with the help of simran and dhyan, is attached to that divine melody within, then it doesn't come down to the senses, because if you get a sweet thing, you don't relish the bitter thing or tasteless thing. If anybody gets emeralds and diamonds, he won't run after baubles. The Lord has kept within every one of us that nectar, the living water. Attachment to that light, that music within, helps us detach ourselves from the senses.

And when I say "a rolling stone gathers no moss," I generally mean that unless we are one-pointed towards the light and sound within, we won't make much progress. If we're always wavering, if our mind runs in every direction – let me go to the temple also, let me go to the church also, let me do this ritual and that ritual, let me follow this path and that path also – you will achieve nothing. You have to be one-pointed towards meditation and towards this path, towards the sound or melody within. No ritual is required, no ceremony is required – everything comes in meditation. You will get nothing by performing austerities, rituals and ceremonies – these are all just a self-deception, you see.

In India, we have a lot of outer rituals for worshipping the Father – it must be the same in every religion. Some people leave home and just dye their clothes in different colours and think that is sufficient to go back to the Father. Some don't wear clothes at all. Some rub a lot of dust on their body, and some pierce their ears or have long hair and all sorts of things. Some people believe in lots of charity work, you see – social work. They think that is sufficient for going back to the Father. Some people think that just reciting holy books or taking baths in holy rivers is sufficient. So in that connection I use the phrase "a rolling stone gathers no moss." If you let your mind run in all these directions and also attend to meditation, you're not going to achieve much. Your rolling stone will gather no moss. You have to be one-pointed towards the sound – only then will the sound be able to pull you. Otherwise, if your mind is wavering, if you have all sorts of doubts, then you're not going to achieve much.

359 Does the master withhold the results of attentive meditation?

You see, sometimes it is not in our interest to have those results, but progress is always there. Every time we attend to meditation, progress is there. But whether the results are being withheld from us is very difficult to say – the result is entirely in his hands. We cannot say that by putting so much time in meditation we have been able to achieve some results and now our progress should be exhibited to us. We can only say that something is being withheld from us when we know that we have earned this much, which we should have got, but we didn't get. He knows best when to give and how to give and how much to give. We have only to knock. The duty of the beggar is to knock, to ask for alms – it is for the owner to open the door and fill his pocket. The beggar can't set the conditions – I have been able to beg so much, so I have earned at least this much now. We shouldn't analyze our meditation from that point of view – that we have been able to earn so much by meditation and the result is being withheld from us. We cannot analyze like that.

360 Is it a fact that we need the body in order to grow spiritually, and that without the body or in the astral region there is no growth whatsoever?

There is growth also in the astral planes.

Is it very slow?

Very slow, that is right, very slow. That is why this body is known as the top of creation. There are also astral forms, astral regions in the creation, but the human body is considered to be the top of creation, because while living in this body we can make better progress, better growth than in those astral regions. But once we have a master, we do make progress from there too, without coming back into the human form.

361 *The other night we were discussing meditation in this world and meditation within, in the astral regions. What is the difference? What is the advantage of meditation in this world over meditation within?*

You make much better progress here than you make there because there is so much agony and misery all around you that you become tired of this creation and want to get out of it. But there, there is no agony, no misery, so your tendency is not much towards meditation. Here the tendency is very much towards meditation, and master is also here in the flesh. The grace is more here than there. But ultimately every soul will be taken back. It just takes more time there.

362 *Maharaj Ji, when one dies and goes to another region, what are the activities of the soul? Are they like anything on this earth?*

I think I explained that to you this morning. There is no activity. The activity is that of love, to make our way up. What I said yesterday is that we make much better spiritual progress by being in this human form than from inside these astral planes, because here we see so much misery around us that we want to escape from it. So we are always thinking about the Lord. We want to go back to him. We do not want to remain here, so we try to work hard to go back to him. Without intense longing we cannot merge back into him. And there, since there is no misery, no birth or death, the yearning to go back is very little.

271

*363 Maharaj Ji, how can a person always have a good envi-
ronment in which to meditate and still not be able to
control his mind to meditate properly?*

Sister, it is not only the environment which helps us; it is the
detachment of the mind from the world that helps us to make
progress within. So unless we are fed up with the world and have
longing to go back to the Father, unless we have devotion and
love within us that is pulling us towards the Father, we won't
make progress. The environment alone won't help us – the pull
should also be from within.

The Lord is there to give that pull to everybody. When he
has sown a seed, it has to sprout sooner or later. If the seed is
not there, there's nothing to sprout. If the seed is there, then it
just needs nourishing to become a big tree. So his grace is there,
and naturally his pull also will be there.

364 Do some people go within more easily than others?

All disciples have their own backgrounds. Some disciples do
hear sounds at the time of initiation, some do see light at the
time of initiation, and some have to work hard to be in touch
with both of them.

And we are told to be good seekers and good knockers.

You see, it's a lifelong struggle. We not only have to continue in
meditation, but continue it for the whole of our life. It is not an
electric switch that you just switch on and off.

*365 Are there different levels of the spiritual path, and as we
progress we go higher?*

You see, the more you progress, the more your love grows. The
more you are on the path, the more you are filled with love and

devotion for the Father, the more you feel the separation, the more you try to be one with him.

366 *Is there any reason why four lifetimes have been chosen for going back, after initiation? We're given a maximum of four lives.*

You mean, why not six?

Yes, four seems a very short time.

You want more, you can take more, if you like.

No. Why is it made so difficult for the master to cram it into four lives?

You see, Soami Ji explains it. One life is for devotion and love of the master. The second life is just for attending to meditation and merging into the shabd and nam, just to live in the nam, always intoxicated with that nectar, with that shabd and nam. The third life is for going across Trikuti, to the second and third stage, from where you don't have to take birth again at all. And the fourth birth is for going back, straight up. That is what the Lord devised, but he does not mean that we have to take four lifetimes. It means if you take it very slow, even then you'll be able to cover the journey within four lifetimes. If one can run, if one can go at jet speed, so much the better.

367 *Maharaj Ji, a person who is fortunate to be initiated, though late in life, might not have had enough time to work out his destiny in this life or to put in enough effort in the spiritual purpose. In either case, he's lagging behind. Now, he may have to be born again in order to continue his noble effort forward. Or will he, by the goodness and grace of the satguru, be allowed to cross*

over, say to the first stage, and from there onwards may
he be allowed to continue his spiritual journey without
being put through the difficulty of being born again?

It depends upon the individual soul. But there's no seniority
in Sant Mat – nobody is late, and nobody is early. That is why
Christ said, the first may be the last, and the last may be the
first.[62] You cannot say who is going to reach there first, who will
be the first one or the last one. It is the sincerity of the mind and
his grace which matter.

If we look to our load of karmas and then calculate how
much effort it would take for us to account for all that, I think
it would be impossible for any soul to go back to the Father.
It is impossible. To burn all the karmas which we have been
collecting by our own efforts – it's impossible. Guru Nanak
himself describes our position. He says: If you go on washing
the earth, there'll be no end to it. You can never reach the bottom. We are made like that.* If we go on accounting for our
karma, there'll be no end to it – we can only stand at your door,
where we are knocking and waiting for your grace. That attitude
should always be there. We have to put in our effort – we have to
knock – but we cannot say that by my effort of so many years,
I'll be able to account for my load of karmas. What to say of four
lives, even twenty lives are not sufficient if we have to account
for all our karmas by our own effort. It's all his grace.

It is with his grace that we attend to meditation, and then
the attitude of our mind towards the creation changes. We don't
remain attached to this creation. That is the main thing. It is
mainly attachment which pulls us back to the level of the creation. By our attitude of meditation our mind gets detached from

---

* *Maati ka kya dhopay swaami, maanas ki gat eihee.* Guru Arjun, Adi Granth,
M5, p. 882.

this creation, and that attitude helps us. No matter how much progress you have made within, no matter how little progress you have, or even if you have no progress to your credit within, the attitude of your mind which you build and develop by following the path, by attending to meditation – that you are not attached to anybody – that helps us a lot, saves us a lot from coming back to this creation. The rest is entirely his grace.

So one should never think that I got too little time to attend to meditation and others got much more time, because it is just his grace. When he pulls, he pulls. There is no question of time limit or age limit with him. We may be concerned with our age, but he's not concerned with our age. He's concerned with the soul. So when he pulls, he pulls. He knows best. We have only to put in an effort.

368 Christ said that many are called, but few are chosen. Of the many you call, what percentage are chosen?

Actually, Christ was giving a parable. He said that when a mystic comes, many are collected, many are called in that life. This means that many are put on the path, are initiated, are filled with love and devotion for the Father, but not everybody will be able to go back to the Father in that particular lifetime. In that lifetime, only a few will be selected.[63] Others may have to take another birth. It's all according to our spiritual progress on the path. We are going towards our destination. Saints initiate thousands. But only the fortunate ones will be able to find their destination in that very birth and go back to the Father. Few are chosen to go back to the Father in that lifetime. Others get an opportunity to improve, to make further progress on the path, and they will also go back to the Father. Everyone who has been called by the Father will ultimately, definitely, reach the Father.

369 *To the extent that we disown the mind, so to speak, to that extent are we at least showing some progress?*

Brother, such a realization by a satsangi is in itself a sign of progress. Then, working for it is progress. Achieving it is still further progress. Merging back into him is the greatest progress.

～ 10 ～

Effort and Grace

Regularity and Punctuality

370 In the books we often see that we should attend to our meditation regularly and punctually. Could you speak about the benefits of regularity and punctuality?

When lunchtime comes, whether we are hungry or not, we quietly go to the dining table, because we have formed a habit of eating at that particular time. In the same way, we have to form a habit of meditation. If I say that I will meditate when I feel the urge, I will perhaps never meditate. If you think, "I will meditate when I feel the right atmosphere – I'll sit in the morning, I'll sit at noon, I'll sit in the evening" – you will always go on giving excuses to yourself and you will never attend to meditation. But just as you have made a habit to go to the office at a particular time, to go for a walk at a particular time, to go to the dining table at a particular time, similarly you should make a habit to go at a particular time for meditation. Then slowly and slowly your mind will become disciplined to attend to that meditation. That is why so much emphasis is laid on regularity and punctuality.

If you say, "Today I don't feel like doing any meditation – I'll sit tomorrow," then tomorrow you'll have some other excuse, and the day after tomorrow again you will have some other excuse. So there will be gaps and gaps and gaps, and you'll real-ize that you have absolutely forgotten to sit in meditation for months and months. But if you force your mind to think, "Even if I can't give proper time, let me give at least half the time, even though I am so busy," then you'll get regularity. Punctuality is also associated with the timing. Say you have selected a particular time, for example 3:00 a.m., 3:30, 4:30. If we know that we have to be punctual in the morning – I have to get up at 3:30 – then you will also be punctual going to sleep in the evening. You will adjust your time in such a way that you can get six or seven hours of sleep before you get up in the morning, otherwise you know that you will miss your morning meditation. So punctuality is essential – it should become a habit with us.

Unless we discipline our mind, it will always find excuses not to sit in meditation. We have been regular in our other daily activities: "I have a time to go to the office, I have a time to go to lunch, I have a time to have a cup of coffee, I have a time to walk in the evening, I have a time to sleep" – then why not also have a time for meditation? That should become part of our life, part of our daily routine. If we discipline our mind, then every day we won't miss meditation. And if you do skip your meditation, you'll feel miserable that day and feel that something is missing, so you will try to find some other time to make up for the morning time. So regularity and punctuality are both very essential.

So regularity and punctuality and everything else that we do will be helpful for a satsangi in leading a Sant Mat way of life?

Naturally. You see, we all try to be regular or punctual in our other daily activities. If you make an appointment with somebody and you are late, you feel guilty; you apologize for being late when you feel that you have not been able to honour the commitment you have made. So we should honour the commitment we have made to the Father to put aside a certain time to attend to the meditation. We have to sit whether our mind is still or not. Whether we have to fight with the mind, that's a different problem; but we have a certain commitment to the Father, and we should try to honour it by giving our time at that particular time to the Father. Just as we are sorry if we are even five minutes late for our worldly commitments – we feel guilty within ourselves – we should also carry that feeling of guilt if we don't attend to meditation. Then if you are late today, maybe next time you won't be late. If you don't feel sorry about being late, then you will get into a habit of coming late all the time. The mind always wants an excuse to run away from meditation, so we have to fight not to give it any excuses. That is why regularity and punctuality always reward us.

371   If I sit for meditation without being able to concentrate at all, do I gain anything? Even if we don't see the light in meditation, should we try to do it anyway?

Sister, whether you concentrate or not is immaterial, but you definitely should sit in meditation because we have to pass through so many phases before we are able to concentrate and enjoy that pull within, its bliss and peace within. You can't straightaway concentrate by simran, but if we won't start, then how will we ever concentrate? You see, we are all born as children, and how many phases do we have to go through before we are able to stand on our own legs, think independently and act independently? We have gone through so many phases right from birth, and you can't eliminate those phases during which we have developed our capacity to think and act independently. Similarly, in meditation we have to pass through so many phases, and every phase is important for our spiritual development. So we have to continue. It is immaterial whether we are able to concentrate or whether we are able to hear the sound or see the light. Our efforts should continue. We should sit in meditation as a matter of duty, even if we don't enjoy that peace and bliss within. Slowly and slowly we do enjoy and we do make progress.

372 *Master, in one of the books there's a mention of 3:00 in the morning as being the time of elixir. Also, you've said that any time, really, that we can put to meditation is okay. Is that right?*

Well, sister, the thing is, any time is good for meditation. Whatever time we give to meditation stands to our credit. There's no wrong time for meditation. Every time is good when we attend to meditation. The morning has certain advantages over other timings, so we try to make use of those advantages. When you get up in the morning, you're absolutely fresh, you are not tired anymore, and you have forgotten all the episodes, the ups and downs of the day before. And your mind is not scattered much. The children are sleeping, there is no hustle and bustle in the streets in the morning hours, and you don't expect any knock on the door or the telephone to ring. Moreover, when you're going to start a day, why not start in the name of the Father? The atmosphere we build by attending to meditation should help us to go through the ups and downs of the whole day. That is the only advantage of the morning time. But if for some reason somebody cannot give time in the morning, he shouldn't think that his whole day is lost. He can attend any time – any time is good.

373 *Master, you said that we have to attach ourselves to shabd and nam. But if our meditation is very dry, how can we depend on the shabd and nam?*

You see, you have to make it tasty. First you have to fight with your mind to attend to your meditation, but the time comes when it becomes very tasty. When a child is sent to school, he weeps and cries and clings to his mother, crying, "I don't want to go to school." But when he's forced to go to the school, he starts reading and writing, and after a while, you can hardly pull him away from his books. Mother is shouting for him to come to dinner or meals, and he says, "Just wait, just wait, just wait." He's the same child. So make your meditation tasty.

374 A friend says she is so ashamed to have failed to obey the master's advice, but now she has been given firm resolve to again attend to meditation. She asks should one medi-tate again and again during the day until two and a half hours are done, even if this means sacrificing all else for that day? And can she be reassured of the master's under-standing and forgiveness of her failures?

Sister, I often advise that the planning of our day is up to each of us, individually. We know our obligations, our responsibilities, our commitments of the day, commitments of life, so we have to schedule our time. We have to give time to meditation, and we have to look to our other responsibilities and obligations also. Only we can decide when to give time to meditation, how much time to give to meditation, and whether to split it in two sittings or whether we have sufficient time for one sitting. Everyone has to decide individually. As for our committing mistakes, well, humans are made like that. We falter, we fall. But if we continue doing meditation, his grace is always there. Meditation is the only way to seek forgiveness for our follies, for our sins, for our mistakes. Meditation is the cure for all such things.

375 Master, I've heard so much about determination on this path, and giving your priorities to the meditation and all of the things that are conducive to meditation. And there doesn't seem to be enough time in the day to really focus on ...

No. For example, how much time does family take each day? You see, there's twenty-four hours in a day, and you have to give only two and a half hours to meditation. And then the whole day is before you. You can plan it. You have to go to a job, you have to do your housework, and you have to adjust your activities accordingly. You can't say that I will do everything and also attend to meditation. You have to adjust your schedule.

376 Mothers know that with newborn babies, they don't find time to meditate. My question is: Is it all right to ignore the baby crying and do the meditation, or should I take care of the baby?

Sister, mothers don't get time to meditate due to their children. But they get time to go to the office, they get time to go to the cinema, they get time to watch TV. They get time to gossip and to have social get-togethers, but they have no time for their children. Children are not always awake or always needing your attention. They also sleep, and you can give your time to meditation if you want to, but not at the cost of the child. You have taken on a certain responsibility and obligation. You have to discharge them. You have to do your duty and also find time for meditation. You have to adjust your schedule. You can do your meditation at the cost of gossip and other social activities. One has to make these adjustments for oneself.

377 Master, will forced meditation bring about good meditation?

Yes, naturally. When you are not in the habit of sitting at all, the first step is to force yourself at least to sit. To sit still is a great credit. When you learn to sit still, then you also have to learn to still your mind. The first problem is to still the body, as the body is always running out and doesn't want to sit in one place for even twenty minutes. So first you get in the habit of stilling the body, and then you get into the habit of stilling the mind. This comes from meditation.

378 *As an initiate, when we miss our meditation at times, is there a way to make up for it?*

Well, sister, the only way to make up the deficiency is to give more time to meditation another day. You see, even if we miss some time, we shouldn't feel too miserable; on another day we can devote more time to meditation. But we should try to give time to meditation every day. Even if we give only a little time on some days, it is all right; another day we can give more time. But we should form the habit of giving time to meditation.

379 *What are the penalties when one misses a day of meditation?*

The penalty is that you have missed the opportunity. There are no penalties in Sant Mat. There are no penalties in devotion. There are no penalties in the way of love. We have missed the opportunity. What greater penalty can there be? When a lover misses the beloved, that in itself is a penalty; and to a real lover, it is the greatest penalty not to be able to be with the beloved.

We should all attempt to sit in meditation every day, regularly and punctually, because this human form is given to us for that very purpose. So, if we do not make use of this opportunity, we are losing something that we should not lose, because we may not get this opportunity so easily again. It is not that if we miss one or two meditation periods we will be penalized or go backwards. That is an absolutely wrong notion. We should try sincerely to give proper time every day, punctually and regularly. If you miss it some day due to some unavoidable circumstances or for any reason, try to make up this deficiency at some other time. The object is that we should get into the habit of doing meditation every day. The question of penalty does not arise on this path.

380 *I was informed that if we miss one day's meditation, we are taken back twenty-four or thirty days. So, if we miss, say, five days that would be equal to not doing any meditation for a whole year.*

Well, you are living at least thousands of miles away from me. Many things can reach you in a different way by the time they reach you here [in America]. Such wrong statements are usually traced to what I call guest house gossip at the Dera, where the guests get together and express their opinions and ideas, and then one of them comes back here and says that is what he or she heard at the Dera. You see, if you try to do a certain thing every day, you get into the habit of doing it. If you neglect it and leave it for some other time – if you postpone it – you get out of the habit of meditation. If you lose this habit, you again have to work hard to get back into it. So that is your own loss. Unless we get into the habit of meditation, we will not achieve any results. When we lose time from daily meditation, we are missing something that we should not miss. But there are no personal penalties.

381 *We are asked to put in two and one-half hours of meditation daily. If in our trials we are not able to do so, I understand we do not fulfil our mission. Is that right?*

You see, we have twenty-four hours in a day, so at least we should try to devote one-tenth of our time to the Lord's devotion. We should not feel guilty if we cannot devote the full two and one-half hours. In the beginning, it is very difficult to sit in meditation for even one hour at a stretch. We should start slowly and gradually, and try to increase the time to this extent. And if we miss sometimes, we should not feel guilty about it. The object is that we should try to be regular and punctual. We should try to devote at least that much time to meditation; but then it depends upon the circumstances of the individuals. That is our endeavour; that is what we should try to do. We should keep that aim in our view. Try for it. If we cannot do it in one sitting, we can divide it into two sittings or three sittings, but slowly and slowly we should try to bring it to only one sitting. However, that needs practice, and the time is increased by and by.

382 *Master, when attempting meditation, the mind continually runs out and runs after trifles. Would you please explain that matter, so we can make corrections?*

Brother, it is a constant struggle with the mind. It is not so easy to control our mind when we have given it such a free rein. It has been spreading into the whole world all of our life, not only in this life but also in previous lives. It has got into the habit of running out and not staying at all in its own place. So naturally, it takes time to curb it, to bring it back, to withdraw the consciousness to the eye centre. It takes time. We want to achieve this in a day or two, but we have to make a regular habit of doing it. When we form a habit of something, automatically we succeed. For example, a child starts learning to climb the stairs. He struggles very hard; sometimes he falls and he may scrape his head, hands, body or feet; he again tries and again falls, but he does not stop trying.

You see, we have all come from the same staircase. We have come down so many steps that we do not feel that we have come from that staircase. In trying to go back up, in the beginning the very first step seemed like the Himalayas for us, but now we do not feel those steps at all. But how? By regular practice. We have made a habit of climbing, and now we climb without even being conscious of it. So we have to make a regular habit of concentrating our mind. That is why saints suggest punctuality and regularity in meditation.

There is no special technique?

Brother, there is no American short cut. [Laughter] You see, Americans are always worrying about how to save time, and how to save dollars and get the maximum. There is no such way in Sant Mat. There is no such way in the devotion of the Lord.

It is slow and steady that wins the race, is that it?

Surely, but we have to be regular and punctual, and live in it. We also have to form a habit of meditation and then slowly and slowly the mind comes back. If every day you do the same thing, ultimately the mind comes back to its own point. It is a constant struggle with the mind, and you cannot fix any time limit or any short cuts on this path.

And it is all up, of course, to 99 percent of one's friends and associations?

Brother, being with them, we are not to be affected by them. We have to detach ourselves by this constant practice. We will be with them, we will move with them, we will work with them, yet we will not be affected by them. They are, of course, pulling strings, trying to pull us outward; but there is much more forceful pulling inside that just withdraws us. When you water a tree and a storm comes with great speed, it uproots it from the ground. So all these group meetings, this hour of discussion, the company of the saints and satsang, this atmosphere of love and devotion, all this is like watering the tree. And when that storm, that severe storm that is shabd or nam, comes, our roots are loosened, and we are off – detached while living our life in this world.

Well, will it not take about a million years?

We are assured that it will take not more than four lives, at the most.

383 *If I may ask – two and one-half hours of meditation a day – I keep harping on this because I feel it sort of catches me forcibly. But if, for discussion's sake, say in one day I had two hours and not two and a half, can I in the next twenty-four hours make it three ...?*

We should go on putting our reserve in the bank. We should not feel guilty if we are not able to give two and a half hours. The main thing is that we should try to be punctual and regular in our meditation. Whether it is one, one and a half, two, or two and a half hours doesn't make much difference in the beginning, provided we are regular, we are punctual – every day. Sometimes, naturally, we give more time, and sometimes our worldly necessities force us to give less time.

The two and a half hours of meditation daily is just general advice. One shouldn't take it blindly that I have got to give two hours and one-half, and then not sit for meditation at all if the full time is not available. We should try to put in two and one-half hours, and if it is ten minutes more or less, that makes no difference.

By regular and punctual, do you mean the same time every day?

287

Habits are easily formed and soon become a part of our daily routine, and then if we neglect them, we start missing those things. Similarly, by giving the same time every day, this meditation should become a part of our daily routine. For instance, whether we are hungry or not, at one o'clock we are at the dining table; or the moment it is eleven o'clock, you rush for your coffee break. It becomes a habit and a routine of life. So meditation should also become a habit and a daily routine. And if you give it secondary importance – "I'll attend to it whenever I feel like it, I'll do it whenever I get time" – then you'll never attend to it at all. So you should make it compulsory.

We develop associations with the time, the place and with the atmosphere. They all help us in building our meditation. For instance, the moment you are in bed, you have an association with sleep. That is why we recommend that you do not try to sit on the bed for meditation, because then you are easily lured to sleep. The moment you are at your desk in the office, you feel like doing your office work. Similarly, we should make meditation a habit and a daily routine. And that can only be if we are punctual and regular in our meditation.

> So we have to train ourselves to get up early in the morning? Because sometimes initially we can get up and be very tired and be half concentrating and half falling asleep. But if we keep on at that time, eventually we will wake up?

That's right. If you fix a particular time and place for your meditation – whether half the time you are doing your meditation and the other half you fall asleep – slowly and gradually you will get into the habit of sitting at that time, and you will not get sleepy. When you are so used to getting up at 3:30 or 4:00 in the morning, then however sleepy you may be, you will at once get up and won't sleep, because you have formed a habit of getting up at that particular time. So we should form a habit to sit in meditation and then there is no problem.

384 *Why does our ability to do our bhajan and to follow the principles of Sant Mat vary so much? Sometimes one goes from one feeling, like one is very capable of doing meditation – and then, for some unexplainable reason, one just cannot do it?*

Ups and downs do come everywhere.

Shall we suffer through it, or shall we feel guilty, or...?

We should never feel guilty at all. We simply should try to put more time in meditation and get through those ugly days.

385 *Master, I cannot do it, but there are people who can – they are constantly in meditation for a fortnight, day and night, day and night. Would that be good?*

We should develop a pattern of life in our meditation. We should not try to close ourselves in a room for meditation for a couple of weeks and then forget about the Lord. The teachings have to be lived. It is a way of life. A pattern of life has to be developed. We should not try to meditate day and night for a couple of weeks and then forget about it for a time. We should devote some time every day to meditation and also carry on our duties at other hours of the day. Our time should be properly distributed and our whole life should be lived like that.

386 *Would there be, at any time, a valid excuse for missing one's meditation?*

If we start justifying our missing the daily meditation period, then there will be no end to it. So I do not want you to find any justification for missing it. We have to put forth all our efforts to give our time every day, but if somehow we miss it, we just miss; but we have missed something that is too valuable to miss. That is all.

387 *Master, who is responsible for our meditation, the disciple or the master?*

Master has to attend to his own meditation, and the disciple has to attend to his own meditation. You see, master has his own load [that he has taken on himself], and the disciple has his own load. When master initiates us, puts us on the path, he tells us to devote time to meditation. If we really love him, we will obey him. We cannot say we love him and, at the same time, not obey his instructions, not live the life he tells us to live. That is not love for the master. If we really have faith in him, if we really love him, we will want to do what he wants us to do. And he wants us to meditate; therefore, we should also try to meditate.

388 *Even if we meditate for a short time, are we achieving anything? Also, are we making progress even though we cannot see or hear anything?*

Every minute, every second, that we devote to meditation is to our credit. We will definitely gain something. We must do our duty, because we are all struggling souls. Only the Lord knows how long we have been separated from the Creator and for how much we have to repent, and how many thick walls or layers of karma are between us and the Father.

Every minute that we attend to meditation is an achievement, is to our credit. Whether or not we hear or see anything, we must give time every day to meditation. Gradually we will be able to pierce through these layers of karmas, and eventually we will be one with the spirit or light within. So we must give time to meditation.

389 *When we are just beginners on this path, doing our simran, and we know that our concentration is very poor and we are not really making very much progress, are we burning away any of our karmas, or does that only happen when we have gone a certain way inside?*

Whatever little time we devote to meditation, that is to our credit. Whatever time we devote to meditation, we are eliminating certain karmas, we are eliminating a certain darkness from our way. So whatever time you devote to meditation, that is always to your credit, whether it is repetition of the five holy names or whether it is listening to the sound. Every minute that we devote in his love, in his devotion, that is always credited to our account and we definitely get the advantage of that in one way or another.

390 *I would like to know, when one is meditating and the mind seems to keep wandering off without one's even realizing it, until finally one catches it, and no matter how hard one tries and keeps telling oneself that it must concentrate, it seems that it just does not want to do so?*

Well, the mind is doing its own work and you have to do your own work. How loyal it is to its superior, Kal, the negative power, when it does not let you concentrate! You have to be as loyal to your own master by trying to concentrate. It is a constant struggle with the mind. You see, by doing a thing every day, punctually and regularly, we get into the habit of doing that. Take smoking for instance: You just start with one or two cigarettes, perhaps out of curiosity, then you find some pleasure in it, and when you continue daily, it becomes a habit. Then you become such a slave to that habit that you cannot leave it. By doing it again and again, you have become a slave to it and that becomes part and parcel of your daily life. You find it difficult even to try to leave it.

Similarly, we have to get ourselves into that habit of meditation, of concentration. Daily, regularly and punctually, we have to go on doing it, and ultimately we succeed. Then we would not like to live with ourselves, we would not feel happy, we would not feel that the day has been rightly spent if we have not given time to meditation. We are creatures of habit, and when once we get into the habit of trying to meditate, then that very habit will help us in concentrating. But in order to achieve this, we must struggle with the mind. It is a constant struggle for light. It is not so easy. From age to age, from year to year, our mind got into the habit of scattering out into this world. Everything is drawing us out, pulling us out. So, naturally it takes time to withdraw the attention back up to the eye centre and to concentrate. We cannot achieve these results with American speed, I would say. [Laughter]

CONTROLLING THE MIND

391 *When I start on my simran, I hold it for a while and my mind wanders out, and there is nothing I seem to be able to do about it. It is concerned mostly with the work I do – my mind keeps going back to it. It is not anything I am attached to exactly; I am interested in it, but I just …*

It is a constant struggle with the mind. The mind has gotten into the habit of wandering about, so through constant struggle we have to bring it back to this point. When you do that thing daily – by practice, practice and practice – you will find that the attention also will begin to stay here, at this point.

392 *Maharaj Ji, the other evening someone asked you about having mental conversations with the master and you said it is just the mind talking to the mind, but just now you mentioned that the Father will put you in an environment which makes you think of him.*

Without the help of our mind, we can never go back to the Father. You see, as I have explained so many times, the seat of the soul and the mind is here at the eye centre, and our mind is pulled downward by the senses. As long as the tendency of the mind is towards the senses, it is our enemy. When we are able to withdraw our consciousness – the mind – to the eye centre and its tendency turns upward, it becomes our best friend. You can never have a better friend than the mind, and you can never have a worse enemy than the mind. So we have to win over this enemy and turn it into a friend, by withdrawing it back to the eye centre and attaching it to that melody and divine light within. We are winning its friendship, and only with the help of that friendship with the mind can the soul go back to the Father.

Unless the mind comes to its own source – Brahm, Trikuti – the soul can never get release from the mind. So the soul is grateful to the mind when the mind is attached to the shabd and starts going to its own source. The mind is our enemy as long as it's pulling us toward the senses, and then it becomes our friend. Guru Nanak gives a very beautiful example: He says when the iron touches the philosopher's stone, it becomes gold. He says that iron is within you and the philosopher's stone is within you, but with the help and grace of the Father or the master, the iron touches the philosopher's stone and becomes gold. The mind is the iron and nam is the philosopher's stone. When the mind touches the shabd and nam within, it becomes gold, it becomes our best friend. So we have to turn it into gold. Now it is iron, as long as it's a victim of the senses.

So we are talking to the mind, to the higher mind, to a better mind. But doing simran is better than talking to your higher mind, because by talking to the master within, you are filling yourself with love and devotion, and the purpose of love and devotion is to attend to your meditation. And if you are attending to your meditation, you are going a step forward. So it is better to attend to simran or to hear the sound rather than just talk to your own mind within.

> So in the first instance, is it when you sort of finally agree that the path is for you – is that purely mind, purely intellect, or is there a little bit of …?

Higher mind, better mind.

> But no spirit, no soul?

You see, the higher the mind rises, the purer it becomes, and then the soul starts shining and shining, shining and shining. Let us say that a bulb has the light of a hundred candles. If you put five, six, or seven black wrappings around it, you won't see any light at all, even though the light is there. But when you start removing the wrappings, the light starts penetrating. Only when all the wrappings are removed do you see the full refulgence of that light. Similarly, when the mind is attached to the shabd and starts going upward, the soul also starts shining. The soul is becoming more and more active now. But the soul can only be absolutely active or free when it leaves the mind. Only when all the wrappings are removed can you see the full light of the soul. But even before that, you see the light, as the wrappings are becoming less and less.

So this is when the master is pulling the strings?

You see, that is a different thing. That soul is becoming better and better; that is, the soul is becoming more and more active. The soul is always immortal and pure, but it is becoming more active because light has started penetrating the mind. But actually the soul is still associated with the mind, so you can call it a higher mind or a better mind – the iron is becoming gold.

And that is when the mind is becoming more friendly towards you?

Yes. Your mind is your best friend when it is attached to the shabd and nam within and starts pulling you upward. Only then can the soul get released from the mind.

393 *In* Philosophy of the Masters *it's very emphatic that the only remedy for controlling the mind is to listen to the sound current; no second way exists. So how can we control the mind if we don't have the sound current? Because we can't do simran unless the mind is controlled.*

Then try to reach to that level to be with the sound current.

But that has a lot to do with grace, doesn't it, if we're making the effort?

Well, the grace of the Lord is that we're on the path. Now we have to make our best efforts to be steadfast and try to achieve. Definitely, unless the mind gets something better than the sensual pleasures, it's very hard for the mind to leave the sensual pleasures. And that something better the Lord has kept within every one of us. That is right at the eye centre – the sound. So we have to try our best to be there in order to be in touch with that sound, so that we may taste that nectar, that living water within. And then our mind won't run to the senses.

Great Master says that you cannot control your mind by austerities, by reading books, by running away from situations, by strong willpower. You can only subdue your mind with the help of the sound. Otherwise, it is just putting a snake in a basket. As long as the snake is there in the basket, we are saved from its poison, from its sting. But how long will we be able to keep that snake in the basket? The moment it comes out, it's going to do mischief again. But if we remove its sting, its poison, it becomes harmless. That is why mystics say: Don't think that you'll be able to control your mind by running away from situations, or by austerities and rituals and ceremonies. That is just putting the snake in a basket. Give the mind a better taste than the sensual pleasures; then it automatically will leave the senses.

Try, just try?

Sister, it's a constant struggle with the mind. It's not a question of one year or two; it's a constant struggle with the mind. Unfortunately, we are not aware of how many ages the mind has been running out, and how much effort and time it will take to withdraw from all that and come to the eye centre. But it is worth the game.

394 *I find that the more that I try to discipline my mind the more that it rebels, and I end up getting angry at my mind, and that doesn't do me any good.*

It's natural, sister. The more we suppress, the more it reacts. That is the habit of the mind. Don't become angry with yourself; just continue with your meditation. The mind doesn't want to be tamed. When you try to attach a *tonga* [cart] to a horse, the horse resists – it doesn't want to lose its freedom – but you must train the horse, and then it becomes all right. Similarly, the mind always rebels and creates all sorts of problems in meditation. It doesn't want to be tamed; it doesn't want to be controlled. So we have to face the situation, but we have to continue in meditation.

395 *Master, we want to hear you say that it's good if we're relaxed, but it seems like it's such a struggle with the mind sometimes that we get very tense and there's such a resistance that it's very difficult to relax.*

Attend to your meditation; it will relax you. The more you are concentrated at the eye centre and your attention is upward, the more relaxed you will feel. The more you are downward, the more tense you will be. You can never be happy as long as the tendency of the mind is always downward and running out. And if you are happy, it will be very short-lived, a very momentary time. The more you are concentrated, the more the mind is turned upward, the more you'll feel relaxed and happy, peaceful and blissful within yourself. It's a lifelong struggle – not just a little struggle but a great struggle.

396 *Even if the mind is strong and meditation is a struggle, one is seeking the help that one needs in order to...*

Well, sister, if the mind is strong, then it's good to put it in meditation. If it is strong, then naturally it will be able to help you to attend to meditation. Only the weak mind runs to the senses. I mean strong from the Lord's point of view, not strong from the senses' point of view. These are our own concepts, our own comparative words: strong and weak. So a strong mind means that it's strong enough to pull itself from the senses and attend to meditation. If that strength in the mind is there, then make best use of it by attending to meditation.

397 Maharaj Ji, when we are with our master and we look at him while we are with his physical form, we feel such love for him. But then at four o'clock in the morning, when it's really time for us to love the master where it counts, all of a sudden the mind says you are so tired, and then you realize that you have no love at all. When we look at you, we know we love you, but then when it really comes to serving you in our meditation, all of a sudden that faith and love just evaporate.

The mind plays its own tricks, but we have to do our duty. If you can't get up at four o'clock get up at five o'clock, get up at six o'clock.

It seems as if the mind is the direct enemy of the inner master within us. It's continually struggling back and forth. Once you said that we fall only to rise again ...

That is why Christ has referred to the mind as a strongman, meaning something within us which is very powerful. And he also has told us how to hold that strongman. He says that if you want to relinquish your house to someone you have to bind the strongman. Then you are the master of that house – you can take anything from that house.[71] That house is the body, and that strongman is within this body. So if we want to get the treasure of nam, the treasure of the Lord, from the body, we have to bind the strongman. And you can bind the strongman only by meditation. Unless the strongman is bound, we cannot get the treasure that the Lord has kept within this body. It is not a very ordinary thing.

398 Maharaj Ji, sometimes in meditation ideas come, and I leave meditation to write them down. Is that wrong? That seems to be the most wonderful time for inspiration.

Well, either you can attend to meditation or you can attend to your problems and inspiration. You can't have both. It's because at the time of meditation, the mind is a little concentrated. So we can get a lot of inspiration, and we can think very clearly. The more the mind is concentrated, the more clearly you can think and solve a problem or analyze that issue.

I'm always afraid that if I go back to meditation and push out the thoughts, I'll forget.

At the time of meditation, we should not allow anything to interfere. At the time of meditation, we should just attend to meditation. When you get into the habit of meditation, you won't let your thoughts scatter too much in this world; but inspirations will come to you even then. This is a trick of the mind to lead us astray, away from meditation. Things which we have forgotten or have never even been conscious of at once project before us at the time of meditation. During the day we never even think about them, but at the time of meditation, all these thoughts project before us. We have to eliminate all that and just attend to meditation.

399 *Maharaj Ji, sometimes in meditation questions come up that demand a lot of attention. And often we offer those questions up to the master inside. Will the master answer those for us, in the sense that during the next day the answer might become clear, or someone speaks to you and all of a sudden your answer presents itself?*

You see, actually we waste too much of our time thinking about all these things at the time of meditation. We should attend to meditation. Meditation is nothing but seeking the solution to all these problems which are tying us down to this creation. Meditation helps us to detach from all the problems of this creation. That is a positive approach, rather than trying to find every little answer to every little problem. If you sit for a couple of hours, and for one and a half hours you are just talking to yourself, then the mind won't become still. It rushes out with all the questions, all the worries, all the problems. Leave those to the Lord to deal with. Just attend to meditation. Because your thinking is not going to solve any problem at all – it will rather complicate it. If you brush the problems aside and attend to meditation, solutions automatically will be there.

400 *When we're doing meditation and our mind wants to run out, should we reprimand it as we would a naughty child, or should we feel like we're in battle?*

Just try to bring it back to the eye centre. What is the sense of reprimanding it? Your mind will run out again. You will accuse the mind, the mind will accuse you – either way, you are projecting. Then you start talking to yourself. The mind projects in so many ways – it becomes the accused, it becomes the complainant. So bring it back into the simran, bring it back, bring it back.

401 *If during meditation a negative thought keeps coming up, should we use energy to suppress it? Or should we let it run through and just try to get back to the meditation?*

No, suppressing it is not the way to keep it out – it will just come back more vigorously. Keep out the thought by putting your mind in a positive direction. Keep your mind in simran. There is only one mind. If it is busy in simran, if it is absolutely absorbed in simran, other thoughts automatically will go. They'll vanish; they'll fade out. If, without doing simran, you try to eliminate them by thinking, "I'm not going to think; I'm not going to think," you can never succeed. Put your mind in a positive direction; think about something positive. That is simran. When your mind is absorbed in that, other thoughts will automatically vanish. There's no other way to keep them out.

402 *Master, when we have a strong thought about a situation, is there any way to eradicate that or to lessen its effect?*

I can tell you a positive thing. Instead of worrying about eliminating that thought, attach yourself to the sound within and you will automatically rise above the thought. It's very difficult to eliminate thoughts one by one. It's impossible. But when we attach ourselves to the shabd and nam within, all these thoughts are automatically eliminated. Instead of cursing the darkness, we should light a candle.

403 *Master, how do we keep impressions from coming into our mind so that we don't have to keep thinking about them during meditation?*

You see, if you try to eliminate the pressure of the world by negative means, you will never succeed. But when you try to create a better impression in your mind, other impressions automatically will go. The mind must form impressions, the mind must think about something. The mind must project in a thousand and hundred and one ways – it can never remain still. But you take a positive step. If you create the impression of light and sound within – in the mind – the other impressions automatically fade out. But if you fight with your mind to eliminate outside impressions, you will never succeed. Your object should be to create in the mind the positive impressions of shabd and light within. Then the other impressions will automatically fade out, if your attention is to that side. Christ said: You can have only one master, either mammon or God.²⁴ Below the eye centre, mammon is our master. Beyond the eye centre, God is our master. We can only worship one – we can't worship both. Either we are below the eye centre or we are above the eye centre. So if you go above the eye centre, those impressions automatically wipe out all the lower impressions. And if you remain below the eye centre, these lower impressions will not help you at all to form the right impressions on the mind.

404 *Master, during the day, negative thoughts come into your mind, and you bring it back to simran, and that keeps happening. At what point are those thoughts creating karma? When you attach to a thought as soon as you are thinking it?*

No, thinking is not a karma. But constant thinking definitely makes a groove on our mind. And that makes a very strong desire, and that desire may pull us back to the creation.

So as long as you just pull it back and don't think about it too much, thinking won't make a groove?

Instead of planning that way, if you take a positive step to think something positive, to keep your mind in simran, automatically that thought will be driven away. The mind is the same. So think something positive with the mind. Instead of eliminating the bad thoughts, fighting to eliminate the bad thoughts, think something positive. In that way bad thoughts will automatically be eliminated.

405 *I was told that just by thinking a particular thought you are taking on more karma. I find myself sometimes thinking that thought, but at the same time my mind is*

*apologizing for doing that. Am I still taking on karma for
thinking and then apologizing?*

I think instead of analyzing all these things, it is better to devote
time to meditation. That will also help you to eliminate such
thoughts from the mind. If the mind is absolutely concentrated
in meditation, such thoughts should not come at all. In meditation nothing should stand between you and the Lord, nothing
should exist, you should not be conscious of anything else in the
world. You exist and he exists. That is meditation. If something
still exists between us, then meditation is not complete, it's not
one-pointed.

406 *Are we permitted any latitude insofar as trying various
methods of repetition and other things?*

There is only one method of controlling the mind, which is
explained to us at the time of initiation. We have to practice it
whether we are an old satsangi or a new satsangi. It makes no
difference. There is only one method to control the mind. There
are not two methods. The mind is fond of pleasures, and unless
it is attached to something better than the sensual pleasures, it
does not detach itself from the senses. So we have to attach it
to something better. Only then will it be detached from these
worldly things.

PRACTICAL QUESTIONS

407 *I have two related questions about simran. How does
mechanical simran get turned into simran with love and
devotion? And does it help to try to repeat the words with
love and devotion if you're not feeling it?*

Brother, first we have to start mechanically. Attending to simran with love and devotion means love and devotion for the master. And his instruction is to attend to your simran. We try to do what pleases our beloved, and we try to abstain from what doesn't please our beloved. Wherever there is love, there's also a fear of offending. It's not fear, it's a fear of offending. That's a part of love. We love them so much that we can't afford to offend them. That is also an expression of love. So if you love the master, you want to please him and you would not do anything which displeases him. He's pleased with our meditation. So we attend to our meditation with love, we don't abstain from our meditation. We don't turn our back to meditation because that may displease him. And we can't afford to displease him because we love him. So this meditation creates love. It strengthens love. Love grows by meditation and grows to the extent that we become one with the Father.

408 Master, what can we do to overcome the disappointment at unfulfilled expectations in meditation?

Brother, we should never sit in meditation with any excitement, with any expectation. We should just sit in meditation with love and devotion – whatever has to come will automatically come. If every day you sit with certain expectations – I am going to see this and I'm going to see that – naturally you will be disappointed and you will not be able to concentrate at all. So we just forget about any excitement, just rise above any type of excitement, and sit in meditation just as a matter of duty. Try to concentrate as much as you can, and when it comes, it just comes.

409 Master, is it necessary to be completely relaxed during meditation? How can we guard against trying to force it?

The results that we will get will be much greater if we attend to our meditation with an absolutely relaxed mind. We should never sit in meditation with excitement – that I am going to see something, something is just going to happen, something is just about to come. Then your mind is always in that excitement of expectation. You should just attend to your meditation with an absolutely relaxed mind. Whatever is to come will come automatically. It comes when you least expect it. And when you are anticipating or when you are excited about it, it does not come at all, because then the mind is not actually concentrated but is scattered in excitement. So we have to attend to meditation in a completely relaxed manner. That is why it is generally advised to sit for meditation in the morning. Usually by morning we forget all that happened to us in the past day and our body is also relaxed physically; besides, there is more quietness and calmness in the atmosphere. So if we try to meditate in that relaxed atmosphere, it is always better.

410 *Like many satsangis, I have some difficulties in medi-*
tation and doing simran. Invariably I fall asleep and
start snoring. Somehow these holy names blend into one
another and form a certain kind of pattern that is con-
ducive to sleep. What advice would you give us to keep
awake, as we all seem to have the same trouble?

Yes, I have understood your question, brother. When we are asleep, we are generally at the throat centre. When we meditate, we try to concentrate at the eye centre. There is very little difference between the method of going to sleep and that of trying to concentrate; so generally our attention at the time of simran slips down from the eye centre to the throat centre and we go to sleep. The reasons can be many, but mostly we have too many activities of mind and body that prevent us from getting the required amount of sleep. I do not know why, but in this modern society, we have so many types of engagements. We do not try to compromise with them, but we do compromise with our sleep and our health in order to fulfil those engagements. We would like to work all day and enjoy sleep all night, and from the sleep time we take our meditation time, disregarding what the body needs.

After proper sleep, leave your bed, move about in your room, wash your face with cold water and sit for bhajan. Then there will be no question of sleep overtaking you. We also have to adjust the intake of our food accordingly. We have to go to bed with a light stomach. I am glad to find that in your country you generally take your supper very early, and so go to bed with a light stomach. The main thing is that the body must get proper sleep; otherwise, we are likely to go to sleep at the time of meditation. If you work all day and rush about at night, when you sit in bhajan early in the morning naturally the body wants to go back to sleep. If you give proper rest to the body, there is no reason why you should fall asleep during meditation.

Generally, it is better if you can leave your bed for meditation because we associate sleep with our bed, so again our mind wants to go to sleep. You should leave your bed, walk about, feel quite alert and yet calm and relaxed before sitting for the meditation. And sit on a separate chair or whatever you have allotted for that purpose – then there are less chances of going to sleep.

411 *Master, the same question asked many times – the problem of sleep in meditation?*

There are so many reasons for it. Either we are overworking the whole day and are too tired, or we try to sit in meditation at the cost of sleep and rest, and we don't want to cut out other daily activities. We only want to cut time from our sleep and rest, or we overeat, or our diet is not balanced. Perhaps we are not careful about our diet and there is insufficient protein in our food, which also makes one very sleepy. Or it can be that we are trying to sit in meditation on our bed. We associate bed with sleep, so that association of the mind again puts us to sleep. Or it can be due to not trying to be alert after leaving the bed. If we sit when we are still half dozing, then sleep overpowers us when we try to meditate. So if you wash your face with cool water, stretch yourself a little or move about in the room and thus refresh yourself, you may be able to avoid that sleepiness. There may be many reasons.

Moreover, there is very little difference between concentration at the eye centre and concentration at the throat centre. Whenever we sleep, our attention is at the throat centre – it drops down to the throat centre. But whenever we try to meditate, we try to hold our attention here, at the eye centre. So when we try to concentrate and are a little inattentive, the attention at once drops down to the throat centre and we are asleep. That is also one of the reasons.

Master, sometimes one's face falls forward – you are not wanting it to fall forward, but it gets very tired of being in one position, and then you seem to drop asleep straightaway.

That is right. Whenever we become a little drowsy, the head naturally will fall forward, so if you are wide awake this will not happen. You can support yourself against some firm surface at the back. You need not sit without a support. You may lean against some support, and if you are alert, then you won't go to sleep.

412 *Maharaj Ji, there's a tendency to fall asleep sometimes during the meetings or satsang. I've heard sometimes – is*

there a special karma that's being worked off or some kind
of transmission going on between the master and disciple?

Sister, in the meetings people sleep because sometimes the meetings are very dull. And in meditation, definitely sleep overpowers us. That is the great fight with the mind — not to sleep at that
time. There are many reasons for it. One reason is that we try
to sit in meditation at the cost of our sleep. The body needs a
certain amount of time for rest at night. It varies with individuals, how many hours they need to sleep, but we try to cut that
sleeping time and then try to attend to meditation, so naturally
sleep overpowers us. Then it can also be caused by our food, our
eating habits. We eat very heavy things and a lot of fat and so
many other things which make us sluggish and make us sleep.
And then sometimes we do so much physical work that we get
too tired and so we go to sleep. And moreover, you see, at the
time of concentration doing simran, we sleep when our attention
slips to the throat centre. We try to concentrate at the eye centre,
and our attention just slips down to the throat centre and we go
to sleep. So we should try to take all available precautions to stay
awake. We can get up and wash our face; we can have a cup of
tea — anything that suits you to warm up and move about for
a few minutes and be a little active, and then sit in meditation.
We should trim our diet also, cut out fats, whatever our doctor
suggests, and also physical exertion should not be too much
because our body can't take it. We can adjust so many things,
but sleep in meditation is a very big fight.

413 *Master, our real work, our real effort is to be able to con-*
centrate. So when we start to concentrate and to collect
the energy back to the eye focus, in passing through the
body and re-collecting this energy, how can we avoid — I
don't know how to call it. You can start to tremble, your

heart beats hard and you start to swallow, and then later
on you reach the peace. But when you reach the peace,
you're really tired. How can we avoid those things?

You see, that is why this process is slow. Withdrawing by the
process of simran is very slow, slowly and slowly. The point is just
to avoid all these things that you are trying to describe. They do
happen, especially at the throat centre. It becomes very dry, as
if you're tired of speaking as your throat has become hoarse, or
there is a deep strain sort of sensation in the throat, which you
cannot explain because there's no sickness at all. That is why
we are told at the time of initiation that we can drink a little
honey liquid or just rub our throat with our hand, and it will
be all right. There is no illness at all. When we withdraw to the
eye centre, we experience many different sensations like these
in our body. Sometimes functions in the body become active,
so that is why we are withdrawing very slowly and slowly. It's a
very slow process.

And I have very great heat. I even start to sweat.

That's right. Sometimes that happens. That is why we sit all
alone in a room. Sometimes it's better to lean against something
solid so that we don't jerk about and fall. Everybody doesn't feel
these things. Some people feel pain, others don't feel it at all.

414 *Would you advise us on whether or not it is good to go to*
     sleep after meditation in the morning?

You must have read about this in *Science of the Soul*. Whatever
atmosphere of happiness and peace we have built within ourselves during meditation, why lose it by sleep? Why not live in
that atmosphere the whole day and cheerfully face the ups and
downs of the day? We definitely gain something of happiness
by meditation, and we should want to enjoy that peace and bliss

the whole day. That is the only idea, not that we lose the effect of meditation if we go back to sleep.

415 *I have another question, Master, about meditation, which is that I find very often when I'm sitting that I will go to sleep without realizing that I'm going to sleep. I think that I'm sitting there doing the simran, and then later on I wake up and find that I've been asleep, but I didn't feel it start to happen. If I feel that it's starting to happen, then I can do something. Do you have any helpful suggestions?*

When you realize you are sleeping and you have awakened, then again you can sit in meditation. Sleep is a great problem, because when we have a little concentration, then sleep overpowers us. At the time of sleep, we are generally at our throat centre. At our throat centre, we go to sleep. We are trying to hold the attention at the eye centre – there's not much difference – but generally our attention slips down and we go to sleep. So everybody has to fight his own battle. We should give proper time to sleep; we should sleep with a light stomach; and when we get up in the morning, we can wash our face or move about to be a little active. Everybody has to adopt his own ways and means to keep awake. Some people take a hot cup of coffee in the morning; some take tea. Whatever suits you.

416 *Because of a disability that I have, I can't sit cross-legged for a long time. I wrote you because of a lot of pain that I was having, and you told me to do the best I could in meditation, and that was sitting in a chair. That was the best I could do. I've given up completely, in my meditation, sitting cross-legged for the two and a half hours, because I have to move around all the time. My question is, will it slow my progress down any if I'm sitting in a chair?*

Well, brother, you may sit in any posture. It is not important at all for meditation or spiritual progress. It is the concentration which matters. Sit in any comfortable posture. Advice about posture given to you at the time of initiation is more from the health point of view than from the spiritual progress point of view. So if you are unable to sit in that particular posture – and many of us cannot – you can sit in any comfortable chair, any comfortable posture. The main thing is that ultimately we have to forget what position our body is sitting in. The main thing is the concentration at the eye centre. It is not the posture which matters, and that is absolutely no hindrance to spiritual progress.

417 *Maharaj Ji, another question please? As we get older, is withdrawal more difficult?*

It depends on how much we have spread our thoughts into this creation. If we have allowed ourselves to just spread out into this creation, naturally it will take more time to pull our mind back from everything. If we have not let our mind run wild in this creation, it becomes easier to pull it back. When you put a muslin cloth on a thorny bush, if it is entangled with just a few thorns, it will be easier to pull it off the thorns one by one. But if thousands and thousands of thorns are there holding the cloth, it will take time to pull it from all that. So it depends upon how many thorns we are entangled with.

But Maharaj Ji, is it easier when we are young?

Well, when we are young we have so many other problems too, those of our youth. But we can do much more meditation when we are young and healthy rather than when we are old and wearing out and tiring out. That is natural. Then again, the struggle is harder at a young age than in old age. So youth has both advantages and disadvantages.

*418 For the hearing and for the respiration, what must we
think of people who are left-handed and right-handed?
There are people who are right-handed, who do everything from the right. So it is with their right ear, but what
about people who are left-handed?*

I'll explain. Our hands and our ears have nothing to do with the
sound. The sound is here, at the eye centre. Since we are used
to hearing with the help of our ears, in the beginning we think
the sound comes from the ears. But even without the help of
our ears, if we concentrate here at the eye centre we will one day
hear the sound. It hardly makes any difference whether you are
left-handed or right-handed. In fact, it makes no difference at
all. The main thing is that your attention has to be here at the
eye centre; your mind has to be stilled here, then automatically
you will be in touch with the sound.

*419 When doing simran, is it possible that when one shuts one's
eyes, one's attention can be outside instead of inside? The
literature speaks of the eyes focusing. You talked about it
the other day, about causing problems with the muscles of
the eyes. If one sees something from a distance with the
eyes shut, like a form, is it possible that this form is on the
outside instead of inside and that the focus could be in the
wrong place?*

At the time of meditation we are just to close our eyes. It is our
attention that is to focus. The physical eyes are not involved at
all. If our attention is outside, we feel that we are outside. We
are contemplating outside. If we forget about the outside world,
if we just close our eyes and hold our attention mentally in the
darkness, we see behind the eyes. My meaning of 'behind the
eyes' is that whenever you close your eyes, you are automatically
in that darkness. Whenever you close your eyes, if you do not

let your thoughts run out, scatter out, you are naturally in this darkness; you are naturally behind the eyes. At that place your attention has to contemplate on the form of the master.

You are not physically to try to invert your eyes nor to try to find any particular point in the darkness. If you do that, you will damage your physical eyes. You are just to forget absolutely about your eyes. Mentally, if you will forget about your eyes and forget about yourself and forget about the outside surroundings, you will be somewhere and that will be within yourself; that will be in the darkness. As you repeat these five holy names while contemplating on the form of the master, you are going within, and you are not going out.

Do not try to visualize someone moving about or running about. If you do, then your attention is scattered outside, and slowly and slowly you will run outside; that is, your attention runs out. Try to eliminate and completely ignore everything that you see going on outside and try to contemplate on the form of the master inside, in the darkness. Whether it appears or not, do not let your thoughts run out, but keep your mind in the repetition of the five holy names. You do not have to think that now you are within or that now you are without. When your attention is in this darkness, you automatically will be within.

Another thing I may add about your question: At the time of simran, we are not to pay any attention to breathing. Some people who have been doing hatha yoga or breathing exercises or different types of yoga sometimes try to mix the simran with breathing. That is wrong. There are many schools which try to teach that principle, but satsangis should never bother with the breathing at all at the time of meditation. I am talking to you; you are listening to me. Neither are you conscious of your breathing, nor am I conscious of my breathing. Breathing is a normal function of the body. At the time of meditation we are just to forget about our breathing, forget about our eyes, forget even about ourselves. Keeping your attention mentally in the darkness, you will automatically be in the centre behind the eyes. You are not to try to locate any particular spot behind the eyes. If you can eliminate thoughts of the outside world, if you can stop letting your mind run out, you will automatically be within yourself, in that darkness, and there you have to contemplate on the form of the master and do the simran and bhajan.

420 *Master, sometimes when I sit in meditation, I might be sore or stiff or have a muscle pain, and I move. When that happens, do I lose whatever concentration I had?*

No, you never lose the concentration. Concentration is an attitude of the mind towards the divine melody within. Concentration is not temporary. Every day that we are trying to concentrate, we're creating a habit of concentration. Moving our limbs or getting up and moving for ten minutes, twenty minutes, then sitting in meditation again doesn't make any difference at all. By doing simran and concentrating every day, we're creating a habit of concentration. This will also remain with us in our daily activities, throughout our whole day. That concentration is not only for a particular time. It becomes a habit to concentrate in everything, in every little detail in your life. We're creating a habit of concentration. So it doesn't make any difference if your hands move or sometimes you have to change your posture or you're interrupted a little, and then again you sit. It doesn't make any difference.

421 *My legs will not permit me to sit in the regular posture. Is there any other way that we can sit, or is there any other proper means?*

Posture has absolutely no relationship with our meditation. This is just for health purposes. We in India are used to sitting without the support of any chairs or cushion, so we can just squat as I am doing now; and if you will squat like this and keep your hands here and straighten your arms, your backbone will naturally be straight. It is always essential to keep the backbone straight in meditation. Then you will not get sleepy, you will feel no discomfort, and there will be no physical trouble in the body as in an incorrect posture. [The squatting referred to here means to sit cross-legged on the floor.]

But if you cannot sit like this, you can make your own comfortable posture for meditation. We should not wrestle with the body; we should sit in a relaxed manner, a relaxed way. Any posture which suits your requirements and your physical fitness is all right. If you can sit like this, it is all right; but posture will not help you in your meditation in any way. It can only help your body so that you can forget about it and do not have to be conscious of it in any way during meditation. Mentally, when you are meditating, you should forget the way you are sitting. You are to become absolutely unconscious of the way you are sitting. The posture does not make any difference, whether you sit on a chair or on the floor or lie on your back. But if you lie on your back, naturally that posture has an association with sleep, so you are likely to fall asleep. And if you do not sit comfortably or in a way which is good for your health, that is not advisable as far as the body is concerned. But in a person's spiritual development, posture does not make any difference at all. We are just to keep our attention here, between the eyebrows, inside, and by repetition and concentration we have to forget about the posture.

422   *Must you have a healthy spine in order to bring in the spiritual energies and to be connected to the sound current?*

315

Our physical body has nothing to do with our spiritual progress. I generally advise people when they sit in meditation to try to keep their spine straight, because generally it is healthier. We don't fall asleep as easily, nor do we feel lazy if our spine is straight. So it is always better to keep the spine straight. But even if you can't keep it straight, you'll make the same spiritual progress.

The posture of your spine or any part of your body won't improve your spiritual progress. Eventually you will have to become unconscious of your body when you sit in meditation. There should be nothing between you and the Father. When you become unconscious of your body, it doesn't make any difference whether the spine is straight or crooked.

423 *When practicing simran, if a satsangi gets tuned into the sound current, is it necessary to change positions for bhajan?*

Posture is not very important from a spiritual practice point of view. Generally it is important mainly from the point of view of health and so that we do not easily fall asleep during that time. You may adopt any posture that conveniently suits you. In India we are quite in the habit of squatting or sitting in that bhajan posture, so it is more practical for us. I don't insist that you in the West should try to adopt the same posture. Whatever posture you can conveniently find, try to make use of that. We should never fight with the body. We should never struggle with the body. If we are always fighting with the body, it becomes difficult to concentrate and be one with the holy word within. So whatever posture suits you, try to make use of that posture.

424 *Maharaj Ji, when the sound within pulls one up, does the body have to have any support? Or does it just fall, just collapse?*

No, the body does not collapse. It will stay as it is now, but you may not be conscious of the body. Normal functions of the body will remain the same, but you will not be conscious of the normal functions of the body.

But if one is sitting in the posture and then it comes, and one just does not move the parts, but just stays?

Sometimes people cannot stand it and they do fall. They just lie down or they begin shivering sometimes. It may happen to certain individuals, but generally one remains in the same posture and just becomes unconcerned or unconscious of the body. But sometimes, when you finish your meditation, you find that you are lying down, whereas when you started, you were sitting. Sometimes the body does fall, but you are not conscious when you are falling. There is nothing to fear about that.

425 *Master, pertaining to the question of posture, what about hatha yoga? The positions that they advocate, would they be beneficial, healthwise?*

Hatha yoga is for health purposes. It has nothing to do with meditation. Hatha yoga, in other words, is a set of physical exercises, just to keep the body fit for meditation, but it is not meditation in itself.

Yes, I realize that; but would it be advisable in certain cases?

There is no harm in doing hatha yoga to keep the body fit. For example, I do some of the hatha yoga exercises because I do not get time to walk or go out. So, for ten or fifteen minutes every day, I do some breathing exercises or hatha yoga exercises just to keep the body fit.

*426 Breathing should be relaxed before starting simran; for
example, yogic breathing? Is this advisable?*

No. Those are physical exercises to keep the body and mind
alert, and that is good, but has nothing to do with meditation.
Any physical exercise to keep the body healthy is good. These
exercises were adopted by the yogis because generally they were
confined to their own small cottages or caves where they used
to give their time to meditation. They would hardly go out, so
they developed certain exercises by which, for half an hour or an
hour a day, even while staying in their cottage, they could keep
their body healthy and strong. They developed all these eighty-
four types of postures and so many breathing exercises to keep
healthy. Sometimes I do these myself for ten or fifteen minutes
a day if I get time; but they have nothing to do with spirituality.

*427 Maharaj Ji, is there ever a time during meditation when
one stops breathing? Would it be dangerous?*

We should not think of breathing at the time of meditation.
Those people who have been doing pranayam, breathing exercises, are generally told at the time of initiation that they should
not interfere with breathing at the time of simran; otherwise, they
are likely to be victims of some breathing difficulty – asthma or
something like that. You are talking to me, I am talking to you.
Neither you are conscious of your breathing nor am I conscious
of my breathing. This is a normal function of the body. Let it
go on. We have to concentrate mentally, here at the eye centre.
We are not to interfere with the breathing at all, and then there
is no danger whatsoever. Some people advise doing simran in
rhythm with each breath inhaled and exhaled. That is not right.
We should pay no attention whatsoever to breathing while doing
simran – in fact, not during the entire meditation period.

428 *Is it not best to do the meditation at the end of the day,*
   when the work is finished, before going to sleep?

Any time is good for meditation. Every time devoted to meditation is to your credit and you should make the best use of that time.
But early morning hours have certain advantages for this purpose,
which other times do not have. In such a big city, at least in the
early morning, there is quiet and calmness in the streets. Your body
is fresh and you have forgotten all that passed in the previous day.
There is no disturbance in the house and you do not have a knock on
your door from any guest or relative. You can very easily and quietly
give that time in the morning to your meditation. In the first place,
if you try to devote that time in the evening, you are tired after the
whole day's work and are likely to go to sleep during meditation.
Also, at that time, all that has happened with you throughout the
whole day will come before you like on a cinema screen. If you could
attain concentration in the morning within one hour, perhaps in
the evening you will need four hours to do it, because during the
whole day your mind has been spinning around. But when we get
up in the morning, we are refreshed, have forgotten the incidents
of the past and naturally have a tendency to concentrate. So we
find concentration much easier in the morning. But if one cannot find time in the morning, one may give time in the evening.
Whatever time we can find for meditation is a good time.

   The time is best if the mind does not wander?

Naturally, the object of meditation is to concentrate the mind. So,
if we start in the morning, it is easier to concentrate than in the
evening. Only from that point of view are the morning hours pref-
erable. Otherwise you can select according to your convenience.

429 *Is there something we can do or should do when we go to*
   bed and meditate?

You mean, to keep awake during meditation?

I am talking about going to bed to go to sleep. Should we repeat the names, or should we concentrate the attention here?

I follow your point. While going to bed, if we keep our attention here at the eye centre and do the simran, the first thing is, there will be no insomnia. You will go to sleep at once. Second, you will have good dreams, and the third advantage is that when you get up in the morning for meditation, your thoughts will not be scattered; it will be easier to concentrate and to be in touch with the sound. So it is always best to do simran while going to sleep.

430 *One of the brothers asked if you would recommend taking certain drugs to keep awake during meditation.*

I am glad he has only asked to take drugs to keep awake. I am glad he did not ask to take drugs to concentrate. [Laughter] People take drugs to keep awake, and then take drugs to go to sleep again. You see the folly of it?

You do not recommend them?

For certain diseases or bodily ailments, drugs are essential. To take them for keeping awake is not right.

431 *Do the saints give any credence to the use of colour meditation as a tuning fork? Light is colour, as I understand it – the different rays or colours are emanations of God, the same as your sound current?*

Sister, it is not the outside colours we have to contemplate on. Those colours are inside. They are a reflection of the five elements. You will understand inside, when you will see those colours.

432 *Master, does it matter whether one repeats the names slowly, or ...?*

Just as you feel like. Do not think that you will get better results by repeating fast or slow. Simply repeat in a relaxed manner, just as you normally speak, but mentally, without the use of the tongue. It is the mind that is to do the repeating.

Master, that brings up the question about the pronunciation. How important is that?

It is of no importance at all. It is the attention that matters.

433 *When I was sick, I could not remember the five words and I was so frustrated. All I wanted to remember was the five words. What does one do in case one cannot remember?*

You cannot help it. You can only do something about it when you are conscious.

434 *Maharaj Ji, it's very difficult when you say that we should not wish for anything, because the mind starts to get carried away and it thinks, "Oh, I'd like this or I'd like that!"*

At the time of initiation we are advised not to use meditation to fulfil our worldly desires. Only use the meditation to reach back to the Father. If we meditate and try to fulfil our worldly desires, or use meditation to fulfil our omissions in life, then we may have to take a birth to satisfy all those desires. Not that you're going to get them fulfilled just now. You will get only what is in your destiny; you're not going to get what you are trying to pray for. But those prayers may bring you back to this world to satisfy all those desires.

OVERCOMING OBSTACLES

435 *Maharaj Ji, in my meditation I strive to have the experience of dying while living, and yet I know that I have a very deep fear of dying. This fear seems to prevent me from giving myself completely to the meditation, and I wonder if you would please help me understand and overcome this fear.*

Well, brother, there's always fear of the unknown in our mind. Something which is unknown to us, we are always frightened of. If you go to a different country, and you don't know anybody at all, there's some sort of fear in you about how you will face things there, how you will conduct yourself in that foreign country. That fear is always there. But when we know we're going to our own destination, we are going back to our own house, there should be no fear at all. There need not be any fear because we are going to meet our own master there. And we are not going alone at all, we are going along with him. That is why we need the master – to not feel frightened of anything unknown to us. He is known to us, and we're happy to be with him, so the question of fear doesn't arise at all. It is only our mind which tries to frighten us. There's nothing to feel frightened about. We are to be met by somebody who knows us, whom we know. Christ said: My sheep recognize my whistle. When I whistle, they all flock to me, run to me, because they know me, they know my whistle – they're not frightened of me.[104] That is the object of knowing the shepherd, of recognizing the whistle. It means I will not feel frightened.

436 *Master, someone asked a question about prayer a few minutes ago. Christ said: Fear not, I am with you always even unto the end. Sometimes I become frightened –*

I know you're my master, yet I still want to cry out for more courage.

Sister, as I have just said to another sister, we should never feel frightened within ourselves. We are never alone. We always have somebody with us, watching us and guiding us and helping us. You mustn't get depressed. You just continue with your meditation. Let anybody appear – don't bother about anybody. You continue with your meditation, and nobody can do you any harm at all.

437 *Maharaj Ji, I would like to thank you for initiation. The experience I have had after initiation has been very difficult. As I go inside my body, in my meditation – not very far – I get very scared because of the pain that I have in my body from the karmas, from the separation I have from you. My response to that fear is to become lazy, to try to leave the vows. I continue, but I become very scared. I'm wondering how you might recommend that I continue in the fear of the darkness, in the fear of the pain.*

Well, brother, I understand. It's very easy to understand Sant Mat, but I know how difficult it is to follow. There is nothing which can harm us inside; it is our own mind which frightens us. You should love the darkness; you should appreciate the darkness. Be in the darkness, do your meditation, and try to eliminate the darkness – don't feel frightened of that darkness. Help automatically will come from within. Just continue.

438 *In London, I asked you about fear of the darkness, and you said that I should learn to love the darkness. My fear of the darkness has left me – I'm no longer afraid. Thank you. But I am having some difficulty learning how to love*

the darkness. The darkness seems to have no substance, so I don't know what to love.

You see, when we are sitting in meditation, we should think that we have no connection with anybody else in the world except this darkness in the forehead. We should cut off from everything in the world and just be in that darkness. This is what I mean by being in love with the darkness – to concentrate here [at the eye centre] in the darkness. Have no other thoughts of the world. Automatically this darkness will change into light.

439 *Master, can you shed some light on the fact that as we meditate, sometimes we go through periods of great lone-liness – not during meditation, but during the day. It may go on for, well, years. I just wondered, how long can it go on?*

Sister, if I rightly follow your question, I have discussed so many times in the meetings that when we try to live the way of Sant Mat and attend to our meditation, follow the path, we lose all our interest in worldly affairs, in worldly people – they do not attract us anymore at all. They don't charm us anymore. So when we get up in the morning, we don't look forward to what used to catch our attention, and within we have not yet been able to make enough progress to hold our attention, so we start feeling the vacuum and loneliness within ourselves. We have to pass through that stage sooner or later because nothing in the world attracts us anymore and we find nothing else within to hold our attention. So we start feeling very lonely, and we feel a void in our life. There is nothing to feel frightened about.

Actually, everybody is lonely in this life – it's a self-deception to think that somebody belongs to you or you belong to somebody. Sooner or later everybody realizes that one is alone in life – to think otherwise is just a self-deception. I think it's a God-given gift when that feeling comes in us. Then we turn to the Father to hold on to something which belongs to us, to which we can belong. And that gives us a sense of peace and bliss and happiness within. Otherwise, on the outside, when we try to belong to somebody or try to possess somebody, nothing but frustration comes, unhappiness comes. So it is the Lord's way of pulling us towards him. If we didn't feel that feeling of loneliness within ourselves, then perhaps nobody would think about the Father. If these outside faces and objects could hold our attention and make us happy permanently, forever, nobody would think about the Father. We react back, we rebound back from all this, and then we turn to the Father to seek that bliss and peace and happiness within.

440 *If we are being responsive to the pull and are drawn to put in more than the allotted time of meditation daily, is there a way that we can avoid the depression that tends to come into the mind?*

Well, brother, depression does come sometimes. I don't deny it. Definitely it comes in meditation sometimes. But we have to pass through that phase also. If we just continue, then we get over it, we rise above it. Then it converts into bliss and peace and happiness. The lover has to pass through so many phases in his love. He doesn't get cake on his plate. So many sacrifices he has to make, so many nights he has to keep awake, and so much depression he has to go through, but he doesn't leave loving – ultimately his love is pure and he succeeds. So similarly we have to pass through so many phases in love, in his love, in his devotion; but we should continue.

441 Master, one of the most difficult things I find, living in the world, is the periods when I feel nothing for the path – no love, no devotion. I know you've spoken of them as dry spells, but I find it almost unbearable sometimes, and I was wondering if you could speak about it.

You mean sometimes you feel devotion and love, and sometimes you feel dry and void? You don't see the sun every day, sister. There are clouds sometimes. And sometimes they are very thick clouds. But that sun is always there. We have to pass through so many phases of our karmas. Sometimes favourable karmas come and we feel full of emotion and devotion for the Father. Sometimes an unfavourable layer of karmas comes and we feel absolutely void and dry. We pass through so many phases of karma.

That's all the more reason why we should attend to our meditation, to get through that dryness. Sometimes also in meditation a stage comes when we feel a great void in our life, because the effect of meditation is that we get detached from all the worldly pleasures, worldly faces. They don't interest us anymore. And nothing holds us inside to catch our attention or our thoughts, so then we feel a void. The world doesn't please us, and we have nothing else to please us within. But we pass through that dry spell. Everybody has to pass through that, so to say. One shouldn't feel discouraged. As long as we were attached to the world, we always had something to look forward to. When we got up in the morning, we'd say: "I'll go to a movie, I'll go to the theatre, I'll go to that party, and I have so many dates and this and that." So you feel attached, and you plan your day and you feel interested in how you will spend the whole day. But when those things don't interest you anymore at all, when you are not being pulled by them in any direction at all, and you are not getting any attachment within, or any enjoyment of meditation or blissful feeling within, then you feel that dryness and void in your life. Practically every seeker has to pass through that period. That's even more reason why we should attend to, cling to meditation.

442 *Master, how can we be happy in this world and keep our balance when meditation is dry sometimes, and also our mind is not getting what it wants in the world anymore?*

Sister, actually we can only be happy when our soul is in love or in devotion with the Father, because the inclination of the soul is always towards its own origin, towards its own source. The more we keep the soul away from its source, from its destination, from the Lord, the more unhappy it remains. The more we are nearer on the path, towards our home, the more joy and bliss we feel within.

There is no pleasure or happiness in the outside worldly objects or worldly achievements. They are all short-lived, temporary, transitory, because there is always danger of losing those things. If you have money which gives you pleasure, there is always a danger in your mind of losing that money. If you have a lovely wife or a lovely husband, there's always the fear of losing him or her. When that fear is in our mind there is always pain and misery, even at the base of these so-called pleasures. So that is no pleasure at all.

Real happiness and pleasure is only to be in love and devotion for the Father, to develop that. The more you build that within yourself, the more happy you will become. Meditation no doubt is dry to begin with, because for ages our mind has been in the habit of running outside towards the senses, towards the worldly objects, towards the worldly achievements. And we are so interlinked with each other, so much attached to each other, that naturally it is not so easy to withdraw the mind from all that and attach it to the shabd and nam within. Naturally it requires a great effort to do it, and meditation to begin with is definitely dry – but it is worth achieving.

443 *Maharaj Ji, when I give in to feelings of emptiness and hopelessness, does the master still help me at those times?*

Well, brother, in the morning when the sun rises, it is there for the whole day. But sometimes thick clouds come and we cannot make use of the light of that sun. It does not mean that the sun is not there – it is just behind the clouds.

So we should not despair. The Lord's grace is within every one of us, but due to our karmas, sometimes thick clouds come within us and we feel that emptiness, that void within ourselves. Not finding anything within and not being attached to anything outside, we feel that void, but that should not cause us to despair at all. That is for our own good, our own advantage. We know the reality of this world, we know our real self, so we try to find the reality. This should help us to attend more to meditation, to overcome that void and emptiness.

The sun is always there. His grace is always there – there is no question of emptiness. Our cup is upside down. His grace is always flowing, so we should try to turn our cup into a position to receive his grace. Our mind is scattered outside. It runs to the senses, it runs to the whole universe through the nine apertures. We should try to withdraw the mind and hold it at the eye centre and make our cup receptive to his grace, to receive that nectar within and to overcome that void and emptiness.

444 *Master, I feel sometimes, especially since I've been at Dera – every now and again I get an overwhelming feeling of everything being a play and unreal, but I feel very*

uncomfortable saying things like that because it makes
me feel empty of something that I have been accustomed
to grasping in life.

Sister, it is very natural when you know that the surroundings
you have to deal with, the environment in which you have
to live, are nothing but a play and you are only a spectator.
You're not attached to anybody, and when you're not attached
to anybody you feel a vacuum within yourself. Then where do
you belong? It's natural to feel empty. Otherwise we would
always deceive ourselves. But still, we always look to someone
or something to hold on to – children, wife, relations, country,
wealth, house, and so many things, so many ways we spend
our time. When we get real conviction and realize that nothing
belongs to us, that it is all a play and we are just spectators, then
naturally you are not attached to anybody. So then you start
feeling that vacuum within yourself. That detachment creates a
vacuum within you; in a way, that is the Lord preparing us for
something to hold on to.

Unless we hold on to the shabd and nam within, it's difficult to remove this vacuum, to remove this feeling of not
belonging to anybody and of nothing and no one belonging to
you. When you hold on to the shabd, then you get that bliss that
you belong now, that your own reality and your real self belong
to you and you are part and parcel of that. Then that feeling of
loneliness or of that vacuum which often frustrates us, dejects
us, vanishes. You see, this has to be. You can't help it.

So then we try to find out: If this is all a play, then what
is the reality? What is my role in that reality? It is actually the
Lord preparing us from within to hold on to something that is
real. He is preparing us, after making us realize the unworthi-
ness of all this – our surroundings, our environment. It is the
Lord preparing us to be one with the reality. Then this vacuum

automatically goes. Then that bliss and peace and happiness fill us. Then we, without any rhyme or reason, remain happy. We then have a sense of belonging to someone and someone belonging to us. And then automatically we become happy.

Maharaj Ji, do we have to experience the vacuum before we can feel that sense of security of which you speak?

Sister, it varies with the individual. Definitely, sooner or later we do have that feeling. Nothing in the world means anything to us anymore, and you've nothing to hold on to. So feeling a vacuum is natural. Sometimes frustration is natural. Dejection is natural. But we pass through this phase also.

445 *Why is it that sometimes when I want to sit in meditation, the mind will try to bring doubts about the teachings?*

The mind is very faithful, because it is the duty of the mind to keep us away from the path and not let us sit in meditation, and to keep us attached to this creation. That is the duty of the mind. So the mind is always faithful to its own master. We should also try to be faithful to our master and sit in meditation in spite of the obstacles created by the mind. We must devote our time to meditation.

446 *Professor talks about having intense longing. When I was a seeker I felt that intense longing, and now that I have been on the path for a while, I feel like the meditation is part of a daily routine, and I am wondering if feeling content with that is a hindrance to the progress.*

No, it doesn't become any hindrance. You see, after initiation we start analyzing ourselves too much, whether we have been able to detach from this object, that face, or not. We analyze too much with ourselves. Before that, we were not conscious of all those things at all. We were rather proud of those attachments. So we don't go backward at all when we are attending to our daily routine, daily meditation. If you are sitting in a dark room, you don't know what is moving about in the room. If a little ray of sun comes in that room through the ventilator, then you realize how many insects are moving about, how many germs are moving about in the room. That little ray of light has been able to expose all that knowledge to you. Before that, you were unconscious of them, you never knew about them. So similarly, after initiation, after we begin attending to meditation, we start analyzing ourselves too much – how much progress we have made, how much we have been able to detach. This calculation doesn't lead us anywhere. We should just continue with our meditation, and detachment is automatically the effect of meditation.

447 Master, I have trouble sometimes reconciling myself – one moment I feel a lot of love and devotion for the master, and the next moment I am off doing something that is just totally lacking in love and devotion. I am just very grateful for all the love that the master has given to me.

Sister, our problem is that we analyze ourselves too much: "Now I am in love, now I have no love, now I am dry." We analyze ourselves too much, which leads us nowhere. The Lord has sown the seed of love, he is nursing that seed of love within us, and it is always developing. The fruit definitely will grow on the tree, but sometimes there is a wind which takes away the fruit – even the flowers fall – but the tree bears fruit again. So we shouldn't try to analyze too much. We should just attend to our meditation and do our duty. If every day you start thinking, "How much love do I have today?" it will lead you nowhere and just confuse you – nothing else.

448 *Maharaj Ji, a central theme of your message seems to be: Don't analyze things so much and don't worry; just do your meditation and the Father will do the rest. Does that mean that we should just sit in meditation and not be concerned whether you appear to us in the radiant form, so long as we continue to do the meditation and follow the rules of Sant Mat?*

You see, we start analyzing ourselves too much: "How much love do I have? Now I have no more faith, yesterday I had too much faith." Every day we judge ourselves. We are the judge, and we are the accused before the judge. The mind is just always running in a circle like this. This self-analysis doesn't lead us anywhere at all. Self-pity – it depresses us sometimes. Let the Lord judge. Let him know what we need. Our work is to do our duty. Our duty is to knock; it's for him to open the door. We can't take on our shoulders his responsibility also. It is for him to open the door. We have to beg; it is for the householder to give.

449 *We are very impatient in this country [U.S.A.]. Everything is hard for us. We try to be kind. In business, people complain because they have no apprentices these days. They will not serve two weeks. They want to be journeymen. So it is very hard to concentrate.*

It is a lifelong struggle.

Is it harder for us here, do you think, than it would be in India?

No, I do not think so. I think, practically, human beings are the same everywhere. They have their own problems, you have your own problems. Probably you are tired because you have too much; they are tired because they have too little. The problem is the same.

EFFORT AND GRACE

450 Most of the events of our lives are predestined, but is the event of reaching home the only event that is not predestined? That is, can we reach this home whenever we put the proper effort into it?

Brother, from that point of view, everything is destined in the sense that when the Lord wants us to go back to him, he creates those circumstances, that atmosphere which makes us think about him, about the path, the way leading back to him. Without his grace we will never come on the path or on the way of devotion; or, in other words, we will never come in contact with the saints at all without his grace. When he wants us to come back and merge into him, only then will all these processes start; only then will we come in contact with the saints; only then will we start meditating. But we ourselves have to work; we have to make ourselves receptive to his grace. He will create the circumstances; he will create the atmosphere for us in which we can work our way back up to our home. So when he wants us to do so, only then do we work. But unless we make the effort and work, we cannot reach our destination.

In other words, no matter how much effort we put into it or how hard we try, if the time is not right, we will never get home?

Brother, it is just like this: A beggar comes to your door to ask you for alms, but first he wants to be assured that he is going to get something from the house before knocking at the door. Otherwise, he is not going to beg. This is a wrong attitude. We are all beggars at the Lord's door. We have to beg. We have to ask, but he always gives. We should not say that when he wants us to meditate we will meditate; otherwise, why bother about it? That is a wrong approach, and definitely a wrong attitude. We are all beggars at his door, so we should all do our best and leave everything to him. Of course, we will only get when and what he wants us to get, but we must make the effort by doing the spiritual practice.

And I assure you, if we really beg from our heart, he is always ready to give. If we come one step, he comes ten steps to receive us. But our devotion must be pure; our longing, our desire to merge back into him must be absolutely one-pointed. We have to love him for his sake. We should not worship him for our children's sake or for the sake of business, money or worldly achievements. That is surely a wrong way to approach him. That is a wrong attitude or motive for meditating on him. We want him, we worship him, we love him because we want to go back and merge into him.

In India some people worship snakes, not because they love them but because they fear their bite. We should not worship the Lord out of fear that if we do not worship him some calamity will befall us or that he will punish us in some way. We should worship him out of love. The basis of religion is not fear; it is absolutely pure love. So we have to base all our worship and meditation on the foundation of love. Only then will we get the best results.

451 *When you know this and know you must develop love – you really do – but there are times of distress when things get away from you, how can you develop this love?*

Brother, practically, it comes when it comes. You do not have the power to develop it. When his grace is there, it just comes; but the practical step that we can take to develop our devotion to the Lord is to meditate, to build that atmosphere around us of devotion for the Lord by reading books, by satsang, by discussion and by having harmonious meetings. By helping each other, we build that atmosphere around us in which, then, we start giving; and we find that the more we give our devotion to the Lord, the more it grows every day. The more love we have, the more it grows. But the only practical step that we can take is to be honest in our meditation, for then devotion and love come automatically.

452 *Are there other ways besides meditation for us to beg for the grace of having more longing for the master, or is meditation the only way to beg?*

Well, brother, other ways are means, not an end. The reality you get only by meditation. The soul is always in love with its Lord; the soul is full of devotion for the Father. But it is helpless due to the weight of the mind. And the mind has become a slave of the senses. So, being mixed up with the mind – rather, dominated by the mind – we do not feel that love for the Father. Love is there in every soul. Potentially, every soul is God. So the more weight we remove from the soul, the more love and devotion we feel for the Father. There's no other way. You see, you have to remove the weight.

The needle is always attracted by the magnet, but if there's a weight over the needle, it becomes helpless. It's not that the needle is not being attracted by the magnet. The attraction is the same as it was before the weight, but it just has become helpless. So all we have to do is remove the weight from the needle; then automatically it goes to the magnet. Similarly, the soul is always in love with the Father, full of love and devotion for the Lord, for its Creator. But it has become helpless due to the weight of the mind, and the mind has become helpless due to being a slave of the senses. So we have to adopt that means and that method by which we can remove the weight of the mind from the soul.

Satsang, discussions, meetings, good company, good literature – they are ways to create longing in us for meditation, for the Father. But achievement can only be done through the meditation. The means create longing in us, strengthen our faith in meditation, but the real achievement we will only accomplish by meditation. So there's no short cut to meditation. That is why Christ said: Sin against the holy ghost can never be forgiven.[46] There's no other way to seek the forgiveness of the Father but to attend to the holy ghost. The devotion is already there, love is there – we are not creating love in the soul, we are only removing the weight of the mind. And then we realize the love from within. It doesn't come from anywhere else. The soul is already anxious to go back to the Father. It's miserable being in separation.

So the question of a short cut doesn't arise. The teachings of the mystics should not remain confined to literature, to discussion, to tapes. They have to be imprinted on our heart – they have to be lived, they have to be followed. The other activities are just means; the main thing is to live in the teachings, in that way of life.

453 *Something has been bothering me. Master, you made the statement that the mind must be made to sit in meditation either by force or love. Now, I have tried to sit in meditation for three and a half years, maybe not too faithfully, but mostly it appears that I have to be forced. Sometimes I enjoy the meditation, but frankly not too often. The question in my mind is, why doesn't the master give his American disciples more glimpses of inner life, so the mind can learn to love meditation and sit for at least the allotted time?*

There are only two ways of attending to meditation. Either you have intense love and desire for meditation, or you make it a habit in your life. You tell yourself: This particular time has to be given to meditation come what may. Only then does it become a habit. Call it force, call it habit, call it a matter of duty – ultimately it comes to the same thing. The other way is intense longing, intense desire and devotion, which forces you to attend to the meditation. That is always best, but if you are not fortunate to have that approach, then naturally we cannot relax in our meditation. We have got to make it a point that certain times in a day have to be devoted to meditation.

As far as glimpses are concerned, when we are honest, when we are doing our duty, we certainly get glimpses here and there. Almost every satsangi gets some glimpses here and there, just to keep us on the path, so that we may continue in that faith, continue on that path. But we have to earn those experiences by our regular meditation, by our devotion, by our faith. You have to start with the ABC's, you have to work your way up in meditation. But we definitely get glimpses if we are really honest about our meditation.

454 *Could you explain what it means for us to be honest in our meditation?*

We have to be sincere with ourselves. We must live with ourselves rather than living for others. We have to put in honest and sincere efforts, then leave the result to the Lord.

455 *Maharaj Ji, is there a difficult way – not a short cut – besides meditation to achieve our goal? [Laughter]*

I don't think there is anything more difficult than meditation. Meditation is the most difficult. It looks so simple, and yet it is so difficult to attend to it. Sant Mat is very simple, but difficult to practice. It's easy to understand, very simple to understand, because the whole philosophy is very simple. But when we put it into practice, many obstacles come in the way. To live that way is a great problem. It's a constant struggle to live the teachings.

456 *Maharaj Ji, it has been said that a great deal of our time doing meditation is only practicing meditation. At what point can we feel that our efforts are really meditation?*

You see, sister, whether you are giving a very soft knock at the door or whether you are giving a very hard knock at the door, whether you are frightened to knock and only shouting, you are at the door and you want the door to be opened to you. Even when we are too nervous to knock, our intention is that the door should be opened and we should get admission. So our effort is there – everybody has a different approach. Everybody who is on the path wants the door to be opened. Effort is when we are sitting in meditation, whether we are too nervous to knock or whether we are knocking. But when the owner of the house sees that you are not interested to get in, he will close the door again.

457 *Professor said yesterday that sometimes we have so many problems in life, so many duties and responsibilities that the master withholds the shabd. So why work so hard – why not just do a little meditation at a time and just wait until we have fewer duties and responsibilities?*

Because it makes you restless if you don't attend to your meditation. You feel guilty. You feel a great weight on your mind if you don't attend to your meditation daily. So you attend to it. You want to enjoy that bliss and peace and happiness of meditation, of that atmosphere. There is no question of why then. You see, master never said that you should not attend to meditation. It is up to the master. He deals with every soul individually. If it is in the interest of a certain soul to discharge certain obligations in this world, everything he has earned from attending to meditation is kept for him, and will be given at the proper time. Master knows the tendency of that soul. So there is no question of our thinking that we should not do it. We have to attend to meditation. Then it is for the master, how he manipulates and how he helps us to get rid of our karmas. We shouldn't try to take responsibility for his duties. We must attend to our own duties.

458 *At the time of initiation, when you take on a large part*
of our karmas, does this change our future from what it
would have been?

You have to clear your own karma. When one goes to a forest, if he has a gun or a sword in his hand he becomes fearless to meet any wild animal. But that doesn't mean that the person who gave him the gun or sword has to come and help him get rid of the wild animals. You have been given a technique of meditation. You have to help yourself. You have to make you own willpower strong to go through all your fate karma. Master also helps you to some extent, but you have to mainly help yourself by meditation. Sometimes when one is feeble, one can lean against somebody, but ultimately he has to walk on his own legs. He can't walk on another person's legs, in another person's shoes – he has to walk in his own shoes. Meditation helps us to clear all those karmas, gives us strength and willpower to go through our present karma, fate karma, and not to be tempted to sow new seeds. So meditation helps in every way. We have to do our duty. That is the main thing.

459 *Simran becomes dry. Is there a way to make it sweeter?*

I can't say whether you can make it sweeter, but you can definitely attend to it with a little strong willpower. Every day you don't see the sun, but the sun rises every day. Sometimes thick clouds are there – sometimes even in the daytime it becomes dark. That doesn't mean the sun hasn't risen today; the sun is always there. His grace is always there, his pull is always there. But thick layers of karmas just sweep us away and we become absolutely helpless. So we should just continue with our meditation with a little strong willpower, and they will pass and you will again enjoy that sunshine.

So then you will be given the strength to come back?

Yes, we have to do our best. Then leave it to him. We shouldn't try to deceive ourselves – that is the main thing. We must do our best and then leave it to him and not worry much.

460 *Master, could you comment on the concept that there's no failure in Sant Mat? I've read it many times, but I'd just like to hear it from you again.*

Failure means that I have done my best to attend to meditation but I couldn't succeed. Failure doesn't mean that I never attended to meditation. That is not failure – that is not even attempting. Failure means I have done my best, I have given my time, I have lived the way of life while I have been trying to build my treasure. From every point of view I have been keeping myself clean, but I have not achieved anything within myself. So this is my failure. That effort will not be lost – that is what is meant by failure. Failure only comes when we are attempting to achieve something and we have not been able to achieve it. When we never attempt to achieve it, then where is the failure? If the child doesn't even try to learn to walk, he will never learn to walk. If the child is trying to learn to walk, he's bound to fall here and there and get bruises. But he's attempting to learn to walk. So our attempt is there, our efforts are there, but the result is not in our hands. From that point of view we can say that we have failed, but that is no failure.

461 *Master, if we try to meditate and our thoughts are still outside all the time, are we really getting anywhere?*

Sister, any time we devote to meditation, howsoever imperfect that meditation may be, is to our credit. It helps. It helps us to grow towards the path. So we should not think that our meditation is not very qualitative. We should think that it should at least be quantitative. Automatically quality comes with quantity. If we don't start, we will never learn to walk. If we start, then naturally we fall also, we get bruises also. But as long as we get up again and start walking again, we will ultimately learn. So every effort made on the path is to our credit. A child, when he grows, has to pass through so many phases. He doesn't just start running after birth. He has to pass through so many phases, and every phase is a step forward. He doesn't even know how to lie down. He doesn't know how to keep his head straight, how to sit, how to stand. He has to pass through so many phases before he learns to stand and run. We have forgotten all those problems now that we are grown, but if we look at childhood, we have so many problems in the beginning.

462 *Master, you said the Father gives the pull from within. He gives you the love and devotion. Why is it that sometimes we don't feel love for the Father and other times we do? Why do we have certain moods when we don't feel love, we don't feel devotion?*

Well, brother, at certain times a layer of karma comes, a cloud of karma comes. When a cloud comes, there is no light from the sun; when the clouds lift, you see the light of the sun. Our Father is always filling us with love and devotion. But when a layer of karma comes, sometimes we don't feel that love and devotion at all. In order to remove that layer of clouds, that layer of karma, we have to attend to our meditation.

463 But is it also correct to say that our initial attempts to meditate are really only by the grace of the master?

Everything is done by the grace of the Father in this world. A seeker can achieve nothing without his grace. Without his grace, a seeker would not even know about the Father, what to say of reaching the Father, what to say of trying to achieve the destination. He would not even know about the Father. Without his grace, we would never be able to take birth in a family in which we could know about the Father. If we take a birth in a certain family, we get that atmosphere of love and devotion for the Father; then we have the company of certain friends who influence us towards our destination.

All this you get by grace, and by his grace we have that longing and desire in us to go back to the Father. We search; we read books; we find the path; we try to tread the path, try to achieve that object. Everything happens by grace. Without his grace, nothing can happen. Unless he wishes, nobody can reach him. We are all blind, groping in the dark. He is the only one who can show us the light out of this darkness. And he has his own ways and means to show that light to us. Nobody can achieve anything without his grace at all. We think that we worship him, that we love him. But he is the one who is pulling us from within, who creates that desire in us to worship him and creates that longing for him. He is the one who is pulling from the back. We are only an instrument, so to say.

464 Master, is the Lord's grace in a person's destiny or karma,
or is that just a gift of the Lord beyond his karma or destiny?

You see, it's very difficult to put any limitation or condition on
the grace of the Lord. We can't say that by doing this, he must
give us grace, he must shower grace on us. He is all-powerful. He
may shower his grace whenever he wants to, wherever he wants
to; there are no conditions to invoke his grace. But normally
what a human being can do is to be good, to be kind, to be nice,
to attend to meditation. We are doing all these things to invoke
his grace. Meditation is nothing but knocking at his door for his
grace, for his blessings, for his mercy, for his forgiveness. That
is the purpose of meditation. And if we are sincere, if we are
successful in knocking, he doesn't withhold his grace. Because
he is the one who has prompted us to knock at his door. He's
pulling us towards him – that is why we are knocking at his
door. If he initiates that longing and is provoking us to knock
at his door, he won't withhold his grace to open the door and
make us one with him – because he has started all this within
us. So naturally he is also anxious that we should be receptive
to his grace and that we should receive his grace.

465 The masters say that there's absolutely no effort without
grace. So I don't understand how – I mean, the way I see
it is that it's all the grace of the master. As you said before
about the food and the plate – if we want to think we are
moving our arm back and forth in order to eat, okay, go
ahead. But really, the way I see it, it says in the books that
there's only grace and no effort at all – it's all impossible
without the master.

It depends on from where you look at things, whether you look
from the higher angle or the lower angle. It depends on from

what stage you are looking. If you look from a very, very high angle, nothing moves without the Father's grace. Without his grace, we would not have gotten human birth. Without his grace, we would not have gotten the environment or atmosphere which pulled us to the path. Without his grace, we would not have developed that love and longing of separation to become one with him. Without his grace, we could not get that environment and the facilities with which to sit in meditation, to put in that effort. So from the higher angle, nothing happens without his grace. He's the one who marks us and he makes us worthy of his marking. He makes us worthy of his test, and he's the one who tests us. He is within us. He worships himself through us, in other words, from that higher angle. From our level, we have to put in effort and then depend upon his grace.

Guru Nanak says: If you look to our karmas, there'll be no end to it. If you go on washing the earth with your hand, how do you expect you'll ever be able to reach the water below?* The water is 200 or 300 feet down. But how can we reach there? The earth between us and the water is the layers of our karma. And this is the way you have made us. So Guru Nanak is telling us that we all depend on his grace – nothing but his grace.

466 *Master, we know that our ultimate goal is God-realization. And we know that realized souls have put in tremendous effort to achieve such a task, while we are living nowadays with family and business duties and just a few hours of meditation. I mean to say, the achievement is so high and our effort is very, very low.*

---

* *Maati ka kya dhopay swaami, maanas ki gat eihee.* Guru Arjun, Adi Granth, M5, p. 882.

Even if we won't put in low effort, as you call it, then what will we achieve? Let us at least put in low effort. Then automatically it will become high effort. With our sincerity, with our honesty in meditation, our quality of meditation increases. It's not the quantity which matters so much; it is the quality of meditation. So our quality will become purer and purer, better and better, with the effort which we try to make, however little it may be. We're trying to improve the quality of our meditation. And then, the Lord's grace is always there to pull us. If we think that with our effort we'll be able to achieve anything, it is impossible. When we improve the quality of our sincerity, our honesty, then we invoke his grace to come to our help, which is never lacking. If sincerity is there, honesty is there – which bring longing in us and create real devotion in us – all these factors provoke his grace, to help us eliminate all that stands between us and the Father. Just by meditation, by effort, I don't think anybody can ever reach back to him. We're trying to make ourselves receptive by meditation. And then he has to fill us. His grace is there.

467 *Master, you said something about when we were brought down to this creation and we didn't have a choice. And I wondered if that is the reason why we love it so much?*

Sister, as Guru Nanak says, if you go on washing the earth, there will be no end to it, you will never be able to reach the bottom, what to say of clearing our karmas, our sins. We are humans, we can't help it. We can escape from this realm only with the Lord's grace. If you say we can escape by our effort, by our intellect – it's impossible. We can do it only by his grace.

We are all condemned to this creation, and we can't help it. We have been made like that. It's not even our fault. We were made like that. Guru Nanak says that we humans will always act like this. If we want to account for our karmas, there will be no limit to it. We will never be able to escape. What we need is his grace. When his grace is there, circumstances combine in such a way that we want to get out of the creation. We come to the path, we get the opportunity to meditate. We get the facilities, the atmosphere. We feel his love, his devotion, and we turn our back to the world and look to him. All these things come just by his grace. It's not that we have done something to deserve all that. We have done nothing. A man can never do anything to deserve all this. We can never do anything to deserve his love. He just gives it and gives it. We are too small-fry to even invoke his grace, because we are so helpless as humans in this creation. It's all his grace. If the master won't come with his grace, then who will? It is nothing but his grace that we get so much pull and love for the Lord from within. Unless he pulls from within, nobody can even think about the Father. Actually, he worships himself through us. When he wants to pull us to his own level, he worships himself through us. We are just helpless.

468 *Master, one evening you said that love is a gift of the Lord. Can you tell us how we can become worthy of this gift?*

Well, if we look within ourselves and think we have become worthy, we never become worthy. We have been here in this creation for generations and generations, and we have been collecting so many karmas every time we have been here. If we must account for all those karmas, it will be impossible to become worthy of the Lord. There would be no end to them. So what we need is the Lord's grace, his forgiveness, nothing else. We can do our best in meditation, pray to him, be sincere with him, be honest with him, but grace depends entirely upon him. We can't say that now, since we have prayed so long, since we have been good for so many years, now we deserve his grace, now we have become worthy of his grace. In no way can we ever become worthy of his grace. He just showers grace – he knows best on whom and when.

469 *How does one develop true spiritual love for the master and satsangis when one has grown rather hard in the business world and has almost forgotten brotherly love?*

Well, when love comes, it just comes. You do not have to build it, you do not have to grow it; it comes. When it is the Lord's grace, it just comes. For putting forth the effort, so to say, we should attend to meditation daily, read literature on Sant Mat, hear satsang and try to be in association with the saints. All these things help us to develop that love. But then, all these things can be done only when his grace is there. So actually it comes back to the same thing, that when he wants us to have it, only then it comes.

470 *Since masters or saints always give their grace, where does the value of effort come on the path?*

The grace forces you to put in effort, unless you want to resist the grace. You see, you will feel the pull from within to sit in meditation, to achieve something within. That is the grace. Now grace is pushing you to make the effort, making you sit in meditation, making you awake early in the morning, and making you feel guilty the whole day if you don't attend to your meditation. That is all grace. That is forcing you to put in effort. So saints have their own way of giving grace.

471 *Maharaj Ji, yesterday in satsang you said that the worship of the spirit is worship of the Father, and that that is the true worship that pleases the Father. And you've also told us in a meeting and told me before that our true surrender won't come until we own that which we can*

surrender to you. So my question is, how do we become more receptive to the ever-flowing grace of the master, and mainly, how do we become good beggars in order to get to that point of surrender?

The more grace he gives us, the more we try to reach him, the more pangs of love we feel within ourselves. Without his grace, nothing can be achieved at all. We are so much involved in this maya, in this illusion, that we hardly know what reality is. Things which are not real, we want them; that which is real – we don't know what is real. We love those who have no reality, and he who has reality – the Lord – we are not even conscious of him. Only he's eternal, only he exists – nothing else exists in this creation. But we are not conscious of him. We are conscious of this creation, which has to perish. It is just by his grace that we realize this hard fact and are able to withdraw our mind from this creation and put our attention toward the worship of the Father. Without his grace, we can achieve nothing.

472 *When we meditate, especially at 3:00 in the morning, is this grace, free will, or destiny or all three?*

It is not just by coincidence that we meet a master or are on the path. If the marking is done by the Father, that marking is a part of destiny. So marking is grace, and our destiny is also grace. If we are destined to follow a path, it is his grace, because he has marked us, allotted us to a certain mystic who will put us on the path. He has given us into the charge of a certain mystic. As Christ says, I of my own will do nothing. I do what my Father wants me to do.[88] So mystics don't pick up souls and initiate them by their own free will. They only pick up those who are marked by the Father; the marked ones will automatically be drawn to that mystic. So nothing happens without his grace.

He is the one who sends the master, he is the one who marks us, and then we are pulled by the master. Everything starts with his grace. And then he also puts in us the urge to make effort, and then we become happy to devote our time to meditation. Everything starts with his grace. But we should also be receptive to the grace and do our best, whatever we can do.

473 *What difference does it make whether I meditate or not, or for how long, since the answer is always please attend to your meditation?*

You see, it's a constant struggle with the mind. Your hunger will increase, your hunger will come when you give your time to meditation. Without hunger, you won't sit in meditation at all, and without meditation you won't be able to increase your hunger. Hunger is there – that is why we sit in meditation. Whether we are able to concentrate or not, that's a different thing. But hunger is there, need is there – that is why we are devoting our time to meditation. There will be more hunger, a greater intensity of hunger, when you give more time to meditation. Hunger automatically will increase.

474 *Is it true to say that progress is in direct proportion to the amount of effort?*

The amount of effort, the amount of his grace, the amount of karma which we have to destroy – so many things affect our progress. If there is only a very little heap of rubbish, it takes only a little time to burn that rubbish. If the heap is big, it will be burned in due course, but it will take more time. It won't be so quick. So you can't say that if two people are giving the same time to meditation they will be able to get the same result at the same time. You can't say that at all.

Everybody has an individual load of karmas, an individual heap of rubbish, to burn. And you also can't know whether this is your first birth on the path or second birth on the path or third birth on the path. You may have burned a lot of rubbish in the last life so you have very little to burn in this life. That is why Christ said, the first may be the last and the last may be the first.[62] There's no seniority, you see, for spiritual progress on the path – that since I have devoted more time and I started meditation earlier, I should have better results than the other person who has come at a later stage on the path and so has devoted less time to meditation. You can't compare like that because you don't know his background. Your background is different than his background; your load of karmas is different than his load of karmas. So you can't compare that with anyone at all.

We should try to do our duty, and then it depends on how much load we have to carry or we have to burn. His grace is there; our effort should be there. His grace is never lacking if our effort is sincere and honest. His grace is never lacking, because once he marks us, once he brings us in touch with a mystic, once we come in touch with the sound or that sweet melody within, then he doesn't withhold his grace. But for that grace, we wouldn't be in touch with that voice of God within at all. We wouldn't be given this human life, we wouldn't be on the path at all, we wouldn't meet a mystic at all, but for his grace. So when he has marked us to be part of a certain fold, of a certain master, he doesn't withhold his grace after that. He's more anxious than we are! So his grace is always there, but we have to do our duty. We just can't look to the grace without even doing our duty. We should do our best; then his grace is always there.

475 *It is mentioned in our talks among satsangis sometimes that we do the work, and the grace comes. Sometimes*

there seems to be confusion between the grace and the effort. Is it not that we should always make the effort? If I put in the effort I will get the grace; the more effort the more grace?

That is right. The more the effort, the more grace we receive. But only through the Lord's grace will we be able to put forth the effort. Without his grace, we will never even think about the Lord. Without his grace, we will never find ourselves on the path. Without his grace, we will never contact a master. Without his grace, we will never be able to devote time to meditation. Everything comes through his grace. But we should not think that only when his grace comes will we give time to meditation. Our duty is to be sincere in our efforts to meditate. When he wants to give his grace to us, he will definitely do so. For instance, if we have a maidservant working in our house and she works honestly and sincerely, we are so pleased that we want to give her a bonus. So when we are working in the name of the Lord, out of devotion to him, he is not unmindful of what we are doing. He will definitely reward us for what we are doing. But supposing a beggar comes to your door and asks you to first assure him that you are going to give him alms, before he asks for them – nobody will bother about him. It is his duty to knock at the door, to beg, to ask. It is for the owner of the house to give or not to give. But when he really asks, he really gets. We cannot put the cart before the horse. So we have to beg. We have to put in the effort. Then the Lord will shower his grace.

476 *How much do our daily activities affect how close we can feel towards the master? Is our life so bounded by destiny that what we do on a day-to-day basis doesn't affect that so much?*

If the seed of love is not planted in us, what can we do? If you don't have that atmosphere and environment, those facilities and opportunities in which you can develop love for the Lord, what can you do? And that is not in our hands; that is in his hands. So he plants the seed of love and he also helps it to grow – grow to the extent that we become one with him. That is also his grace, because he provides that opportunity, that facility, the environment, the atmosphere, which are very essential for that love to grow so that we can become him. And that is entirely in his hands. So this feeling which we have within us, that our love should grow, that is also planted by him, that is also a part of destiny, that is also part of his grace. You would like the love to grow only when you want it to grow. This wanting it to grow is not in your hands; that is in his hands. That he's pulling you and you feel that your love should grow more and more – that is in his hands.

477 *Isn't it true that we can do nothing on our own, that we are entirely dependent on grace?*

That is true. We will get his grace only when he wants us to get it. It is always there, but we are not always receptive to it, and it is he who makes us receptive. By his grace, we can have his love. We have to make the effort, do our spiritual practice, and it is for him to give us grace. He does not withhold his grace when we are sincere and honest in our love and devotion. And all this meditation, all these spiritual practices, are simply to make us receptive to his grace. But only with his grace will we get such an atmosphere, such circumstances, that we can devote time to meditation and that we will long to meet him. He is within us, every one of us. Being within us, he gives us his own love. We think we love him, but actually he loves us. It is he who creates that love in us. We are just responding to his love. The more we respond to his love, the more we feel his love in us. In fact, it is the Giver who is giving this love. We are not doing anything. We are just responding to what he gives us. The more receptive we become, the more love and devotion we feel within ourselves for the Lord.

But the progress is in the hands of the master, is it not?

As we have just discussed, it is a matter of grace. We have to put in our efforts. The master helps us, the Lord helps us, but we must make the effort. Progress we do get accordingly. As we make more effort, we get more grace to make more progress.

478 Master, how can we possibly clear all our karmas?

By meditation. That is the only way. You see, brother, the Lord's grace is not lacking; our efforts are lacking, our sincerity is lacking, our faith is lacking. The Lord's grace is not lacking. He is more anxious to pull us than we are anxious to go back to him. But for that we would not be on the path at all today. It is because of his pull that we find ourselves on the path.

479 We have been told that the Lord helps those who help themselves. Suppose a person becomes helpless and cannot help himself?

We are helping ourselves when we are in meditation day and night. His grace will also be there. If we refuse to meditate and are always expecting his grace, we do not deserve it. If a beggar is not going to knock at the door, how is the owner of the house going to give anything to him? If a child does not weep, the mother also does not pay much attention. For example, in our country, generally we have maidservants, and one takes the child out to play so that the mother can do her work. If the child weeps and cries for the mother, the maidservant tries to humour him. She tells him fairy stories, or she may give him toys to play with, or she may give him some sweets. She tries to engage his attention. But if the child refuses everything and just weeps for the mother, and wants only the mother and nothing else, the mother cannot resist it. She runs from the house and embraces him.

Similarly, we are all children playing in this world with the material or worldly faces and all that. We are so attached to them and absorbed in playing with them that we do not even think about the Lord. We are away from him. But when we have real longing and devotion for him alone and want only him, we withdraw our attention from everything else. Then he cannot bear it, comes to meet us with open arms and embraces us as he receives us.

Mostly we do not try to meditate for his sake. We meditate for worldly possessions. Even if we meditate, we do not pray to him for his grace, but we pray for worldly things to satisfy our worldly desires and cravings. We want him to fulfil our desires and nothing else. We do not want him for his sake. In Sant Mat we are just to pray to him for him, to merge back into him. When we do our duty with love and devotion, he will also help us. When we are helping ourselves, we will get his help, too.

480 *Sometimes a glimpse is seen during bhajan which does not recur for a month or so. What could be the reason?*

Sometimes, with the grace of the Lord, we get a glimpse of the master or we have some inner experiences, just to keep us straight on the path. Then again, sometimes we become shaky and do not try to give our time to meditation. We do find such experiences within ourselves. This is actually just a reminder, a push given to us to keep us steady on the path. But we still have to practice and earn all those experiences, because we have not earned these experiences yet. It is only with the grace of the Lord or the Father that we get these experiences so that we may continue on the path.

481 How does the idea of grace fit into this business of karma?

Sister, without grace nothing can happen. Grace means the grace of the Lord. Only by his grace will we come into a certain atmosphere where we can work our way up. Without his grace we can never even think about him, and we would never know that the Lord exists. But he does not come into this world directly. He sends his grace through some means, through some instruments, through the masters. As you have often read in the Bible, Christ said, I have been sent by my Father. I have been sent for those marked souls, those particular souls who are ready to go back to him.[128] That is his grace. When the Lord wants those sheep, those particular souls to be collected to come back to him, his grace is there, and the master is sent to collect them. Without his grace, the saints or masters would not come into this world.

Without his grace, we would not even think of the Lord, much less try to meditate. His grace is the first step in meditation. Without his grace, nothing can happen. But when we are sincere, when we want to work our way up, his grace also comes. If we go one step, he comes ten steps to meet us, but we have got to be sincere in our efforts. He always receives us with open arms, provided we want him, we long for him. Mostly we do not try to seek him; mostly we do not try to have real devotion for him. Even if we turn to him, it is not for meeting him but to achieve some worldly aims, desires and possessions. We want him to fulfil all that our mind wants. We do not want him for himself. Very few people want him for his sake. Most people have ulterior motives; they want him because he can be a good instrument for fulfilling their desires. That is not wanting him, that is not invoking his grace.

We should worship him because we want him, we love him. The basis of religion is not fear, but love. We do not want to worship him to escape from the woes of the world. We worship him because we are in love with him. And when you are in love with anybody, you just want to be with him for the sake of love, and not for the fulfilment of any desires or worldly things. So unless that real longing, that real yearning, comes within us and that real devotion takes place in our heart, we cannot achieve our destination.

People hardly pray to him for his grace, for his blessings, for helping them to merge back into him. They usually pray to him for their sons, their litigations, their wealth, their health, and for so many other worldly desires to be fulfilled. They never pray to him for his sake, for him. They only want to make him their means, an instrument to satisfy their desires. And who creates the desires? The mind creates the desires. And to whom are we praying to fulfil them? We are asking the Lord to fulfil our desires. We are not explaining to our mind to abide by the will of the Lord. We are trying to explain to the Lord to abide by the will of the mind. We then serve the mind, not the Lord. Unless we completely surrender ourselves to him, driving all these desires out of our mind, we cannot achieve our destination, because he will always give us what we want. We will have to surrender to him. When we just want him from him, only then can we merge back into him. So we have to create within ourselves that real longing and desire for him, devotion to him.

482 Has the master the power to help the disciple open the inner eye while the disciple is meditating, or is it just that we have to be purified so much until it automatically

opens of its own accord and then the master helps us to
open it?

Brother, it takes both. We have to put in the effort, and the grace of the master is always there. My master used to tell us that if a disciple goes one step forward, the master comes ten steps to receive him. If we go ten steps, he comes a hundred steps to receive us. If we are sincere and honest in our devotion, in our efforts, he never withholds his grace. It is always there.

483 *Maharaj Ji, it is said that if the disciple takes one step*
towards the master, he takes nine steps toward the dis-
ciple. Can you say something about the nature of that
one step?

Actually it is the Lord who pulls us from within. We are so tied down with the attachments of this creation that it becomes difficult for us to take even one step. We are so engrossed in this creation, so attached to this creation. Our roots have gone so deep into this creation that it is not so easy to uproot them. So even our one step is a great step. Without his grace, we can never get out of this creation. So even our one step is sufficient for him to pull us.

484 *Do you think contemplation can be attained by anyone,*
by an ordinary person?

Everybody should try it, and everybody can try it. And that is what the Lord wants. But we can try only when he wants us to. That is what I said – without his grace nothing can be done. But we have to make the effort and not try to justify our failure to do so by thinking that when the Lord wants us to, we will contemplate on him. We cannot put a condition that we will only beg of the Lord if we are sure that he is going to give to us. But it is entirely at his mercy; he can give to us whenever he likes. When anybody in this world asks us for anything four or five or six times, we feel like giving it; so how can the Lord be unmindful if we are really begging at his door? The thing is that we must beg at his door. And we can beg only if we find the door of the Lord, and that door is here, between the eyes. We should come here – concentrate all our attention here – and beg from him, and he will definitely give us what we want.

485 What I don't understand is – where does the effort come from? Does it not come from grace?

They both go together. Without grace, effort will not come, and without effort, you will not get grace. Without the Lord's grace you would never be on the path and would never meet the master, nor would you be filled with the desire to meditate. So first came his grace and now should come the desire for meditation.

When you are giving your time to meditation, you are getting more and more grace from the Lord. Grace is to eliminate the sinchit karmas which stand between the soul and the Father. These will be eliminated through meditation. So meditation is nothing but asking the Lord for his grace to eliminate that veil of darkness from our way. The mind then becomes receptive to that divine melody within.

486 How are we brought to meditation?

By the grace of the Lord. There is no other way. We may say that we have become devotees of the Lord because we have found the right teachings, we have found the path, we have found the master. It would be quite wrong to think so. Actually, when he wants to put us on the path, when he wants to give us his devotion, he creates such circumstances that we have no option but to follow that path. We are ultimately drawn to the path. It is all in his hands. When he wishes it, everything becomes clear to us. First is his grace. With his grace we will meet a master. Through contact with the master we will be put on the path, and with our efforts we invoke his grace to travel on that path until ultimately our practice will lead us to our home and we merge back into him. Everything is interconnected. Without the Lord's grace, nothing can happen.

487 Could you please explain something of the love and mercy that a master has for a disciple that produces the desire for inner darshan?

Well, brother, when a beggar knocks at the door for alms, he's asking for mercy. So knocking at the door invokes the mercy of the house owner. Attending to meditation, we are trying to invoke the mercy of the Father, the grace of the Father. What is the grace of the Father? To pray to him that whatever stands between us and the Father should be eliminated and that we should become one with him. That is the mercy we are trying to seek, that is the forgiveness we are trying to seek. Our own ego, our own load of karma – our mind – stands between us and the Father. So we are trying to seek his forgiveness, asking him to forgive us for whatever stands between us and the Father. Meditation is nothing but invoking the mercy of the Father.

By our own efforts, we will never be able to account for all the karmas, all the rubbish which we have collected all through, right from the beginning of the creation. It's only his mercy which can pull us back to his level. Without his grace and mercy, we would never have even thought about the Father. We would never get an opportunity even to think about him. Our circumstances, our environment would not be conducive to our meditation at all without his grace and mercy. So he's the one who's pulling us from within. He's the one who makes us receptive to his grace. He's doing everything.

488 Is not God's grace the power to shape all that we are destined to become?

God's grace is always there, but, brother, we have to become receptive to his grace. If it is raining very heavily and your cup is upside down, not a drop of water will get into it. You have to put that cup with the right side up, and then it will be filled with rain water. God's grace is always there, within every one of us, but we have to be receptive to that grace, and by receptive I mean that we have to withdraw our consciousness to that point where his grace is coming day and night. Unless we attach ourselves to that and unless we are filled with that love and devotion for the Lord, naturally these desires and attachments of the world will not go out of us. There is no limit to his grace, which is everywhere, but we have to be receptive.

489 Maharaj Ji, you say that we should be receptive to the grace. What is the best way to be receptive to it?

Well, the best way to be receptive is, when the Lord would like us to be receptive, we will become receptive. He knows the ways and means to make us receptive. But we have to read the literature, attend the meetings, help each other, and devote the required time every day, regularly and punctually, to the spiritual practice. We have to live in Sant Mat, in that atmosphere. All these are means to be receptive to his love.

> *But, Maharaj Ji, if it is the master who makes us receptive, then we need not have a feeling of guilt for being bad satsangis?*

Sister, we should never entertain the guilty feeling of being a bad satsangi. As I told you, there are no failures in Sant Mat. You are going ahead. You have to go ahead. But we have to be satsangis – do not forget that. We should not forget the definition of a satsangi, and do our best to live up to it. The principles on which we have to stand, the time which we have to devote, these are prerequisites of being a satsangi, what is expected of a satsangi. If we are real satsangis, we should have no feeling of guilt. Whether you are considered good or bad makes no difference, as long as you remain a satsangi in the true sense of the word.

490 *Maharaj Ji, on the special occasions when grace and mercy are bestowed on the disciple, is that an intervention by the master?*

The whole life of a disciple is a special occasion. When the marked soul takes a new birth, the saint becomes responsible to take the soul back to the Father. He becomes responsible after giving it a new birth to help the child grow to become one with the Father. So every step, every occasion, is a special occasion for the disciple. The Lord's blessing and grace is always there with the disciple, but it is up to us to be receptive to that grace. If a cup is upside down, however hard it rains, not a drop can get in. If the cup is in the right direction, it can be filled.

Master's grace is always there. He doesn't withhold his grace after initiation. A gardener does his best to see that a tree yields fruit. He puts the right type of nutrients in the soil and waters, cuts and prunes the tree because he's anxious for it to yield fruit once he has taken responsibility for it. The master is always anxious that the disciple should go – the sooner the better – back to the level of the Father. When he's so anxious, he doesn't withhold his grace. We have to make use of that grace by becoming receptive, and meditation makes us receptive to his grace. Whenever we attend to meditation, that's a special occasion to get the grace. Otherwise his grace is always there.

RESPONDING TO THE INNER PULL

491 *So you can't say how much meditation you want to do? You don't have any willpower about how much medita-tion you want to do? That's not in your hands either, how much meditation you can do?*

Well, brother, actually it is not in your hands at all. If there is no pull from within for meditation, you will not even sit for medita-tion. When the pull is there to become one with the Beloved, you can't help sitting in meditation. When day and night the pull is within, that I should become one with my Beloved within, I should be with the radiant form of the master within, that I should become one with that infinity within, the pull will be so strong in you that you can't help sitting in meditation. You will set aside the whole world and you will give your time to meditation because there is such a strong pull from within to become one with him.

And if that pull is not there, you may do your best to sit in meditation, but you will not be able to sit for five minutes. And that pull is not in your hands; that pull is in the Lord's hand. So you can say that you are sitting in meditation, but actually there's someone else who's forcing you to sit in meditation.

You see, a lover is running after his beloved. He thinks that he's running after the beloved. But for that love, would he run after that beloved? This love is forcing that lover to run after that beloved and to make any sacrifices to become one with the beloved. But for that love, he would not make even the slightest sacrifice for her. So he's not doing it; the love makes him do all these things. Minus love, he would not do anything. He would not give her even a glance or a look or even talk to her. There are thousands like her. But there is something in him making him helpless to run after the beloved, and that something is not in his power. That is in the hand of the Lord.

So when he makes us restless to become one with him, we all become helpless to sit in meditation. We devote our time. We read Sant Mat books. We try to dissolve our doubts. And we're not happy with ourselves unless we give our time to meditation. We don't find that bliss anywhere else. Nothing, no company of the world, attracts us. We find misery in the most glamorous company, from a worldly point of view. We become miserable with them, because there's something within us which is forcing us towards the Lord. So it is not in your hands to do all those things. He who is pulling you is within you. He will make you sit in meditation; you can't help that.

In a shabd by Guru Nanak, after explaining the whole Sant Mat teaching, he says: We're all helpless; nothing is in our hands; everything is in your hand. So please have your mercy, have grace on us. Everything is in your hand; we are all puppets.

And what is meditation? The realization of this very fact: that we are puppets, we are helpless and he does everything. This realization can only come when you're able to eliminate the ego from you. As long as the ego is there, your individuality is there, your identity is there, you think you are doing everything – who can make you dance? And when with the help of meditation that ego is eliminated, then we know our insignificance before that mighty Father. Who am I? What am I? Then you realize all that, and that realization is the real knowledge which can come only by meditation, and meditation is entirely in his court, in his hands.

And if he has marked you to become one with him, you can't help running after him. Without his marking, you may do your best to run after him to find the path, but you will never succeed. You will have all sorts of doubts; all sorts of intellect will come in your way; a hundred and one circumstances will force you out of it. You can't help it. So everything is in the hands of the Father.

492 Master, isn't love a gift of the Lord? Or do we have to earn it by effort?

Sister, to be very frank, love is a gift from the Lord. Unless the Lord wishes, we can never think about him. Unless he pulls us towards himself, we can never search for him at all. We think we are loving the Lord, we think we are finding the Lord. Actually he is the one who's pulling us from within, giving us facilities, opportunities, environments, creating all that atmosphere within us so that we think about the Lord and try to make a search to go back to the Father. He is the one who's giving all that to us. Without him, we can never think about the Father at all. So it is a gift given to us by him. And the more we love, the more it grows. Of course, it starts with the Father; but then we try to search for him, and our love grows and grows. The more he gives, the more it grows. The more effort we make, the more love we feel; the more his grace is there, the more effort we make. These will always go side by side.

493 Master, I have heard that it's gratitude which promotes that receptivity to meditate. How can we develop a greater sense of gratitude, so that we can be more receptive?

By attending to that pull from within. The more effort you make, the more receptive you will become. The more receptive you will become, the more effort you will be able to make. We have to build that atmosphere in which we can build our

treasure in heaven. You see, atmosphere counts a lot for meditation. That is why there is so much literature which we read,
so many meetings, satsangs, discussions. All that is just to
build that atmosphere for meditation, to help us be a source of
strength to each other, so that we can help each other attend to
our meditation. These are all means, strong means to that end.
All these things make us receptive to that meditation.

494 *Maharaj Ji, earlier in the session, when answering a
question about grace and effort, you made the analogy
of the Lord providing or giving us hunger...*

Hunger is there. That is why you are putting in effort. Hunger
is forcing you to put in effort. Longing is there within. He is
pulling you from within. So you are putting in effort to reach
there. If there is no food on the plate and you are hungry, you
have nothing to eat, what will you do? If there is food on the
plate and you have no hunger, even then you won't eat. Your
hands will only work when there is delicious food on the plate
and you're hungry. Then you automatically eat. So effort comes
with the hunger. And then there is also something to eat.

Similarly, the Lord has kept that food within every one of
us here at the eye centre. And now he gives you the hunger to taste
that living water, to taste that nectar, and that hunger is making
you put in effort to reach to that level of consciousness where you
can taste that nectar, satisfy your hunger. So the Lord has kept
that food within you and has given you that hunger. And that
hunger is forcing you to taste that food. If the hunger is not there,
the food is still within everyone, but nobody tries to put in effort
to eat it. If you are thirsty, then you will search for a well. If you
are not thirsty, you will not care to search for a well. And if you
are thirsty and you see the water in the well, you will try to adopt
a hundred and one means to pull the water out to drink.

That hunger is in the Lord's hand, and he also gives the food. He is the giver of the food and he is the giver of the hunger. That is why Christ said, blessed are those who mourn; for they shall get rest.[8] Those who miss the Lord, who feel the separation from the Father, who feel that pull from within, who have that hunger to become one with the Father, they are the blessed ones. Ultimately their hunger will take them to the destination. Hunger will force them to put in effort and they will find the destination.

495 *Maharaj Ji, the question is, when someone very much wants the master, but circumstances or other things in one's life prevent this, what can one do?*

Well, sister, master is not anywhere outside, as I just told the other lady. Master is within every one of us and that divine word is our real master. So we should pray to him within for guidance and for help. The pull has to come from within, and then we are automatically pulled towards him, even outside. The pull has to come from within. We can only worship the Father by his grace. Nobody can worship him without his grace. We can only worship him if he wants us to worship him. Actually, he worships himself through us. When he wants us to worship, then he gives us that pull from within and we become restless to become one with him, we become restless to worship him. Nobody can worship him without his grace, without his pull from within. So even when we attend to meditation, it is nothing – it is not so much our effort but just his grace that we are attending to meditation.

I often give an example that if one is hungry and there is no food on the plate, then there is nothing to. And if there is delicious food on the plate and you are not hungry at all, your hands won't move. But, if there is delicious food on the plate and you are also hungry, your hands automatically start moving from the plate to your mouth. It is not in your hands to have that food on the plate and to have that hunger. It is in the Lord's hands. When he wishes, he will give us delicious food on the plate, and he will also give us that hunger. Our hands will automatically start moving. We think that we are worshipping him. Actually, he is worshipping himself. When he wants us to worship him, then he gives us that hunger, he gives us that thirst within, and he also puts us on the path, to quench our thirst, to fill our stomachs. He also gives us that food, and then we start enjoying that bliss and peace within.

496 *Maharaj Ji, love and devotion and grace, I believe, are all that count. And you say that to get love and devotion, you just meditate more. But my mind is very active and it's very difficult, extremely difficult to sit in meditation and concentrate. It's very difficult to even sit still. What can souls that are – to use a term – 'out of it' like myself do to try to stimulate that sense of grace and love and devotion?*

Well, brother, if the Lord's pull were not there, we would not even think about the Father. When his pull is there from within, there is a seed of love and devotion within us, which he has created. He has sown that seed of love and devotion within us by pulling us, by marking us. Now we have to develop that seed, with his grace, by attending to meditation. And slowly and slowly, we do. When we feel we have no love, it means we are not satisfied with the depth of love that we have. That doesn't mean that you have no love at all. Otherwise you wouldn't think about it. When you feel you have no love, you have love, but you want more and more of it. You want it to grow. We're not satisfied with the depth of it. Love is there, otherwise you wouldn't bother about it, you would never even think about it. When we are conscious that we have no love, it means love is there. We want to grow it, we want to strengthen it.

497 You say that we should try not to resist the pull from within. But is there a part of us that is resisting that call?

Yes, resisting in the sense that shabd is always vibrating here at the eye centre. And our mind is spread into the whole creation and running toward the senses. So we are not attending to that call within. We are resisting it, we are turning our back to that call. As Christ said, don't turn your back to the holy ghost, don't sin against the holy ghost.[46] The shabd is calling every one of us.

> *So during the day, would it be good for us to try to listen to the sound, even if we're not hearing it, for a minute here or there throughout the day – would that be not resisting that inner call, if we consciously made that effort?*

Please give your time to shabd and bhajan and simran every day. Then that attitude of the mind will develop, that practically all our time is spent in meditation. You see, meditation is an attitude of the mind. Also it means devoting our time to hearing the sound and doing simran. Then that habit of attending to meditation also creates an attitude of our mind, that our whole tendency and intention should always be towards meditation, whatever we may be doing in this creation. We have to change the attitude of our mind by meditation. Now the attitude of our mind is outward – downward and outward. Then the attitude of the mind becomes inward, upward. We have to change our attitude of mind.

> *I think it was yesterday you said that if we really want to come inside, we must draw everything from the outside inward. For myself personally, I notice that my mind goes out. I love to read and to study and to go to seminars, and I feel myself mentally spreading out. Is it best to draw back in?*

Sister, whenever we are in, we are never out. Whenever we are out, we are never in. Whenever our consciousness is spread outside, we are not there where we can be in touch with that sound. Whenever we have that little concentration within, we are at once in touch with that light and sound. Whether our concentration is low or little or just for a short time, we will be at once in touch with that light and sound.

Should we be giving more than two and a half hours a day to meditation?

You don't have to give so much time. Give the time which is told to us at the time of initiation; two and a half hours is sufficient to train our mind, to create a tendency towards meditation. The mind is being trained to attend to meditation. It starts getting pulled within. It starts losing interest outside.

498 *Maharaj Ji, you've spoken to us now about love and practice – about faith and practice. How does love come into it? Does it develop along with our faith?*

Well, when it comes, it just comes. It comes from within. Actually it is not in our hands, it's all with God's grace. If we say that I am building love, that's wrong. He's always pulling us from within. That is why Christ says, I have come for the marked souls. The marking was done by the Father. I have just come to collect them.[128]

So the one who is pulling from within is creating that love within us, he's creating that devotion in us, he's creating that yearning in us, that longing to go back to our home. He is the one who's pulling us from within. Without that pull from within we would never have any love for the Lord. We would never even think about the Father. We would never even dream of going back to him. He is the one who's pulling us from within.

We think that we are seeking him, we are loving him, we are trying to develop faith in him, we are trying to practice to go back to him, but actually he is the one who is working from within. He is creating all that pull, all that atmosphere, all that environment. He is creating all that light in which we can see and get out of this illusion. He is the one who is doing everything from within. We have to be receptive to his pull. That is the maximum we can do. And that's a great thing to be receptive to the pull. But the pull must come from within.

That is why Christ says, my teaching is not meant for everybody. I talk in parables. Those who are meant to understand, they will understand. Those who are not meant to understand, they will never understand my parables.[49] Those who were meant to understand me, those who are meant to be pulled by the Father from within, automatically they will find themselves on the path.

Automatically they will feel the pull to try to reach or try to seek the destination. That marking, that pull, has to come from within. So actually the love is nothing but the grace of the Father. It is not in our hands at all.

499 *Maharaj Ji, when I saw you this morning, I was not carried away as I have so often heard about, and you mentioned it's only through meditation that we develop that longing. Would you explain all that again?*

Well, brother, one passes through so many phases in life. Sometimes you feel dry and sometimes you feel full of emotions. One passes through so many phases in one's life. Meditation always strengthens our love. Actually meditation creates love. Then it strengthens our love. Then with the help of meditation our love grows – grows to the extent that we become one with the Father. All meditation helps.

*I understand one doesn't go without the other. It's almost
a question of which comes first.*

If he had not put that spark of love in you, you would not have
thought of meeting the Lord at all. He is the one who is pulling you
from within. So the spark starts, the love starts within us. Then we
try to seek him, search for him. And that searching and seeking,
with his grace, puts us on the path. And then when we try to follow
the path, he gives us strength to follow the path. He strengthens
our faith, he strengthens our love with the help of meditation and
by our following that path. He is the one who's pulling us from
within. We sometimes think that we worship him or that we are
in love with him. Actually, he is in love with us. But for that we
would never be in love with him at all. As Christ says, I have come
for the marked souls, for the allotted souls.[128] So that marking and
allotment has been done by the Father. And what is that marking
and allotment? Creating that spark of love in us which makes us
restless to become one with him. That is his marking.

500 *Can I hear something about faith and devotion and why
mystics expect faith from their disciples while they are the
creators of that faith?*

Unless we have love for somebody, we don't have any faith in
him at all. Love creates faith in the person. And faith leads us to
the practice of obeying the instruction of the person. So they're
all essential. If we have love for the master, we will naturally
have faith in him. And if we have faith in him, then we like to
please him by following his instructions. Then we will attend to
our practice, what he teaches. The whole remedy lies in practice.
But for that, faith and love are required.

*Why do they ask their disciples to have faith while they
are the creators of that faith?*

The Lord creates his own love within us. We're just an instrument. We feel that we love him, but actually he is the one who is pulling us from inside. He's the one who is creating that love within us. We become restless to become one with him. The pull starts with him. But we should at least be receptive to the pull. We shouldn't resist the pull, we should be receptive to the pull. The Lord worships himself through us, in other words. Because he's the one who pulls; he's the one who makes us receptive to the pull. He's the one who pulls us to his own level, within. But we have a certain part to play, so the part is being played through us. Without his grace, nobody can worship him, nobody can love him – because we are all blind. We are lost in this illusion. And we could never think about the Lord unless he creates those facilities, that opportunity, that atmosphere in which we can build our meditation. If that atmosphere is not there, that opportunity is not there, that environment is not there, what can we do? So he has everything in his hands.

501 *Master, we're constantly encouraged to develop love, faith and devotion for the master on the path. Many times for me it seems that's something I play in my imagination – I try and yet it's something intangible. When we come to see you, in your physical presence, then it becomes very tangible and feels much more real inside. Can you speak to us a little bit about the role of love, faith and devotion?*

Well, brother, even if we live in imagination, live in love even in imagination, it is worth it. If we don't have the real love, the real devotion, but perhaps we imagine we have, even that imagination is worth living – because that will create real love someday. Love is the Lord's gift. You don't create it. You get it by his grace, because unless he pulls from within, we don't feel the separation from him. We don't feel that pang to become one with another person, another being, unless his pull is there. So we have to be receptive to that pull. And then it grows and grows, the longing to become one with the Father. He is worshiping himself through us. Without his grace, nobody can worship him. So if he gives it to us, let us receive it. Let us be responsive to it.

502 *Master, last night you said that yearning and suffering for the Lord was rare. Why is this rare?*

It's a rare privilege given to certain souls. It is only given to those whom the Lord wants to get back. Unless he loves the soul, the soul can never go back to the Father at all. The love starts with him. He marked the soul. He anoints the soul to come back to him. It means the love is on his side first. We also feel that love when the marking is there, and then we go back to him. Actually, love starts with the Father, not with the soul at all. If the Father didn't want the soul to love him, we would never think about the Lord at all. The pulling is always from him. He's within us and pulling us towards him. We think we love him, but actually he's loving us. We think we are suffering in separation and all that. He has given us this feeling of separation, of longing, of love. He has given us this gift. We think we love him, but actually he's pulling us.

503 *Maharaj Ji, after we are given the five names, we have to meditate and follow the master's instructions to get back to the Father. That is the only way – isn't that correct?*

Absolutely 100 percent. You see, we are all part of this creation and all lost in this illusion. It is not within our hands at all to go back to Father, unless he pulls us up to his level, and he has his own ways and means of pulling us to his level. It's not for the soul to go back to the Father; it's for the Father to pull the soul to his level, and he has his ways and means to do it.

Now there's another thing: It's all one-sided. You are one who loves us very much, but we can't return that love. Is that right?

The Father creates his own love in us because we are lost in this illusion; we are in love with this creation and we have forgotten the Creator, even though he is within every one of us. The Creator is nowhere outside – he is right within us, but we don't know where he is, and we have absolutely forgotten him, lost him, and we also have no inclination to become one with him because we are so lost in this illusion. So unless he pulls us up, we cannot go back to him at all. He makes his presence known to us. He sows that seed of love within every one of us and it develops, and then we become restless to become one with him.

504 *Maharaj Ji, on Saturday you said something to the effect that the Lord expresses his love for himself through his disciples. I was wondering if you might explain that a little further.*

Well, brother, I think I was trying to be very clear that if not for his grace, nobody would even think about the Father. We are so mixed up with this mesh of maya, so involved in worldly and sensual pleasures, that we would never even think about the Father but for the pull which he creates within every one of us. First we start with his grace that he starts pulling us, then he makes us worthy of his pull, he makes us receptive to his pull, and then we attend to that pull – we try to achieve our destination.

With his grace we go back to him. So who is doing it? Isn't he worshipping himself through us? We were ignorant of him, we were slaves of worldly love, worldly sensual pleasures. He created that fire within us, he created that pull within us, he gave us the opportunity, he gave us that good company, he put us on the path, gave us the company of the mystics and saints and made us more restless to become one with him – so restless that day and night we're thinking about him, trying to worship him and meditating on him. So when we achieve our destination, who's worshipping whom? Through our body he's worshipping himself, because without his pull, without his grace, without his making us receptive, without his giving us the opportunities and facilities to meditate, nobody would do anything at all.

505 *Do we have a choice here, by saying that I choose not to*
go back to the Father?

You have no choice. The Father forces you to meditate. He creates that desire in you to meditate to go back to him, and that is forcing you to meditate. You think you are meditating in order to go back to the Father, but you forget the One who's pulling from the back. He is creating that desire in you, making you think that without meditation I will never be able to go back to the Father, so I must attend to meditation. He has given you the intellect to know that without meditation you will never be able to go back to the Father. He has given you that understanding. If he denies you that understanding, you will never meditate. So that is also not in your hands. Then he gives you the opportunities, the facilities, the atmosphere in which you can build your meditation, in which you can build your treasure. That is also not in your hands. So where is the free will?

506 *Master, can you make too much effort?*

You see, a man who's not used to sitting five minutes in a day for meditation, perhaps he thinks ten minutes is too much for him. And one who is giving two hours and thirty minutes every day may think six or seven hours is too much for him. So it's comparative, what the mind thinks is too much. Nothing is too much on the path. There is nothing too much in love and devotion. Meditation is nothing but building love and devotion for the Father. A lover never thinks that he has been able to give too much love. And if he calculates in that way, he's not a real lover at all. A lover never calculates. He's always absorbed in his love, happy in his love. He would like to utilize every minute in love and devotion; so it is never too much for him. He can't say, I have too much love, now I want to go. He's never satisfied and he never calculates. So in love there is never too much. The more he gives, the more it grows.

People become rich by getting something from somebody. In Sant Mat you become rich by giving. The more you give, the more it grows, the richer you are in love and devotion.

~ 11 ~

Path of Action

507 What do you mean by 'atmosphere of meditation'?

The atmosphere of love and devotion which you build within you by meditation, and then you always remain in that atmosphere. You always remember the atmosphere of Sant Mat and you keep that around you, in your daily dealing with people, daily mixing with people. It's not only that for two or three hours in a room we attend to meditation, and then when we come outside, we are worse than even animals. That is not the point. That atmosphere, the qualities which we build by meditation, the peace which we share with meditation, we have to also share that with others in our daily dealings, in our mixing with people, in attending to situations throughout our whole day. That atmosphere of meditation should always be guiding us and should always be there.

508 Maharaj Ji, does only that meditation count which is done while concentrated at the eye centre? What about meditation when you're scattered – does that count?

Sister, meditation – it is not the simran, not the dhyan, not only the hearing of the sound. Meditation is living the life of Sant Mat. The whole of life is a meditation; making the mind pure – that is meditation. Because karmas only have association with the mind, when the mind becomes pure and the soul gets released from the mind, then all these karmas become ineffective. They cannot pull the mind down. They may remain in the mind, but the soul is the one who is getting punished due to this karma. When the soul gets released from the mind, all these karmas become ineffective and they cannot pull the soul back. So you can say then that your karmas have been burned, your karmas have been destroyed.

So whatever makes your mind pure, that is meditation. Because when the mind becomes pure, only then can the soul get released from the mind. So whatever makes your mind pure is your meditation – good living, right type of living, living by the teachings, having good relations with everybody, having a sympathetic nature – and also giving your time to meditation. That is all meditation, you see. Meditation is not closing yourself in a room for a couple of hours and then forgetting where God is and where you are. That is not meditation at all. We have to live in meditation day and night. That is real meditation.

509   *What actually does the master mean when he says we should take our meditation with us into the world so that it is for twenty-four hours rather than just two and a half hours?*

You see, we must not forget meditation when we start our worldly activities during the day. Its effect should remain with us. It fills us with certain noble ideas, noble thoughts, noble principles, and we shouldn't start compromising with them during our daily activities. Our meditation must reflect in all our activities in life. It automatically makes you kind, makes you humble, makes you loving, makes you helpful. You don't try to cheat anybody, you don't try to deceive anybody, and you don't want to hurt anybody. It must reflect in our daily activities – this is our way of life.

510 What is the most practical way of leading a life?

We should try to face our day-to-day problems remembering our destination, remembering the path. Our problems are of our own making. We may not be creating them now, but we have created them in the past. We have sown the seeds and we are here now to face the result of those seeds. Since we created them, we should try to go through them cheerfully and lovingly.

If you meditate, you build an atmosphere around you, an atmosphere of bliss, happiness and contentment. And then you can pass through all these ups and downs of the world without losing your balance. But if that atmosphere of meditation is not with you, then naturally you get confused. That is why saints advise us to try to give morning time to meditation.

Morning is not the only time for meditation – any time can be given to meditation – but the morning time has certain advantages. The main advantage is the atmosphere you build in meditation that helps you to go through the ups and downs of the whole day. Then, generally, you don't lose your balance because you have with you that atmosphere of bliss and happiness which you yourself have built in the morning hours. So if that atmosphere is around you, it won't be difficult for you to face these problems.

511 I have felt that when I attempt to meditate in the centre between the eyes, it becomes rather mechanical and I get

*the feeling that I am sort of twisting God's arm mentally
or, without actually saying so, depending on some inner
experience. But if I try five minutes of simple prayer, I feel
as if I am closer and please God much more.*

Well, brother, that is why I always say that mechanical meditation
will not help us so much. We have to live in meditation, we have
to build up that atmosphere of meditation, of that bliss and peace;
live in that meditation, live in that bliss and peace. The mechanical meditation we do need in order to concentrate our mind. If
you do a thing every day, you get used to it and develop it into a
habit. Similarly, mechanical meditation, as you may call it, if we
do it every day, we get so much into the habit of concentration that
we forget whether we are doing it mechanically or we are doing it
with love and devotion. Until the real love and devotion comes
to us, we hardly feel that we are doing anything. We hardly feel
we are in love, doing that mechanical meditation. But in order to
create that habit within us, we have to start some way or another.
Mere mechanical meditation will not help unless you live in that
meditation, become part of that meditation, merge into that
meditation. Your whole life should be that of love and meditation, and not just one or two hours of trying to concentrate.

512 *The initiate may divide the two and one-half hour meditation period into several periods until he can sit for the
full two and one-half hours at one stretch. Does initiation help one to sit in meditation for two or three hours
at one time?*

I have discussed this question many times. Normally, we should
devote one-tenth of our time to meditation. We, in India, have
a practice we call seva. This initiation into giving of our time to
meditation is also giving our seva to the Lord. In seva we always

like to give one-tenth of what we have. So one-tenth of our time is to be devoted to meditation of the Lord. And if we are not lucky enough to give two hours and thirty minutes daily, which comes to one-tenth of our day, at one time, we can easily do it in two or three sittings. But we should try, slowly and slowly, to do it all in the morning at one stretch. Till we can do it all at one stretch, there is absolutely no harm in doing it in two or three sittings. Every moment that we spend in his memory, in his love, in devotion and meditation, is accounted for and credited to us, and we get its benefits.

So, whatever time we can give, we should try to give it. And this is not only the mechanical meditation of giving two hours and thirty minutes and then forgetting it the rest of the time. Our whole day, every day, should be lived in Sant Mat. We have to live in meditation in our whole life, in our dealings with everybody. It is not only that particular time spent in sitting in meditation that matters; it is our whole living that matters. We have to live the teachings. We have to live in Sant Mat, for Sant Mat, in that atmosphere, day and night. That helps in the long run, not only the daily two hours and thirty minutes. It must be a part of our life. We have to live it.

513 *Is it correct to say then that ultimately our meditation or remembrance of the master really becomes a twenty-four hour job? I mean, that's really the only way, isn't it, to avoid running to the senses?*

Well, for the lover, love is a twenty-four-hour sickness. He doesn't have a specific time to love or to think about the beloved. He is in love twenty-four hours, no matter what he's doing, where he is. He is mentally with his beloved twenty-four hours. He doesn't specifically fix the time – this is my time for love. His mind is always there, no matter what he's doing, where he may be. So similarly, the Lord should always be there in our mind, no matter where we are, no matter what we are doing. That remembrance should reflect in our actions, our dealings. We should never forget him at any cost. That is why I say Sant Mat is a way of life. It is not closing yourself in a room for a couple of hours for meditation and then forgetting about it. The Lord should become part and parcel of your life.

514 *Ultimately, aren't we saved by God's grace? In meditation, there seems to be sort of a technique – it seems almost as if one is pushing buttons?*

No. I follow your question. Excuse me for interrupting. Meditation is not mechanical. We have to work upon it hard. We have to build the atmosphere of meditation around us. It is not a matter of snatching one or two hours every day and forgetting all about it the rest of the day. We practice because we want to live with it. We live in that atmosphere which we build around ourselves through meditation. That is our fort, which saves us from all the temptations and vices. Meditation is not a push-button affair. It is not physical. You see, it is trying to stop our thoughts from running out. This is just a means. The real meditation is to be in touch with the sound inside. By this method and means we try to withdraw to this point, the eye centre. The actual meditation is to be attached to that sound inside. That is real meditation. But this is a very strong means, and most important to that end.

515 *Maharaj Ji, my meditation is so poor that I feel that it doesn't even count as meditation.*

Well, you can count all twenty-four hours in your meditation. If you build around you an atmosphere of meditation, every breath you breathe is meditation for you. If you build that atmosphere of meditation and you live in that atmosphere of meditation, then meditation is always around you in one way or another. If the Lord is always in your heart in one way or another, then every breath is meditation. Meditation is not closing yourself in a room for a couple of hours – meditation is a way of life.

516 *Master, when we do our daily work with an attitude of love for the master, will he accept it as a kind of seva?*

If your master is within you, if you're always surrounded with love and devotion for the Father, then whatever you do in this world, it's all meditation, it is all seva. You should not forget him at all, even for a moment. He should reflect in your every activity, your every word. Then every breath is meditation. What is meditation? It's knocking at the door for grace so that we may be able to live in his love and devotion and our mind doesn't go to anything in the creation, only towards him. Meditation tilts you towards him, pulls you towards him, and if he's always with you and if he is reflected in all your actions, that is all meditation. That's why I say: It is a way of life.

517 *In the Bible Jesus says something about remembering the Lord day and night. Is that simran and dhyan together? Is that the same as remembering?*

You see, remembering the Father day and night means that we are not to attend to our meditation just for an hour or two by closing ourselves in a room. It should be part of our life for the whole day. Devotion for the Lord should be part of our life, in all our activities in this world, whether we are eating, whether we are sleeping, whether we are dealing with people, whether we are doing our official work. It should be part of our life, our way of life. Meditation should become a way of life for us. That is remembering the Lord day and night, not sitting for a couple of hours in a room and then coming out and hurting people, abusing and cheating people, deceiving people. That is no meditation at all. Its effect should be there with you in all the activities of the day. That is remembering the Father day and night. We always think about people we love day and night. We have to build that type of love and devotion within us, lest we annoy the Father who is in them. And we should do those things which please the Father and avoid those things which annoy him. That is remembering the Father day and night.

518 *Maharaj Ji, does one first have to attain the two and one-half hours a day meditation before he becomes an initiate?*

No, sister. There is a little misunderstanding about it. We should try to devote two hours and thirty minutes in our meditation. But if you think that from the very day you start you can sit for two hours and thirty minutes, it is not possible. It is not possible at all. You are not used to giving so much time to meditation. So you can start with one hour, and slowly and slowly increase your time and gradually add to your daily time. Your target should be at least two hours and thirty minutes. It is not that if we cannot sit for two hours and thirty minutes the very first day, we should not come to the path. We have to fight with our mind to give more and more time to meditation. It is a constant fight with the mind. And if some days we cannot give it, we should not feel guilty about it because it is not the mechanical meditation that helps us so much as the atmosphere of meditation which we build around us by meditation. We have to live in that atmosphere of meditation. The whole day is to be spent in that atmosphere. It is not the two hours and thirty minutes sitting in meditation and then forgetting all about Sant Mat and letting the mind run loose here or there. That is not the right attitude. By devoting our time we have to live the whole day in that Sant Mat atmosphere. So we should try to increase our time gradually every day.

519 *Master, is constant simran all day when you're not doing anything difficult that you have to concentrate on – that really is a form of meditation also, isn't it?*

Sister, anything we do towards achieving our end is a part of meditation. You see, when a child takes birth, it has to go through so many phases of life, phases of development, before he can start running. He can't just take a birth and start running. Every little step a child takes after birth is progress for him.

So after initiation, whatever efforts we are making – doing simran, reading Sant Mat books, attending meetings, having good discussions, becoming a source of strength to each other, filling each other with love and devotion for the Father – these are all strong efforts toward our spiritual development.

We should just continue and then leave it to the Father. We should just continue. Everything is meditation as long as we are progressing towards our goal. That is why I say that meditation is a way of life. Meditation is not closing yourself in a room for a couple of hours and then forgetting about it. It is a way of life. Your whole pattern of life is changed; your attitude of life is changed. That is meditation.

520 *Maharaj Ji, apart from simran, can you give some advice about how, in our daily routine, we can keep the mind poised for meditation when we sit? In our daily life, how can we keep the mind primed?*

You see, sometimes simran becomes too mechanical during the day and your thoughts are not with your simran. That will not purify your mind. But sometimes you build up your meditation in the morning time and, along with it, automatically you build up that bliss and peace and happiness within yourself, and the whole day you are just happy in that atmosphere which you have built in the morning. You keep yourself in that atmosphere, and you don't let your mind go astray at all.

By meditation we have to build our own atmosphere in which we have to spend the whole day. Then the next morning we have to recharge the battery, recharge the battery again. And then we get into the habit of living in that atmosphere of meditation. Then our meditation reflects in all our daily activities automatically because our consciousness becomes very pure and nobler, higher, and we hesitate to do anything wrong. So naturally the effect of meditation starts reflecting in our daily routine.

So if you can retain that atmosphere of meditation during your daily activities, you may or may not do simran at all the whole day. You see, sometimes simran during the whole day becomes just mechanical. But if your mind is in that atmosphere, in that bliss, then you don't let it go astray at all, and automatically all your activities will reflect your meditation. Actually, it's very difficult to analyze these things. This has to be experienced more or less by one's own self. It's very difficult to explain what I'm trying to tell you, very difficult to explain.

DOING SIMRAN ALL DAY

521 Master, what is the practical use of doing simran all day?

The practical use is that when we sit in meditation after having done simran during the day, we are able to concentrate much better, sooner. Otherwise, if we let our thoughts spread into the whole creation for the other twenty-two hours, it becomes difficult to concentrate in just one and a half or two hours. So when we don't let our thoughts go out in the world and keep our mind in simran, at the time of sitting, it becomes easier to concentrate and we concentrate sooner. We get concentration very soon then. That is the only advantage. Unnecessarily we are thinking the whole day and making ourselves miserable about things we can't control, which we can't help, which have passed. We are always thinking – thinking about either our future or about the past. By thinking those things, we're always worrying. You can save yourself from all that worry by keeping your mind in simran.

522 *Maharaj Ji, is doing simran during the day – other than during meditation – does that have any effect on the burning of karma, or does that get cleared only in meditation?*

You see, all these are strong means to an end. When you are doing simran the whole day, your mind will at once be in touch with the sound when you sit down to meditate. Actually, the sound is always coming. The sound and the light are always coming, but when you devote time to simran and dhyan, you are going towards the sound. You are purifying your mind to be one with the sound. Unless you purify your mind, how can you become one with the sound? These are all steppingstones. Actually, what is burning karma? When the soul gets released from the mind, then all those karmas become ineffective. Then the karmas cannot pull back the soul. That is burning karmas. The soul can only get released from the mind when it is in touch with the sound; without being in touch with the sound, the soul cannot get released from the mind. So the real burning of karmas is just by the sound, in bhajan.

523 *Master, we're told that there's no short cut to meditation. And yet we're also told at the same time that there is a kind of a legitimate short cut by doing simran during the day. I've been on the path now for sixteen months, and I'm only just beginning to realize the importance of that constant repetition during the day. And it's awfully dry. Is there any kind of set time before it starts to become automatic, or is it just, like everything else, a matter of attitude?*

You see, this constant simran helps our attitude towards meditation, helps to draw our mind towards meditation. That helps when we sit in meditation because we are developing a certain attitude towards Sant Mat, towards the teachings, towards the path. It helps a lot. It may be dry, but if you leave your mind alone, it will have other, worldly thoughts. It won't be still. It will always think something or other. So why not give it something better? Why let it go so astray, why not pull it back? We are helping it not to run very astray and wild. The more it runs astray and wild, the more difficult it becomes to pull it back. That is why whenever we get time or we are mentally free, we do simran.

524 *Is there any value in doing simran throughout the day, even if we don't put our full attention and love into it?*

For one thing, we won't feel tortured by thinking about our past, about our weaknesses, about our guilt; our mind is busy in simran. Another thing is that when you do sit in proper meditation, you will at once be able to withdraw back to the eye centre and be in touch with the sound. Otherwise, if you let your consciousness scatter into the world for twenty-one or twenty-two hours during the day, in just an hour or so you will not be able to withdraw back to the eye centre. So you are not letting your thoughts run out if you keep your mind in simran at odd times. So that advantage is always there.

525 *Two days ago you said that doing simran while we are outside in the world keeps our mind from thinking. Is this all the simran does outside in the world?*

Simran helps us to keep our thoughts from running wild. Simran during our meditation is for concentrating at the eye centre. That we do with concentration. But when we are doing simran while moving about, travelling, going from here to there, we may not be able to concentrate at all sometimes. But this helps us to keep our mind from running wild, thinking worldly things. You see, the more we let our mind run wild, the more effort we will have to make to bring it back. So indirectly you are helping the mind not to run out and to concentrate. The more you let it scatter, the more effort and time you will need to concentrate.

526 *Would you please explain the benefits of what I call the individual repetition of the names, simran, while we are eating, or working at a desk, which does not require too much concentration?*

Our mind is never still and is always thinking about something. It is always thinking about worldly faces, worldly objects, and it is never still. So if we want to forget those things, we have to direct the mind into a different channel. In order to do that, we should repeat the name of the Lord while moving about or doing our work. There are two things that we are usually thinking about. Mostly we are unhappy thinking about what has been our past. We generally think about that and have a sense of guilt about it, and then we are sorry for what we have done and are always worrying and repenting, or feeling sorry for ourselves and trying to justify our actions. Secondly, we are always bothered about our future and that is always making us frustrated and unhappy. If you keep your mind constantly in simran, you will not have this sense of guilt or frustration or unhappiness; and, when you sit for your meditation period, because you have not allowed your thoughts to be scattered out into the world, you will easily be able to withdraw your attention back up to the eye centre and will be in touch with the sound.

If you are always thinking about the world, then by spending only one or two hours a day in simran, you cannot possibly concentrate or withdraw your thoughts to the eye centre because it needs a similar amount of time to withdraw it as the time it has taken to scatter out. So saints always advise that when we are mentally free, when we are walking about, when we have nothing to do, we can keep our attention in simran. We should get into the habit of simran to such an extent that even if we are talking to someone, it should automatically go on within us. The advantage is that we will be able to detach ourselves easily from the worldly things, or the nine apertures of the body, and come back to the eye centre, and can then easily attach ourselves to shabd.

Simran is a dry and insipid process, but a very, very essential process. We can hear the sound without first doing simran, and we will be happy to hear that sound, but at that stage the sound will not pull us. Unless we are able to withdraw our attention up to this point [the eye centre], the sound will not take us up. We will hear it, we will enjoy it, but we will remain where we are. So, especially in the beginning, we should give more time to simran and less time to hearing the sound. When we are sufficiently withdrawn with the help of simran, then we should try to give more time to hearing the sound and less time to simran.

Simran is the means to contact shabd, and to go up with its help is the end. So simran is a very important means of withdrawing to this point, the eye centre, and to be in touch with the sound. Therefore, we should try to give more time to simran in the beginning and less time to the sound. But when the sound is clearly audible and strong, and it is pulling us up, we are enjoying it, then we should switch from simran to hearing the sound and just submit ourselves to the sound. Ultimately the sound, and not the simran, is to pull us up. Simran ceases to exist when we cross the first stage.

527 *Master, am I correct in understanding that even though an initiate has followed the metaphysical path most of the time and leaned heavily upon mental affirmation and declaration of the truth as he understood it, in times of stress and to solve problems and just to keep the mind clear, he should and will benefit by leaving all that and relying on simran of the five holy names, even during the day – from time to time – when work does not require his concentration?*

I have not exactly followed your question, sister. But whenever we are free, mentally, we should try to devote time to simran. We will feel the definite advantage of it when we are giving proper time to our meditation, for we will have much better concentration, quicker concentration, and we will be in touch with the sound sooner. If during the whole day we are absorbed in doing simran, two definite advantages are there. First, we are not letting our thoughts be scattered too much, so we will be able to concentrate in a shorter time when we sit for meditation. Second, mostly we are unhappy in thinking about what has passed, and our future is always bothering or worrying us. So, when we are absorbed in simran, we will be at least safe from all this unnecessary worry. We should, therefore, try to make use of our time in doing simran whenever we are free mentally. That has definite advantages.

LIVING THE PRINCIPLES

*528   Would you explain the two-fold purpose that Great Master
said each American satsangi has – to do our meditation
and lay the foundation for Sant Mat in America?*

You are at the other end of the world from India, so it is really
a special grace of the supreme Father that certain marked souls
here could have their contact or blessing through the Great
Master, who happened to be born in India. Without that grace
it was impossible, as you know, to search for a master or to know
anything about him or to find such a great, living master in the
world at that time, living in India. It is really the special grace
of the Lord that the marked souls in this country [U.S.A.] came
in contact with the Great Master and were put on the path.

Every soul, as Maharaj Ji [the Great Master] said, has
two great purposes. The first is to prepare your own way, to
work on your own spiritual development, to get rid of illusion
of the mind and make your soul purer. Just to know ourselves
and merge back into the Lord – that is the function of every
marked soul. These souls are selected just for this purpose, so
that they may get the opportunity or get those facilities to make
themselves pure, make themselves worthy to go and merge back
into the Lord.

And then, when we are on the path and meditating, our
influence naturally affects others in our surroundings, our
relations and our friends. By being a living example of a good
satsangi, we naturally influence our surroundings and people
who come in contact with us. By being a good example, we will
influence them much more than by discussing or explaining
the teachings to them. They find that radiance, they find that
peace, they find that bliss, that contentment in us. They find
us absolutely changed human beings as far as they can see, and

naturally they are anxious to know what has come into us, what has brought about that wonderful change in us. Also, when they have found out that we are better human beings, they are naturally influenced by the way we live. So we can put others on the path in a much better and finer way by ourselves becoming an example of Sant Mat, an example of being a true initiate.

Every soul has a two-fold purpose: First, to help ourselves, to get redemption from the mind, to get release from the mind, to make ourselves purer; and second, to help others to come on the path. Naturally, when anyone gets something very precious, he is always anxious to share it with those whom he loves. He is anxious to share that treasure with his friends and with the people in whom he is interested. All satsangis, I know from my own experience, are always anxious to share the path, that enlightenment, that wisdom of the path, with all their associates, with all their friends. In this way every soul has a two-fold purpose: to work for himself and to work for others by being a living example, which is befitting a disciple of a great master.

529 *During the course of the day we probably spend thousands and thousands of seconds and have thousands of actions that we do. Some of them are reactions. These actions are seemingly very quick. How can we do them in the name of the master? Is this automatic to a satsangi, or does it have to be an automatic projection of some kind to perform everything in the name of the master?*

To do everything in the name of the master is to remain within the principles which he has laid down for us – to live our lives according to the principles of Sant Mat and devote our time every day, regularly and punctually, to meditation. If we do everything with that Sant Mat atmosphere around us, then we are doing it in the name of the master. We do it in the name of the master when we take our 'selves' out of ourselves. As long as the self is in us, we try to justify our actions in the name of the master. Actually, what we are doing is following the instinct of the mind. When you withdraw yourself from the mind, then you will subdue your mind with the help of meditation and submit yourself unconditionally to the master inside, and then whatever you do will be in the name of the master. As long as we are slaves of the mind, and the mind is a slave of the senses, and we are running about outside, how can we say we are doing it in the name of the master?

It is automatic then, after one has accomplished release from the mind?

Yes.

530 *Maharaj Ji, in* Die to Live *it says that everything that we do during the day should consciously prepare us for the next meditation. It seems to me that if one were able to live one's life with that degree of concentration and attention, then there would be very little difference between our daily life and our meditation. Is that correct?*

The idea is that whatever we do in our daily activities should be arranged in such a way which helps us at the time of meditation. And we shouldn't spend our day in such a way which becomes a hindrance to us at the time of meditation.

What does it mean that our daily life should "consciously prepare us"?

That is, consciously prepare yourself for meditation. Consciously, we are not letting our thoughts go so astray or letting ourselves get so lost in the senses and worldly pursuits that it becomes difficult for us to attend to meditation and to concentrate at the time of meditation. So we are consciously preparing for meditation the whole day. We avoid situations where we are pulled apart and we prefer situations which help us to meditate.

531 *Master, you spoke yesterday about trying to see the light in meditation – spending our whole life in meditation. In leading a life as a woman, does one burn off sinchit karmas as much as someone would if she just sat down and attempted to do simran and bhajan, and will the progress come through?*

You see, you forget one thing – that it is the meditation which invokes the Lord's forgiveness, and if we build on a strong foundation, naturally we will build a very strong building. If we keep to the principles and attend to the meditation, only then will we achieve results in meditation, and only that will burn our sinchit karmas. Only leading the Sant Mat way of life will not help you to burn those karmas or to get the forgiveness of the Father. But the way of life will lead you to meditation also. If you lead a Sant Mat way of life, naturally you will attend to meditation. Without attending to meditation, you can never lead a Sant Mat way of life. And meditation will help you to invoke his forgiveness.

532 *Maharaj Ji, I'm afraid I've asked this question in a way several times, but what is the relationship between obedience of the disciple to the master – by that I mean living the principles of Sant Mat – and progress towards concentration and meditation?*

You see, that obedience will lead to concentration. The Sant Mat way of life will lead you to concentration and your progress. That is the foundation on which you have to build. The way of life is the foundation on which you have to build your meditation. Without a foundation, how will you build your treasure? We have to build on a rock – we have to lay the foundation on a rock, and that foundation is the Sant Mat way of life. That's why Christ said, if you believe in me.[92] Believing in the master means if you lead my way of life, follow my instruction, live my instruction, live in the way that I will tell you to live. That is believing in Christ. And that automatically will lead you to progress.

533 *What can the disciple do to clean the vessel? Just meditate?*

Simran, dhyan, and shabd. That makes us receptive also. And being steadfast on the principles of Sant Mat. That is the foundation on which we have to build our meditation, build our treasure in heaven. A foundation is very essential. You can't build on a weak foundation.

A CONSTANT STRUGGLE WITH THE MIND

534 *Master, you mention in your teachings that if we attend to our meditation, our willpower becomes so strong that we'll be able to face the ups and downs of life. But I'm still being thrown off balance by things – the hardships of life – and at the same time, I've felt that I was doing the best I could in meditation. So where did I go wrong?*

You see, we don't go wrong anywhere, but it is a constant struggle with life. We have to continue that struggle our whole life. You can't say that my struggle is over now and everything is a piece of cake for me. You have to watch yourself your whole life; it's a constant struggle with the mind. Nothing is wrong with us.

535   *In order to reach the radiant form, what kind of sacrifice
is really necessary in this worldly life?*

Well, sister, the question is withdrawing your consciousness to
the eye centre and attaching yourself to the shabd within. That
is the only sacrifice we have to make. For withdrawing to the
eye centre, you can imagine what sacrifices are required. The
main thing is that we should attend to our meditation and not
compromise with the principles of Sant Mat. As Christ said:
If you build on sand, when a rainstorm comes, the house will
fall. If you build on rock, a rainstorm won't move it.[70] So the
foundation has to be strong. The way of life in Sant Mat is very,
very essential. We must stand firmly on our principles, then
build our treasure on that foundation. In order to hold up this
ceiling and roof, you can imagine how strong the foundation is.
If the foundation were weak, you and I couldn't sit under this
roof at all. So similarly, we have to build a strong foundation
for building our treasure in heaven.

536   *Sometimes we have a particular way of thinking about
something, certain worldly things that we shouldn't do.
And sometimes you give us two different answers about
a whole category of things. Is it okay for a representative
to give us an opinion?*

Sister, fundamentally we are told only four things in Sant Mat.
As long as you base your meditation on that foundation, you
can do what you feel like. If you base your meditation on the
three fundamental principles, you will never do anything bad
at all – your mind will not let you do anything bad at all. Our
problem is that we don't try to base our treasure on that foundation. We attend to meditation but we keep our foundation very
weak. We build, but we build on sand, not on a rock – that is the

problem. As I said, meditation fills us with love and devotion for the Father. And when love and devotion come in us, all the positive qualities of human beings come like cream on the milk.

Are you saying that we automatically know what we should do?

Yes, we have to make our own judgment. When our mind is more clear, more pure, then it gets a detached view of a situation and we can make our judgment.

But what if we don't have a detached view of the situation?

Meditation will give you that. If you are attending to meditation, then it will make you like that. You always know whether what you are doing is right or wrong – if you just listen to yourself. If you don't want to listen, that is a very different thing. The mind itself warns us, and mind itself also forces us to do that. That is also the mind which warns us that what we're going to do is wrong. And it is also the mind that forces us to do that wrong thing. There's a struggle and a conflict in the mind always, but we always know what is good and what is bad.

537 *Does failure have any value?*

Naturally failure has value, provided we make another determination not to fail again. Then, naturally so many failures ultimately lead you to success.

538 *I think it might be of some consolation to our brother over there, Master, if we tell him that it's been repeated again and again that there are no failures in Sant Mat. Isn't that so?*

When he's bold enough to walk, there's a chance of him falling also. We should take all these failures as our pillars of strength, provided we get up and walk again. If we don't get up again, that is different. We are full of weaknesses, so pitfalls are there. But we should always be steady on the path. Our destination should always be before us, and we should try to get up again, and again walk. Ultimately we succeed. So there's no failure at all.

539 *Master, it appears that a satsangi who is able to think clearly from a Sant Mat point of view would never fall prey to negative emotions. Would you comment on that?*

Well, sister, intellect doesn't help here much. Intellectually we all know that this path leads us back to the Father. But what about our karmas? When a strong wave of karma comes, it just pushes us away from the path, shakes our feet from the path. We become very shaky. And again we are pulled back to the path. Intellectually we know, even when we commit sins, intellectually we know it is wrong, that what we are doing is wrong. It's not right what we are doing. But do we resist? We always fall prey to it. We are helpless then. Intellectually we know it's not good to do this thing and not good to do that thing. Ultimately we find we are doing the same thing. Mind is so strong, so powerful. Your conscience may be telling you it's not right, but yet you are a victim, a slave of that weakness. So just merely knowing the path doesn't keep us straight on the path. Only meditation gives us that strength, that strong willpower, to keep us steadfast on the path. And even if we fall, we again get up and keep to the path. But if we don't attend to the meditation and only intellectually try to know that this is the right path, then we never know when we will be swept away from the path. So meditation, even if we fall, pushes us back again to the path – if we keep to the meditation.

Even if the meditation is poor?

Every meditation is poor. Meditation is meditation – effort, effort, effort. Ultimately it becomes strong. A child doesn't start running right after birth. He has to pass through so many phases before he learns to walk, and then he learns to run. We also have to pass through so many phases in meditation.

540 *I would like to know why we have to struggle so much on the path.*

Why do we have to struggle? Is there any work in life for which we don't have to struggle? Tomorrow you would like to know why, after birth, you have to struggle to walk, to talk, to eat. You have passed through so many phases before you could walk, before you could talk, before you could eat, and now you don't feel that struggle at all. Is there any work in the world which we learn without struggle? So then, why not struggle on the path?

541 *Master, when we were initiated, you took some of our karmas onto your shoulders. What we are doing now after initiation – is that on your shoulders also?*

Sister, that's a wrong concept. Master may stand as a ransom for you to go out of the realm of Kal, but you have to bear your own load on your own shoulders. You have to fight for your own karmas. You have to do your meditation to get rid of those karmas. You can't just have this idea that master has taken the karmas and I have become absolutely free now. That's a wrong concept. You see, if a soldier is equipped to fight the enemy, he has to fight the enemy. He can't say, my general who has equipped me, he should fight the enemy. His general is there at his back to tell him how to fight. He's there to equip him.

He's there to help him, to command him. But the fighting has to be done by the soldier. This is a wrong concept. Master may take anything, master may do anything, but we are responsible for our karmas, to help ourselves get rid of them. Master only takes the responsibility that the soul is not to go back to the Kal anymore; it has to go to the Father. But unless you are able to clear all that, you cannot get out of that.

How can we possibly clear all our karmas?

By meditation. That is the only way. The Lord's grace is not lacking. Our effort is lacking. Our sincerity is lacking. Our faith is lacking. The Lord's grace is not lacking. He's more anxious to pull us than we are anxious to go back to him. But for that, we would not be on the path at all today. It is because of his pull that we find ourselves on the path.

> *You don't overcome anything – you don't overcome lust, you don't overcome anger. Years go by, and you don't overcome anything.*

You have to do your duty. You can't escape from your responsibilities, what you are supposed to do. You see, a command is given by a general, but he has to go through the soldier. We have to fight with our mind. And we have been well equipped to fight with our mind, with the load of our karmas. The help is there, command is there, guidance is there. But you can't say that I am not going to fight, you also fight for me. That is wrong.

It's discouraging when you fight and you lose every battle.

In Sant Mat you never lose, you always win. You never lose. Maharaj Ji [Maharaj Sawan Singh] used to say, if you can't bring me your success, bring me your failures.

We have a lot of them.

Well, we all are struggling souls, and I don't deny it. But at least we are putting in effort. If a child won't try to put in an effort to stand on his legs, how will he ever learn to run? The mother helps the child, but the child has to put in effort. He needs help, all sorts of guidance, but ultimately the child stands up and then runs. The mother is anxious that the child should learn to run at once, but the child has to play his part. We must put in our effort.

542 Does the master really love our failures when he sees the soul struggling and failing?

You see, it means that those who fail are making an honest attempt to succeed and he couldn't, so he fails. Master loves the attempt you make to succeed. The mother wants the child to learn to walk, but the child falls. He has scratches and bruises, but he gets up again. Again he tries to learn, again he gets up, again he tries to learn. The child has to pass through that phase before he can learn to walk and run. So similarly, we also have our own human failings when we are on the path, but if we get up again, and again are steadfast in trying to succeed, we may fall again, but again we try to succeed. Naturally those failures are an attempt to go forward, not backward. Every failure reminds us of our success, of where we are lacking. So we should go on putting in our best effort, and then if we fail, we shouldn't be so dejected, but we should try to follow the path again. But if we just fail and don't try to make another attempt to succeed, then of course the master won't love the failures.

543 Master, could you talk about the type of courage required to be a good satsangi?

Well, brother, at every step we need courage. We are all struggling souls, and it's a big fight. It is a very strong fight with the mind. It's not so easy to fight the mind. Our enemy is within all of us. Our enemy is not anywhere outside. He is right within us. And we never know when he may deceive, when he may betray us, when he may put us off the path. So we always have to be conscious of our own enemy. Sometimes it plays the role of a friend. Sometimes it plays the role of an enemy and frightens us, makes us nervous, shakes us from the path, from our faith. So we have a constant struggle with the mind. We have to be watchful. We have to watch its activities every day, every moment. We can't just be lulled into thinking that we have conquered it. It is a struggle, a constant struggle for our whole life. So unless we are strong, well equipped to fight the mind, how can we win the battle? We have to be strong.

There are human failings, but that doesn't mean that we have not to rise again and fight again our enemy. Soldiers in a war get wounded, but they get up again, take up their arms and fight again. We shouldn't have a defeatist attitude if we have fallen, if we have become a victim of human failings. When a child starts running, how many times does he fall? How many times does he get bruises? But he rises again, gets up again, again starts running. We have all passed through that same phase, and now walking or running is no problem for us. So in the same way, we are tempted, and we do fall, we do become a victim of human failings. But that doesn't mean that we have to submit to the mind, that we have to lose the battle. We have to carry on. Ultimately, success is ours if we just struggle, just carry on.

544 *Maharaj Ji, when one reaches the point of truly living in the will of the master, will that soul feel any kind of suffering at all in the body – when he's truly living in the will of the master?*

Well, sister, when you're in love with anybody, do you bother about the suffering of the love, or are you happy in that love? If you are in love with somebody, do you count how much you suffer for it, or are you happy that you are in love with the person? There's no question of calculation here. A lover never calculates the gains in love. He's in love because he loves. Whatever sacrifice he has to make, whatever he has to sacrifice, whatever he has to go through, he's very happy. A woman never thinks about the pains when she delivers a child. She's the happiest person to deliver a child. If she were always thinking: "I'm going to feel pain and this will be terrible," she would never have a child. But she's anxious to have a child, she never bothers about the pain, she never even calculates. The lover never calculates what suffering he has to go through. He's happy in his love. That's all that he needs; that's all that he wants.

545 *Maharaj Ji, there's a poem by Saint Paltu that says: When becoming a lover, first dig a grave for thyself; then only think of becoming a lover. Can you explain that?*

He says, you have to dig your own grave, you have to face a living death in this creation, in this world. You have to abstain from all the sensual pleasures, all those attractions which are pulling your mind toward the creation. You have to withdraw from everything. It is not so easy if you want to become the lover of the Lord. You have to turn your back on the creation. Only then can you face him.

546 *There is a part in the* Sar Bachan *that I would like you to discuss, if you would, please. It's Part Two, number 163: "Disciples of saints feel no pain at the time of death. Rather they face it bravely because they have already kept death in mind and have taken part in the affairs of the world only as much as was absolutely necessary. They*

have already struck at the roots of the world in them. The worldly life of the satsangis of a saint is like short-lived greenness of a tree which has been cut down." What particularly interests me is what Soami Ji means by "the roots of worldly activities have already been cut off."

By our meditation, we cut our roots. That's what Christ meant when he said, I have come with a sword.[39] The work of the sword is to cut the roots, the chains.

So the cut isn't done with one slice at initiation then; it is done continually after initiation?

If you are to uproot a tree from the dirt, can you do it just in one slice? The roots sometimes go deep down into the ground. It depends which tree is to be uprooted. Some trees are just like grass – it takes no time to uproot those. Just with a little weight, they fly out. Others, how much time does it take to uproot them? It varies with individuals. So we are all attached to this creation. These attachments are our roots in this creation. Unless they are cut, nobody can go back to the Father. Meditation is for nothing but to cut those roots which pull us back to this creation again and again.

So cutting them then is happening during meditation rather than their being cut once you connect to the shabd?

Yes. Connecting with shabd is giving you an axe. Now cut the roots of the tree. If you won't use the axe, then what is the use? A farmer takes an axe to pull out a tree, to cut its roots, but if he doesn't want to use the axe, doesn't want to labour, doesn't want to work hard, how can he cut the tree and cut the roots of the tree? He has to work. He has to use the axe. He is well equipped to do it.

So mystics equip us to fight with our mind, fight with our attachments to the creation, and we have to play our part. The general equips his soldiers to fight the enemy, and he wants each soldier to fight. He is at the back to guide him, to equip him, to give him his ammunition, to look after all his needs, but the soldier has to fight. The soldier can't tell his general to come and fight in the front lines for him. We have to do our part. We have to play our part. And we are equipped to play our part – we have to fight with our enemy, our mind, which is attached to this creation. So naturally, meditation will help you to uproot yourselves from this creation. We always try to find out ways by which we may not have do anything. We always try to interpret our books and mystic sayings so that we may not have to do anything.

547 *Master, in the book* Die to Live, *in the chapter "Be Bold Enough to Struggle," you say, "You have to sacrifice a lot in life." Now with one corner of my heart, I still love the world, and with another corner of my heart, I love the Lord. And my question is, what can I do to heal that split?*

Meditation, sister. It is the same with every one of us. Our heart is not wholly and solely in the meditation. Our heart is not wholly and solely with the Father. It is also with the family, it is also with the world, it is also with the pleasures of the world. And it also has something in it which yearns to go back to the Father because there is a natural instinct in everyone for the Father. The soul's inclination is always towards the Father. But the direction of the mind is outside into the world. So both things are there. Mind is pulling outward; soul is pulling upward.

> *Yes, but my question is, how can I get more of the tendency to sacrifice and more inclination towards love for the Lord?*

Well, sister, the time we give to meditation is a sacrifice. And we have to abstain from society so that we can give our time, adjust our time for meditation. We shun certain company which we don't relish anymore, which we don't like anymore, which distracts us from the Father, which pulls us, which is slippery. This is the type of sacrifice we have to make.

Sometimes the result is loneliness, and my experience is that loneliness is not always conducive to meditation.

Sometimes it's not. And sometimes it's very conducive to meditation. Sometimes we yearn for loneliness. We run to the mountains; we run to the solitary places; we are tired of the world; we try to find some silent corner to sit alone and be with ourselves. Sometimes we don't like anybody's company; we just want our own company. But sometimes, definitely we want company; we want to be with people.

548 *I often get very depressed about my weaknesses and faults. Should we really accept these as master's grace, too?*

No, just do your best. You put in effort; you do your best. You be receptive to his grace. You put in effort, but you will get what he wants to give you. You see, he creates that atmosphere, the environment in which we know about the Father, in which we become restless to become one with the Father. And we start worshipping him, start seeking him. He creates that environment, that atmosphere, that family background – many things combined together condition our mind to worship him. And that is all entirely in his hands. Nothing is in our hands.

Actually, we are puppets. But this ego doesn't let us think we are puppets. We think, I am doing it, I have done it. And this ego is binding us to this whole creation. The only difference between a realized soul and the unrealized soul is that the realized soul realizes that he's absolutely a puppet. Nothing is in his hands – it's all the Father's grace. The unrealized soul thinks: "Who can make me do anything? It is me who is doing everything – who else can make me do these things?" He's a victim of ego, while another man has been able to eliminate ego. They may look alike, but one realizes he is a puppet and the other does not.

549 *Maharaj Ji – I think it's in* Sar Bachan *– what is meant by the phrase: In Sant Mat, we must live the life of a warrior?*

A warrior is never frightened of death, and he sacrifices so many things. He doesn't look back at all. He never worries: What will happen to my wife, what will happen to my son, and if I'm killed, how will they live? His only aim is to fight and conquer and be victorious. Similarly, our aim in meditation should be to be like a warrior. We shouldn't worry: If I leave this creation what will happen to my children, what will happen to my wife? I've collected so much wealth – what will happen to it? We must absolutely pull our mind from all these things and be prepared to sacrifice anything to achieve our end. A warrior is always ready to fight, so we should always be ready to fight with our mind, to conquer our mind and be prepared to sacrifice anything in order to achieve our end – like a warrior.

550 *Could you explain if there's any difference between being a warrior on the path and being a satsangi?*

Being a warrior on the path is just a way of expressing the idea that you have to fight with the mind, with your senses, just as a warrior fights with the enemy, and he's not frightened, even of his death. No matter how much hardship he has to go through, he wants to fight, he looks ahead. Similarly, our attitude should be to fight with the mind, fight with our senses, fight with our weaknesses like a warrior. That's only a way of expression.

There's no distinction, then, between a warrior and a satsangi?

Every satsangi is a warrior.

551 *Maharaj Ji, in all the books and even in Professor's talk this evening is the idea that we have no love, that this is a gift of the master.*

I think we have to start right from the beginning to answer this question. Why should we be separated from the Father at all? We have to start from there. Now we are in the middle of the battle; now we can't think about the beginning. We have to start right from here – that we are in the middle of the battle and we have to win it. Why have we entered this battle? We have no answer to that at all now, at this stage – it's too late to think about it. Once you are in the battle, you have to fight. Before entering the battle we could think, why enter the battle? Probably that was not our choice, and there is no sense in thinking about that now. Now, the only solution is that we have to fight the battle.

552 *Master, it seems impossible to win the battle with the mind.*

Guidance is always there within. The soldier is always armed to fight, the general is always there to command him, to help him, to guide him to fight, but the soldier has to fight. He can't tell the general: "Now you have equipped me with all the armaments, and now you also have to fight for me." He has to fight. We have to fight with our enemy, which is right within every one of us. We are fully equipped to fight the enemy, so why should we feel frightened about it? Our enemy should feel frightened because even if we run away from the situation, our enemy is going around with us. We can't escape from the enemy – it's right within us. We never know when it may deceive us. We have to confront whatever situation it creates, so by running away we don't solve any problem at all.

REMAINING IN HIS DISCIPLINE

553 Maharaj Ji, how is discipline connected with love, and what is the difference between discipline and love?

Well, sister, to remain in the Father's love actually is to remain in his discipline. To submit ourselves to him – that is to remain in the discipline or to remain in his love. Anything which takes us away from his love makes us undisciplined, so whatever keeps us within his love, within his devotion, that is a discipline for us that we have to follow.

554 Maharaj Ji, I don't have this together. With your help I can get this together – I know my own level. I remember reading something in one of the books about some form of detachment, that our thoughts should be at such a stage that we have no desire for this world or the next. Does that mean that at this stage we do meditation for the sake of loving God and for no other reason?

You see, religion is not based on fear, but it should be based on love, devotion. We're not to worship the Father out of fear of punishment, out of fear of coming back to this creation again and again. That is one approach. The positive approach is to become one with the Father. We have so much love and devotion for the Father that we worship him, we cannot live without him. That's the positive approach. So the basis of religion is love, not fear. But the human mind is such that unless we are frightened of something, we never do anything. Even in our daily course of life – you go to any city – if you think that nobody's going to challenge you, you won't stop your car at a red light. You'll just go right through it. But if you have a fear that if you don't stop at the red light you'll be punished, you'll be fined, out of that fear you'll stop the car. But if you are told that everybody should stop, look around, and then go, but there would be no punishment for not doing so, nobody would stop.

So if we are not disciplined out of love, then we have to be disciplined out of fear. Mystics sometimes tell both sides: that the best way to approach the Father is out of love, but if this approach doesn't appeal to you, then don't forget what you have to go through if you have to come back to this creation. So they also depict this side: the misery of this world, of this creation, and they also fill us with love and devotion for the Father. Whatever approach appeals to you is good. The main thing is that we must worship the Father.

555 *I've heard that there's so much pain involved in the Sant*
     Mat path as far as denial of worldly things. Can this be
     a path of joy also?

Well, you mean to say that those people who do not follow the path are happy? Go to all the mental asylums and find whether they're happy or not. People are just miserably living in comfort, nothing else. Those who deny themselves the pleasures of the world, they may be the happiest ones. They are much happier than those who have become slaves of the pleasures of the world. Pleasure lies in pulling away from the senses, not becoming a

411

slave of the senses. That's a wrong concept, that there's pain in following the Sant Mat path and there's pleasure in going away from it. If there had been pleasure, nobody would come to the path. People only run to the path because they have become miserable without it. They try to seek pleasure in the senses and they find themselves more miserable. We can only get peace and pleasure by denying ourselves these pleasures rather than by becoming a victim of them.

556 There is a statement – I believe in Spiritual Gems – *that's a little bit puzzling. It says that a saint considers it fortunate if he can find one true disciple in his ministry. Can you explain that?*

You see, a true disciple is one who really worships the Father for the sake of the Father, who is full of love and devotion for him and not concerned with anything else in the world. We become that real disciple of a master when we cross the stage of Brahm, the second stage – when the soul gets released from the mind. Then we are really true disciples of the master. Before that we are more or less disciples of the mind.

We become the real disciple of the master, the real slave of the master, Guru Nanak said, when nobody else exists between me and the Father, me and the master. If anything else exists, then I am not wholly a disciple of the master yet. When nothing exists between me and the Father or me and the master, then I am a true disciple of the master. If my children exist or property exists or ego exists or worldly pleasures exist, then I am not a true disciple of the master. That is what Maharaj Ji [Maharaj Sawan Singh] is trying to say. What he actually means is that it is very difficult, very rare, to find a true disciple. Everybody is anxious to go back to the Father, but we have our own weaknesses, we have our own attachments, which we have to overcome. We are all struggling souls, but those who have struggled enough and have reached beyond the realm of struggle, they're the real disciples.

557 What if you don't get very far at it, then when you die, does that mean you'll only be in darkness?

Well, if you are in darkness now, then what else can you expect after death? But then, as we discussed, there is grace – we can always depend upon that. You see, if the student is very obedient in class, and very disciplined, the master, the professor, is always anxious to pull him through with one excuse or another. So if we are not intelligent enough to secure that high standard, let us at least be disciplined and good and obedient so that we can invoke his grace to get through. The one who has pulled us to the path, who is pushing us on the path, he doesn't forget us after death.

558 Maharaj Ji, from a master's point of view, what are some of the characteristics of a good disciple?

Well, I don't know who is worthy to go back to the Father or who is worthy to be his best disciple. But one who stands firm on the principles of Sant Mat and is attending to his meditation and living in the will of the Lord, naturally he's the right type of disciple.

OVERCOMING WEAKNESSES

559 It is depressing to see how full of weaknesses we are and how unsuccessful our efforts are to overcome them.

To go back to what you said about many people being very nice, though not being satsangis, satsangis probably try to analyze themselves too much, thinking that they have too many bad qualities in them. If this room is filled with darkness, you do not know how much that darkness covers up; but if a little ray of light comes in, you know instantly that this whole room is filled with small particles. Similarly, when we do not know about or are not on the path, we are not aware of our bad points. Rather, we take pride in our habits. But when we are on the path, that ray of light comes within us. Then we analyze ourselves and find that we have many very bad habits. In fact, the bad habits were there before, but now we are in a position to analyze them, to realize them. So we feel a little guilty about them. Actually, it is a sign that we are improving because this consciousness has come in us to help us discriminate between what is good and what is bad. That light of discrimination has come to show us that we are really bad and we should get rid of these bad habits. Before that, we never knew it and we even took pride in these things. So one should not feel guilty about it. Rather, we should try to know our weaknesses and then do our best to overcome them.

I always say that when we are conscious of our faults, half the battle is won because then we begin to do something about them. But when we are unaware of our faults, we delude ourselves into thinking that what we are doing is right, which causes us to travel still farther in the opposite direction. We should therefore be grateful that the Lord's grace is enabling us to avoid these pitfalls and travel straight on the path leading back to him.

560 I have believed, believed sincerely, backslid, believed again, believed sincerely, backslid again, believed sincerely, backslid. How many times does this go on?

Well, brother, the temptation is always there. As long as you believe you have sinned, you realize your weakness and try to rise above it. The very realization that we are committing a sin and are the victim of this weakness, that very realization is a great step toward getting rid of that weakness. If we don't realize we are committing sins, we will never be able to get rid of those sins at all. But when you know you're committing a sin and try to help yourself, the Lord's grace will also be there to help you. It is good to know that you are committing a sin because then, naturally, you will try to get rid of it.

561 *Master, sometimes I come to situations where I know right from wrong. I know what the appropriate behaviour is, but I don't seem to be able to get into the place where I can do what I know is the right thing. It's confusing sometimes.*

You see, the purpose of the Sant Mat teachings is to clean our mind, to help us understand what is right, what is wrong, and then to fight the situation accordingly. That is the purpose of all this – satsang, the meetings, the literature, the Sant Mat way of life. We are conditioning our mind to discriminate between what is good and what is bad and to know how to eliminate the bad and how to hold on to the good. This is the purpose of satsang, of these meetings, of reading all this literature.

Well, it's frustrating when you know right from wrong and you can discriminate, but yet when you go do the action, the negative action occurs.

The mind is very powerful. As long as you understand it is wrong, then naturally when you realize it's wrong, you'll fight with the mind not to repeat that behaviour. If you don't understand that it is wrong, then how can you rise above that weakness? If you start justifying that, then you will always remain a slave of that weakness. But once you start realizing it is wrong, once that consciousness has come into you that what you are doing is wrong, then naturally the time will also come when you'll fight with yourself to do what is right. But if you start justifying your wrong behaviour and taking pleasure and pride in that, then you will always remain a victim of that weakness. That is the first step to fight the weakness, to realize that I am absolutely wrong.

562 *Maharaj Ji, sometimes we see our own imperfections and our own shortcomings, and we know that these are keeping us from being one with the Father. Yet is there a danger of us being too hard on ourselves for having weaknesses?*

There is no danger of being hard on ourselves at all. We have been too soft with ourselves all through – that is why we are part of the creation. If we had been a little hard or strong with ourselves, we would not be here today. We have been too soft. We always try to justify our weaknesses and then we become a slave of them. And then we find we are part of this creation. So we should try to be hard with ourselves.

563 *Maharaj Ji, I never understand the difference between discrimination and tolerance, for instance. I don't know where tolerance starts and discrimination begins.*

There's a lot of difference, sister. If you will consult the Oxford dictionary, tolerance is something different.

No, but let's say I don't like a person because I find that this person is very negative. But then I remember that Sant Mat says you have to be tolerant. And then I remember also that I have to be discriminating. So, I am really confused.

Sister, the question is rather that we are negative to others. We are negative to certain people, so we think they're being negative to us. We have to improve ourselves, we have to become positive. Why should there be any thought in our mind about anybody being negative? Why should it affect us at all? There is some weakness hidden in us that causes it to affect us. If we are strong, then nothing affects us; so nobody is negative to us. You see, evil is there. I don't say that evil is not there. But if we are strong, there's no evil. Now, crime is there, but if you don't commit a crime, for you there's no punishment. The jails are full of criminals, and there are so many police and guards, but if you are a good citizen, that doesn't affect you at all. There may be many policemen and many jails, but you're not frightened because you're a good citizen. We should not be affected by anybody's negative thoughts or positive thoughts.

Now, the words negative and positive are very comparative. But we should not be affected by anybody – we should be strong within ourselves. Then this negative tendency won't exist for me at all. If I am weak, then I am easily lured by other people's company; so the weakness lies in me, not in the other person. You see, weakness lies in us, that we are tempted by evil. Weakness doesn't lie in the evil. Weakness lies in us, that we are influenced by evil company, the evil tendencies of another person. It is our weakness that we are a victim of. We have to get rid of that weakness, and then evil intentions won't affect us at all.

564 *Maharaj Ji, I heard on a tape you telling a disciple that not only was everything in this life already chalked out, but even the way we think is not in our hands, that we are made to think in a certain way to go through our destiny. After hearing that, I wondered if it's totally*

meaningless and a waste of time for us to judge and con-
demn ourselves for our human weaknesses and maybe
even our failures as disciples?

With meditation our willpower becomes so strong that even if
our mind has been wrongly conditioned and wrongly influenced
in childhood, we can become a saint. That influence of childhood is there on the mind, no doubt, but still sometimes we get
better company, or by the Lord's grace we realize that our mind
has been wrongly conditioned, and we are able to rise above it
and not act according to the conditioning of our mind. We act
independently of the conditioning of the mind.

565 *We all realize, of course, that one day this life must come*
to an end. One who is initiated by a master – will the
master definitely meet him at death?

If we remain within the commandments and we practice and
we do not want to come back to this world, definitely the master
will meet us at the end and will take us up. But if we compromise
with the principles and we do not want to meet the master, then
it is for him to come or not to come. We cannot demand it. We
have to deserve it, but somebody has to come to take you at
the time of death. Naturally, an initiate who does his spiritual
practice cannot go with the negative power, which is Kal. Who
else is there to come and take you back? We want assurances,
perhaps from the point of view that we may do whatever we feel
like and that the master will still come and take us back. We
perhaps want to justify our weaknesses, justify our not doing the
spiritual practice. I think from that point of view this approach
is not right. It is for the master to come or not to come, but we
should work hard. We must do our duty, and then naturally he
must come and take us.

If a child commits any mischief, does not behave properly, even breaks the law, the father never hands him over to the police. A father never likes his son to go to jail, but all the same the father wants to put him on the right path, so he punishes him, though he may not hand him over to the police or to the jail. That does not mean that if we do not practice, even then we will be accepted and taken back. We have to get punishment – sometimes perhaps the father's punishment is more severe than that of the police – but all the same, there is love coupled with the idea of discipline behind this punishment; there is no revenge in the father's heart. His object is to improve the son, to make him a better human being; but he will not hand him over to the police or the district jail. Similarly, for those who come on the path, the question of their going back to the negative power does not arise; but if they do bad karmas, if they do not practice the right thing, they are punished. Punishment is there.

Maharaj Ji [Maharaj Sawan Singh] often used to explain to us that a potter always keeps his hand under the clay which he is trying to mould. He spanks from above, probably to expand it. But his guiding hand, his helping hand, is always at the bottom, just to give it shape. Similarly, we get punishment, but the guiding hand is always there. There are no failures on the path. When we want to run, want to achieve some destination, we try to run, we fall, we get up, we run, we fall again, but as long as we know the destination is there and we sincerely try, we have got to achieve it. On the other hand, if you do not make a start at all, of course there may not be any falls, there may not be any pitfalls, but you definitely are not going towards the destination. You are not going any distance. When we try, there are sometimes pitfalls here and there, but his guiding hand, loving hand, is always there to set us right, to put us right and to help us overcome our weaknesses, to rise above them, follow the path and merge back into him.

419

The seed once sown is never destroyed. If the field is fertile and the seed is there, it is only a question of time till it comes up. It may take one rain or two rains or three rains. It may need watering, but it is a seed that must sprout. So we, who are only a part of the master, must see to it that we merge back into him. He does not just initiate us and then forget about it; he is responsible to take our soul back to the Lord. But we have to do our part. Without doing our part, we are not entitled to go back. But with his grace, he also makes us do our part and we achieve what we want to achieve.

FALLING AND GETTING UP

566 Do you think a person, an initiate who follows this path, will be released in four lifetimes? If he is not scheduled to be released in this lifetime, will he still taste the bliss of nam?

Well, brother, I will discuss tomorrow the parable of sowing of the seeds. Christ himself has given a beautiful parable. When a farmer goes to a field, some seeds fall on barren ground, some seeds fall on rocky ground, some seeds fall among thorns. Some seeds go to fertile ground. The seed which goes to fertile ground yields 100 percent results, or 70, 60 or 50 percent results. But the seeds are scattered everywhere by the farmer.[48]

In this way, saints come to this world. They initiate so many people. So many people are drawn by them. But sometimes a seed goes on barren ground. Sometimes a seed goes on rocky ground. Sometimes a seed goes on marshy ground. Sometimes a seed goes to fertile ground. That seed which goes to fertile ground will, in this very lifetime, get 100 percent results, or 70 percent results. This means they will not come back again.

They will get the full result of their meditation. Other people will have to take another birth to improve their spiritual level, to improve their spiritual progress, to have that experience. So every lifetime you improve more and more, and ultimately you are able to go back.

Not every initiate, in this very lifetime, will be able to go back to the Father. Everybody has their individual karma which they have to clear. Some have a very light load. They are more receptive. They will be able to succeed in this very lifetime. Others may have to take another birth.

567 What is meant by the saying in the Bible: Many are called, but few are chosen?

When Christ says that many are called but few are chosen,[63] he means that few are chosen in this very lifetime to go back to the Father. Whoever has been called, ultimately, will be chosen to go back to the Father, but not necessarily in this very lifetime. He may have to take another birth, another birth, and another birth to get an opportunity to improve. And then, ultimately, his soul may shine and go back to the Father.

Saints come and call many seekers, initiate many seekers. But few are chosen in this very lifetime to go back to the Father. Christ gives a very beautiful parable to explain this point. He says that when a farmer takes seeds to a field to plant, some seeds just fall on barren ground and people come and crush them under their feet, and that's the end of that seed. And other seeds fall on rocky ground where there's not much soil or moisture. Plants come up, but with the heat of the sun they wither and die. A third type of seed, while being taken to the field, falls on some marshy ground and sprouts along with the tares, the weeds. And some seed falls on fertile ground. Those seeds give a 100 percent results, 70 percent results, 80 percent results.[48]

Then he says: Many are called; few are chosen. Wherever the seed has gone, it must sprout, but only the seed which has gone to the fertile ground will be able to get 100 percent results, which means that, in that very lifetime, that soul will be able to go back to the Father. Whether the soul goes to the third, fourth or fifth stage is 70, 80 or 100 percent results, but the soul goes on its way towards the Father.

Christ explains the other seeds – there are many types of seekers. Some people just by circumstance happen to come into the company of mystics, and as long as they are in their company, they're influenced by them and want to follow the path. They feel love and devotion for the Father. But the moment they leave the mystic, they absolutely forget and again become like worldly people. That is the seed which has fallen on barren ground.

Another type of person, as long as they remain in the company of the mystic, they meditate, and they're good and honest. But the moment they leave the mystic's company, they too are taken away by sensual pleasures and worldly ambitions, and they just forget about the path. Their seed has fallen on rocky ground.

The third type of person is very sincere, devoting their time daily to meditation. They're full of love and devotion for the Father, but they're also ambitious from the worldly point of view. They want to attain worldly achievements, and they have also certain weaknesses which they can't shed. They are building their treasure in heaven but, on the other hand, weeds are also growing – they're also doing bad deeds. Both are progressing, good deeds and bad deeds, meditation and the sensual pleasures – they're victims of these. These are the seeds which have fallen on marshy ground. Ultimately, what happens to these people? They have done good deeds; the time they have devoted to meditation will take care of the evil deeds which they have been tempted to do. Whatever meditation is left in their balance, they will get credit for that.

The fourth type is where the ground is absolutely fertile. These people attend to their meditation; they are full of love and devotion for the Father, and they absolutely make progress during their lifetime. They will go back at once to the Father after death.

Everybody will go back. But everybody is not equal in their progress because the ground is not the same. One ground is barren; one ground is rocky; another is marshy and another is fertile. The seed is the same – soul is the same, but progress also depends upon the fertility of the ground.

When Christ says that many are called but few are chosen, he means that few are chosen in this very lifetime to make progress and go back to the Father. But, he says, whoever has been called will ultimately go back to the Father, but the first may be last and the last may be first.[63] There's no seniority on the path.

568 *Maharaj Ji, could an initiate do anything so bad, even if it is against the master or Lord personally; or could anything be done to an initiate; or is there any force or evil in the world that could damage or destroy the bond of initiation between the Lord and the disciple, between the master and the disciple?*

Well, brother, this relationship is such that it can never be destroyed. Once the seed has been sown, it has to sprout and bear fruit. Once we come on the path, we have to follow it and find the destination. No matter how much we go right or left, ultimately we will again find ourselves on the path. In Christ's example of the sowing of the seed, once the seed has fallen on the ground, no matter how little earth there may be under it, it has to sprout. Once the seed has been sown, it cannot be destroyed. The marking has been done by the Father, the pull has been created by the Father, and by his grace, once that pull has been created, it is bound to pull us to his level sooner or later. That relationship cannot be destroyed at all.

We have human failings. We are all struggling souls, but we again get up and again we start walking. That doesn't mean that, if we have left the path, we can never come back on the path again. When you fly a kite – you have seen people flying kites – the string is always in the hand of the kite-flyer. When he sees the kite going right and left with the wind, he pulls that kite back. Similarly, with the wind of karmas, we go astray right and left, but our string is in the hand of the master, and he again pulls us back to the path.

569 *Maharaj Ji, in the last four years you've showered immense grace on me, and I had no understanding of what it meant. At some point I turned my back on you in a very ugly way. And I don't know if there'll be another possibility in this lifetime that you'll forgive me.*

Sister, the Lord is always showering his grace on us. He's always pulling us from within. We have to be receptive to that pull, we have to be receptive to his grace and be grateful to him for that pull, for that grace. No doubt, sometimes we do go astray here and there because our destiny is such – we have a strange load of karma which just puts us off the path. But I give the example of a kite, which, when we fly it, goes right and left. As long as the string is there in the hand of the flyer, it will be pulled back to the level of the flyer. The kite has nothing to worry about. We do go astray here and there, but that pull of the shabd and nam is always there, that seed is there within us. It has to sprout sooner or later. And that puts us on the path again.

We are all beggars at the Father's door. Our duty is to beg, to knock at the door. It is for the giver to see if we are worthy to receive what he has to give. But we must do our duty. We must knock, we must beg. He is a very good giver, but we are very poor beggars.

570 *Master, perhaps I just don't understand anything, but I think we've all seen our brother and sister satsangis who, after many years on the path, sometimes have gone completely off of the vows. It frightens me a little because I know that they're helpless to be or do anything other than what they are. And my question is: If it is in one's karma to go through such an intense karma that you can't even meditate or do anything like that, if that satsangi is truly devoted, really wants to be devoted to master and really desires to do your will, can he pay off that same karma without having to go off the path, so to speak?*

It is not in his hands, whether to pay off the karmas without going off the path or by remaining on the path. It's not in his hands at all. He has no control over his karmas at all – he is a slave of those karmas. When we become the master of our karmas, then it's different. Then we rise above them. But now we're all slaves of our karmas. As I said a couple of days ago, sometimes clouds do come and we don't see the sunlight at all, but that does not mean that the sun is not there. Ultimately the clouds fade out and the sun comes again. We are definitely all struggling souls on the path. We're definitely swayed away from the path, due to our weaknesses, our karmas, our sins – give them any name. But ultimately, we again are pulled back on the path. When you fly a kite with a strong wind, it goes right and left – it looks absolutely out of control. But the person who is flying the kite has its string in his hand. When he thinks it is going too much out of control, he pulls it back to his own level. So our string is in the Lord's hand, the master's hand, and we're never allowed to go so far away that we cannot be pulled back. Definitely this wind of strong karmas does flow and take us away from the path.

> *Why isn't it handled in such a way that the master would make us meditate more rather than our being carried off by our karmas, which we then have to burn off in meditation?*

Sister, if you had certain karmas to go through by going off the path, then who will account for that? It's very difficult to analyze these things. We should just do our best and not worry at all. There's no 'why' here.

571 *Master, sometimes disciples seem to go off the path and they stop their meditation and they break other vows. Is this necessary for their spiritual progress? Do they have to go through these karmas in order to proceed on the path?*

I can't say it's necessary, but sometimes the wind of karmas is so strong that we are swayed off our feet, and we find that we are away from the path. But then we are pulled back to the path again. The sun shines every day, but sometimes thick clouds come and we don't see that sunlight; we don't feel the warmth of that sun even though the sun is always there.

> *Would that mean that a person comes straight again on the path in this life, or would it mean…?*

There's no question of time and space with the disciple or with the master. There's no question of this life or that life. He knows best.

572 *Master, I think we are arriving at the stage where our main concern is trying to receive your grace and your*

mercy concerning all these things. We understand that one of the principles of Sant Mat is that the master sometimes administers what would be fatal sword stabs as pinpricks. I wonder if this also coincides with the words of Jesus in the Lord's Prayer: Lead us not into these awful temptations of our karma, but, Master, deliver us from them – we know you can because you're the kingdom and the power and the glory forever.

Well, brother, when by his grace, by the grace of the Father, the master puts us on the path, he doesn't withhold his grace. His grace is always there. The more we are becoming receptive to his grace, the more grace we are receiving within. As I said yesterday, the gardener is more anxious that the tree should yield fruit. Master is anxious to finish his responsibility, anxious that all the souls allotted to him should go back to the home of the Father. He doesn't withhold his grace at all.

Our concept of grace is about material things in life, but that is not the concept of grace that we have in Sant Mat. That concept of grace is about spiritual progress, about how many pitfalls we are saved from, how much we are saved at every step. That grace is there when the master puts us on the path. He's there within us always, to guide us. He never lets us go so far astray that we cannot come back to the path, that he cannot lead us back to the Father.

People flying a kite have the kite string in their hand. The kite is running this way and that, with the wind. But the kite flyer always holds the string in his hand, and when he thinks it's getting out of his control, he pulls it back. So that is the duty of the master. It is his responsibility after initiation to take the soul back to the Father. We have to play our part, and he has to play his part.

573 So we feel the master's grace even in the midst of our failures?

We feel his grace at every step. A child feels the guiding hand, the helping hand, of his mother at every step in his upbringing, his development. Without the mother's helping hand a child can never develop. Master's helping hand is always there for our spiritual development. We could never spiritually develop at all without his guidance, whether outside or inside. His helping hand is always there with the disciple, for his spiritual development.

We're never allowed to go so astray that we can't come back to the path and ultimately find our destination. The marking has been done, and those who have been marked must ultimately go back to the Father. Christ gives a very beautiful example. He says: The shepherd has been entrusted with a hundred sheep. One sheep goes astray out of the fold. The shepherd leaves ninety-nine sheep and runs after that one particular sheep and even physically lifts that sheep on his shoulder to bring it back to the fold because he's responsible for all hundred sheep, not ninety-nine sheep.[57] He cannot think or say that ninety-nine are certain, so why should I bother if one has gone astray? He's responsible for all hundred of the sheep.

Similarly, the master is responsible for all the allotted souls, the ones marked for the master – not only the good ones, but every one. As Christ said, ultimately there'll be one shepherd and one fold.[107] Everybody has to be in that fold, all those who are marked. So naturally his guiding hand is always there, whether we are conscious of it or not conscious of it. For our spiritual development, he is always there to help us in every way.

Are you saying, then, that it's impossible to resign from the path?

Unfortunately, you are right. The marking is so deep, that in spite of your best efforts, you will not be able to erase it.

574   *I'd also like to ask: When you come to a crossroads in your life and you can make a decision that is either going to take you away from the master or towards the master, as satsangis, do we have that freedom of choice, or will we still have to go through, let's say, making a bad decision in order to go through that karma?*

Actually, sister, we have no choice at all in this creation, and we never go away from the master. We may feel that we have gone away from the master, but because master never goes away from us, how can we go away from him?

What about when we do something against the Sant Mat principles?

Well, children are not always obedient to their parents; they rebel, they become mischievous. But the parents love them just the same.

575   *In* Quest for Light, *there is mention of the gates of hell being wide open for certain very bad sins, and it is also said that the Lord and the saints come for the fallen ones. Sometimes when I feel very sinful, I feel like, "Oh well, I might go to hell," and other times, when I feel like I have a chance, I feel like maybe I'll go with my master. How should I think about this?*

You see, we are all supposed to be good citizens, so if we misbehave, we have to go to jail. But for a person who is behaving, neither the police exist for him nor the jails exist for him. But in order to remain a good citizen, you have to be told what the consequences are if you don't behave properly. So master gives us love, nothing but love. The father always loves the child, but also frightens him by telling him that if he misbehaves, he will have to face such and such punishment. Sometimes the father may even exaggerate just to keep the child straight. He may not mean it at all, but he wants that child to be disciplined, and that fear helps the child to become a good citizen and a loving son.

Some letters are written with a very particular purpose. You see, if a satsangi is going absolutely wild and is trying to justify his follies, you have to shake him from the roots to bring him back to the path. You can't be very lenient in your letters. He has to be shaken to make him realize the consequences of his behaviour. So these letters are always in reference to particular situations.

576 *Master, when initiates break the vows that they take before the Lord at the time of initiation, could you explain how that makes the master's work harder?*

When a child doesn't remain disciplined, doesn't obey his parents, of course the parents never hand him over to the police, but they do give him a good thrashing. And a mother will never pick up a dirty child; she may give him a good wash and clean the child before she picks him up. It's not that she doesn't love the child, but she wants the child to be clean, to be pure. So if we break the vows, if we go astray from the path, we are punished. It's not that we are not punished – sometimes we are punished even more severely. But there is a love behind that punishment. The master wants us to be absolutely clean because unless we are clean, unless our souls shine, we cannot merge back into the Father. So that is the purpose of our punishment, to keep us straight on the path.

577 *Master, based on the reality that we must reap what we've sown, if the satsangi is successful in stilling the mind and at the same time performs his social duty in the world, living morally in his professional and personal life, how can he extricate himself from the world if he incurs this good karma, and bad karma as well?*

You see, when you learn to walk, learn to run, you fall many times, but you get up again, and again you start running. It doesn't mean that if you have fallen once, you will not get up and try again. Slips are there. And the mind is very powerful. It sways us off our feet to the right and left. But if we continue in meditation, we become firm again on the path. A child doesn't mind how many times he has fallen. He falls, he cries, he gets up again and he starts doing the same thing over again.

We have so many pitfalls in life which we have to face, very unpleasant things. But if we keep our destination before us, the path before us, and the determination to follow it and reach the destination, then you are able to do it.

578 *Maharaj Ji, if a person is very interested in spiritual growth and his environment is such that he is constantly attacking a hurdle and is constantly, from what he recognizes, pushing, in that he is trying to get around in every honourable, possible way, and he himself has digressions; if this environment is constantly holding one back, what must one do to overcome this?*

Brother, we are all struggling souls in this world. When we have our destination in view, we know the path leading to the destination and we travel on that. There are falls – we fall, we get up and again we run. There are no failures on the path. One who does not make a start at all has no chance of falling, but then he is not getting anywhere. One who runs has a chance of falling, but he only falls to get up and run again. Pitfalls here and there do pull us back, but as long as we try to overcome those weaknesses, we again get up and again go ahead. We have to do our best under the circumstances. When we are sincere, the Lord comes to our aid and nature also helps us in our environment, in our atmosphere, in our circumstances. The Lord's guiding hand is always there whether we are conscious of it or not.

We should never lose heart when we have pitfalls or when we have fallen or think that we are being driven from the path. He never leaves us. Momentarily, we may feel that we have left the path, and at another time we may feel that we are again on the path. We explain to ourselves that we have left it. Actually, we do not leave it; we cannot leave it. We are so strongly bound, so strongly got hold of, that we cannot leave it, we cannot go astray. But naturally it takes time to learn to walk and then to run. So we should try not to analyze too much. We should do our duties while living in this world, try to give our time to meditation, try to live to the best of our ability, and then slowly but surely, with the Lord's grace, we will become successful in our endeavour.

Would that mean that is part of our karma, too, when we have these pitfalls as we travel on the path?

Well, sister, sometimes definitely it is due to our karma, and at other times there are so many things in the way. These are Kal's devices to keep us away from the path, to make us frustrated, to frighten us from going ahead, to tempt us in so many ways. Sometimes we become their victims; but as long as we are conscious that we are victims, conscious of our destination – that we are on the path and want to travel on the path – then we do succeed. The master's guiding hand is always there to steer us through all those pitfalls, to steer us through all those weaknesses. We pierce through and we do come to the light. There are many factors to that.

579 *Sir, a disciple back home has been suffering from rather severe depression, and I was wondering if you might be able to say some words that I might send along to him.*

You see, why curse the darkness? Why not light the candle? We often curse the darkness rather than lighting the candle. We are worrying about our past, what we have done. When we can't take credit for all that we have done – if we have done anything bad, we should try to improve ourselves for the future. That is the main thing – instead of worrying about the past. That doesn't solve any problem at all. One must look ahead and make best use of the present so that we don't repeat such mistakes again. Otherwise, carrying guilt on your conscience doesn't solve any problem. Sometimes we can't help it, we feel so guilty. But it is okay, if we don't repeat the same mistake again.

580 *How can we know when we're doing the right thing? How can we become better disciples when you say that we have no free will? Yet we have to make that one step, and then the master takes a hundred to us?*

Well, you must take that one step. We are more anxiously waiting for his hundred steps rather than our one step. We should not hesitate to take one step, and he never hesitates to take a hundred steps to pull us. But even our one step is in his hands, not in our hands, because he's the one who sows the seed of his love and devotion within us. He's the one who pulls us from within, and then we take that one step. We have limited free will, conditioned free will, not absolute free will.

Being a friend

*581   Master, when one has been initiated and has broken all
the vows, to the extent of giving up the diet and so forth,
to what extent should the association of satsangis with
that person be changed? Or should it be changed? Should
they eat with him?*

I have already covered that point in another answer, that still
he is better than a noninitiate. When we meet with all other
types of people, in all sorts of atmospheres, who know nothing
about Sant Mat and spirituality or even about God, we never
hesitate to mix with them. Then why should we hesitate to mix
with one who has strayed from the path, but still feels that the
path is right? He is a victim of his own weaknesses and cannot
help that. He is to be pitied and helped. Rather, we should give
him more love and consideration to bring him back to the path
instead of boycotting him. It is not the right attitude not to mix
with or help such people. We should have no hatred toward
anybody. Our hearts should be receptive – open to everyone
who wants to come into the fold.

*Master, I did not mean it like that. I mean, should we
ever say anything to him about it? Or should we take the
position that we are ignoring him?*

It may depend upon your relationship with him. If you think
he will take advice from you, wants help and a certain moral
strength, you should not hesitate to give it to him. If you think
he would resent it, that he would like to avoid it, then why fuss
over it? We should definitely try to help each other. What is the
object of these meetings? What is the object of satsangis meeting
together? It is to get help to keep straight, to remain on the path.
In satsang, which really means true meeting, true association,

we get so much moral strength, moral support, from each other to remain in the realm of Sant Mat. So the true teachings expressed in love and harmony are paramount qualities and should always be given and open to everybody. But if anybody resents that, do not bother about it or be hurt about it, but go on doing your duty lovingly and devotedly, leaving him to his own fate. We should never try to force any advice on anyone, even with the best of intentions. Example is better than precept, and such a person will eventually reform when those bad karmas are finished, or when he lives up to the teachings and is helped over them [the karmas] by the grace of the master.

582 *Master, how should a satsangi brother or sister help another satsangi brother or sister who has strayed off the path?*

Well, the first thing that helps anybody is to be a living example to another person. Then, lovingly, we should try to talk to them, without showing off or making them too conscious of their weaknesses, because we don't want to drive them farther away – we want to pull them back. Because we don't want to drive them away, we first have to make them receptive to what we want to say. It depends upon our individual approach. We shouldn't try to show off that we are superior. We are all struggling souls. We do fall here and there. We should be a source of strength and help to one another no doubt, but in a way that we are able to pull a person back rather than drive him away by making him more conscious of his weaknesses or by showing our own superiority over him.

583 *Just as a baby lion gets a slap from its mother when it walks into a dangerous pen, is it not right for us, as*

grown-up children, to sometimes slap our brother with the truth? I think it is not love to accept everything that is given to us. Buddha has said, "I do not accept the gift that evil gives. I will not accept it." Is it always love to accept, or is it good to incur the hatred of someone whom we correct, and to stand away from it and not to hate them?

Brother, nobody will mind if it is a slap of love. Nobody will mind being corrected if there is love behind it and if you approach him with affection, with love, with devotion and with understanding. If you try to boss over him and think that you are superior to him and he is inferior to you, that is not the right approach. He will not understand. He will never be on the path again. But, by your example, by your own love, by your own devotion, you can always set him right without hurting him or driving him away from the path. Rather, he needs more love. Everybody needs love, and some people need more love. So we should give him more love, more understanding to put him on the path, and then the question of slapping does not arise at all.

I mean, should they be told the truth?

The truth must be explained with love. If the other person knows everything is for his own good and it is explained with love, he will understand it. But when there is bossing, when there is hatred or when we try to inflate our own ego and try to appear superior, then we are not helping him. Instead, we are driving him off the path. We should be helpful to each other, but always with love and with respect. We should be an example of love and devotion and be generous-hearted, open-hearted. Then even the worst criminal could benefit.

We should have no hatred against anybody. For example, a mother does not hate a child when she spanks him and the child thinks that she is displeased. Actually, she is happy when the child is set right again for there is an inner love in her heart, and she wants to see the child become good and prosperous in the world. Sometimes, though, she has to scold and spank him, but she does not give vent to her anger or ego; that should not be there. It is only with the purpose of correcting the child, and the child knows that his mother loves him very much and he should do what she wants him to do. When that feeling is there, the child will receive what she wants to give.

On the other hand, when the child feels that his mother hates him, whatsoever she may do, he will never accept it. So if we give anything with love and devotion, it will always be accepted in earnest, straightaway. That is why Christ said that we must first forgive others before we ask the Lord for forgiveness.[21] It means that our heart must be pure; we must be receptive to his grace. If we have any ill feeling against anybody, it means that our heart is not ready for his grace and his love. We have first to give love to people before we can receive his love.

584 *Maharaj Ji, if we know somebody who has actually gone off the path for a while, what is the best thing we can do to help them?*

You should yourself become an example to the person, so that he can take advantage of your example. And then you can lovingly explain to him and bring him back to the path. You shouldn't taunt him or try to expose his weaknesses and show your superiority to him or make him feel that he's inferior because he couldn't keep to the path.

Christ has given a very beautiful parable about this. He says that servants asked their master, if the seed was good, the field was good, where did the tares – weeds – come from? The master said, the enemy had sown them. Then a servant asked, should I go and pull up those tares? The master said, no, because pulling up the tares may shake the roots of the crop and destroy it. The servant asked, then what should we do? The master said, at the time of the harvest, first we will cut all the tares and destroy them, and then we will collect the crop, whatever remains.[50]

So saints initiate us. We are quite sincere about that. The seed is good and the soil is good, but we are tempted by Kal, so to say, by the negative power, by sensual pleasures, and we go off the path and become a victim of the senses. Naturally other disciples feel for that disciple, that initiate. But if we taunt him or try to expose his weaknesses, he will shun you and run away from you forever. You know that his weakness is there; but still, he's trying to meditate, he's trying to come to the meetings, he's trying to do his best. So we should encourage him, not try to expose his weaknesses. We should lovingly try to strengthen his faith and pull him out of what he's involved in so that he can follow the path again.

If you make him conscious of his weaknesses, he will leave your company; he will leave the meetings; he will never even see you because he is self-conscious about his weaknesses. So why should we make him conscious of his weaknesses? In a practical way we should help him to come out of those weaknesses rather than try to show him our superiority and his inferiority. That is the meaning of Christ's parable.

MAKING DEVOTION OUR PRIORITY

585 *How can we strengthen our attachment to the Lord to the point that we can overcome all the worldly pulls?*

We always try to give that time to the Father which is of no use to us at all. When we are rejected by society, by our children, by our friends, then we want to devote our time to the Father. But we have to give the best time of our life to the Father. Mostly our time is spent in growing up. Then we start getting education and training, and then we give ourselves to family life and the senses and pleasures of the world. And then we become old and everybody rejects us. Our senses don't go along with us. Even our eyes refuse to cooperate, our ears refuse to cooperate, our limbs refuse to cooperate with us. Then we want to worship the Father. We lose the best opportunity, and the time which is of no use to anybody is what we want to devote to the Father. Then we want to be a lover of the Father. The main purpose of this human birth is to go back to the Father, so that should always be kept in view. Keeping that view, other things should fall in line.

586 *Maharaj Ji, we can find the answers to many of the questions we ask in the literature. What can we satsangis in America do to propel us on our spiritual path? What do we need here in America to help us on our spiritual path?*

You are right, brother. There is hardly any question which I have answered since I came here to which an answer cannot be found in the books. Rather, they are answered in the books in a much more elaborate way. They have been written, and here I am speaking. That is the only difference. But I have nothing particular for Americans to do. The meditation is the same, but some people have different circumstances, different environments where they have been placed. Meditation is not different for Americans than for others. Some people have a greater instinct of possession, they are more possessive. They have to realize that and rise above such things. As I said this morning, like a spider we weave our own web, and soon we find that the web is complete and we are caught in it. We are imprisoned in a net of our own making and cannot get out of it. We create desires and cravings and work hard for material achievements and possessions, and when we get them, ultimately we find that we are being possessed by them. We have become prisoners of them. That is the way I find Americans today.

These things of the world are meant for our use; we are not meant for their use. We should possess them; they should not possess us. What I feel, from what I have been able to see, is that the very objects we possess are possessing us now. We have become so much their slave that we have forgotten the object of our birth, the object of our coming into human form. We have lost the end or goal and have become involved in the means. We have to rise above these things. We have to realize that these things are meant for us; we are not meant for them. All these scientific inventions are for our convenience, to give us more leisure, to allow us to enjoy ourselves and be happy. If we cannot find leisure and happiness as a result of all these scientific achievements, which today are to our credit, I think our purpose in achieving them is no good, is of no use at all. We have to see whether these things have made us happy; or have they, on the other hand, just made us more frustrated and more unhappy, in which case we should realize how to overcome this – how to possess them and not be possessed by them.

For example, what people used to do with their hands in ten hours, now our modern machinery does in perhaps two or three minutes. All this was done to save those nine hours and fifty-seven minutes. But after inventing that machinery, where are those extra nine hours and fifty-seven minutes? It is nowhere. We have invented all these devices to save time, to have more leisure for ourselves so that we can think about our self and think about the Lord. That is good. I am not against it, but we must have that leisure for which we have worked so hard to achieve these inventions, these so-called timesavers. We have forgotten that purpose for which we have worked so hard. That has been absolutely forgotten. We have become just like a prisoner in a spider's web. We have beautifully woven it, and ultimately we find we are a prisoner of it and cannot get out of it, so we have to work harder to get rid of this net now. The means by which we can get rid of it is nothing but meditation.

So, whatever you do, keep your destination and purpose in view. Keep your home in view and try to achieve it. Do not forget your destination. Do not forget the purpose of human birth. We should always keep that in view. Work in this world, live in this world and enjoy yourself in this world, but never forget that destination nor leave the path we have to tread in order to get there. Where we want to go – that goal should always be there in front of us. Keeping that goal in view, going towards that goal, do not become a slave of worldly achievements and forget your real home. That is the only thing I can say.

587 We are living in a country here where the vast majority of the people are suffering in agony and we are privileged parties – we have a certain amount of economic and intellectual power which perhaps we should use for the benefit of those less fortunate than ourselves. But it seems to me that the satsangi path emphasizes one's own enlightenment, not the serving of one's fellow man. Isn't it selfish to focus just on gaining peace for oneself?

The masters' only concern is with the souls and to lead them back to the level of the Father. Everybody is miserable in separation – though some may be comfortable in their misery – so they want to find peace within themselves. When we are able to achieve that peace within ourselves, wherever we go, we will radiate peace. If you go to a happy person, he will make you happy in no time; if you go to a miserable person, he will make you miserable in no time. So first we must obtain that peace within ourselves; we must live with ourselves. When we are able to obtain that peace within ourselves, naturally we will radiate peace wherever we go. We will also create it in other people's minds and hearts, but unless we have achieved it ourselves, we cannot radiate peace at all. So Sant Mat disciples are not self-ish. Actually, unless they have achieved it, how can they radiate peace to others?

588 *Master, someone told me the other day that last summer he met someone who said of someone visiting the Dera: "Look at him, how lazy he is, sitting down there enjoying this holiday. He should be working to rescue the starving millions of India." How should one respond to that?*

You see, in that way people definitely accuse us of being self-ish. They say this meditation and God-realization are nothing but selfishness with no concern for humanity. But they don't understand that actually we are helping our fellow man. The closer we are to the Lord, the more unselfish we are becoming, because the Lord belongs to everybody, so we also start belonging to everybody. Now we are selfish – we belong to a particular person, particular family, particular country, particular nation, particular tribe. And then we get out of this selfishness because the Lord belongs to everybody and we are getting nearer to him, so we are getting nearer to his creation. We can help them much better that way. So God-realization or meditation is not selfish at all because we can actually only help others when we have helped ourselves.

Now, when we try to help the starving millions, we just share their misery, share their miserable plight and condition. Instead of there being ten miserable people, now an eleventh has joined them. But if you help yourself, then you may be able to radiate your happiness to them, your peace and bliss to them, because you can share only what you have. So if you have developed that peace and happiness within yourself, you can help them much better; you won't lose your own balance and yet you will help them. But when we have not helped ourselves and try to help others, instead of one, there are more miserable people. So meditation or following a path is not a selfish attitude at all.

589 *I have found that in being a satsangi, one gets a feeling of selfishness.*

By meditation or by our devotion to the Lord, we become self-centred or concentrated on that side and try to ignore the other side. Is that what you mean?

Yes. Don't we forget a lot of important things?

No, brother, I do not agree with you. I feel that the more time we give to meditation, the nearer we are to the Lord and the closer we are to our destination; so we go higher and higher. The higher we go, the more space we are covering to look upon. Rather, we are expanding ourselves; from a part, we are becoming the whole. When we merge into the Lord, we become the Lord. And when we become the Lord, we become everybody. I would say that now, as long as we are slaves of the senses, we are self-centred. And we are self-centred as long as we try to fulfil our desires for anything except to merge back into the Lord. As we go nearer to him, our vision becomes broader and broader, and we belong to more and more people. We come to love more of humanity as we go nearer to the Lord. When we love him, we automatically love his creation, and then we belong to everybody. When we belong to him who belongs to everybody, we then also belong to everybody. It is a very wrong conception to think that our meditation will lead us to selfishness.

What is selfishness? To think about yourself? Everybody thinks about himself or herself. Do we think we are selfish when we have clothes while many other people do not have clothes to wear? Are we not then thinking about ourselves? We have houses to live in and many people do not have a roof over their head. We have cars to ride in, while other people are walking. Are we not selfish from that point of view? From that point of view, everybody in this world is selfish. But when we start our devotion to the Lord, when we are going nearer to our home, we are rather getting out of this selfishness. We are then coming into the whole; our vision becomes much broader and we know that we belong to everybody. We then realize that we were attaching ourselves unnecessarily to a few and that when we belong to the Lord, who belongs to everybody, we also belong to everybody. I think we are getting rid of selfishness by our devotion to the Lord.

590 Are we able to live in this world without being selfish?

Nobody can live in this world without being selfish. Everybody is selfish. So we should also be selfish to find our goal in life. Why are we not selfish in that regard? We have so many considerations: family ties, relations, friends, fellow citizens. If we say otherwise, we are marked as selfish. But we should also have that instinct of being selfish to find our goal, yet we ignore that aspect. Being selfish means looking to your own personal interest. When this human birth is given to us to go back to the Father, and it is a rare opportunity which we don't get so easily, we should also have that selfish instinct to realize that goal during this span of life. It's correct that nobody can be without any selfishness in this world. All relationships are nothing but selfishness.

591 *Master, please, will you speak about the quality of discrimination and how best to develop it and use it for protection?*

Sister, we can only develop our power of discrimination by meditation. The purer the mind becomes, the better able we are to discriminate between what is good and bad for us. The more we are a slave of the senses, the more our mind is conditioned by the senses, by the sensual pleasures, the less discretion we have to select what is good and bad for us. Sometimes we say that someone has been brainwashed. No matter what you tell him, it has no effect on him. He has become so much a victim of the senses that no matter how much you shake him, he won't understand. He has no sense of discrimination.

You see, this electric bulb gives a lot of light – and we see it and make use of it. But if we put a lot of wrappings around it, we don't see the light. It doesn't penetrate through those wrappings, so we can't make use of that light. The light is there, it is shining, but due to the wrappings we can't make use of it, we can't see. But if you remove the wrapping, the light will start to penetrate. You can only see the full light when there is no wrapping around the bulb at all. Similarly, when our mind becomes purer and purer, the light of the soul starts penetrating. More light, more sense of discrimination comes in us. The mind is becoming purer. It is going to its own origin, so we have a better sense of discrimination then.

592 *Maharaj Ji, would you please explain the difference between clear thinking, discrimination, and analyzing?*

Well, if you had referred to the Oxford dictionary, it would have been better because everybody has his own concept of clear thinking. Even a thief thinks that he's absolutely clear in what he's going to do. Everybody is always just analyzing themselves. No matter what we do or don't do, we are always analyzing within ourselves. As for discrimination, we have to develop a sense of what's right for us and what's wrong for us. What can I explain? There are no do's and don'ts. We have to develop discrimination so that we can make the right decisions and reject the wrong ones.

It's like another sense then that happens?

No, discrimination is a development of the mind. They're all mind: Thinking is mind, discrimination is mind, and analyzing is with the mind. The mind projects in many ways, but we have to utilize this faculty of mind in a better direction, not downward to the senses, but upwards in the love and devotion of the Father.

Could you explain discrimination, what that means?

You see, humans have a sense of discrimination: "This is good, that is bad; I should do this, I should not do that; I am hurting somebody, I am giving love to somebody." We always know. We can know what is good, what is bad, what is right, what is wrong. That is a sense of discrimination.

If we don't know, then should we just kind of push on and hope for the best?

If we don't know, we should try to know by meditation. Our sense of discrimination will become very sharp, accurate and to the point with the help of meditation. But even otherwise, we always know. The Lord has given us that sense to know what is good and what is bad in a broader sense.

LOVING NOT CALCULATING

593 *Master, when we sit in meditation and put in the effort,
but our mind does not concentrate, are sinchit karmas
still being paid off?*

Sister, never calculate in meditation how much you have been
able to clear today, and how much you have to sit in meditation
to clear so much of your karmas. Never calculate. Calculation
will lead you nowhere. You do your duty. Leave it to the Lord
how the karma is cleared, when it is cleared and where it is
cleared. That is his job. Calculated meditation won't take you
anywhere. It is not wages you are demanding. You are meditating because you are in love with him, you want to become one
with him. A lover never loves because he wants the wages of
his love. If a lover wants the wages of his love, he is not a good
lover at all.

594 *Master, if someone isn't doing simran and they are singing shabds to the master with a feeling of devotion, is
that as good as simran?*

You see, we should not do our meditation on a calculated basis.
We are so fond of getting wages for anything we do. We say, I
have done simran for so long, what advantage will I get? Love
never demands any wages. Love itself is an effect of wages. The
Lord has given you that love to love him. What more wages
could one demand from the Lord? A lover doesn't demand any
wages at all. He just wants to love. But we hardly sit in meditation and our sole aim is: How much have I been able to gain,
how many karmas have I been able to wash today? You wash
nothing; if that is the calculation, you wash nothing. When that
love comes, you don't want any reward for your wages. You are

447

filled with love, and you are happy in your love, and you just love, and you want nothing but love. All karmas automatically are washed.

595 *Master, is there any point at which a disciple becomes aware that he has love for the master, or, if he has realized it, then it would be true?*

That reminds me of the funny story of a girl who asked her mother, "Please wake me up when I'm delivering a child." You think you will not be aware when you are in love with the master? And you want to know how you are in love with the master? Is love such a dead thing?

> *But then, Master, why do so many of us come here – I'll speak for myself – why do I come here and struggle with meditation day after day, and yet I feel so empty of love and devotion?*

Because we analyze ourselves too much, or our ideal seems to be very high, or we want to know that we are in love. We want to be sure that we are in love, so we are always trying to analyze: "Are we in love?" Without that pull, how could anybody come to the path? But then, it depends upon the seed, whether it has been sown in the ground, whether it has just sprouted or it has taken root and become a tree. The seed is the same. Some seeds have become trees while other seeds are still just in the ground, fighting to come up out of the earth. But that seed has to sprout.

596 *How should we try to love the master without expectancy?*

How do you know reward is not there? And moreover, you see, you never bargain in love. I've never found that bargain in love. You never love somebody because you expect something from the other person. You love because you're helpless to love, irrespective if the other person loves you or not. If you want love in return, then that is no love at all. That may be your desire, but that is not a bargain. But how do you know that you love the master? The master may be pulling you from within to love him. You may just be responding to his pull. You see, love always starts with the Father. Unless he pulls us from within, we can never worship or love the Father at all. Love always starts with the master; it never starts with the disciple. The pull is always from within – you may not be conscious of it – then we become restless. So the question of reward doesn't arise at all. We have only to be receptive to the pull. And it is also he who makes us receptive.

597 *The other night, Professor was reading about love for the master, and how we must love the master for his sake. We shouldn't ask him for anything, not even Sach Khand – we should want just the master. But I'm sure many of us love the master for our own sake. We're tired of the creation, and the master is the means by which we can get out of it.*

You see, these are just ways of expression. Actually, in love we never demand anything. In love we always give. If we demand anything, that is no love at all. Love is giving. Losing your identity, becoming another being, that is love. Love is not making another person merge in you. Love is not making another person lose his identity in you. *You* have to lose your identity. *You* have to merge in another person. *You* have to become another being. That is love. So love is always giving; it is never taking. You don't love for the sake of any gain. If you love to get some calculated gain, that is no love at all.

Well, then I guess it would be accurate to say that a lot of us have no love at all for the master.

Well, you are judging on that scale. It is said that God is love and love is God, because the characteristic of God is love. We become one with him. We lose our own identity – we merge in him; we become another being. We don't exist anymore; only he exists. That is the characteristic of love. Then we always want to do what pleases another person. We never want to do anything which displeases another person because we don't exist – for us, only he exists; we have no ego of our own at all. We want to do what pleases him and avoid what displeases him – that is love. Then where are we? Where is the sense of any gain from that love? There is no bargain in it. It is just giving and giving. And when by giving we can become God, what else is left? If by giving yourself – as a drop you become an ocean – have you gained or lost? If in losing your own identity you become the Father, have you gained or have you lost? That is love.

You see, this intellectual love doesn't take us very far. These intellectual emotions don't take us far. They are good to push us on the path, but that doesn't take us very far. Only meditation can generate love. Love can grow only by meditation. The more we lose ourselves, the nearer and nearer we become to the Father. And the nearer we are to the Father, the nearer we are to each other. The farther away we are from the Father, the farther away we are from each other. Then brotherhood can never come. Brotherhood will come in humanity only when everybody's focus is the same. Those who are in love with the Father are nearer to each other. Christ said: Love thy Lord with all thy body, with all thy mind, with all thy heart. When you absolutely lose your own identity and just become the Lord, your 'self' is now nothing but the Father. He then says: Love thy neighbour as thyself.[67] Now, what is your 'self'? Not this body. You have lost everything; you have become one with the Father. That is your 'self' now. Then you see the Father everywhere in this whole creation, and then the whole creation is your neighbour. Then we see him everywhere. Then that sense of brotherhood comes, that sense of affinity with each other. Then we find, as Christ said, that ultimately there will be one shepherd and one fold.[107] Then he is the shepherd and we are the fold. That is real brotherhood. That is real relationship. A worldly relationship is just a karmic relationship. We need each other, but we don't belong to one another. We belong only to him.

598 *Master, I was visiting a church where the people believe in the forgiveness of sins. How can I explain to them how it really works?*

You see, you don't have to ask the Father at all. You have only to love him, and you are automatically forgiven. You don't need to ask for forgiveness. A child loves his father. His father looks after him, educates him, marries him, puts him on his feet, ultimately gives him all his wealth because the son loves the father. A loving child never has to ask his father for what he needs. His father is anxious to look after his needs because the son loves his father. That is why Christ said: O ye of little faith[25] – you're always asking from the Father bread, butter, all the worldly ambitions and desires. He says, you have no faith in the Father at all. If you love your Father, he knows your needs and he will automatically give you what you need. When the Lord looks after the insects and the stones, won't he look after you, you being the top of creation?

So we don't have to ask him, we have to love him. But we are always asking him for favours – we don't love him at all. We want a reward for our asking: "I have said so many prayers, I have asked him a thousand times, four thousand times; now it's his duty to give to me." We think we have laboured to pray to him and that now it is for him to fulfil our desires. But that is the wrong attitude. Christ says that he knows. Without your saying, he knows what you need. If you become a loving son, he'll give you more than you need.

So we don't want to love him – we only want all the boons of life from him. But there's no bargaining with him at all. You have just to give yourself to him, and then he gives you everything. He makes you himself. He makes you God; he makes you the Lord.

DO IT NOW!

599 Sir, is there an assurance of meeting the Lord and going home in one life, or four lives?

Why limit ourselves? Why think about four lives? Why not try to do it in one life? We should do our best to achieve our destination in one lifetime. If we do not succeed in this life, the Lord will give us another life, and two or three more if necessary, but the assurance is there that when we are trying sincerely to meet him, we will definitely meet him, and every life will be better and more conducive to our spiritual progress than the previous one.

600 Master, is there any exception to the rule that once you're initiated you will then come back for four lives? Does it ever happen that a satsangi will have to come back for more lives?

We should never think about the four lives at all. We should only think that this is our last life and we must go back to the

Father. We should never console ourselves that we have sufficient opportunity in the future. That is the wrong concept. This is the time when we have to become one with him.

601 *A gentleman asked about reincarnation and the intellect. If the intellect could prove scientifically that reincarnation is true, could this work to the detriment of the soul? Could it be that, if the intellect could prove to itself scientifically that reincarnation is true, it might try to work on improvements for the next birth here and not try to go back home?*

No. But how can we be sure that we will be able to practice, have more spiritual practice, if we get an extra human birth? Rather, we should make use of this birth. Why not make use now of what we are trying to postpone to another birth? This is just an excuse to escape the duties in this life.

602 *Does it ever happen that a soul that has been initiated by a perfect master and is reborn as a human being can't come in contact with a perfect master in the next life?*

Why think of coming back at all? Make best use of this life. Whatever you want to achieve next time, try to achieve now. You are taking a chance in assuming you'll be a human next time, but now you are sure you are human, so make use of your human birth now.

Appendix

DIVINE LIGHT, LETTER 439

You have asked me a very pertinent question about the eating of non-fertile eggs and have tried to rationalize that unfertilized eggs are vegetarian food. God made eggs for conveying life; so every egg, whether fertilized or unfertilized, has a potential life factor. Besides, as you must have read in *The Inner Voice,* an egg, whether fertile or infertile, is a food which excites animal instincts, interferes with concentration and thus works against our spiritual progress.

In this connection, I might at the outset tell you that we recognize that on this earth, life subsists on life. The big fish eat small fish, the wild animals eat smaller game, and the smaller animals eat insects and plants. None of these living beings appear to survive on stones or sand. Therefore, in the scheme of things, we recognize that life must subsist on life by extinguishing other life which is used as food. However, the extinguishing of life for nourishing our life affects the structure of our mind. Although operating from a focal point between and behind the eyes, our mind is scattered all through the body as well as the entire world outside, of which the mind gets awareness through sense perception.

Saints and sages who have achieved practical realization have all given indication that the path to God- or to self-realization lies within ourselves and that we must collect our attention within, at the eye centre, rather than scattering it without. Our attention being the only available part of our consciousness which we can manipulate, our spiritual practice requires the concentration of attention at its natural focal point, which is between and slightly above the eyes.

Food, like actions, affects the mind and therefore its capacity to concentrate at its natural focal point. Killing a man causes a severer mental reaction than killing a goat. Similarly, killing a goat causes a severer mental reaction than plucking an apple from a tree. Concentration of mind would therefore be, as a rule, proportionately more difficult in the case of a man who has committed murder than in the case of a man who has killed a goat or one who has plucked an apple from a tree. The reason is that the manifest form of life in a man, in a goat, and in an apple tree has different degrees of consciousness or awareness. Accordingly, the extinguishing of life in each of them causes varying degrees of mental reaction, and therefore obstruction to spiritual concentration of the mind.

The food we eat also implies the extinguishing of life of the category to which the food belongs. Thus the eating of animal food (flesh) makes spiritual concentration more difficult than the eating of fish and fowl, while the eating of fish and fowl (including eggs) makes spiritual concentration more difficult than the eating of plants (vegetables and fruits). It is for this reason that we recommend all practitioners on the spiritual path to extinguish life of the lowest degree for their nourishment. In other words, we recommend a strictly vegetarian diet.

You have drawn a distinction between the fertile and non-fertile eggs. In fact, nature has made an egg for the hatching of the chick. The mere fact that life is prevented in the egg by artificial means does not make the egg a different category of food. You have said that a non-fertile egg has no life. That way you could also say that a goat that is already killed has no life and similarly the rooster dressed up for sale in the grocery store has no life.

The question is not whether the food has life at the time when you eat it, but whether it was intended to be a vehicle of life, and the category of life to which it belongs. The laws of nature are fairly obvious and those which are not so obvious are being made obvious by the work of man, and it will not be difficult to see how nature has made the egg as much a vehicle of life as a hen or a rooster.

I would therefore recommend that eggs, whether fertile or infertile, being an 'exciting' food and of the category intended for conveyance of life, should be avoided in order to successfully practice the spiritual methods of concentration and realization.

INDEX TO BIBLE QUOTES

According to the King James Version of the Bible

1   **Psalms 37:11** But the meek shall inherit the earth; and shall delight themselves in the abundance of peace. [*i.*266]

2   **Proverbs 17:22** A merry heart doeth good like a medicine: but a broken spirit drieth the bones. [*i.*399]

3   **Matthew 3:2** And saying, Repent ye: for the kingdom of heaven is at hand. [*i.*70, *i.*87, *i.*97, *i.*128, *i.*239, *i.*309, *i.*333, *iii.*259]

4   **Matthew 3:10** And now also the axe is laid unto the root of the trees: therefore every tree which bringeth not forth good fruit is hewn down, and cast into the fire. [*i.*125]

5   **Matthew 3:16** And Jesus, when he was baptized, went up straightway out of the water: and, lo, the heavens were opened unto him, and he saw the Spirit of God descending like a dove, and lighting upon him: ... [*i.*84]

6   **Matthew 4:10** Then saith Jesus unto him, Get thee hence, Satan: for it is written, Thou shalt worship the Lord thy God, and him only shalt thou serve. [*i.*306, *ii.*215]

7   **Matthew 5:1** And seeing the multitudes, he went up into a mountain: and when he was set, his disciples came unto him: ... [*i.*507, *iii.*403]

8   **Matthew 5:4** Blessed are they that mourn: for they shall be comforted. [*i.*25, *i.*290, *ii.*102, *ii.*366, *iii.*63, *iii.*65, *iii.*70, *iii.*77]

9   **Matthew 5:5** Blessed are the meek: for they shall inherit the earth. [*iii.*231]

10   **Matthew 5:9** Blessed are the peacemakers: for they shall be called the children of God. [*i*.395, *i*.493, *iii*.417]

11   **Matthew 5:14** Ye are the light of the world. A city that is set on an hill cannot be hid. **15** Neither do men light a candle, and put it under a bushel, but on a candlestick; and it giveth light unto all that are in the house. **16** Let your light so shine before men, that they may see your good works, and glorify your Father which is in heaven. [*i*.381]

12   **Matthew 5:17** Think not that I am come to destroy the law, or the prophets: I am not come to destroy, but to fulfil. [*i*.322]

13   **Matthew 5:18** For verily I say unto you, Till heaven and earth pass, one jot or one tittle shall in no wise pass from the law, till all be fulfilled. [*i*.308]

14   **Matthew 5:21** Ye have heard that it was said by them of old time, Thou shalt not kill; and whosoever shall kill shall be in danger of the judgment: … [*ii*.59]

15   **Matthew 5:23** Therefore if thou bring thy gift to the altar, and there rememberest that thy brother hath ought against thee; **24** Leave there thy gift before the altar, and go thy way; first be reconciled to thy brother, and then come and offer thy gift. [*iii*.134, *iii*.261]

16   **Matthew 5:25** Agree with thine adversary quickly, whiles thou art in the way with him; lest at any time the adversary deliver thee to the judge, and the judge deliver thee to the officer, and thou be cast into prison. [*i*.124, *i*.399, *iii*.257]

17   **Matthew 5:28** But I say unto you, That whosoever looketh on a woman to lust after her hath committed adultery with her already in his heart. [*i*.113]

18   **Matthew 5:39** But I say unto you, That ye resist not evil: but whosoever shall smite thee on thy right cheek, turn to him the other also. [*i*.302, *i*.314, *iii*.363]

19   **Matthew 6:1** Take heed that ye do not your alms before men, to be seen of them: otherwise ye have no reward of your Father which is in heaven. **2** Therefore when thou doest thine alms, do not sound

a trumpet before thee, as the hypocrites do in the synagogues and in the streets, that they may have glory of men. Verily I say unto you, They have their reward. [*iii*.156, *iii*.403]

20   **Matthew 6:6** But thou, when thou prayest, enter into thy closet, and when thou hast shut thy door, pray to thy Father which is in secret; and thy Father which seeth in secret shall reward thee openly. **7** But when ye pray, use not vain repetitions, as the heathen do: for they think that they shall be heard for their much speaking. **8** Be not ye therefore like unto them: for your Father knoweth what things ye have need of, before ye ask him. [*ii*.134]

21   **Matthew 6:10** Thy kingdom come. Thy will be done in earth, as it is in heaven. **11** Give us this day our daily bread. **12** And forgive us our debts, As we forgive our debtors. [*i*.497, *i*.505, *ii*.437]

22   **Matthew 6:21** For where your treasure is, there will your heart be also. [*i*.275, *i*.392, *i*.490, *iii*.297, *iii*.299, *iii*.331]

23   **Matthew 6:22** The light of the body is the eye: if therefore thine eye be single, thy whole body shall be full of light. [*i*.209, *i*.239, *i*.299, *i*.309, *i*.333, *i*.388, *i*.476, *ii*.15]

24   **Matthew 6:24** No man can serve two masters: for either he will hate the one, and love the other; or else he will hold to the one, and despise the other. Ye cannot serve God and mammon. [*ii*.105, *ii*.111, *ii*.302, *iii*.10, *iii*.161, *iii*.299]

25   **Matthew 6:25** Therefore I say unto you, Take no thought for your life, what ye shall eat, or what ye shall drink; nor yet for your body, what ye shall put on. Is not the life more than meat, and the body than raiment? **26** Behold the fowls of the air: for they sow not, neither do they reap, nor gather into barns; yet your heavenly Father feedeth them. Are ye not much better than they? **27** Which of you by taking thought can add one cubit unto his stature? **28** And why take ye thought for raiment? Consider the lilies of the field, how they grow; they toil not, neither do they spin: **29** And yet I say unto you, That even Solomon in all his glory was not arrayed like one of these. **30** Wherefore, if God so clothe the grass of the field, which to day is, and to morrow is cast into the oven, shall he not much more clothe you, O ye of little faith? **31** Therefore take no thought,

saying, What shall we eat? or, What shall we drink? or, Wherewithal shall we be clothed? 32 (For after all these things do the Gentiles seek:) for your heavenly Father knoweth that ye have need of all these things. [*i*.263, *i*.380, *ii*.131, *ii*.133, *ii*.144, *ii*.451, *iii*.201]

26   **Matthew 7:1** Judge not, that ye be not judged. [*iii*.250]

27   **Matthew 7:3** And why beholdest thou the mote that is in thy brother's eye, but considerest not the beam that is in thine own eye? [*iii*.244]

28   **Matthew 7:6** Give not that which is holy unto the dogs, neither cast ye your pearls before swine, lest they trample them under their feet, and turn again and rend you. [*ii*.254]

29   **Matthew 7:7** Ask, and it shall be given you; seek, and ye shall find; knock, and it shall be opened unto you: ... [*i*.288, *i*.329, *i*.476, *ii*.159]

30   **Matthew 7:11** If ye then, being evil, know how to give good gifts unto your children, how much more shall your Father which is in heaven give good things to them that ask him? [*iii*.202]

31   **Matthew 7:17** Even so every good tree bringeth forth good fruit; but a corrupt tree bringeth forth evil fruit. 18 A good tree cannot bring forth evil fruit, neither can a corrupt tree bring forth good fruit. [*i*.121]

32   **Matthew 7:21** Not every one that saith unto me, Lord, Lord, shall enter into the kingdom of heaven; but he that doeth the will of my Father which is in heaven. [*iii*.80]

33   **Matthew 10:8** Heal the sick, cleanse the lepers, raise the dead, cast out devils: freely ye have received, freely give. 9 Provide neither gold, nor silver, nor brass in your purses,... [*i*.312]

34   **Matthew 10:16** Behold, I send you forth as sheep in the midst of wolves: be ye therefore wise as serpents, and harmless as doves. [*iii*.178]

35   **Matthew 10:19** But when they deliver you up, take no thought how or what ye shall speak: for it shall be given you in that same hour what ye shall speak. 20 For it is not ye that speak, but the Spirit of your Father which speaketh in you. [*i*.317]

36   **Matthew 10:22** And ye shall be hated of all men for my name's sake: but he that endureth to the end shall be saved. [*i*.318]

37   **Matthew 10:28** And fear not them which kill the body, but are not able to kill the soul: but rather fear him which is able to destroy both soul and body in hell. [*iii*.41]

38   **Matthew 10:30** But the very hairs of your head are all numbered. [*i*.130, *i*.131, *i*.413]

39   **Matthew 10:34** Think not that I am come to send peace on earth: I came not to send peace, but a sword. [*i*.51, *i*.58, *i*.312, *i*.339, *i*.384, *i*.392, *i*.490, *ii*.405, *iii*.5, *iii*.203, *iii*.279]

40   **Matthew 10:35** For I am come to set a man at variance against his father, and the daughter against her mother, and the daughter in law against her mother in law. [*iii*.279]

41   **Matthew 10:36** And a man's foes shall be they of his own household. [*iii*.280]

42   **Matthew 10:37** He that loveth father or mother more than me is not worthy of me: and he that loveth son or daughter more than me is not worthy of me. [*i*.201, *i*.222, *i*.442, *i*.461, *i*.464, *i*.473, *iii*.22, *iii*.279]

43   **Matthew 11:5** The blind receive their sight, and the lame walk, the lepers are cleansed, and the deaf hear, the dead are raised up, and the poor have the gospel preached to them. [*i*.192, *i*.506]

44   **Matthew 11:25** At that time Jesus answered and said, I thank thee, O Father, Lord of heaven and earth, because thou hast hid these things from the wise and prudent, and hast revealed them unto babes. [*i*.265]

45   **Matthew 11:28** Come unto me, all ye that labour and are heavy laden, and I will give you rest. [*i*.399]

46   **Matthew 12:31** Wherefore I say unto you, All manner of sin and blasphemy shall be forgiven unto men: but the blasphemy against the Holy Ghost shall not be forgiven unto men. [*ii*.103, *ii*.336, *ii*.368, *iii*.30]

47   **Matthew 12:47** Then one said unto him, Behold, thy mother and thy brethren stand without, desiring to speak with thee. **48** But he

answered and said unto him that told him, Who is my mother? and who are my brethren? **49** And he stretched forth his hand toward his disciples, and said, Behold my mother and my brethren! **50** For whosoever shall do the will of my Father which is in heaven, the same is my brother, and sister, and mother. [*iii*.221, *iii*.280, *iii*.292, *iii*.294, *iii*.303, *iii*.306]

48   **Matthew 13:3** And he spake many things unto them in parables, saying, Behold, a sower went forth to sow. **4** And when he sowed, some seeds fell by the way side, and the fowls came and devoured them up. **5** Some fell upon stony places, where they had not much earth: and forthwith they sprung up, because they had no deepness of earth. **6** And when the sun was up, they were scorched; and because they had no root, they withered away. **7** And some fell among thorns; and the thorns sprung up, and choked them. **8** But other fell into good ground, and brought forth fruit, some an hundredfold, some sixtyfold, some thirtyfold. [*i*.424, *i*.440, *ii*.420, *ii*.421]

49   **Matthew 13:13** Therefore speak I to them in parables: because they seeing see not; and hearing they hear not, neither do they understand. [*i*.403, *i*.408, *i*.415, *ii*.370]

50   **Matthew 13:24** Another parable put he forth unto them, saying, The kingdom of heaven is likened unto a man which sowed good seed in his field. **25** But while men slept, his enemy came and sowed tares among the wheat, and went his way. **26** But when the blade was sprung up, and brought forth fruit, then appeared the tares also. **27** So the servants of the householder came and said unto him, Sir, didst not thou sow good seed in thy field? from whence then hath it tares? **28** He said unto them, An enemy hath done this. The servants said unto him, Wilt thou then that we go and gather them up? **29** But he said, Nay; lest while ye gather up the tares, ye root up also the wheat with them. **30** Let both grow together until the harvest: and in the time of harvest I will say to the reapers, Gather ye together first the tares, and bind them in bundles to burn them: but gather the wheat into my barn. [*ii*.438, *iii*.6, *iii*.121, *iii*.372]

51   **Matthew 15:4** For God commanded, saying, Honour thy father and mother: and, He that curseth father or mother, let him die the death. [*iii*.307]

52 **Matthew 15:24** But he answered and said, I am not sent but unto the lost sheep of the house of Israel. [*ii*.7]

53 **Matthew 16:23** But he turned, and said unto Peter, Get thee behind me, Satan: thou art an offence unto me: for thou savourest not the things that be of God, but those that be of men. [*i*.505]

54 **Matthew 17:12** But I say unto you, That Elias is come already, and they knew him not, but have done unto him whatsoever they listed. Likewise shall also the Son of man suffer of them. **13** Then the disciples understood that he spake unto them of John the Baptist. [*i*.467]

55 **Matthew 17:20** And Jesus said unto them, Because of your unbelief: for verily I say unto you, If ye have faith as a grain of mustard seed, ye shall say unto this mountain, Remove hence to yonder place; and it shall remove; and nothing shall be impossible unto you. [*ii*.124]

56 **Matthew 18:3** And said, Verily I say unto you, Except ye be converted, and become as little children, ye shall not enter into the kingdom of heaven. [*iii*.205]

57 **Matthew 18:12** How think ye? If a man have an hundred sheep, and one of them be gone astray, doth he not leave the ninety and nine, and goeth into the mountains, and seeketh that which is gone astray? [*i*.404, *ii*.428, *iii*.4, *iii*.6, *iii*.18, *iii*.132]

58 **Matthew 18:13** And if so be that he find it, verily I say unto you, he rejoiceth more of that sheep, than of the ninety and nine which went not astray. **14** Even so it is not the will of your Father which is in heaven, that one of these little ones should perish. [*iii*.4]

59 **Matthew 18:20** For where two or three are gathered together in my name, there am I in the midst of them. [*iii*.106, *iii*.115, *iii*.126]

60 **Matthew 18:26** The servant therefore fell down, and worshipped him, saying, Lord, have patience with me, and I will pay thee all. [*iii*.258]

61 **Matthew 19:24** And again I say unto you, It is easier for a camel to go through the eye of a needle, than for a rich man to enter into the kingdom of God. [*i*.267, *i*.392, *iii*.143, *iii*.146]

62   **Matthew 19:30** But many that are first shall be last; and the last shall be first. [*i*.97, *i*.430, *ii*.274, *ii*.350]

63   **Matthew 20:16** So the last shall be first, and the first last: for many be called, but few chosen. [*ii*.275, *ii*.421, *ii*.423]

64   **Matthew 20:28** Even as the Son of man came not to be ministered unto, but to minister, and to give his life a ransom for many. [*i*.498]

65   **Matthew 22:14** For many are called, but few are chosen. [*i*.429]

66   **Matthew 22:21** They say unto him, Caesar's. Then saith he unto them, Render therefore unto Caesar the things which are Caesar's; and unto God the things that are God's. [*i*.47, *i*.83, *i*.89, *i*.103, *i*.109, *i*.499, *iii*.225, *iii*.354]

67   **Matthew 22:36** Master, which is the great commandment in the law? **37** Jesus said unto him, Thou shalt love the Lord thy God with all thy heart, and with all thy soul, and with all thy mind. **38** This is the first and great commandment. **39** And the second is like unto it, Thou shalt love thy neighbour as thyself. **40** On these two commandments hang all the law and the prophets. [*i*.174, *i*.393, *i*.485, *ii*.58, *ii*.102, *ii*.450, *iii*.130, *iii*.261, *iii*.389]

68   **Matthew 26:42** He went away again the second time, and prayed, saying, O my Father, if this cup may not pass away from me, except I drink it, thy will be done. [*iii*.73]

69   **Mark 8:18** Having eyes, see ye not? and having ears, hear ye not? and do ye not remember? [*i*.284, *i*.289, *i*.468, *ii*.30, *ii*.206]

70   **Luke 6:48** He is like a man which built an house, and digged deep, and laid the foundation on a rock: and when the flood arose, the stream beat vehemently upon that house, and could not shake it: for it was founded upon a rock. [*ii*.397]

71   **Luke 11:21** When a strong man armed keepeth his palace, his goods are in peace: ... [*ii*.298]

72   **John 1:1** In the beginning was the Word, and the Word was with God, and the Word was God. **2** The same was in the beginning with God. **3** All things were made by him; and without him was not any thing made that was made. **4** In him was life; and the life

was the light of men. 5 And the light shineth in darkness; and the darkness comprehended it not. [*i*.27, *i*.29, *i*.116, *i*.175, *i*.178, *i*.284, *i*.298, *ii*.14, *ii*.230]

73 **John 1:6** There was a man sent from God, whose name was John. [*i*.428, *i*.443, *ii*.14]

74 **John 1:14** And the Word was made flesh, and dwelt among us, (and we beheld his glory, the glory as of the only begotten of the Father) full of grace and truth. [*i*.451, *i*.464]

75 **John 1:27** He it is, who coming after me is preferred before me, whose shoe's latchet I am not worthy to unloose. [*i*.516]

76 **John 2:16** And said unto them that sold doves, Take these things hence; make not my Father's house a house of merchandise. [*i*.315]

77 **John 3:3** Jesus answered and said unto him, Verily, verily, I say unto thee, Except a man be born again, he cannot see the kingdom of God. [*i*.309, *i*.517, *ii*.16, *ii*.23, *ii*.24, *iii*.352, *iii*.377]

78 **John 3:8** The wind bloweth where it listeth, and thou hearest the sound thereof, but canst not tell whence it cometh, and whither it goeth: so is every one that is born of the Spirit. [*i*.298, *i*.309, *i*.476]

79 **John 3:14** And as Moses lifted up the serpent in the wilderness, even so must the Son of man be lifted up: 15 That whosoever believeth in him should not perish, but have eternal life. [*ii*.234]

80 **John 3:17** For God sent not his Son into the world to condemn the world; but that the world through him might be saved. 18 He that believeth on him is not condemned: but he that believeth not is condemned already, because he hath not believed in the name of the only begotten Son of God. [*i*.428, *iii*.11, *iii*.16, *iii*.26]

81 **John 3:29** He that hath the bride is the bridegroom: but the friend of the bridegroom, which standeth and heareth him, rejoiceth greatly because of the bridegroom's voice: this my joy therefore is fulfilled. [*iii*.418]

82 **John 4:14** But whosoever drinketh of the water that I shall give him shall never thirst; but the water that I shall give him shall be in him a well of water springing up into everlasting life. [*i*.200, *iii*.151]

83   **John 4:23** But the hour cometh, and now is, when the true worshippers shall worship the Father in spirit and in truth: for the Father seeketh such to worship him. [*i*.344, *ii*.24]

84   **John 4:24** God is a Spirit: and they that worship him must worship him in spirit and in truth. [*i*.305]

85   **John 5:14** Afterward Jesus findeth him in the temple, and said unto him, Behold, thou art made whole: sin no more, lest a worse thing come unto thee. [*i*.201, *i*.409, *ii*.22, *ii*.155]

86   **John 5:25** Verily, verily, I say unto you, The hour is coming, and now is, when the dead shall hear the voice of the Son of God: and they that hear shall live. [*i*.477]

87   **John 5:27** And hath given him authority to execute judgment also, because he is the Son of man. [*i*.448]

88   **John 5:30** I can of mine own self do nothing: as I hear, I judge: and my judgment is just; because I seek not mine own will, but the will of the Father which hath sent me. [*i*.418, *i*.443, *ii*.348]

89   **John 5:35** He was a burning and a shining light: and ye were willing for a season to rejoice in his light. [*i*.467]

90   **John 6:27** Labour not for the meat which perisheth, but for that meat which endureth unto everlasting life, which the Son of man shall give unto you: for him hath God the Father sealed. [*i*.448]

91   **John 6:38** For I came down from heaven, not to do mine own will, but the will of him that sent me. **39** And this is the Father's will which hath sent me, that of all which he hath given me I should lose nothing, but should raise it up again at the last day. [*i*.444]

92   **John 6:40** And this is the will of him that sent me, that every one which seeth the Son, and believeth on him, may have everlasting life: and I will raise him up at the last day. [*i*.439, *i*.465, *ii*.29, *ii*.396, *iii*.34, *iii*.352]

93   **John 6:44** No man can come to me, except the Father which hath sent me draw him: and I will raise him up at the last day. [*ii*.6, *ii*.10]

94   **John 6:53** Then Jesus said unto them, Verily, verily, I say unto you, Except ye eat the flesh of the Son of man, and drink his blood, ye have

no life in you. **54** Whoso eateth my flesh, and drinketh my blood, hath eternal life; and I will raise him up at the last day. [*iii*.43]

95   **John 6:63** It is the spirit that quickeneth; the flesh profiteth nothing: the words that I speak unto you, they are spirit, and they are life. [*iii*.46]

96   **John 7:37** In the last day, that great day of the feast, Jesus stood and cried, saying, If any man thirst, let him come unto me, and drink. **38** He that believeth on me, as the scripture hath said, out of his belly shall flow rivers of living water. [*i*.329, *i*.408, *i*.416]

97   **John 8:28** Then said Jesus unto them, When ye have lifted up the Son of man, then shall ye know that I am he, and that I do nothing of myself; but as my Father hath taught me, I speak these things. [*iii*.38, *iii*.40]

98   **John 8:32** And ye shall know the truth, and the truth shall make you free. [*iii*.260]

99   **John 8:34** Jesus answered them, Verily, verily, I say unto you, Whosoever committeth sin is the servant of sin. **35** And the servant abideth not in the house for ever: but the Son abideth ever. [*i*.151]

100   **John 8:50** And I seek not mine own glory: there is one that seeketh and judgeth. [*i*.518]

101   **John 9:1** And as Jesus passed by, he saw a man which was blind from his birth. **2** And his disciples asked him, saying, Master, who did sin, this man, or his parents, that he was born blind? **3** Jesus answered, Neither hath this man sinned, nor his parents: but that the works of God should be made manifest in him. [*i*.98]

102   **John 9:4** I must work the works of him that sent me, while it is day: the night cometh, when no man can work. **5** As long as I am in the world, I am the light of the world. [*i*.191, *i*.466, *i*.475]

103   **John 9:39** And Jesus said, For judgment I am come into this world, that they which see not might see; and that they which see might be made blind. [*i*.486, *i*.505, *iii*.403]

104   **John 10:4** And when he putteth forth his own sheep, he goeth before them, and the sheep follow him: for they know his voice. [*i*.404, *i*.405, *i*.406, *i*.407, *ii*.322, *iii*.43]

105   **John 10:8** All that ever came before me are thieves and robbers: but the sheep did not hear them. [*ii*.236]

106   **John 10:14** I am the good shepherd, and know my sheep, and am known of mine. [*i*.466]

107   **John 10:16** And other sheep I have, which are not of this fold: them also I must bring, and they shall hear my voice; and there shall be one fold, and one shepherd. [*i*.451, *i*.452, *ii*.237, *ii*.428, *ii*.451, *iii*.10, *iii*.98, *iii*.101, *iii*.292, *iii*.306]

108   **John 10:17** Therefore doth my Father love me, because I lay down my life, that I might take it again. **18** No man taketh it from me, but I lay it down of myself. I have power to lay it down, and I have power to take it again. This commandment have I received of my Father. [*i*.107, *i*.444, *i*.447, *i*.510, *i*.511, *ii*.215, *ii*.229]

109   **John 10:27** My sheep hear my voice, and I know them, and they follow me: ... [*ii*.6]

110   **John 10:28** And I give unto them eternal life; and they shall never perish, neither shall any man pluck them out of my hand. **29** My Father, which gave them me, is greater than all; and no man is able to pluck them out of my Father's hand. [*i*.511]

111   **John 10:30** I and my Father are one. [*i*.169, *i*.195, *i*.207, *i*.447, *i*.449, *i*.453, *i*.462]

112   **John 10:34** Jesus answered them, Is it not written in your law, I said, Ye are gods? [*i*.171]

113   **John 10:38** But if I do, though ye believe not me, believe the works: that ye may know, and believe, that the Father is in me, and I in him. [*i*.448, *i*.476]

114   **John 11:25** Jesus said unto her, I am the resurrection, and the life: he that believeth in me, though he were dead, yet shall he live: ... [*i*.497]

115   **John 13:34** A new commandment I give unto you, That ye love one another; as I have loved you, that ye also love one another. [*i*.386, *i*.389, *iii*.134, *iii*.145, *iii*.363]

116   **John 14:2** In my Father's house are many mansions: if it were not so, I would have told you. I go to prepare a place for you. [*i*.276, *i*.329, *i*.476]

117   **John 14:3** And if I go and prepare a place for you, I will come again, and receive you unto myself; that where I am, there ye may be also. [*ii*.216, *iii*.35]

118   **John 14:4** And whither I go ye know, and the way ye know. [*iii*.31, *iii*.67, *iii*.69, *iii*.72]

119   **John 14:9** Jesus saith unto him, Have I been so long time with you, and yet hast thou not known me, Philip? he that hath seen me hath seen the Father; and how sayest thou then, Shew us the Father? [*i*.464, *ii*.55]

120   **John 14:10** Believest thou not that I am in the Father, and the Father in me? The words that I speak unto you I speak not of myself: but the Father that dwelleth in me, he doeth the works. **11** Believe me that I am in the Father, and the Father in me: or else believe me for the very works' sake. [*i*.81, *i*.404, *i*.462, *i*.478, *ii*.55]

121   **John 14:16** And I will pray the Father, and he shall give you another Comforter, that he may abide with you for ever; **17** Even the Spirit of truth; whom the world cannot receive, because it seeth him not, neither knoweth him: but ye know him; for he dwelleth with you, and shall be in you. **18** I will not leave you comfortless: I will come to you. **19** Yet a little while, and the world seeth me no more; but ye see me: because I live, ye shall live also. **20** At that day ye shall know that I am in my Father, and ye in me, and I in you. **26** But the Comforter, which is the Holy Ghost, whom the Father will send in my name, he shall teach you all things, and bring all things to your remembrance, whatsoever I have said unto you. [*i*.307, *iii*.33, *iii*.69]

122   **John 14:20** At that day ye shall know that I am in my Father, and ye in me, and I in you. **21** He that hath my commandments, and keepeth them, he it is that loveth me: and he that loveth me shall be loved of my Father, and I will love him, and will manifest myself to him. **23** Jesus answered and said unto him, If a man love me, he will keep my words: and my Father will love him, and we will come unto him, and make our abode with him. [*ii*.194, *ii*.225, *ii*.231, *iii*.29, *iii*.37, *iii*.42, *iii*.44, *iii*.46, *iii*.95, *iii*.294]

123 **John 15:4** Abide in me, and I in you. As the branch cannot bear fruit of itself, except it abide in the vine; no more can ye, except ye abide in me. [*i*.474]

124 **John 15:20** Remember the word that I said unto you, The servant is not greater than his lord. If they have persecuted me, they will also persecute you; if they have kept my saying, they will keep yours also. [*iii*.248]

125 **John 15:22** If I had not come and spoken unto them, they had not had sin: but now they have no cloke for their sin. [*i*.93]

126 **John 16:7** Nevertheless I tell you the truth; It is expedient for you that I go away: for if I go not away, the Comforter will not come unto you; but if I depart, I will send him unto you. [*iii*.66, *iii*.67, *iii*.72]

127 **John 16:16** A little while, and ye shall not see me: and again, a little while, and ye shall see me, because I go to the Father. **17** Then said some of his disciples among themselves, What is this that he saith unto us, A little while, and ye shall not see me: and again, a little while, and ye shall see me: and, Because I go to the Father? **18** They said therefore, What is this that he saith, A little while? we cannot tell what he saith. **19** Now Jesus knew that they were desirous to ask him, and said unto them, Do ye enquire among yourselves of that I said, A little while, and ye shall not see me: and again, a little while, and ye shall see me? **20** Verily, verily, I say unto you, That ye shall weep and lament, but the world shall rejoice: and ye shall be sorrowful, but your sorrow shall be turned into joy. **21** A woman when she is in travail hath sorrow, because her hour is come: but as soon as she is delivered of the child, she remembereth no more the anguish, for joy that a man is born into the world. **22** And ye now therefore have sorrow: but I will see you again, and your heart shall rejoice, and your joy no man taketh from you. **23** And in that day ye shall ask me nothing. Verily, verily, I say unto you, Whatsoever ye shall ask the Father in my name, he will give it you. **24** Hitherto have ye asked nothing in my name: ask, and ye shall receive, that your joy may be full. **25** These things have I spoken unto you in proverbs: but the time cometh, when I shall no more speak unto you in proverbs, but I shall shew you plainly of the Father. [*i*.47, *i*.475, *ii*.127, *ii*.235, *iii*.59, *iii*.62, *iii*.99, *iii*.190]

128   **John 17:9** I pray for them: I pray not for the world, but for them which thou hast given me; for they are thine. [*i*.405, *i*.416, *i*.426, *i*.427, *ii*.355, *ii*.369, *ii*.371]

129   **John 17:11** And now I am no more in the world, but these are in the world, and I come to thee. Holy Father, keep through thine own name those whom thou hast given me, that they may be one, as we are. **22** And the glory which thou gavest me I have given them; that they may be one, even as we are one: **23** I in them, and thou in me, that they may be made perfect in one; and that the world may know that thou hast sent me, and hast loved them, as thou hast loved me. [*i*.110, *i*.305, *i*.405]

130   **John 20:9** For as yet they knew not the scripture, that he must rise again from the dead. [*i*.477, *i*.506]

131   **1 Corinthians 15:31** I protest by your rejoicing which I have in Christ Jesus our Lord, I die daily. [*ii*.226, *ii*.244, *ii*.245, *ii*.246, *ii*.247]

132   **2 Corinthians 6:16** And what agreement hath the temple of God with idols? for ye are the temple of the living God; as God hath said, I will dwell in them, and walk in them; and I will be their God, and they shall be my people. [*i*.174, *i*.239, *i*.329, *i*.476, *iii*.170]

133   **Galatians 6:7** Be not deceived; God is not mocked: for whatsoever a man soweth, that shall he also reap. [*i*.50, *i*.54, *i*.56, *i*.75, *i*.115, *i*.125, *i*.132, *i*.138, *i*.151, *ii*.59, *iii*.224, *iii*.260]

134   **Ephesians 1:3** Blessed be the God and Father of our Lord Jesus Christ, who hath blessed us with all spiritual blessings in heavenly places in Christ: ... [*i*.494]

135   **Ephesians 2:18** For through him we both have access by one Spirit unto the Father. [*i*.29]

136   **1 John 4:8** He that loveth not knoweth not God; for God is love. [*i*.284, *i*.461, *ii*.97]

137   **1 John 4:16** And we have known and believed the love that God hath to us. God is love; and he that dwelleth in love dwelleth in God, and God in him. [*i*.289, *ii*.102]

138   **Exodus 20 (The Ten Commandments)** 1 And God spake all these words, saying, 2 I am the LORD thy God, which have brought thee out of the land of Egypt, out of the house of bondage. 3 Thou shalt have no other gods before me. 4 Thou shalt not make unto thee any graven image, or any likeness of any thing that is in heaven above, or that is in the earth beneath, or that is in the water under the earth. 5 Thou shalt not bow down thyself to them, nor serve them: for I the LORD thy God am a jealous God, visiting the iniquity of the fathers upon the children unto the third and fourth generation of them that hate me; 6 And shewing mercy unto thousands of them that love me, and keep my commandments. 7 Thou shalt not take the name of the LORD thy God in vain; for the LORD will not hold him guiltless that taketh his name in vain. 8 Remember the sabbath day, to keep it holy. 9 Six days shalt thou labour, and do all thy work: 10 But the seventh day is the sabbath of the LORD thy God: in it thou shalt not do any work, thou, nor thy son, nor thy daughter, thy manservant, nor thy maidservant, nor thy cattle, nor thy stranger that is within thy gates: 11 For in six days the LORD made heaven and earth, the sea, and all that in them is, and rested the seventh day: wherefore the LORD blessed the sabbath day, and hallowed it. 12 Honour thy father and thy mother: that thy days may be long upon the land which the LORD thy God giveth thee. 13 Thou shalt not kill. 14 Thou shalt not commit adultery. 15 Thou shalt not steal. 16 Thou shalt not bear false witness against thy neighbour. 17 Thou shalt not covet thy neighbour's house, thou shalt not covet thy neighbour's wife, nor his manservant, nor his maidservant, nor his ox, nor his ass, nor any thing that is thy neighbour's. [*i*.448, *i*.479, *ii*.54, *ii*.58]

Subject Index

accident, *i*.78, *i*.108, *i*.109, *i*.146

actions. *See also* karmas
cause of, *i*.243
desireless, *i*.107, *iii*.154–58
ends don't justify means, *ii*.87

Adam and Eve, *i*.16

adversity, *iii*.226

advertising. *See* proselytizing

Ages (Golden, Silver, Copper, Iron),
i.34

ahankar. *See* ego

Alakh, Agam, Anami, *ii*.213

alcohol, abstaining from, *ii*.78–84

ambitions, *iii*.178, *iii*.179. *See also* job

amrit, *ii*.153

analyzing, *ii*.330–32, *ii*.446, *ii*.448,
iii.370

angels. *See* gods and goddesses

anger, *i*.255, *iii*.242–55, *iii*.313
effects of, *iii*.252, *iii*.253

animals/pets, *iii*.330–3
creating or clearing karma, *i*.93
state of, *i*.198

apertures, nine, *i*.223, *i*.489, *ii*.15,
ii.114, *ii*.151, *ii*.158, *ii*.171,
ii.199, *iii*.388

apologizing, *iii*.251, *iii*.262, *iii*.264,
iii.265

appreciation. *See* praise

army. *See* military service

art, *i*.257, *iii*.273, *iii*.275

arti, *i*.311. *See also* rituals and
ceremonies

asceticism, *i*.224

association(s)
in dreams, *i*.256
in Par Brahm, *ii*.229
mental, *iii*.27
of mind and soul, *ii*.155, *ii*.217,
ii.227
of past. *See* sanskaras
with animals, *iii*.331
with family in past, *i*.76, *iii*.325
with masters in previous lives,
i.434–36, *i*.439
with path in past, *ii*.17, *ii*.201,
ii.262
with sleep, *ii*.288, *ii*.315

astral plane, *i*.248, *ii*.214, *iii*.343

astrology, *i*.148–50

attachment(s), *i*.67, *i*.73, *i*.190,
i.273–82, *i*.422, *ii*.198,
iii.392
breaking, *i*.217, *i*.281
by meditation, *i*.222, *ii*.108,
ii.266, *ii*.405

create detachment, *i.*167, *i.*210,
    *i.*212, *i.*222, *i.*225, *i.*229, *i.*246,
    *i.*250, *i.*273, *i.*275, *i.*463, *ii.*110,
    *ii.*166, *ii.*268, *iii.*171, *iii.*281,
    *iii.*289
  analogy of bulldozer, *i.*278,
    *i.*426, *iii.*295, *iii.*297, *iii.*300
  creation of, *i.*86, *ii.*158, *ii.*187,
    *iii.*385
  deceptions of, *i.*348, *ii.*265
  types of, *i.*168, *i.*278, *i.*279, *ii.*210,
    *iii.*179, *iii.*284
    of relatives, *i.*162, *iii.*286,
      *iii.*295–99, *iii.*304
    to physical form of master, *iii.*71
    to sound, *ii.*199
    to the world, *i.*51, *i.*58, *ii.*405,
      *iii.*408
attachments and duties, *iii.*163,
    *iii.*168, *iii.*279–308
  analogy of married girl, *iii.*159,
    *iii.*286
attitude
  changes in perception, *iii.*374–77
  detached, *iii.*282
  positive, *i.*369, *ii.*301, *ii.*302, *ii.*417,
    *ii.*433, *iii.*246, *iii.*367–73
  towards creation, *i.*58
  towards elderly, *iii.*319
audible life stream. *See* shabd
austerities, *i.*211, *i.*213, *i.*224, *i.*225,
    *iii.*170

Baba Jaimal Singh Maharaj
  sitting in meditation during battle,
    *ii.*88
balance, *ii.*108, *ii.*117, *ii.*136, *ii.*175,
    *ii.*177, *ii.*379, *ii.*396, *iii.*160,
    *iii.*161. *See also* life, balanced

Barah Maha, *i.*310
beggars, *i.*74
bhajan, *ii.*185–86, *ii.*199–211. *See also*
    meditation
  burns karma, *ii.*387
  deafness and, *ii.*206, *ii.*207
  how to do, *ii.*209
  physical ears and, *ii.*207, *ii.*312
  plugging ears, *ii.*205
  preliminary sounds, *ii.*199, *ii.*204
  time for, *ii.*201–3, *ii.*208, *ii.*210
Bible, *i.*297, *i.*327, *i.*328, *i.*477
birth control, *i.*80
black magic, *iii.*345, *iii.*346
body
  dissolution of, *i.*171, *i.*177, *i.*179,
    *i.*237. *See also* elements, five
  makeup of, *i.*20, *i.*176
  mind's effect on, *iii.*337, *iii.*342
  stilling, *ii.*283
  taking care of, *iii.*335, *iii.*337
  temple of God, *i.*173, *i.*174, *iii.*390
  transmigration of, *i.*208
  withdrawal from, *i.*183, *ii.*248.
    See also withdrawal
books
  misconstruing of, *i.*331
  purpose of, *i.*333, *i.*334, *ii.*157,
    *iii.*114, *iii.*115
bossing, *ii.*436, *iii.*104, *iii.*138, *iii.*149
Brahm, *i.*237, *ii.*213
breathing, *ii.*184, *ii.*313, *ii.*318
brotherhood, *ii.*450, *iii.*123
Buddha, teachings of, *i.*296, *i.*319,
    *i.*323
burial or cremation, *i.*160, *iii.*302,
    *iii.*364, *iii.*365

calamity. *See* karmas, types of, group
calculation, *iii*.68, *iii*.239
  in meditation, *ii*.108, *ii*.447
castes, creeds and colours
  Maharaj Charan Singh's memories
    of caste distinction, *iii*.124
  no distinctions of, *i*.289, *i*.299,
    i.322, *ii*.110, *iii*.94, *iii*.145,
    iii.150
celibacy, *ii*.92, *ii*.96
chakras
  analogy of starting at middle of
    hill, *ii*.160, *ii*.161, *ii*.163, *ii*.167,
    ii.180
Charan Singh Maharaj
  describing village life of olden
    days, *iii*.270
  his nephew becoming vegetarian,
    ii.70
  memories of caste distinction,
    iii.124
  pushed into world after love for
    master grew, *iii*.160
charity, *i*.105, *i*.382, *ii*.442, *iii*.154–58.
    See also helping others
  accepting, *iii*.184
  deception of, *i*.74, *iii*.156, *iii*.157
  expectation of reward, *iii*.183,
    iii.184, *iii*.239
chaurasi. *See* cycle of eighty-four
children, *i*.134, *iii*.320–30
  born with handicaps, *i*.98, *i*.101,
    iii.154
  born with special knowledge, *i*.138
  death of, *i*.67, *i*.72, *i*.98
  discipline of, *iii*.329
  duty towards parents, *iii*.301
  explaining Sant Mat to, *iii*.321,
    iii.323–25, *iii*.327

  influence of initiated parents,
    iii.322, *iii*.323, *iii*.325
  on vegetarian diet. *See* vegetarian
    diet, children and
  responsibility to, *ii*.282, *iii*.320,
    iii.328
  when life enters into, *i*.186
choices, *i*.118, *i*.137, *i*.412, *i*.425,
    ii.429. *See also* free will
chosen people. *See* soul(s), marked
Christ, teachings of, *i*.296, *i*.302,
    i.319, *i*.322, *i*.329, *i*.338, *i*.474
circumstances. *See* life,
    circumstances
citizens, good, *ii*.429, *iii*.180
civilization, *i*.267, *i*.376–78. *See also*
    worldly achievements
clear thinking. *See* discrimination
coincidence. *See* path, coming to
Comforter. *See* shabd
communication, *i*.376–77, *iii*.393
communion, *iii*.82
company
  good, *iii*.246
  of mystics, *i*.443
  of satsangis, *ii*.434, *iii*.116, *iii*.186
  our own, *iii*.93, *iii*.276
compassion, *iii*.289, *iii*.379–85,
    iii.397
concentration, *i*.112, *ii*.171, *ii*.173,
    ii.199, *ii*.244–45, *ii*.314, *ii*.395
  analogy of rolling stone gathers no
    moss, *ii*.269
condemnation, *i*.428
conditioned free will. *See* free will,
    limited
conflict, human. *See* creation,
    imperfections of
conscience, *i*.241, *i*.254, *ii*.399

consciousness
at time of death, *i.*111
before birth, *i.*161
levels of, *i.*180, *ii.*184, *ii.*219, *ii.*228,
*ii.*242, *iii.*11
contemplation. *See* dhyan
contentment, *iii.*21, *iii.*73, *iii.*195,
*iii.*229
conversion, religious, *i.*291,
*i.*292, *i.*302, *i.*320, *i.*420.
See also proselytizing
conviction, *i.*22, *i.*421, *iii.*115, *iii.*177
correcting others, *iii.*248
courage, *ii.*402
cowardice, *iii.*164
creation
as God's play, *i.*24, *i.*37–43, *i.*430,
*iii.*307
analogy of puppet show,
*i.*38–41, *i.*417
as God's projection, *i.*26–31, *i.*178,
*i.*186
continuation of, *i.*32–37, *i.*57, *i.*412,
*i.*416
getting out of
analogy of man in well, *i.*13, *i.*52
imperfections of, *i.*32, *i.*35, *i.*54,
*i.*56–59, *i.*400
impermanence of, *i.*168
one with God, *i.*208
purpose of, *i.*11–20, *i.*56, *i.*173
within man, *i.*186
creative power. *See* shabd
Creator. *See* God
criticism, *iii.*242–55
cursing, *iii.*254
cycle of eighty-four, *i.*154,
*i.*188–91, *i.*197, *i.*343.
See also transmigration

darkness
in forehead, *ii.*324
master pulls us through, *ii.*225
region of, *ii.*213, *ii.*217, *ii.*225
darshan, *iii.*47–60, *iii.*104
calculating, *iii.*47, *iii.*53
clearing karmas and, *iii.*51,
*iii.*55–58
distance from master and, *iii.*50,
*iii.*52, *iii.*68
increases devotion, *ii.*192, *iii.*54,
*iii.*56
inner and outer, *ii.*191, *iii.*50–58,
*iii.*66
of successor, *iii.*50
death, *i.*260, *ii.*229, *iii.*204
destined, *i.*137, *i.*144
facing, *iii.*350–66
help from master at, *i.*438, *ii.*413,
*ii.*418, *iii.*352, *iii.*357
hindering progress in, *iii.*363
knowing beforehand about,
*iii.*352, *iii.*358
pain of, *ii.*247, *iii.*350
analogy of removing cloth from
bush, *ii.*244
physical, *i.*237, *ii.*243, *iii.*359
readiness for
story about buffalo with bucket,
*i.*233
spiritual. *See* meditation, dying
while living
decisions, *i.*142, *ii.*398, *iii.*189–94.
See also discrimination
deities. *See* gods and goddesses
delusion. *See also* illusion
freedom from, *i.*374, *iii.*103
self-deception and, *i.*372

Dera, *i.*338, *i.*382, *ii.*284, *iii.*93, *iii.*94, *iii.*97, *iii.*124, *iii.*157, *iii.*176
leaving, *iii.*91
desireless actions. *See* actions, desireless
desires, *i.*112, *i.*240, *i.*245, *i.*250, *i.*273–82, *ii.*104. *See also* sanskaras
difference from necessity, *i.*274
elimination of, *i.*280, *i.*281, *ii.*105
fighting by meditation
analogy of dam in river, *ii.*106
analogy of snake in basket, *ii.*105
for God, master, *i.*281–82, *i.*306, *i.*351, *iii.*24, *iii.*71
fulfilment of, *i.*153, *i.*164, *i.*165, *i.*273–75, *i.*280, *ii.*321, *iii.*195
destiny, *i.*63–81, *i.*125, *i.*130, *i.*134, *i.*137, *i.*138, *i.*141–43, *i.*154. *See also* karmas, types of, fate
accepting, *i.*145, *i.*147, *ii.*132, *ii.*138, *ii.*139, *ii.*143, *ii.*147, *iii.*207, *iii.*210, *iii.*229
and free will. *See* free will
changing, *i.*110, *i.*145, *i.*147, *ii.*108, *iii.*200, *iii.*201
interconnected, *i.*145, *i.*146, *iii.*200
remission of, *i.*47, *i.*130
responsibility for, *i.*132, *i.*140
detachment, *i.*217, *iii.*172. *See also* attachment(s)
from role in life, *i.*135
from those who have died, *iii.*363
from worldly relationships, *iii.*281
devil, *i.*44. *See also* Kal
devotion, *i.*81, *i.*214, *i.*218, *i.*251, *i.*252, *ii.*176, *ii.*334, *ii.*335, *ii.*438–46, *iii.*7, *iii.*208. *See also* emotions

one-pointed, *iii.*10
dhyan, *ii.*173–83, *ii.*186–99, *ii.*202–3, *ii.*209. *See also* meditation
bhajan and, *ii.*190, *ii.*191
how to do, *ii.*188, *ii.*191, *ii.*193, *ii.*196
inner light and, *ii.*194–96
love and, *ii.*196
of own master, *ii.*195
of statues and pictures, *ii.*178, *ii.*187, *ii.*192, *ii.*197, *iii.*48
purpose of, *ii.*186, *ii.*188, *ii.*192, *ii.*196, *ii.*197, *ii.*233
radiant form and, *ii.*174, *ii.*189, *ii.*194. *See also* radiant form
diet, affects meditation, *ii.*308, *ii.*310
disciple(s), *i.*427, *i.*435, *i.*482. *See also* soul(s), as real disciple
and grace, *i.*429
characteristics of good, *ii.*412, *ii.*413
giving advice, *ii.*436
no testing of, *i.*255, *iii.*11
two-fold purpose of, *ii.*392
discipline, *ii.*410–13, *ii.*416
discrimination, *i.*41, *i.*140, *i.*246, *ii.*398, *ii.*414, *ii.*415, *ii.*445, *ii.*446
dissatisfaction, *i.*369
dissolution and grand dissolution, *i.*27, *i.*28, *i.*35, *i.*36, *i.*106, *i.*177, *i.*417. *See also* elements, five
divorce, *ii.*95, *iii.*286, *iii.*311, *iii.*315
doctors, *iii.*188, *iii.*334
doubts, *ii.*9, *ii.*42
dreams, *i.*255
as spiritual experience, *i.*256, *ii.*224
getting instructions in, *i.*248

drugs
  abstaining from, *ii*.78–84
  inner experiences and, *ii*.79
  medicine and, *ii*.82
  spiritual harm of, *ii*.79, *ii*.81–83
  to keep awake, *ii*.320
duties, *i*.101–4
  meditation as duty, *ii*.280
  performed with detached attitude.
    See attachments and duties
  towards children, *iii*.320. *See also*
    children, responsibility to
  worldly, *ii*.339, *iii*.163, *iii*.164,
    iii.166, *iii*.173, *iii*.319
dying while living. *See* meditation,
  dying while living

East and West
  holding satsangs and, *iii*.105,
    iii.110
  initiation and place of birth, *i*.407
  outlook on religion, *i*.364
  spirituality vs materialism, *i*.364,
    i.366
effort
  and grace, *i*.431, *ii*.260, *ii*.333–62,
    ii.347, *ii*.357, *ii*.358, *ii*.364.
    See also grace
  analogy of beggar knocking on
    door, *ii*.333, *ii*.338, *ii*.343,
    ii.351, *ii*.357, *ii*.359
  in meditation, *ii*.290, *ii*.291, *ii*.337,
    ii.345, *ii*.347, *ii*.349, *ii*.400,
    ii.402
  analogy of child weeping for
    mother, *ii*.353
  of one step, *ii*.433
  to seek within, *i*.387, *ii*.407
eggs. *See* vegetarian diet

ego, *i*.266–73, *i*.391, *ii*.120, *ii*.407
  as attachment, *iii*.220, *iii*.234
  eliminating, *i*.266, *i*.271, *i*.393,
    ii.119, *ii*.363, *iii*.173, *iii*.232,
    iii.241, *iii*.249
    analogy of cutting off head, *i*.341
  from sharing spiritual experiences,
    ii.250
  in garb of humility, *iii*.240
  spiritual, *iii*.236–38
elements, five, *i*.20, *i*.120, *i*.170, *i*.171,
    i.176, *i*.195, *i*.230, *i*.237, *ii*.115
  dissolution of, *i*.28
  soul giving life to, *i*.156
  vegetarian diet and, *ii*.56
emotions, *i*.234, *i*.236, *i*.251, *i*.253,
    iii.271
  as passion or devotion, *i*.252, *i*.253
  need to channelize, *ii*.254, *ii*.256
environment for meditation, *i*.70,
    iii.171
equanimity. *See* peace, of body, mind
  and soul
ethics. *See* morality
evil, *i*.51, *i*.52, *ii*.417. *See also* good
    and evil; karmas, types of,
    good and bad
  definition of, *i*.51, *i*.53
  effect of, *i*.133
  responsibility for, *i*.125
  spirits, *iii*.345–47
evolution, *i*.28, *i*.156
experiences. *See* inner experiences
eye centre, *i*.239, *i*.299, *i*.476, *ii*.159.
    See also withdrawal
  concentration at, *ii*.164
  location of, *ii*.160, *ii*.168, *ii*.169
  physical eyes and, *ii*.169
  reaching, *ii*.158–71

seat of mind and soul, *i.*225, *i.*235,
  *i.*245, *i.*257, *ii.*167, *ii.*170, *ii.*171
spiritual heart, *i.*236
staying at, *iii.*412

failures, *ii.*398, *ii.*403, *ii.*419, *ii.*431
analogy of child learning to walk,
  *ii.*402
as grace, *iii.*241
none in Sant Mat, *ii.*341, *ii.*361,
  *ii.*399, *ii.*401, *ii.*428, *ii.*431,
  *iii.*371
faith, *i.*434. *See also* intellect, satisfying
dissolving of questions by, *ii.*127
intellectual and true, *ii.*123
phases of, *ii.*126, *ii.*127
  analogy of driving between two
    cities, *ii.*125
through experience, *ii.*122–29
faith healers, *iii.*338
family. *See also* worldly relationships
feuds, *i.*383
family life, *iii.*309–20.
  See also marriage
attending family religious
  practices, *iii.*316–18
caring for elderly people
  story of grandfather and
    blanket, *iii.*319
Father. *See* God
faults. *See* weaknesses
fear, *ii.*322, *ii.*323, *iii.*16
of darkness, *ii.*323
of losing what we have, *i.*371,
  *i.*372, *iii.*194
of offending, *ii.*304, *iii.*17
female saints, *i.*459
five elements. *See* elements, five
five names. *See* simran

five passions. *See* passions, five
flowers, *iii.*274
forgiveness, *iii.*255–67
karma and, *ii.*136, *iii.*256, *iii.*258
seeking by forgiving others, *i.*399,
  *ii.*437, *iii.*135, *iii.*257, *iii.*261,
  *iii.*263, *iii.*266, *iii.*267
Christ's parable of servant and
  his loan, *iii.*258
seeking through meditation,
  *ii.*103, *ii.*104, *ii.*145, *ii.*281,
  *ii.*336, *ii.*359, *ii.*395, *ii.*451,
  *iii.*256, *iii.*259, *iii.*369
four lives. *See* lives, four
free will, *i.*126–51, *i.*413, *ii.*375
limited, *i.*118, *i.*127, *i.*131, *i.*135,
  *i.*136, *i.*140, *ii.*433
friends, *iii.*187, *iii.*344, *iii.*393.
  See also worldly relationships
future, *i.*95, *i.*100, *iii.*200, *iii.*373.
  See also karmas, types of,
  future

ghosts. *See* evil, spirits
gifts, *iii.*81, *iii.*181, *iii.*182, *iii.*185,
  *iii.*186
God
beyond description, *i.*284
blessings of, *iii.*243
conceals himself in creation, *i.*34
concept of, *i.*20–26, *i.*56, *i.*94,
  *i.*175, *i.*182, *i.*186, *i.*284, *i.*476,
  *ii.*450, *iii.*26
doer and giver of everything, *i.*164,
  *i.*427, *ii.*141, *ii.*144, *ii.*146,
  *ii.*372, *ii.*425, *ii.*451, *iii.*202
analogy of giving food and
  hunger, *i.*55, *i.*415, *i.*416, *i.*431,
  *i.*463, *ii.*365, *ii.*407

analogy of puppets and
puppeteer, *i*.135–36, *i*.142,
i.345, *i*.413–14
faith in his omnipresence, *iii*.334
forgiveness of. *See* forgiveness
marks souls, *i*.216, *i*.403, *i*.409,
i.412, *i*.414, *i*.418, *i*.423, *i*.433,
ii.23, *ii*.344, *ii*.348, *ii*.371,
ii.373. *See also* soul(s), marked
names of, *i*.283–85
projected in creation. *See* creation,
as God's projection
pulling from within, *i*.463, *ii*.342,
ii.424, *ii*.425
reality of, *i*.11, *i*.22, *i*.23
remembrance of, *ii*.382, *ii*.383
will of. *See* will of God
worshipping himself through us,
ii.346, *ii*.374
God-realization, *i*.101, *i*.152,
i.199–209
before self-realization, *i*.174, *i*.271
gods and goddesses, *i*.198, *ii*.215
good and evil, *i*.51–61. *See also* evil
grace, *i*.221, *i*.361, *i*.419, *i*.432, *i*.433,
ii.427, *iii*.395. *See also* inner
pull; effort, and grace
all done by, *ii*.342, *ii*.344, *ii*.345,
ii.348, *ii*.352, *ii*.355, *ii*.357,
ii.359, *ii*.374
always flowing, *ii*.328, *ii*.343,
ii.360, *ii*.427
becoming worthy of, *ii*.114, *ii*.346,
iii.279
invoking, *i*.431, *ii*.136, *ii*.413,
iii.368, *iii*.369
of master, God, *i*.83, *iii*.228,
iii.240, *iii*.408
Granth Sahib, *i*.330

gratitude, *i*.274, *iii*.399–402
Great Master
facing opposition, *i*.317, *iii*.175
first photo for public, *iii*.49
story of beloved thugs, *iii*.306
with tear in his eyes at partition,
i.445
grooves on mind, *i*.113, *i*.164, *i*.280.
See also desires; sanskaras
group meetings. *See* satsangs
grudges, *iii*.136, *iii*.251, *iii*.261, *iii*.262
guilt, *ii*.279, *ii*.285, *ii*.287, *ii*.289,
ii.338, *ii*.361, *ii*.389, *ii*.433.
See also weaknesses,
awareness of
gurmukh, *i*.41, *i*.345, *i*.413
guru, meaning of, *i*.447
Guru Nanak, teachings of, *i*.331

habit
forming of, *i*.309, *ii*.78, *ii*.288
of creating problems, *i*.456, *ii*.9,
ii.51
of meditation, *ii*.17, *ii*.152, *ii*.202,
ii.249, *ii*.277, *ii*.283, *ii*.284,
ii.288, *ii*.292, *ii*.299, *iii*.356
of mind, *ii*.173, *ii*.175, *ii*.186, *ii*.190,
ii.194, *ii*.197, *ii*.234, *ii*.296
of simran, *ii*.390
happiness, *i*.229, *i*.232, *i*.250, *i*.352,
i.364–78, *i*.396, *ii*.443, *iii*.21,
iii.376, *iii*.409–19
accompanied by fear, *i*.371, *i*.372
in adjustment to events, *iii*.204,
iii.211, *iii*.212
analogy of weather changes,
ii.143
real, *i*.172, *i*.347, *i*.370, *i*.373, *ii*.121,
ii.327, *ii*.411, *iii*.226, *iii*.418

analogy of child at fair, *i*.390
sharing, *i*.372, *i*.373, *i*.379, *i*.383
through worldly achievements.
    See worldly achievements
harmony among satsangis, *iii*.104,
    iii.108, *iii*.120, *iii*.125, *iii*.128,
    iii.130, *iii*.131, *iii*.137–39
hatha yoga. *See* yoga, types of
hatred, *i*.281, *iii*.134, *iii*.261
    from co-workers, *iii*.174
    indifference to, *iii*.175
healing, *iii*.337, *iii*.339
    spiritual, *iii*.5
health, *iii*.117, *iii*.334–48
heaven and hell, *i*.60, *i*.61
helping others, *i*.105, *i*.110, *i*.378–80,
    i.382, *i*.512, *ii*.86, *ii*.442,
    iii.154–58, *iii*.250, *iii*.362,
    iii.384. *See also* seva; charity
    and creating karma, *iii*.155
    by first helping ourselves, *i*.426,
        iii.154, *iii*.156
    dying person, *iii*.358–60
    fellow satsangis, *i*.354, *ii*.434–36,
        iii.121
    older people, *iii*.301
    our relations, *i*.422, *i*.426, *iii*.301,
        iii.302
helplessness
    analogy of puppets, *i*.40, *ii*.363
    to look at master, *iii*.50, *iii*.52, *iii*.91
hobbies, *iii*.273. *See also* pleasures,
    innocent
holy books. *See* scriptures
holy ghost, *i*.307. *See also* shabd
holy names. *See* simran
honesty, *ii*.85
human being
    basic requirements of, *iii*.199

can be worse than animals, *i*.192,
    i.193
not improved by civilization, *i*.376,
    i.377, *i*.385
top of creation, *i*.193–96
human form, *i*.188–99, *i*.439
    analogy of man in maze, *i*.343
    combination of good and bad
        karmas, *i*.57, *i*.245, *iii*.205,
        iii.225, *iii*.270
    opportunity of, *i*.190
    purpose of, *i*.173, *i*.194, *i*.244,
        ii.122, *ii*.439, *ii*.440, *ii*.444,
        iii.367
humility, *i*.266, *iii*.146, *iii*.231–42
    of masters, *iii*.38
humour and laughter, *iii*.275, *iii*.415
hurrying
    story of man with newspaper,
        iii.276
hurting others, *iii*.249, *iii*.258,
    iii.264, *iii*.265
    unintentional, *iii*.264
hypnotism, *i*.258

ill-feelings, *i*.399, *ii*.437, *iii*.261
illness, *ii*.115, *iii*.200, *iii*.335.
    See also suffering
illusion, *i*.24, *i*.109, *i*.374, *i*.497, *ii*.35,
    ii.348, *ii*.372, *ii*.373, *iii*.291.
    See also delusion
    about path, *i*.293
imagination, *i*.257, *ii*.194, *ii*.220–23,
    ii.233–34, *ii*.372
impressions
    deep. *See* sanskaras
    of light and sound, *ii*.301
India/Indian culture. *See* East and
    West

indifference, *iii*.391
  to people's remarks, *iii*.246
individuality
  losing, *i*.27, *i*.180, *i*.182, *i*.254,
    i.269, *i*.272, *ii*.119, *ii*.194,
    ii.262, *ii*.394, *ii*.449, *iii*.12,
    iii.14, *iii*.68, *iii*.76, *iii*.218
  analogy of candle and flame,
    i.179, *i*.181
I-ness. *See* ego
initiation, *i*.196, *ii*.12–31.
    See also path, coming to
  age requirement, *ii*.25–27
  as new birth, *ii*.24, *iii*.82
  karmic barriers before, *i*.100
  never destroyed, *iii*.6
    analogy of sown seeds, *i*.423–
    424, *ii*.420–424
  of physically handicapped, *ii*.30,
    ii.31
  preparation for, *ii*.11–12, *ii*.16–17,
    ii.24–28
  protection before, *i*.406, *i*.424,
    i.435, *ii*.10
  purpose of, *i*.67, *ii*.13, *ii*.15, *ii*.16,
    iii.105
  responsibilities after, *i*.99
  result of many lives, *i*.411
  sponsor, *ii*.21
  through representative, *ii*.18–20
inner experiences, *i*.256–57, *ii*.218–21,
    ii.223, *ii*.228, *ii*.337, *ii*.354–55.
    See also progress
  as imagination, *ii*.221
  before coming to path, *i*.424
  corroboration of, *ii*.222
  digesting within, *ii*.250–57
  for encouragement, *ii*.224, *ii*.354
  meeting past masters, *ii*.236

  sharing, creates ego, *ii*.250–54
inner guidance, *iii*.47. *See also*
    master(s), helping disciples
inner journey, *i*.183, *ii*.154, *iii*.172.
    See also soul(s), return to God
inner pull, *i*.215–16, *i*.414, *ii*.6–11,
    ii.362–76, *iii*.372. *See also*
    path, coming to
  by grace of God, *i*.427–34
inner regions, *ii*.211–29
  falling from higher, *ii*.267
  five, *ii*.213
  rulers of, *ii*.215
  sound and light, *ii*.218. *See also*
    shabd, sound and light
inside, definition of, *ii*.249
intellect, *i*.11–14, *i*.263, *i*.264
  going beyond, *i*.263, *i*.265
  limitations of, *i*.11–16, *i*.155, *i*.260,
    i.262, *i*.414, *ii*.41, *ii*.42, *ii*.126,
    ii.258, *ii*.399
  satisfied, produces faith, *i*.22,
    i.264, *ii*.48
  satisfying, *ii*.31–52, *iii*.115
    analogy of driving between two
    cities, *i*.261, *ii*.36, *ii*.43
intellectuals, *i*.261, *i*.344, *i*.432, *ii*.39,
    ii.46, *ii*.51, *iii*.103, *iii*.115
intention, *i*.117, *i*.120
intuition, *i*.256, *i*.259

jealousy, *iii*.74–75, *iii*.104, *iii*.131–37
job
  involvement, *iii*.165–67, *iii*.173–74,
    iii.187–88. *See also* duties
  satisfaction, *iii*.179, *iii*.272
journey of soul. *See* inner journey
joy. *See* happiness
judging, *iii*.244, *iii*.249

justice and injustice, *i*.75, *i*.76, *i*.79,
  i.80, *i*.340, *iii*.257, *iii*.260
justification. *See* karmas, creating

Kabir, *i*.340, *i*.341
Kal, *i*.43–50, *i*.305. *See also* mind;
  universal mind
  boons of, *i*.36
  deceptions of, *i*.45, *i*.340, *ii*.225,
    ii.432
  duty of, *i*.50
  fear of, *i*.46–49
  God's agent, *i*.44, *i*.47–48
    analogy of head of state, *i*.44,
      i.48
    analogy of jail warden, *i*.49
kam, ii.96. *See also* lust
karmaless, *i*.107, *i*.108
karmas, *i*.65, *i*.68, *i*.87, *i*.91, *i*.107,
  i.109, *ii*.341, *iii*.224
  analogy of killing thousand
    chickens, *i*.63, *i*.65, *i*.86, *i*.100
  association with mind, *i*.82, *i*.106,
    iii.224
  changing. *See* destiny, changing
  clearing, *i*.66, *i*.82–100, *i*.124,
    i.125, *i*.128, *i*.205, *i*.221, *ii*.107,
    ii.108, *ii*.135, *ii*.247, *ii*.274,
    ii.340, *ii*.345, *ii*.395, *ii*.400,
    iii.227, *iii*.262
    by meditation, *i*.93, *ii*.339,
      ii.447, *ii*.451, *iii*.51
    help from master, *i*.89, *i*.99,
      i.439, *i*.498, *i*.508, *i*.511–13,
      ii.339, *iii*.12
    in one life, *i*.88–89, *i*.99,
      i.147–48, *i*.221, *ii*.421
    through repentance, *i*.87, *i*.97,
      ii.136
  creating, *i*.74, *i*.75, *i*.86, *i*.113,
    i.114–26, *ii*.302
    by justifying actions or
      indifference, *i*.73, *i*.95, *i*.101,
      i.118, *i*.123, *i*.384, *ii*.95
    first karma, *i*.114–16, *i*.132, *i*.136
    new seeds, *i*.84, *i*.85, *i*.122–25,
      i.130, *i*.141, *iii*.193
    sowing and reaping, *i*.63–68,
      i.70, *i*.75, *i*.86, *i*.102, *i*.104,
      i.110, *i*.115, *i*.121, *i*.122, *i*.127,
      i.131, *i*.139, *i*.152, *i*.375
  of going off path, *ii*.424–26, *ii*.429,
    ii.432
  rising above, *i*.64, *i*.66, *i*.82–85,
    i.87, *i*.106, *i*.107, *ii*.387
  theory of, *i*.155, *i*.156
  types of, *i*.95, *i*.118, *i*.122, *i*.123,
    ii.326, *ii*.399, *iii*.193
    fate, *i*.64, *i*.66, *i*.70, *i*.85, *i*.117
    future, *i*.65, *i*.100
    good and bad, *i*.90–92, *i*.104,
      i.115, *i*.118, *i*.121, *i*.153, *i*.188,
      i.189, *i*.245, *iii*.208
    group, *i*.76–79
    individual, *i*.77–80, *i*.112
    reserve, *i*.64, *i*.86, *i*.88, *i*.89, *i*.94,
      ii.103
    three types, *i*.63, *i*.84, *i*.85, *i*.127
karmic impressions, *i*.106, *i*.183,
  i.204. *See also* mind;
  sanskaras
karmic relationships, *i*.76–79, *i*.102,
  i.405, *iii*.193, *iii*.257–59,
  iii.282–286, *iii*.307, *iii*.335.
  See also worldly relationships
  self-deceptive and real, *iii*.291,
    iii.293
  with adversary, *i*.72–73, *i*.124

with relatives, *i.*71–73, *i.*103,
    *iii.*280, *iii.*283, *iii.*305–7
killing, *i.*53–54, *i.*78–80, *i.*393–94
    avoiding, *ii.*58, *ii.*73, *iii.*332
    insects, pests, etc., *i.*120–21,
        *iii.*332–33
    in war, *i.*103, *ii.*88
    unavoidable, *iii.*333
    unintentionally, *i.*120
kindness, *i.*106, *iii.*18, *iii.*155, *iii.*382,
    *iii.*383. *See also* compassion
knowledge, *i.*263. *See also* intellect
kriyaman karma. *See* karmas, types
    of, future
kundalini. *See* yoga, types of

langar, *iii.*145
laughter. *See* humour and laughter
lawyers, *iii.*188
leela. See creation, as God's play
letters written to master, *iii.*190
liberation, final, *i.*277. *See also* soul(s),
    return to God
life
    balanced, *iii.*159–88, *iii.*199
    circumstances, *i.*241, *i.*275, *ii.*40,
        *iii.*163. *See also* karmas
    adjusting to, *ii.*117, *ii.*138,
        *iii.*199–200, *iii.*205
    difficult, *ii.*89, *iii.*169, *iii.*178,
        *iii.*188, *iii.*191
    karmic, *i.*65, *i.*118, *i.*141
    leading towards the path, *ii.*7,
        *ii.*333, *ii.*346
    happy, relaxed, *iii.*195, *iii.*200,
        *iii.*267–77
    normal, natural, *i.*378, *iii.*159, *iii.*165
    purpose of, *i.*14, *i.*101, *i.*173, *i.*193,
        *i.*344, *i.*396, *ii.*441

reality of, *i.*23, *i.*363, *ii.*348, *iii.*96,
    *iii.*209
simple, *iii.*179, *iii.*268
light. *See also* shabd
    flashes of, *ii.*230, *ii.*240–241
    merging into, *i.*206–9
    of God, *i.*208–9
    of sun and moon, *ii.*230
    within, *i.*208–9
line of masters. *See* master(s),
    successorship
lives, four, *i.*159, *i.*163, *i.*167, *i.*185, *i.*221,
    *i.*423, *i.*430, *ii.*107, *ii.*273, *ii.*420,
    *ii.*421, *ii.*452, *iii.*373. *See also*
    initiation, never destroyed;
    reincarnation, after initiation
living in monastery, *iii.*170–71
living Sant Mat, *ii.*377–386, *ii.*393–
    95, *ii.*408. *See also* meditation,
    atmosphere of; Sant Mat, way
    of life
    as warrior, *ii.*408
loans, *iii.*184–85
loneliness, *i.*21, *i.*31, *i.*171, *i.*347–49,
    *i.*358, *i.*359, *i.*490, *ii.*324,
    *ii.*329, *ii.*407, *iii.*21
    as grace, *i.*349, *i.*359–63
longing, *iii.*60–78
    created and satisfied by God,
        *i.*431–33
    same effect as darshan, *iii.*67
    tears of, *iii.*70, *iii.*71
    to return to God, *ii.*11
        analogy of crying child, *i.*353
Lord. *See* God
love
    analyzing, *iii.*393, *iii.*396
    as gift from God, *ii.*347, *ii.*364,
        *ii.*369, *ii.*372, *iii.*385–99

capacity for, *ii*.257
Christ's saying 'love thy
  neighbour', *i*.174, *i*.393, *i*.485,
  ii.58, *ii*.450, *iii*.130, *iii*.261,
  iii.389–90
concept of, *i*.206, *ii*.256, *ii*.381,
  iii.18, *iii*.386
  merging into another being,
    i.182, *i*.214, *i*.254, *i*.268, *i*.461,
    ii.449
creates faith, *ii*.371, *iii*.22
developing, *ii*.122, *ii*.171, *ii*.335,
  ii.367, *ii*.450, *iii*.395
  by meditation, *i*.206, *ii*.97–104,
    ii.256, *ii*.272, *ii*.304, *ii*.364,
    ii.370, *ii*.376, *iii*.29–31, *iii*.387,
    iii.388
different from lust, *ii*.93, *ii*.111
dramatizing, *ii*.256, *iii*.24, *iii*.78
erases hatred, *iii*.262
for God vs world, *i*.313, *i*.357,
  i.386, *i*.441, *i*.461, *ii*.354,
  iii.291, *iii*.292, *iii*.375, *iii*.379,
  iii.388–91, *iii*.398
for master, *i*.143, *ii*.290, *ii*.448,
  iii.22–30, *iii*.40, *iii*.41, *iii*.101,
  iii.160
  his physical form, *iii*.54, *iii*.65,
    iii.66
for master's successor, *iii*.102
higher type of, *iii*.387, *iii*.388
in relation to mind, *i*.213, *i*.236,
  ii.342, *iii*.13, *iii*.386
  devotion or emotion, *i*.214,
    i.215, *i*.218–19, *i*.251, *i*.252,
    ii.406
  intellectual, *ii*.450
pain of, *ii*.404, *iii*.73.
  See also separation, pain of

analogy of woman delivering
  child, *ii*.404, *iii*.73
true religion, *i*.292. *See also* religion
unconditional, *ii*.448, *iii*.26,
  iii.220
within everyone, *i*.314
lover, *iii*.73, *iii*.378, *iii*.394, *iii*.396
  never calculates, *ii*.376, *ii*.404,
    ii.447, *ii*.449, *iii*.24, *iii*.60,
    iii.76
loving heart, *iii*.380, *iii*.382
lust, *i*.225, *i*.254, *ii*.93, *iii*.168

Maharaj Sawan Singh. *See* Great
  Master
Maha Sunn, *i*.183–84, *ii*.225.
  See also darkness, region of
malice, *iii*.135, *iii*.250
manmukh, *i*.41, *i*.345, *i*.413
mantras, *ii*.184
marked souls. *See* soul(s), marked
marriage, *i*.125, *ii*.93, *ii*.94, *iii*.168,
  iii.309–20. *See also* family life
  as duty, *iii*.295
  children and, *iii*.313
  legal, *ii*.89, *ii*.96
  partner's reaction to path, *iii*.310,
    iii.314
  pulling through storms, *iii*.312
  role of love in, *iii*.309
  spiritual progress and, *iii*.294,
    iii.315
master-disciple relationship, *iii*.3–32,
  iii.41, *iii*.133, *iii*.240. *See also*
  master(s), living, need for
  analogy of moth and light,
    ii.232–33
  analogy of mother and child, *iii*.17
master(s). *See also* saints

all same, *i*.282, *i*.460, *iii*.36, *iii*.98,
    iii.101
    as waves of ocean, *i*.437, *i*.450,
        i.452, *ii*.237, *iii*.35, *iii*.36
always alive for disciple, *i*.466,
    ii.426, *ii*.429, *ii*.432, *iii*.97,
    iii.99, *iii*.100
analogy of gardener, *ii*.361
analogy of philanthropist and
    prisoners, *i*.491, *i*.502
as doer of everything, *ii*.262, *iii*.75
as mirror, *iii*.25
as one with God, *i*.170, *i*.305,
    i.448, *i*.462, *iii*.45
as ransom, *i*.46, *ii*.400
collect marked souls, *i*.403, *i*.417,
    i.427, *i*.437, *i*.478
coming to world again, *i*.436,
    i.451, *i*.453, *i*.509
do not improve world, *i*.384, *i*.490,
    i.492, *i*.502, *iii*.203, *iii*.226.
    See also world, improving
finding master in next birth,
    i.435–37, *i*.440
follow laws of nature, *i*.497
helping disciples, *i*.109, *i*.499, *i*.500,
    ii.239, *ii*.334, *ii*.355, *ii*.357,
    iii.46
    analogy of flying kite, *i*.406,
        ii.424–27, *iii*.3
    parable of hundred sheep, *i*.404,
        i.498, *ii*.322, *ii*.428, *iii*.3, *iii*.131
karmas and, *i*.507–13
living, need for, *i*.442, *i*.461–83,
    i.488, *ii*.19
looking after predecessor's
    disciples, *iii*.98, *iii*.101
merging into, *ii*.194, *ii*.198, *ii*.211,
    iii.45

nearness or distance from,
    iii.87–89
need a master, *i*.509, *i*.514–18
never accepts anything from
    disciples, *iii*.153, *iii*.182
never exposes our weaknesses,
    iii.25
number in world, *i*.514, *i*.517
passing of, *iii*.97–102
persecution of, *i*.315–18, *i*.455,
    i.494–96, *iii*.73
pleasing or displeasing, *ii*.304,
    iii.14–17
presence of, *iii*.27, *iii*.86–97
purpose of, *i*.58, *i*.392, *i*.483–502,
    i.505–6
recognize, how to, *i*.429, *i*.457,
    ii.3–5
responsibility of, *i*.18, *i*.405, *i*.416,
    i.426, *i*.438, *i*.488, *ii*.428,
    ii.441, *iii*.354
running after, *iii*.78–80
sent by God, *i*.428, *i*.443, *i*.446
shabd is real form of, *i*.438, *i*.441,
    i.444, *i*.446, *i*.448, *i*.451, *i*.484,
    iii.32–40, *iii*.41–46, *iii*.67,
    iii.72, *iii*.98, *iii*.102
share disciples' karmas.
    See karmas, clearing
show emotions, *i*.445
successorship, *i*.282, *i*.303, *i*.304,
    i.452, *i*.459, *i*.460, *i*.472,
    i.514–16
suffering of, *i*.501, *i*.508, *i*.512,
    iii.19
talking to inner, *i*.247, *i*.248, *ii*.137,
    ii.236, *iii*.28, *iii*.40
types of, *i*.454, *i*.459, *i*.510, *i*.512,
    i.516

hidden, *i.*472
what is, *i.*441–49, *i.*487, *iii.*45
where found, *i.*456–58
materialism. *See* worldly achievements
maya. See illusion
media, *i.*377
medicine, *iii.*334, *iii.*339
with animal substances, *iii.*340
meditation. *See also* bhajan; dhyan;
simran
as struggle, *ii.*272, *ii.*289, *ii.*332,
*ii.*337, *iii.*112
as true prayer. *See* prayer
atmosphere of, *ii.*365, *ii.*377–86,
*ii.*394, *iii.*92, *iii.*93
before initiation, *i.*470
benefits of, *i.*373, *ii.*104–22,
*ii.*399, *ii.*446, *iii.*212, *iii.*376.
See also progress
brings peace, happiness, *i.*217,
*ii.*116, *ii.*117, *ii.*386, *iii.*337,
*iii.*416. *See also* peace
clears karmas. *See* karmas,
clearing
creates detachment.
See attachment(s), breaking
generates love. *See* love,
developing
God-realization. *See* God-
realization
influence on children in womb,
*iii.*324
makes us receptive.
See receptivity
strengthens discrimination,
*i.*246, *ii.*100, *ii.*445.
See also discrimination
strengthens willpower.
See willpower

definition of, *ii.*165, *ii.*363, *ii.*368,
*ii.*378, *ii.*383, *ii.*385
desire for, *ii.*336, *ii.*375
analogy of hunger, *i.*3, *i.*55,
*i.*415–16, *i.*431, *i.*463, *ii.*349,
*ii.*365–77
dry, *i.*215, *ii.*281, *ii.*324–30. *See also*
vacuum
dying while living, *ii.*226,
*ii.*243–50, *iii.*355
excessive, *iii.*165
expectation, *ii.*304, *ii.*305
mechanical, *ii.*379–83
no danger in, *ii.*214
no substitute for, *iii.*28, *iii.*30
obstacles, *ii.*299, *ii.*300, *ii.*322–32
pain and sensations. *See* withdrawal
phases of, *ii.*267, *ii.*279, *ii.*325,
*ii.*341, *ii.*400
practice, *ii.*151–58, *ii.*159, *ii.*303,
*ii.*371
with love, *i.*205, *ii.*97–104,
*ii.*304, *iii.*370
with relaxed mind, *ii.*305
purpose of, *i.*85, *i.*199, *i.*206, *i.*209,
*i.*216, *i.*353, *ii.*102, *ii.*107,
*ii.*108, *ii.*114, *ii.*117–20, *ii.*155,
*ii.*441, *iii.*95, *iii.*196
quantity brings quality, *ii.*341,
*ii.*345
regularity and punctuality,
*ii.*277–92, *ii.*337, *ii.*338
support for, *ii.*157, *ii.*382, *ii.*385,
*ii.*395–97, *iii.*112, *iii.*140.
See also habit
technique. *See* meditation, practice
time, *ii.*203, *ii.*280–82, *ii.*287,
*ii.*319, *ii.*369, *ii.*379, *ii.*381,
*ii.*384, *ii.*438, *iii.*167

way of life, *ii.*289, *ii.*384, *ii.*385.
　See also Sant Mat, way of life
meekness. *See* humility
mental illnesses, *iii.*343, *iii.*344
mercy killing, *iii.*332, *iii.*361–62
military service, *i.*103, *ii.*88
　as profession, *ii.*87
mind, *i.*210, *i.*223, *i.*241, *i.*245–65
　attributes and faculties of, *i.*204,
　　*i.*245, *i.*257–59, *i.*279, *ii.*446
　to think and visualize, *ii.*174.
　　See also dhyan; simran
　blanking of, *ii.*165–66
　controlling, *i.*202, *i.*212, *i.*216,
　　*i.*224–27, *i.*239, *i.*270, *ii.*111,
　　*ii.*283, *ii.*292–303, *ii.*388
　analogy of dam in river, *ii.*112
　creates desires, *i.*245, *ii.*356, *ii.*440.
　　See also desires
　creates problems, *i.*262, *ii.*297
　deceptions of, *i.*240–49, *i.*305,
　　*ii.*177, *ii.*183, *ii.*299, *ii.*330,
　　*ii.*446
　different from soul, *i.*176, *i.*218,
　　*i.*234
　enemy or friend, *i.*223–27, *i.*251,
　　*i.*260, *ii.*227, *ii.*293, *ii.*403,
　　*ii.*410
　everything comes through, *i.*218,
　　*i.*219, *i.*251, *i.*266
　feeling devotion with, *i.*213–15,
　　*i.*252
　higher and lower, *i.*241, *i.*247,
　　*i.*254, *i.*257, *ii.*294
　never appeased, *i.*251, *i.*368
　story of rishi with bow and
　　arrow, *i.*242
　projections of. *See* mind,
　　deceptions of

purifying, *i.*224, *i.*255, *i.*257, *ii.*378,
　*ii.*387, *ii.*396, *ii.*415, *ii.*445,
　*iii.*152, *iii.*336
　analogy of water evaporating
　　from mud, *i.*234
　reactions of, *iii.*169, *iii.*172
　release from, *i.*227, *i.*244
　scattered in creation
　　analogy of cloth on thorny
　　　bush, *ii.*311
　slave of senses, *i.*212, *i.*219,
　　*i.*226–43, *i.*252, *ii.*335, *ii.*404,
　　*iii.*10
　source of, *i.*210
　strong, *ii.*297, *ii.*298
　struggle with, *i.*249, *ii.*285, *ii.*291,
　　*ii.*292–303, *ii.*396–410.
　　See also meditation, as
　　struggle
　　analogy of soldier and general,
　　　*ii.*400, *ii.*406, *ii.*409
　subconscious, *i.*113, *i.*167, *i.*204,
　　*i.*279
　suppressing. *See* suppression
　talking to, *i.*249
　thinking of past and future, *ii.*389
　training of, *ii.*278, *ii.*380, *iii.*206
　unhappiness of, *i.*228
miracles, *i.*505, *i.*506, *iii.*402–9
　as individual experience, *iii.*404–7
　as related to sharing inner
　　experiences, *ii.*250, *ii.*253
　of Christ, *iii.*403
　of master, *i.*501–7, *iii.*5, *iii.*402–5
　worldly vs spiritual, *iii.*404, *iii.*405
misery, *ii.*411, *ii.*441, *iii.*200
misunderstanding, *iii.*251, *iii.*266
monastery, *iii.*169–71
morality, *i.*386, *ii.*85–96

motive. *See* intention
behind criticism, *iii.*250, *iii.*251
music, *i.*257, *iii.*110, *iii.*274–75
mystical literature, *iii.*115.
See also books
mystics. *See also* master(s); saints
teachings and personalities,
*i.*335–42

nam. *See* shabd
*nam bhakti, i.*310
names, five. *See* simran
natural instincts, *iii.*296
negative power. *See* Kal
negativity, *ii.*417
nine apertures. *See* apertures, nine
*nirat, i.*298, *ii.*168
nirvana, *i.*323
nonviolence, *ii.*59, *iii.*260

obedience, *ii.*84, *ii.*290, *ii.*395, *ii.*413,
*ii.*429, *iii.*218
obligations. *See* duties
obsession, *i.*113, *i.*114, *iii.*164, *iii.*380
old age. *See* youth, advantages and
disadvantages
*om, ii.*184
organ donation and transplantation,
*iii.*340, *iii.*341
original sin. *See* karmas, creating

pain
as pleasure, *ii.*117
of separation, *i.*359
Par Brahm, *ii.*229
parshad, *iii.*80–86
passions, five, *i.*255, *ii.*215, *ii.*404
expressions of ego, *i.*268
fighting by meditation, *ii.*112

analogy of snake and
sandalwood tree, *ii.*110
slow elimination of, *ii.*264
past
brooding over, *iii.*196, *iii.*370
knowledge of, *i.*162, *i.*203, *i.*204,
*i.*217, *ii.*216
not remembering, *i.*37.
See also Kal, boons of
path. *See also* Sant Mat
always the same, *i.*450, *i.*454, *i.*478
bringing others to, *i.*419, *i.*420,
*ii.*393
bringing somebody back to,
*ii.*434–37
coming to, *i.*366, *i.*424, *i.*433,
*ii.*6–10. *See also* inner pull
automatically, *i.*403–6, *i.*412
determined by karma, *i.*423
due to association with saints in
previous life, *i.*434, *i.*435
inner guidance, *ii.*5–12
in next life, *i.*436
not coincidence, *i.*404, *i.*434
reasons for, *i.*81, *i.*408, *i.*419, *i.*439
spiritual experiences before, *ii.*10
through master or teachings,
*i.*411
conviction for, *ii.*31.
See also intellect, satisfying
finding right one, *i.*402, *i.*434,
*i.*440, *i.*456
going off, *i.*404, *ii.*50, *ii.*399,
*ii.*424–28, *ii.*432, *iii.*4, *iii.*6
need for, *i.*344
phases of, *ii.*370, *iii.*371
steadfastness on
analogy of rolling stone gathers
no moss, *iii.*42–45, *ii.*269, *iii.*10

peace, *i*.197, *i*.250, *i*.386–402
    how achieved, *i*.397, *i*.400
    in world, *i*.395, *i*.401, *iii*.270
    not possible as long as ego is there,
        i.394
    of body, mind and soul, *i*.217,
        ii.108, *ii*.114–17
    radiating, *i*.391, *i*.493, *ii*.442
    searching for, *i*.352, *i*.367, *i*.396
        worldly vs spiritual approach,
            i.387, *i*.389
peacemakers, *i*.493, *iii*.417
perversions. *See* passions, five
pets. *See* animals/pets
philanthropy, *i*.375
philosopher's stone, *ii*.293
physical exercise, *ii*.317, *ii*.318
pictures, *i*.464, *iii*.40, *iii*.85
    story of Great Master and his first
        photo for public, *iii*.49
Pind, *ii*.228
pineal gland, *ii*.168. *See also* eye
    centre
pitfalls, *ii*.431
pleasures
    innocent, *iii*.273, *iii*.274
    sensual. *See* passions, five
politics, *iii*.180, *iii*.181
positive thinking. *See* attitude,
    positive
possessiveness, *i*.140, *i*.269, *i*.270,
    i.383, *ii*.439, *iii*.135, *iii*.398
posture, *ii*.311, *ii*.314–17
poverty, *i*.382
praise, *i*.409, *iii*.156, *iii*.239, *iii*.246
pralabdh karma. *See* karmas, types
    of, fate
pranayam. *See* yoga, types of
prayer, *i*.248, *ii*.129–49, *ii*.356

asking for reward, *ii*.139, *ii*.451,
    iii.201
benefits of, *ii*.130, *ii*.132, *ii*.138,
    ii.139, *ii*.143, *ii*.145, *ii*.147
for others, *ii*.141, *ii*.142, *ii*.147
karma and, *ii*.147
sincerity in, *ii*.137, *ii*.139, *ii*.142
submission through, *ii*.131,
    ii.133, *ii*.135, *ii*.147, *ii*.148.
    See also submission
predestination. *See* destiny
presents. *See* gifts
pride. *See* ego
priests, *i*.495, *i*.496
prince of this world, *i*.44, *i*.45.
    See also Kal
principles, four. *See* vows, four
privilege of returning to God, *ii*.373
problems, *i*.354, *ii*.332. *See also* life,
    circumstances; suffering
    rising above, *ii*.118, *iii*.174, *iii*.203
    solving of, *iii*.162, *iii*.189, *iii*.212,
        iii.213
progress, *ii*.258–76. *See also* inner
    experiences
analogy of child learning to walk,
    ii.341, *ii*.385, *ii*.400, *ii*.403,
    ii.431
depends on many factors, *ii*.272,
    ii.349, *iii*.372
in inner planes, *i*.159, *i*.167, *i*.276,
    ii.228, *ii*.270, *ii*.271, *iii*.67
is always there, *ii*.260, *ii*.270
is in God's hands, *ii*.260
means for, *iii*.80
measuring, *ii*.259, *ii*.263, *ii*.266
obstacles to, *i*.258, *i*.269, *ii*.42
question of reincarnation and,
    i.275, *iii*.304

signs of, *i.*217, *ii.*23, *ii.*109, *iii.*410.
    See also meditation, benefits of
    time required to achieve, *ii.*263,
    *ii.*275, *iii.*377
    without master, *i.*482
proselytizing, *i.*320, *iii.*108, *iii.*140
psychologists, *iii.*344, *iii.*345
public opinion, *i.*317, *iii.*248
pull. *See* inner pull
punishment, *ii.*411, *ii.*430
    as discipline, *i.*94
    analogy of father not handing
        son to police, *ii.*419
    analogy of potter moulding clay,
        *ii.*419
puppet. *See* God, doer and giver of
    everything
pure-hearted, *i.*399

Rabia Basri, *i.*60
Radha Soami, *i.*285. *See also* God
radiant form, *ii.*194, *ii.*230–38, *ii.*397,
    *iii.*33, *iii.*356
    does not leave disciple, *i.*475, *ii.*235
    purpose of, *ii.*231, *iii.*29
    recognizing, *ii.*237, *ii.*238, *iii.*37
    talking to, *i.*247, *i.*248, *iii.*379
reality, *i.*22–24, *ii.*329, *iii.*36, *iii.*111,
    *iii.*282
reaping. *See* karmas, sowing and
    reaping
reasoning, *i.*22, *ii.*35, *iii.*191, *iii.*393
receptivity. *See also* inner pull
    developed by meditation, *ii.*100,
        *ii.*345, *ii.*364, *iii.*29
    for grace, *ii.*343, *ii.*349, *ii.*352,
        *ii.*360, *ii.*361, *ii.*424, *ii.*427,
        *ii.*437, *iii.*230, *iii.*250

reincarnation, *i.*151–68, *ii.*217.
    See also transmigration
    after initiation, *i.*158–68, *ii.*420–21,
        *ii.*452–453, *iii.*102, *iii.*353–54
    due to attachments, *i.*71, *i.*92,
        *i.*166, *i.*221, *i.*275, *i.*277, *i.*278,
        *i.*339
    due to karmic relationships,
        *iii.*322. *See also* karmic
        relationships
    into animals, *i.*94, *i.*153, *i.*156, *i.*157
    into same family, *i.*162, *iii.*303
    keeping same mind and soul,
        *i.*243, *i.*260
    on other planets, *i.*168
relaxation, *iii.*198, *iii.*267, *iii.*268,
    *iii.*273
    by meditation, *ii.*115, *ii.*297, *iii.*269.
        See also meditation, benefits of
    movies and theatre, *iii.*274
religion
    basis of, *i.*299, *i.*320, *ii.*410
    conflicts in, *i.*314
    essence the same, *i.*287
    exploitation of, *i.*294, *i.*312
    killing in name of, *i.*301, *i.*315
    limitations of, *i.*292, *i.*313
    no need to change, *i.*293, *i.*320
    true, *i.*286–99, *i.*300
remission. *See* destiny, changing
renunciation, *ii.*113, *iii.*170–72,
    *iii.*296. *See also* suppression
repentance, *i.*88, *i.*97, *ii.*104,
    *iii.*196, *iii.*256, *iii.*259.
        See also karmas, clearing
research, spiritual, *i.*29
resignation. *See* submission
responsibilities. *See* duties

restlessness, *ii*.363. *See also* soul(s),
    inclination of
resurrection, *i*.157, *i*.465, *i*.497, *i*.498,
    iii.364
revenge, *iii*.250, *iii*.260, *iii*.261,
    iii.263
riches, *iii*.179. *See also* worldly
    achievements
rituals and ceremonies, *i*.287, *i*.295,
    i.301, *i*.304, *i*.309–12, *i*.478,
    ii.269, *iii*.80

Sabbath, *i*.310
Sach Khand, *i*.183
sacrifices, *ii*.397, *ii*.407, *ii*.408
sahaj marg, *iii*.166
Sahansdal Kamal, *i*.482
saints, *i*.336. *See also* master(s);
    mystics
  all have same message, *iii*.112
  difference between masters and,
    i.447
sangat, *iii*.96, *iii*.109
sanskaras, *i*.111, *i*.112, *i*.424, *i*.438,
    ii.217
Sant Mat, *i*.287. *See also* path
  does not discriminate based on
    gender, *i*.187
  explaining or giving lecture on.
    See satsang, format of
  explaining to seekers, *ii*.33
  Granth Sahib and, *i*.331
  in America, *ii*.392
  needs to be experienced, *i*.257
  not meant for everybody, *iii*.177
  purpose of, *ii*.415
  religion and, *i*.318–27
  resignation from, *ii*.429
  turning into organized religion,

    i.302, *i*.338
  way of life, *ii*.278, *ii*.381, *ii*.395,
    iii.87, *iii*.104, *iii*.167. *See also*
    living Sant Mat
Sat Lok, *i*.183
Satan, *i*.44. *See also* Kal
Satnam, *ii*.213
satsang
  appropriate topics, *iii*.111, *iii*.116,
    iii.117, *iii*.122, *iii*.126, *iii*.128
  benefits of, *iii*.9, *iii*.106, *iii*.113,
    iii.141
  definition of, *iii*.113
  food and drink at, *iii*.107, *iii*.123,
    iii.128, *iii*.138
  format of, *iii*.107–10, *iii*.113, *iii*.116,
    iii.125, *iii*.126, *iii*.128
  gossiping and recreation at, *iii*.107,
    iii.123
  helping seekers and new initiates
    at, *iii*.104, *iii*.108, *iii*.119,
    iii.127, *iii*.138, *iii*.139
  importance of, *iii*.103–20
  master's presence, *iii*.103, *iii*.114
  place for, *iii*.123, *iii*.139, *iii*.142
  purpose of, *ii*.434, *iii*.104–6, *iii*.112,
    iii.118, *iii*.124–26, *iii*.139
    creating atmosphere for
      meditation, *iii*.120–42,
      iii.140, *iii*.142
  rituals at, *iii*.107
  speakers, disagreement with,
    iii.126, *iii*.127
satsangis, *i*.109. *See also* disciple(s)
  attending meetings of different
    societies, *iii*.129
  getting master's attention
    according to their needs,
    iii.133

494

staying or coming closer to master,
   iii.133
scientific inventions, *ii*.440
scientists, *ii*.46
scriptures, *i*.29, *i*.327–34
search for God, *i*.431, *i*.432
seekers, *ii*.33, *ii*.39
   if die before getting initiated, *i*.438
   protected from birth, *i*.424
   types of, *ii*.422
self
   know thyself, *i*.202, *i*.212, *i*.234,
      i.263, *i*.265
   loss of. *See* individuality, losing
self-centredness, *ii*.443, *ii*.444,
   iii.269. *See also* ego
self-confidence, *iii*.193, *iii*.337
self-deception, *i*.349, *i*.370, *i*.374.
   See also delusion
self-importance. *See* ego
selfishness, *ii*.442–44
selflessness, *iii*.231. *See also* humility
self-pity, *iii*.370
self-realization, *i*.199–209, *iii*.20
   before God-realization, *i*.200
   definition of, *i*.199
seniority on path, *i*.97, *i*.430, *ii*.274
   Christ's saying 'first may be last',
      ii.350, *ii*.423
senses, *i*.228
   purpose of, *i*.13
   withdrawing from, *i*.225
separateness from body, *ii*.249, *ii*.262
separation, *ii*.372, *ii*.441, *iii*.60–78
   as gift, *ii*.373
   cause of misery, *ii*.363
      analogy of child at fair, *i*.351
   pain of, *i*.354, *i*.368, *iii*.62,
      iii.69–78

analogy of woman delivering
   child, *iii*.62, *iii*.73
story of Mira Bai and her love
   for guru, *iii*.63, *iii*.64
service. *See* helping others; *See* seva
seva, *ii*.380, *iii*.143–49, *iii*.151, *iii*.206
   attitude in, *iii*.144–49
   benefits of, *iii*.144
   influence on meditation, and,
      iii.112
   meditation as, *iii*.150–53
   no calculation in, *iii*.147
   opportunity and amount of, *iii*.149
   question of clearing karmas and,
      iii.151
   types of, *iii*.150–53
shabd, *ii*.96
   audible, *ii*.208
      from left or right, *ii*.204, *ii*.205
      outside of meditation, *ii*.207
   controls mind, *i*.270
   creative power, *i*.28, *i*.177, *i*.178,
      i.298
   detaches us from creation, *i*.486,
      ii.210
   does not pull noninitiates up, *ii*.201
   experiencing, *ii*.239–43
   five sounds of, *ii*.200, *ii*.226
   is God, *i*.178
   master projects himself from,
      i.178, *ii*.235, *ii*.238.
      See also master(s), shabd is
      real form of
   portrayed as dove, *ii*.243
   purifies mind, *ii*.227, *ii*.241
   purpose of, *ii*.185
   seeing and hearing, *i*.289
   sound and light, *i*.298, *i*.309, *ii*.106,
      ii.111, *ii*.218, *ii*.241, *ii*.242

within everyone, *i*.178
shabds, singing of, *iii*.109
sharan. *See* surrender, unconditional
short cut, *i*.147, *i*.292, *i*.446, *ii*.286,
     ii.336, *iii*.51, *iii*.174
silver cord, *ii*.214
simran, *ii*.171–205, *ii*.208–210.
     See also names, five;
     meditation
   as call to master, *ii*.184
   as means to contact shabd, *ii*.179,
     ii.387, *ii*.390
   as test of internal entities, *ii*.177,
     ii.182
   at bedtime, *ii*.208, *ii*.320
   connection with master, *ii*.179
   doing all day, *ii*.386, *ii*.386–91
   forgetting, *ii*.321
   helps attitude towards meditation,
     ii.388
   how to do, *ii*.169, *ii*.171, *ii*.173,
     ii.175, *ii*.179, *ii*.182
   in company of ill person, *ii*.175
   mechanical, *ii*.304, *ii*.386, *ii*.390
   of the world, *ii*.173
   power of, *ii*.184
   purpose of, *ii*.172, *ii*.176, *ii*.180,
     ii.185, *ii*.186, *ii*.190, *ii*.389–91
   speed of, *ii*.183, *ii*.321
   sweetness of, *ii*.339
   time for, *ii*.201, *ii*.203, *ii*.208, *ii*.210
   while imagining presence of
     master, *ii*.181, *ii*.187, *ii*.188
sin, *ii*.52. *See also* guilt; karmas
sincerity, *i*.81, *ii*.337, *ii*.353, *ii*.357
sinchit karma. *See* karmas, types of,
     reserve
single eye. *See* eye centre
slander, *i*.150, *i*.376, *iii*.175, *iii*.265

sleep, *ii*.306–10
social reformers, *i*.390, *i*.416
sorrow, *iii*.212, *iii*.225. *See also*
     karmas, types of, good and
     bad karmas
soul mate, *i*.187, *iii*.312, *iii*.315
soul(s)
   as real disciple, *i*.438, *i*.446, *i*.464,
     ii.237, *iii*.32–34
   at time of death, *i*.160
   concept of, *i*.21, *i*.157, *i*.168, *i*.176,
     i.182, *i*.185, *i*.227, *i*.236, *i*.346
   coverings over
     analogy of wrappings around
       light bulb, *ii*.294, *ii*.445
   descent into creation, *i*.15–19, *i*.26,
     i.178, *i*.182, *i*.425, *i*.430
   direct perception of, *i*.183
   dominated by mind, *i*.218, *i*.220
   entering into body, *i*.186
   gives life to body, *i*.171, *ii*.226
   group, *i*.76. *See also* karmic
     relationships
   has no religion, *i*.291
   inclination of, *i*.21, *i*.22, *i*.83, *i*.217,
     i.348–50, *i*.352, *i*.358, *i*.490
     analogy of needle and magnet,
       i.353
   individuality of, *i*.182, *ii*.119, *ii*.218
   light of, *i*.184
   lost, *i*.185
   marked, *i*.184, *i*.362, *i*.402–27,
     i.478, *ii*.7, *ii*.344, *ii*.423, *ii*.428
     come to path automatically,
       i.405, *i*.408, *i*.409, *i*.412, *i*.436,
       i.437
     reasons for, *i*.216, *i*.402, *i*.410,
       i.411, *i*.433
   number of, *i*.19, *i*.159

proof of existence, *i*.30
realized vs unrealized, *ii*.407–8
  analogy of puppets, *i*.39–41,
    i.135, *i*.140–42, *i*.345, *i*.413,
    ii.407–8
  relationship to body and mind,
    i.176, *i*.210–44, *i*.234, *i*.241,
    i.251, *i*.254, *ii*.218, *ii*.229
  relationship to God, *i*.169–87,
    i.194, *i*.203, *i*.215, *i*.289, *i*.346,
    i.422
    analogy of child at fair, *iii*.411
    analogy of drop and ocean,
      i.169, *i*.171, *i*.181
    analogy of moth and light,
      i.204, *ii*.219
    analogy of needle and magnet,
      i.205, *ii*.335
    analogy of rays and sun, *i*.175
  released from mind, *i*.87, *i*.200,
    i.210, *i*.231, *ii*.261, *ii*.295.
    See also mind, release from
    analogy of water evaporating
      from mud, *i*.201
  return to God, *i*.17–19, *i*.169, *i*.171,
    i.179–84, *i*.196, *i*.418
    analogy of bricks of the house,
      i.345, *i*.412
sound current. *See* shabd
sowing seeds. *See* karmas
spectator, living as, *ii*.261, *ii*.329,
    iii.209, *iii*.210
spirit, *i*.175. *See also* God; soul(s)
spiritual experiences. *See* inner
  experiences
spiritualism, *i*.259, *i*.260
spirituality
  basis of religion, *i*.295, *i*.322, *i*.496,
    iii.111

  analogy of golden frame, *i*.299
  exploited by politicians, *i*.389
  of India, *i*.304
  searching for, *i*.367
spiritual love, *i*.214. *See also* love, in
  relation to mind
spiritual powers, *ii*.250–54
spiritual progress. *See* progress
steadfastness, *i*.84, *ii*.42, *ii*.52, *ii*.295,
    ii.396, *ii*.399, *ii*.402, *iii*.214
sterilization, *i*.80
stilling the mind. *See* concentration
struggle. *See* mind, struggle with
struggle for existence, *i*.393
submission, *ii*.410, *iii*.74, *iii*.218, *iii*.398
  meditation and, *iii*.30
  to master, *ii*.394, *iii*.220
successorship. *See* master(s),
  successorship
suffering, *i*.57, *i*.197, *i*.356, *i*.359
  as grace, *i*.359–63
  as means to return to God, *i*.356
  karmas and, *iii*.224
  of body, mind and soul, *i*.230–32
  relativity of, *i*.355
    story of man walking on hot
      sand, *iii*.400
suicide, *iii*.348–50
sun and moon (as light), *ii*.230
superiority, *ii*.435, *iii*.237, *iii*.238,
    iii.249
suppression, *i*.213, *i*.222, *ii*.113, *ii*.296,
    ii.300, *ii*.301, *iii*.164, *iii*.166,
    iii.271. *See also* renunciation
  analogy of dam in river, *ii*.166,
    iii.171
  analogy of snake in basket, *ii*.106,
    ii.296, *iii*.169
  in children, *iii*.323

of lust, *i.*225, *ii.*93, *iii.*168, *iii.*295
*surat, i.*298
surat shabd yoga. *See* yoga, types of
surrender, *iii.*214–21
   and idea that everything belongs
     to master, *iii.*216
   intellectual, *iii.*218
   unconditional, *iii.*153, *iii.*215,
     *iii.*216, *iii.*219

talents, *iii.*274
teachings
   arrested into religion, *i.*299–318
   commercialization of, *i.*312
   distortion of, *i.*294, *i.*296, *i.*321,
     *i.*328, *i.*338
   how masters convey, *i.*308,
     *i.*335–42, *i.*369, *i.*449, *i.*478,
     *i.*480, *i.*485, *ii.*224, *iii.*109
   in traditions, *i.*310
   meant only for marked souls, *i.*403
   not forcing on others, *ii.*51, *iii.*314,
     *iii.*318
   remain the same, *i.*308
   understanding of, *i.*408, *iii.*103
   universal, *i.*302, *i.*308, *i.*311, *i.*326
telepathy, *i.*259
temptations, inside, *i.*255
   analogy of house with five stories,
     *ii.*211
Ten Commandments, *i.*310, *i.*385,
     *i.*479, *ii.*53–54, *ii.*58
tension, *ii.*115, *ii.*116, *iii.*198.
     See also worry
thankfulness. *See* gratitude
third eye. *See* eye centre
thoughts
   controlling, *ii.*387, *ii.*389–91.
     See also simran, doing all day

spreading out, *ii.*152
throat centre, *ii.*305–10
time, lacking, *iii.*180. *See also* worldly
   achievements
tolerance, *ii.*416. *See also* forgiveness
tragedy. *See* karmas, types of, group
transmigration, *i.*113, *i.*151, *i.*154,
     *i.*157, *i.*168, *i.*188, *i.*190, *i.*191.
     See also cycle of eighty-four;
     reincarnation
Trikuti, *i.*82, *i.*210, *i.*237, *ii.*213,
     *ii.*216–19
trust, *iii.*193
truth
   as excuse to humiliate another,
     *iii.*247
   rarely accepted, *i.*446
   sharing, *i.*381
twins, *i.*73. *See also* karmic
   relationships

ultimate goal, *i.*169, *i.*238, *i.*344,
     *ii.*431, *ii.*439, *iii.*368. *See also*
     soul(s), returning to God
understanding. *See also* discrimination
   as gift, *ii.*375
universal mind, *i.*228, *i.*237. *See also*
     Brahm; mind
urge for following path. *See* path,
     coming to

vacuum, *ii.*174, *ii.*188, *ii.*192, *ii.*196.
     See also meditation, dry
vegetarian diet, *ii.*56–78
   animals and, *ii.*74, *ii.*75, *ii.*76
   children and, *i.*69, *i.*71, *ii.*70, *ii.*71,
     *ii.*78, *iii.*326
   hair-splitting and, *ii.*72
   health of soul, *ii.*62

illness and, *ii.*62
infertile eggs and, *ii.*63
karma theory and, *ii.*59, *ii.*61
serving meat or alcohol to others,
    *ii.*64–68
should not compromise, *ii.*69
spiritual progress and, *ii.*58, *ii.*59
straying from, *ii.*64
wearing leather and, *ii.*76, *ii.*77
working in restaurant and, *ii.*65
virtues, *i.*260, *i.*401, *iii.*398
visions, *i.*162, *i.*424, *ii.*125, *ii.*189,
    *ii.*224, *ii.*248, *ii.*320.
    See also inner experiences
visualization. *See* dhyan
visualizing worldly objects, *ii.*152.
    See also dhyan
    analogy of cinema screen, *ii.*158,
        *ii.*186
void. *See* meditation, dry
vows, four, *ii.*52–96, *iii.*398
    breaking, *ii.*430, *ii.*434, *iii.*189.
        See also karmas, of going off
        path
    foundation for meditation, *ii.*396,
        *ii.*397
    moral life, *ii.*84–96

war
    caused by lacking inner peace,
        *i.*383
    justifying, *i.*384
    suffering collectively. *See* karmas,
        types of, group
    weaknesses, *ii.*399, *ii.*407, *ii.*417,
        *ii.*432, *ii.*434, *iii.*11, *iii.*192
    awareness of, *ii.*264, *ii.*265, *ii.*414
        analogy of ray of light in dark
            room, *ii.*264, *ii.*331, *ii.*413

going off path, due to, *ii.*425
justifying, *ii.*415, *ii.*416, *ii.*418,
    *ii.*430
not exposing, *ii.*435, *ii.*437, *iii.*250
    Christ's parable of weeds amidst
        crop, *iii.*6, *iii.*121
overcoming, *ii.*112, *ii.*409, *ii.*413–20
positive approach, *iii.*369
weapons, possessing, *i.*242
weeping and laughing, *iii.*272.
    See also emotions
will of God, *i.*54, *i.*138, *i.*497,
    *iii.*223–30
    living in, *ii.*140, *ii.*142, *ii.*144,
        *ii.*145, *ii.*148
will of master, *iii.*222
    vs will of mind, *iii.*214, *iii.*222,
        *iii.*230
willpower. *See also* mind
    losing, *i.*258, *ii.*399
    strengthening, *i.*64, *i.*257, *ii.*138,
        *ii.*139, *ii.*143, *ii.*339, *ii.*418,
        *iii.*192
wisdom, *i.*263, *i.*265
withdrawal, *ii.*244, *iii.*324.
    See also concentration
    analogy of cloth and thorny bush,
        *iii.*351
    analogy of thousand candle bulb,
        *ii.*244
    numbness of, *ii.*248
    of attention, *ii.*247–48
    pain of, *iii.*351
    to eye centre, ii.153, ii.158, ii.171,
        *ii.*247, ii.328, *ii.*397
word. *See* shabd
world
    end of, *i.*33, *i.*35
    field of karmas, *i.*68

improving, *i*.378–86, *i*.392, *i*.401,
i.491. *See also* social reformers
analogy of thorns and strong
shoes, *i*.380
desire for, *iii*.164
job of social reformers not
mystics, *i*.375
living in but not attached, *iii*.159,
iii.375
place of misery and war, *i*.172,
i.352, *i*.374, *i*.383, *i*.385, *i*.386,
i.394, *i*.395, *i*.490, *i*.493
why it exists, *i*.37, *i*.39
worldly achievements, *i*.367, *i*.368,
ii.440
happiness and, *i*.364, *i*.365, *i*.375,
i.376, *i*.378, *i*.382, *i*.391, *iii*.131
worldly relationships, *ii*.451, *iii*.283.
See also karmic relationships
and love for God, master, *iii*.280,
iii.281, *iii*.289
as thieves, dacoits and thugs,
iii.306
duties for, *iii*.286, *iii*.287.
See also duties
loving without attachment, *iii*.289,
iii.290

story of mystic who kissed
dancing girl, *iii*.288
worry, *ii*.118, *ii*.387, *ii*.433, *iii*.194–98,
iii.301
about future, *iii*.196
as lack of faith in master, *iii*.197
attitude towards, *iii*.196, *iii*.197
habit of, *iii*.198
passing it on to God, *iii*.195, *iii*.198
worship, *i*.304
different approaches to, *i*.306,
ii.410
only through grace, *i*.431, *ii*.366
out of love, *ii*.103, *ii*.334, *ii*.356

yearning of soul. *See* soul(s),
inclination of
yoga, *ii*.160, *iii*.117
difficulty of, *ii*.248, *iii*.342
hatha, *iii*.342
kundalini, *ii*.162
pranayam, *ii*.185, *ii*.318, *iii*.342
surat shabd, *i*.285, *ii*.163, *iii*.341
youth
advantages and disadvantages,
ii.311

Addresses for Information and Books

INDIAN SUB-CONTINENT

INDIA
The Secretary
Radha Soami Satsang Beas
Dera Baba Jaimal Singh
District Amritsar, Punjab 143204

NEPAL
Capt. S.B.B. Chhetri (Retd.)
Radha Soami Satsang Beas Nepal
Gongabu 7, P. O. Box 1646
Kathmandu
☎ +977-1-435-7765

PAKISTAN
Mr. Sadrang Seetal Das
Lahori Mohala, Larkana, Sindh

SRI LANKA
Mr. Chandroo Mirpuri
Radha Soami Satsang Beas
No. 45 Silva Lane
Rajagiriya, Colombo
☎ +94-11-286-1491

SOUTHEAST ASIA

FOR FAR EAST
Mrs. Cami Moss
RSSB-HK
T.S.T., P.O. Box 90745
Kowloon, Hong Kong
☎ +852-2369-0625

MALAYSIA
Mr. Bhupinder Singh
Radha Soami Satsang Beas
29 Jalan Cerapu Satu, Off Batu 3 ¼
Jalan Cheras, Kuala Lumpur 56100
☎ +603-9200-3073

THAILAND
Mr. Harmahinder Singh Sethi
Radha Soami Satsang Beas
58/32 Ratchadaphisek Road, Soi 16
Thapra, Bangkok Yai, Bangkok 10600
☎ +66-2-868-2186 / 2187

INDONESIA
Mr. Ramesh Sadarangani
Jalan Pasir Putih IV/16, Block E 4
Ancol Timur, Jakarta
DKI Jakarta 14430

Yayasan Radha Soami Satsang
Jalan Transyogi KM. 5, Jatikarya
Pondok Gede, DKI Jakarta 17435
☎ +62-21-845-1612

Yayasan Radha Soami Satsang
Jalan Bung Tomo
Desa Pemecutan Raya
Denpasar, Barat 80116
☎ +62-361-438-522

PHILIPPINES
Mr. Kay Sham
Science of the Soul Study Center
9001 Don Jesus Boulevard
Alabang Hills, Cupang
Muntinlupa City, 1771
☎ +63-2-772-0111 / 0555

SINGAPORE
Mrs. Asha Melwani
Radha Soami Satsang Beas
19 Amber Road, Singapore 439868
☎ +65-6447-4956

ASIA PACIFIC

AUSTRALIA
Mr. Pradeep Raniga
Science of the Soul Study Centre
1530 Elizabeth Drive
Cecil Park, New South Wales 2178

NEW ZEALAND
Mr. Tony Waddicor
P. O. Box 5331, Auckland

Science of the Soul Study Centre
80 Olsen Avenue, Auckland
☎ +64-9-624-2202

GUAM
Mrs. Hoori M. Sadhwani
115 Alupang Cove
241 Condo Lane, Tamuning 96911

HONG KONG
Mr. Manoj Sabnani
Radha Soami Satsang Beas
3rd Floor, Maxwell Centre
39-41 Hankow Road
Tsim Sha Tsui, Kowloon
☎ +852-2369-0625

JAPAN
Mr. Jani G. Mohinani
Radha Soami Satsang Beas
1-2-18 Nakajima-Dori
Aotani, Chuo-Ku, Kobe 651-0052
☎ +81-78-222-5353

KOREA
Mr. Haresh Buxani
Science of the Soul Study Group
613, Hopyeong-Dong
R603-18604 Sungbo Building
Nam Yangju, Gyeong Gi-Do
Nam Yangju Kyung-gi
☎+822-315-117-008

TAIWAN, R.O.C.
Mr. Haresh Buxani
Science of the Soul Study Group
Aetna Tower Office, 15F., No. 27-9
Sec.2, Jhongjheng E.Rd.
Danshuei Township, Taipei 25170
☎+886-2-8809-5223

NORTH AMERICA

CANADA
Mr. John Pope
5285 Coombe Lane
Belcarra, British Columbia V3H 4N6

Mrs. Meena Khanna
149 Elton Park Road
Oakville, Ontario L6J 4C2

Science of the Soul Study Centre
2932 -176th Street
Surrey, B.C. V3S 9V4
☎ +1-604-541-4792

Science of the Soul Study Centre
6566 Sixth Line, RR 1 Hornby
Ontario L0P 1E0
☎ +1-905-875-4579

MEXICO
Radha Soami Satsang Beas
Efrain Gonzalez Luna
2051 Col. Americana
Guadalajara, Jalisco 44090
☎ +52-333-615-4942

Radha Soami Satsang Beas
Circuito Universidad S/N
Lomas Del ProgresoEL Pitillal CP 48290
☎ +52-322-299-1954

UNITED STATES
Mr. Hank Muller
P.O. Box 1847, Tomball, TX 77377

Dr. Vincent P. Savarese
2550 Pequeno Circle
Palm Springs, CA 92264-9522

Dr. Frank E. Vogel
275 Cutts Road
Newport, NH 03773

Dr. Douglas Torr
P.O. Box 2360
Southern Pines, NC 28388-2360

Science of the Soul Study Center
4115 Gillespie Street
Fayetteville, NC 28306-9053
☎ +1-910-426-5306

Science of the Soul Study Center
2415 Washington Street
Petaluma, CA 94954-9274
☎ +1-707-762-5082

CARIBBEAN

FOR CARIBBEAN
Mr. Sean Finnigan
R.S.S.B. Foundation
P. O. Box 978
Phillipsburg, St. Maarten, N. A.

Mrs. Jaya Sabnani
1 Sunset Drive South
Fort George Heights
St. Michael BB111 02, Barbados

BARBADOS, W.I.
Mrs. Mukta Nebhani
Science of the Soul Study Center
No. 10, 5th Avenue
Belleville BB11114
☎ +1-246-427-4761

CURACAO, N.A.
Mrs. Hema Chandiramani
Science of the Soul Study Centre
Kaya Seru di Milon 6-9
Santa Catharina
☎ +599-9-747-0226

ST. MAARTEN, N.A.
Mr. Prakash Daryanani
R.S.S.B. Foundation
P. O. Box 978, Phillipsburg
☎ +599-547-0066

GRENADA, W.I.
Mr. Ajay Mahbubani
P.O. Box 820, St. Georges

GUYANA
Mrs. Indu Lalwani
155, Garnette Street
Newtown Kitty, Georgetown

HAITI, W.I.
Ms. Mousson Finnigan Pierre
P.O. Box 2314, Port-au-Prince

JAMAICA, W.I.
Mrs. Reshma Daswani
17 Colombus Height
First Phase, Ocho Rios

ST. THOMAS
Mrs. Hema Melwani
P.O. Box 600145
USVI-VI00801-6145

SURINAME
Mr. Ettire Stanley Rensch
Surinamestraat 36, Paramaribo

TRINIDAD, W.I.
Mr. Chandru Chatlani
20 Admiral Court
Westmoorings-by-Sea, Westmoorings

FOR CENTRAL & SOUTH AMERICA

Mr. Hiro W. Balani
Paseo De Farola, 3, Piso 6
Edificio Marina
Malaga, Spain 29016

CENTRAL AMERICA

BELIZE
Mrs. Milan Hotchandani
4633 Seashore Drive
P.O. Box 830, Belize City

PANAMA
Mr. Ashok Tikamdas Dinani
P.O. Box 0301
03524 Colon

ADDRESSES FOR INFORMATION AND BOOKS

SOUTH AMERICA

ARGENTINA
Ms. Fabiana Shilton
Leiva 4363 Capital Federal
C.P. 1427 Buenos Aires

BRAZIL
Mr. Guillerme Almeida
RUA Jesuino Arrvda 574/51
Sao Paulo 04532-081

CHILE
Mr. Vijay Harjani
Pasaje Cuatro No. 3438
Sector Chipana, Iquique

Fundacion Radha Soami Satsang Beas
Av. Apoquindo 4770, Oficina 1504
Las Condes, Santiago

COLOMBIA
Mrs. Emma Orozco
Asociacion Cultural
Radha Soami Satsang Beas
Calle 48 No. 78A-30, Medellin 49744
☏ +574-234-5130

ECUADOR
Dr. Fernando Flores Villalva
Radha Soami Satsang Beas
Calle Marquez de Varela
OE 3-68y Avda. America
P.O. Box 17-21-115, Quito
☏ +5932-2-555-988

PERU
Mr. Carlos Fitts
P.O. Box 18-0658, Lima 18

Asociacion Cultural
Radha Soami Satsang Beas
Av. Pardo #231
12th Floor, Miraflores, Lima 18

VENEZUELA
Mrs. Helen Paquin
Radha Soami Satsang Beas
Av. Los Samanes con
Av. Los Naranjos Conj, Res. Florida 335
La Florida, Caracas 1012

EUROPE

AUSTRIA
Mr. Hansjorg Hammerer
Sezenweingasse 10, A-5020 Salzburg

BELGIUM
Mr. Piet J. E. Vosters
Driezenstraat 26, Turnhout 2300

BULGARIA
Mr. Deyan Stoyanov
Radha Soami Satsang Beas
P. O. Box 39, 8000 Bourgas

CYPRUS
Mr. Heraclis Achilleos
P. O. Box 29077, 1035 Nicosia

CZECH REPUBLIC
Mr. Vladimir Skalsky
Maratkova 916, 142 00 Praha 411

DENMARK
Mr. Tony Sharma
Sven Dalsgaardsvej 33, DK-7430 Ikast

FINLAND
Ms. Anneli Wingfield
P. O. Box 1422, 00101 Helsinki

FRANCE
Mr. Pierre de Proyart
7 Quai Voltaire, Paris 75007

GERMANY
Mr. Rudolf Walberg
P. O. Box 1544, D-65800 Bad Soden

GIBRALTAR
Mr. Sunder Mahtani
RSSB Charitable Trust, 15 Rosia Road
☏ +350-200-412-67

GREECE
Mr. Themistoclis Gianopoulos
6 Platonos Str., 17672 Kallithea, Attiki

ITALY
Mrs. Wilma Salvatori Torri
Via Bacchiglione 3, 00199 Rome

THE NETHERLANDS (HOLLAND)
Mr. Henk Keuning
Kleizuwe2, Vreeland 3633AE

Radha Soami Satsang Beas
Middenweg 145 E
1394 AH Nederhorst den Berg
☎ +31-294-255-255

NORWAY
Mr. Manoj Kaushal
Langretta 8, N - 1279 Oslo

POLAND
Mr. Vinod Sharma
UL. Szyprow 2M12, 02-654 Warsaw

PORTUGAL
Mrs. Sharda Lodhia
CRCA Portugal
Av. Coronel Eduardo Galhardo
No.18 A-B
Lisbon 1170-105

ROMANIA
Mrs. Carmen Cismas
C.P. 6-12, 810600 Braila

SLOVENIA
Mr. Marko Bedina
Brezje pri Trzicu 68, 4290 Trzic

SPAIN
Mr. J. W. Balani
Fundacion Cultural RSSB
Fca Loma del Valle S/N
Cruce de Penon de Zapata
Alhaurin De la Torre, Malaga 29130
☎ +34-952-414-679

SWEDEN
Mr. Lennart Zachen
Norra Sonnarpsvägen 29
SE-286 72 Asljunga

SWITZERLAND
Mr. Sebastian Züst
Weissenrainstrasse 48
CH 8707 Uetikon am See

UNITED KINGDOM
Mr. Narinder Singh Johal
Radha Soami Satsang Beas
Haynes Park
Haynes, MK45 3BL Bedford
☎ +44-1234-381-234

AFRICA

BENIN
Mr. Jaikumar T. Vaswani
01 Boite Postale 951,
Recette Principale Cotonou 01

BOTSWANA
Dr. Krishan Lal Bhateja
P. O. Box 402539, Gaborone

CONGO
Mr. Prahlad Parbhu
143 Kasai Ave., Lubumbashi

GHANA
Mr. Murli Chatani
Radha Soami Satsang Beas
P. O. Box 3976, Accra
☎ +233-242-057-309

IVORY COAST
Mr. Veerender Kumar Sapra
Avenue 7, Rue 19, Lot 196
Trechville, Abidjan 05

KENYA
Mr. Surinder Singh Ghir
Radha Soami Satsang Beas
P.O. Box 15134
Langata 00509, Nairobi
☎ +254-20-890-329

LESOTHO
Mr. Sello Wilson Moseme
P. O. Box 750, Leribe 300

LIBYA (G.S.P.L.A.J.)
Mr. Abhimanyu Sahani
P.O. Box 38930, Bani Walid

MADAGASCAR
Mr. Francis Murat
Lote 126B
Amnohiminono, Antanetibe
Antananarivo 101

MAURITIUS
Dr. I. Fagoonee
Radha Soami Satsang Beas Trust
69 CNR Antelme /Stanley Avenues
Quatre Bornes
☎ +230-454-3300

NAMIBIA
Mrs. Jennifer Carvill
P. O. Box 449, Swakopmund 9000

NIGERIA
Mr. Nanik N. Balani
G.P.O. Box 5054, Marina, Lagos

RÉUNION
Ms. Marie-Lynn Marcel
5 Chemin 'Gonneau, Bernica
St Gillesles Hauts 97435

SIERRA LEONE
Mr. Kishore S. Mahboobani
82/88 Kissy Dock Yard
P.O. Box 369, Freetown

SOUTH AFRICA
Mr. Gordon Clive Wilson
P.O. Box 1959
Randpark Ridge, Gauteng 2156

Radha Soami Satsang Beas
P.O. Box 5270, Cresta 2118
☎ +27-11-792-7644

SWAZILAND
Mr. Mike Cox
Green Valley Farm, Malkerns

TANZANIA
Mr. Manmohan Singh
99 Lugalo Street
Dar-Es-Salaam 65065

UGANDA
Mr. Sylvester Kakooza
Radha Soami Satsang Beas
P. O. Box 31381, Kampala

ZAMBIA
Mr. Surinder Kumar Sachar
6 Mutondo Crescent
Riverside, Copper belt, Kitwe

ZIMBABWE
Mr. Gordon Clive Wilson
P.O. Box 1959
Randpark Ridge
Gauteng 2156, South Africa

MIDDLE EAST

BAHRAIN
Mr. Iqbal Kundal
P.O. Box 76091 - Juffair

ISRAEL
Mr. Michael Yaniv
Moshav Sde Nitzan 59
D.N. Hanegev 85470

KUWAIT
Mr. Vijay Kumar
Yousef AL Badar Street
Bldg 28, Block 10, Flat #8, Salmiya

U.A.E.
Mr. Daleep Jatwani
P.O. Box 37816, Dubai
☎ +971-4-339-4773

BOOKS ON THIS SCIENCE

SOAMI JI MAHARAJ
Sar Bachan Prose
Sar Bachan Poetry

BABA JAIMAL SINGH
Spiritual Letters

MAHARAJ SAWAN SINGH
The Dawn of Light
Discourses on Sant Mat, Volume I
My Submission
Philosophy of the Masters (5 volumes)
Spiritual Gems
Tales of the Mystic East

MAHARAJ JAGAT SINGH
Discourses on Sant Mat, Volume II
The Science of the Soul

MAHARAJ CHARAN SINGH
Die to Live
Divine Light
Light on Saint John
Light on Saint Matthew
Light on Sant Mat
Quest for Light
The Path
Spiritual Discourses (2 volumes)
Spiritual Heritage
Spiritual Perspectives (3 volumes)

BOOKS ABOUT THE MASTERS
Call of the Great Master – Daryai Lal Kapur
Heaven on Earth – Daryai Lal Kapur
Treasure beyond Measure – Shanti Sethi
With a Great Master in India – Julian P. Johnson
With the Three Masters (3 volumes) – Rai Sahib Munshi Ram

MYSTICS OF THE EAST SERIES
Bulleh Shah – J. R. Puri and T. R. Shangari
Dadu: The Compassionate Mystic – K. N. Upadhyaya
Dariya Sahib: Saint of Bihar – K. N. Upadhyaya
Guru Nanak: His Mystic Teachings – J. R. Puri
Guru Ravidas: The Philosopher's Stone – K. N. Upadhyaya
Kabir: The Great Mystic – Isaac A. Ezekiel
Kabir: The Weaver of God's Name – V. K. Sethi
Mira: The Divine Lover – V. K. Sethi
Saint Namdev – J. R. Puri and V. K. Sethi
Sant Paltu: His Life and Teachings – Isaac A. Ezekiel
Sarmad: Martyr to Love Divine – Isaac A. Ezekiel

BOOKS ON THIS SCIENCE

Sultan Bahu – J. R. Puri and K. S. Khak
The Teachings of Goswami Tulsidas – K. N. Upadhyaya
Tukaram: The Ceaseless Song of Devotion – C. Rajwade
Tulsi Sahib: Saint of Hathras – J. R. Puri and V. K. Sethi

SPIRITUALITY AND SANT MAT
Honest Living – M. F. Singh
In Search of the Way – Flora E. Wood
The Inner Voice – C. W. Sanders
Liberation of the Soul – J. Stanley White
Living Meditation: A Journey beyond Body and Mind
   – Hector Esponda Dubin
Message Divine – Shanti Sethi
The Mystic Philosophy of Sant Mat – Peter Fripp
Mysticism: The Spiritual Path – Lekh Raj Puri
The Path of the Masters – Julian P. Johnson
Radha Soami Teachings – Lekh Raj Puri
A Spiritual Primer – Hector Esponda Dubin

THE MYSTIC WAY AND WORLD RELIGIONS
Adventure of Faith – Shraddha Lietz
Buddhism: Path to Nirvana – K. N. Upadhyaya
The Divine Romance – John Davidson
The Gospel of Jesus – John Davidson
The Holy Name: Mysticism in Judaism – Miriam Caravella
Jap Ji – T. R. Shangari
The Odes of Solomon – John Davidson
The Prodigal Soul – John Davidson
The Song of Songs – John Davidson
A Treasury of Mystic Terms,
   Part I: The Principles of Mysticism (6 volumes) – John Davidson, ed.
Yoga and the Bible – Joseph Leeming

BOOKS ON MISCELLANEOUS THEMES
Empower Women: An Awakening – Leena Chawla
Life Is Fair: The Law of Cause and Effect – Brian Hines
One Being One – John Davidson
A Soul's Safari – Netta Pfeifer

VEGETARIAN COOKBOOKS
Baking Without Eggs
Creative Vegetarian Cooking
The Green Way to Healthy Living
Meals with Vegetables

BOOKS FOR CHILDREN
The Journey of the Soul – Victoria Jones
One Light Many Lamps – Victoria Jones

For Internet orders, please visit: www.rssb.org

For book orders within India, please write to:

Radha Soami Satsang Beas
BAV Distribution Centre, 5 Guru Ravi Dass Marg
Pusa Road, New Delhi 110 005